*Microsoft*®

W9-AWZ-039

# Inside Microsoft Dynamics™ AX 4.0

*Hans J. Skovgaard*
*Arthur Greef*
*Michael Fruergaard Pontoppidan*
*Lars Dragheim Olsen*
*Palle Agermark*
*Per Baarsøe Jørgensen*
*Thomas Due Kay*
*Karl Tolgu*
*Mey Meenakshisundaram*
*Bjørn Møller Pedersen*

PUBLISHED BY
Microsoft Press
A Division of Microsoft Corporation
One Microsoft Way
Redmond, Washington 98052-6399

ISBN-13: 978-0-7356-2257-9
ISBN-10: 0-7356-2257-4
Library of Congress Control Number 2006928843

Printed and bound in the United States of America.

1 2 3 4 5 6 7 8 9  QWT  1 0 9 8 7 6

Distributed in Canada by H.B. Fenn and Company Ltd.

A CIP catalogue record for this book is available from the British Library.

Microsoft Press books are available through booksellers and distributors worldwide. For further information about international editions, contact your local Microsoft Corporation office or contact Microsoft Press International directly at fax (425) 936-7329. Visit our Web site at www.microsoft.com/mspress. Send comments to mspinput@microsoft.com.

**Acquisitions Editor:** Ben Ryan
**Project Editor:** Maureen Williams Zimmerman
**Technical Editor:** David W. Robinson
**Copy Editor:** Crystal Thomas
**Indexer:** Brenda Miller

Body Part No. X12-41754

# Contents at a Glance

## Part IV     Appendixes

# Table of Contents

## Part I    A Tour of the Development Environment

### 1    Architectural Overview

## Part IV  **Appendixes**

# Foreword

In the course of our engagement with numerous partners and customers, and also in personal experiences, we have come to realize two things.

First, we have learned how much developers enjoy working with Microsoft Dynamics AX 4.0. We love Dynamics AX, and our partners love its powerful set of development tools, which provides an affordable adaptability story for ERP systems that is second to none. Some of the examples that you will see in this book can be performed in 10 minutes or less, such as making and exposing custom data sets to external applications through a Web service. The very same examples would take at least a week to complete in other ERP systems.

We have also realized how difficult it is to provide adequate information to developers during their very first experiences with implementation and setup of the application. We are painfully aware of the difficulties that we faced in the past in our efforts to provide developers with initial resources to help them become proficient quickly in the Dynamics AX tool set. For those of us who have had to learn Dynamics AX the hard way, it is a special pleasure to have been able to convince (admittedly with some use of force) a group of application experts to write this book. We believe that this book, which aims to provide good information on advanced concepts to experienced developers, can make your entry into the powerful tool set for building business applications a much smoother and more digestible learning experience. We hope that this book will be received as an insightful resource for many people working with Dynamics AX 4.0.

I wish you success with your implementation and customization of Microsoft Dynamics AX 4.0.

*Hans J. Skovgaard*
Product Unit Manager
Microsoft Corporation

# Acknowledgments

We want to thank all the people who assisted us in making this book become a reality. The list of people is long—if we inadvertently missed anyone, we apologize. A special thanks goes to the following people on the Microsoft Dynamics product team:

- Mette Nyberg, who worked with authors, their idiosyncrasies, and non-native English to get the book in a shape that would allow the Microsoft Press editors to actually start editing. She also made sure that the deadlines were kept within a safe horizon.

- Hal Howard and Niels Bo Theilgaard, who sponsored the project.

- The product team reviewers, who provided valuable feedback that made the book more accurate and a whole lot better:

| | |
|---|---|
| Michael Costello | Niels Sejer Pedersen |
| Ajay Aggarwal | Jyoti Gawade |
| Hari Pulapaka | Peter Villadsen |
| Kenneth Puggaard | Jens Klarskov Jensen |
| Lachlan Cash | Niels Erik Møller |
| Laurent Ricci | David Aichele |
| Lei He | Ramana Parimi |
| Mark B. Madsen | Jeppe Oskar Meyer Larsen |
| Morten Jensen | Hua Chu |
| Per Vikkelsøe | Kim Moerup |
| Srikanth Avadhanam | Anna Lomova |
| Sune Gynthersen | David Pokluda |
| Uffe Kjall | Jens Møller-Pedersen |
| Steen Sloth Christensen | |

- We would also like to thank our external reviewers, who took time out of their busy schedules to add value to this book:

  Martin Fruergaard Laursen

  Anders Hauge

  Oliver Morrison

Of course, we also want to thank the people at Microsoft Press who helped support us throughout the book writing and publishing process:

- Ben Ryan, who championed the book project at Microsoft Press.

- Maureen Zimmerman, who was the most patient project editor we could have asked for. This was our first book project, so we had a lot of questions and probably made life a bit more difficult for Maureen during the course of this project.

- David W. Robinson, the technical editor, who asked the authors all the painful (and right) questions as he made his way through the numerous code examples in the book. We owe him a lot for this effort.

- Crystal Thomas, who did a phenomenal job on our book. The life of an editor is never easy, and we are fortunate that Crystal worked on our book.

In addition, we want to thank Ole Jauch from our partner, thy:development, for his support and sponsorship of Chapter 18, "Upgrade and Data Migration."

*The Microsoft Dynamics AX author team*

*Top row from left to right: Palle Agermark, Karl Tolgu, Hans J. Skovgaard, Mey Meenakshisundaram, Arthur Greef, Bjørn Møller Pedersen, Lars Dragheim Olsen. Front row from left to right: Per Baarsøe Jørgensen, Michael Fruergaard Pontoppidan, Thomas Due Kay.*

# Introduction

We understand if you are a bit skeptical when we tell you that you are about to fall for a piece of software. But you will love Microsoft Dynamics AX 4.0 by the time you finish reading this book. We want you to know up front that our intention is to show you all the wonderful and amazing benefits that Dynamics AX 4.0 has to offer your business.

## Who Is This Book For?

This book delves into the technology and tools of Dynamics AX 4.0. New and experienced developers are the intended target audience, and consultants will also benefit from reading this book. The intention is not to give any guidance on application functionality, but rather to offer as much technical information between the two covers as possible. It is also beyond the scope of this book to include the details regarding installation, deployment, and sizing of production environments. Please refer to the extensive installation and implementation documentation supplied with the product for details on these topics.

To get full value from this book, you should have knowledge of common object-oriented concepts from languages such as C++, C#, and Java. Knowledge of Structured Query Language (SQL) is also an advantage. SQL statements are used to perform relational database tasks such as data updates and data retrieval.

 **Note** If you do not have the Dynamics AX license that provides developer rights, you will not be able to perform most of the actions in this book. The current MSDN version comes with developer rights for one developer.

## The History of Microsoft Dynamics AX

Historically, Microsoft Dynamics AX envelops more than 20 years of experience in business application innovation and developer productivity. The business knowledge represented in the product stems from the predecessors XAL and C4. These products were developed by a company called Damgaard Data; following a merger with Navision, the company was acquired by Microsoft in 2002. To clarify a few aspects of this transition, the authors contacted the people who participated in the early stages of the Dynamics AX development cycle.

How was the idea of using X++ as the programming language for Dynamics AX conceived?

"We had been working with an upgraded version of XAL for a while called OO XAL back in 1996/1997. At some point in time, we stopped and reviewed our approach and looked at other new languages like Java. After working one long night, I decided that our approach had to change to align with the latest trends in programming languages, and we started with X++."

*Erik Damgaard, co-founder of Damgaard Data*

Of course, there were several perspectives among the developers on this breakthrough event.

"One morning when we came to work, nothing was working. Later in the morning, we realized that we had changed programming languages! But we did not have any tools, so for months we were programming in Notepad without compiler or editor support."

*Anonymous developer (but among the authors of this book!)*

Many hypotheses exist regarding the origin of the original product name, Axapta (now AX). However, it is a constructed name, and the only requirement was that the letter X be included, to mark the association with the predecessor XAL. With the latest release, the product was rebranded to Microsoft Dynamics AX 4.0.

# Organization of This Book

Part I is mainly for people new to Dynamics AX. It describes the application architecture from the perspective of development, deployment, and administration. Part I also provides a tour of the internal Dynamics AX development environment to help new developers familiarize themselves with designers, tools, the X++ programming language, and the object-oriented application framework that they will use to implement their customizations, extensions, and integrations.

Part II is largely devoted to illustrating how developers use the Dynamics AX application framework. Through code samples written for a fictitious bicycle sales and distribution company, this part describes how to customize and extend Dynamics AX. The examples show how the fictitious company customizes, extends, and integrates the application to support its online make-to-order sales, distribution, and service operations. Part II also explains how developers deploy and administer their Dynamics AX solutions.

Unlike the first two parts, Part III takes a close look under the hood of Dynamics AX 4.0, and it consists of chapters that can be read separately and in random order. The chapters cover areas such as the Enterprise Portal, configuration and security mechanisms, and the database transaction layer. Part III also explains how you can use advanced features such as reflection, system classes, and unit testing. With special focus on enhancing customer and partner experiences, this part provides deep insight into improving performance in customizations for Dynamics AX. The last chapter is devoted to upgrading and data migration. We asked a partner (the company thy:development) to write this chapter because this is, after all, where partners feel at home and are the experts in the product.

# Reading Guide

If you are an experienced Dynamics AX developer, you might want to skip the tour of the development environment after reading Chapter 1, "Architectural Overview," and move straight to Part II. However, before you move on, you might just want to take a look at two new additions to Dynamics AX 4.0 that are described in Chapter 4, "The MorphX Development Tools": the Visio Reverse Engineering tool and the Version Control tool. Also, the interoperability with the Microsoft .NET CLR system described in Chapter 5, "The X++ Programming Language," is interesting reading.

Obviously, seasoned software developers and development managers will benefit most from reading Part III, which discusses advanced technical subjects.

## Product Documentation

In addition to this book, you can read thousands of topic pages of product documentation on application and system issues in the online Help. Exhaustive documentation on installation and implementation is available in the Microsoft Dynamics AX SDK and the Microsoft Dynamics AX Implementation Guide, both supplied with the product. You can also find the product documentation on MSDN. And if you have an installation of Dynamics AX 4.0, you have access to the following topic areas on the Help menu: Administrator Help, Developer Help, and User Help.

## Product Web Site

This new user portal for the Dynamics AX product encompasses product and purchase information, as well as guidelines on how to use the product. For more information, visit the site:

*http://www.microsoft.com/dynamics/ax*

## Naming

With the latest version of the application, the name of the product changed to Microsoft Dynamics AX 4.0. The previous product version was called Microsoft Axapta, but you might find some marketing material that uses the name Microsoft Dynamics AX 3.0. For easier reading, this book refers to the 4.0 version of the product as Dynamics AX and makes specific reference to earlier versions where appropriate.

## Code

All relevant code examples are available for download. For details on the Web site, see the section later in this Introduction called "Code Samples." Note that the code samples might need some degree of modification to be executed; this is described either in the .xpo files themselves or in the readme file associated with the code samples on the Web site.

# Glossary

Like all software, Dynamics AX involves the use of many abbreviations, acronyms, and technical expressions. Much of this information is available in a glossary that you will find at the end of the book. For a more exhaustive list of terms and abbreviations, refer to the glossary provided with the product documentation.

# Special Legend

To distinguish between SQL and X++ statements, this book uses the common practice for SQL keywords, which is to display them in all capital letters. The following code shows an example of this in connection with nested transactions, where a transaction is started in X++ and later sent to a SQL server.

```
boolean b = true;
;
ttsbegin; // Transaction is not initiated here
update_recordset custTable
    setting creditMax = 0; // set implicit transactions on
if ( b == true )
    ttscommit; // COMMIT TRANSACTION
else
    ttsabort; // ROLLBACK TRANSACTION
```

# System Requirements

You will need the following hardware and software to build and run all the code samples for this book:

- Microsoft Dynamics AX 4.0: Business Connector .NET, Microsoft Dynamics AX 4.0 Rich Client, AOS (up and running)

- Microsoft Windows XP with Service Pack 2, or Windows 2000, or Microsoft Windows Server 2003 with Service Pack 1 (for Microsoft Dynamics AX 4.0 Rich Client)

- Microsoft Windows Server 2003 with Service Pack 1 (AOS Server)

- Microsoft SQL Server 2000, SQL Server 2005, or Oracle Database 10g

- Microsoft Windows SharePoint Services Service Pack 2 (to run the Enterprise Portal)

- Microsoft Visual Studio 2005

- Minimum 600-MHz Pentium or compatible processor (1-GHz Pentium recommended)

- 1 GB RAM or more recommended
- Video: at least 1024 × 768 High Color 16-bit
- CD-ROM or DVD-ROM drive
- Microsoft mouse or compatible pointing device

# Pre-Release Software

This book was reviewed and tested against the April 2006 Virtual Machine pre-release version of Dynamics AX 4.0. The April pre-release was the last preview before the final release of Dynamics AX 4.0. This book is expected to be fully compatible with the final release of Dynamics AX 4.0. If there are any changes or corrections to this book, they will be collected and added to a Microsoft Knowledge Base article. For details, see the "Support for This Book" section in this Introduction.

# Technology Updates

As technologies related to this book are updated, links to additional information will be added to the Microsoft Press Technology Updates Web site. Visit this site periodically for updates on Visual Studio 2005 and other technologies:

*http://www.microsoft.com/mspress/updates/*

# Code Samples

All code samples discussed in this book can, where relevant, be downloaded from the book's companion content page at the following address:

*http://www.microsoft.com/mspress/companion/0-7356-2257-4/*

# Support for This Book

Every effort has been made to ensure the accuracy of this book and the companion content. As corrections or changes are collected, they will be added to a Microsoft Knowledge Base article. To view the list of known corrections for this book, visit the following article:

*http://support.microsoft.com/kb/922316*

Microsoft Press provides support for books and companion content at the following Web site:

*http://www.microsoft.com/learning/support/books/*

# Questions and Comments

If you have comments, questions, or ideas regarding the book or the companion content, or questions that are not answered by visiting the sites mentioned earlier, please send them to Microsoft Press via e-mail:

*mspinput@microsoft.com*

You may also send your questions via postal mail to

Microsoft Press
Attn: *Inside Dynamics AX 4.0* Project Editor
One Microsoft Way
Redmond, WA 98052-6399

Please note that Microsoft software product support is not offered through these addresses.

# Part I
# A Tour of the Development Environment

# Chapter 1
# Architectural Overview

The objectives of this chapter are to:

- Introduce the Microsoft Dynamics AX 4.0 architecture.
- Provide an overview of the operations environment.
- Explain the design of the Enterprise Portal.
- Describe how Dynamics AX applications are developed through application modeling and program specification.
- Provide an overview of the application model layering system.
- Provide an overview of the application framework.

## Introduction

Dynamics AX 4.0 is an extremely productive development and run-time environment for enterprise resource planning (ERP) application developers. Much of this productivity is enabled by a software design methodology that is based on developing a model of an application, rather than programming the specification of an application. This model-based methodology is part of the Dynamics AX architecture that helps application developers focus more attention on meeting domain requirements and less attention on meeting technology requirements. For example, the Dynamics AX architecture can help you spend your time meeting financial, production, and logistics domain requirements rather than meeting user interface, client/server, and database access technology requirements.

Dynamics AX makes this possible by satisfying technology requirements for the following core set of application developer tasks:

- Connect database and calculated data to user forms and reports.
- Connect user-entered data and calculated data to database tables.
- Navigate users between forms and reports in response to menu item selections.
- Exchange database and calculated data with external applications.

The following scenario illustrates how productive you can be when you use tools that support a model-based architecture. Suppose you need to implement a feature to edit and batch print account number and account name data. MorphX, the Dynamics AX integrated development environment (IDE), allows quick definition of the required application model using nothing more than mouse clicks.

In this scenario, you first use MorphX to define a database table with two fields that will store account number and account name data by following these steps:

1. Open the Application Object Tree (AOT) modeling designer (one click).
2. Navigate to the *Tables* node and add a table element and two field elements (four clicks).
3. Navigate to the *Extended Data Types* node (two clicks).
4. Drag extended data types onto the previously defined field elements (three clicks). The table elements in the application model are automatically synchronized with the database schema when it is saved.

Then you define a rich client form that hosts a grid control, as described in the following steps. The data in the grid control is bound to the fields in the previously defined table.

1. Navigate to the *Forms* node (two clicks).
2. Add a new form element (two clicks).
3. Add the previously defined table element to the form's data source element (two clicks).
4. Add a grid control to the form design element (four clicks).
5. Drag table field elements onto the grid control columns (seven clicks).

This task can be completed with approximately 27 mouse clicks, which illustrates an unparalleled strength of Dynamics AX.

Rich client forms have a built-in reporting feature that sends the form data to a screen view, a printer, or an e-mail account. The rich client reporting feature also has a built-in batching capability. These built-in features and the AOT allow you to fulfill the domain requirements of the scenario without having to spend any time on the technology requirements.

Figure 1-1 illustrates the key functional areas of the Dynamics AX architecture that enable a high level of productivity.

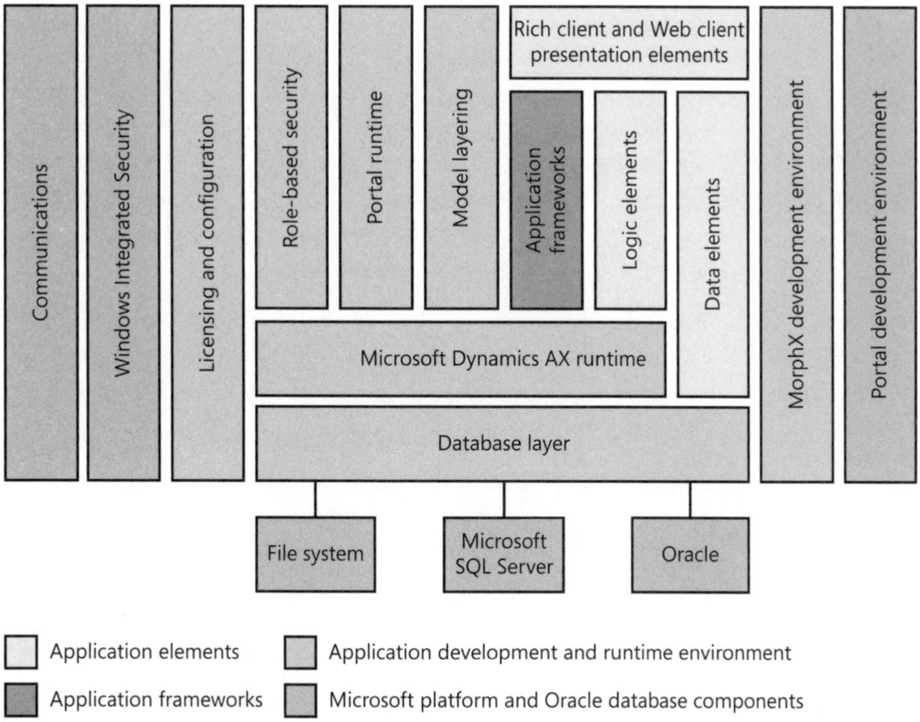

**Figure 1-1**   The Dynamics AX architecture.

You specify the structure and configurable behavior of an ERP application by defining rich client and Web client presentation elements, business logic elements, and data model elements using MorphX. You program the domain-specific and customer-specific behavior of an application in X++, an object-oriented programming language native to MorphX. These model elements and the X++ source code that comprises an object's definition are called application elements, and they are managed with the development tool known as the Application Object Tree (AOT). The AOT is a user control in the MorphX environment that manages a dictionary of application elements, including object definitions, license and configuration keys, resources, references, menus, and jobs.

**Note**   The name *Application Object Tree* is something of a misnomer. Application objects are actually only instantiated by the Dynamics AX runtime, and their definitions are developed with the help of the AOT. The tree also contains resources and references in addition to application object definitions. This book uses the abbreviation AOT to refer to the *tree* control, but it describes the nodes in the tree as mapping to application elements contained in a dictionary.

An X++ application framework provides built-in technology capabilities such as batching, number sequence generation, and error logging. An application model can also be read by application objects using the built-in model reflection capability of the X++ programming language and the model dictionary API. Reflection is the ability of an application to inspect and query its own structure. Refer to Chapter 14, "Reflection," for a discussion of this topic. This capability makes it possible to validate the application model before it is used by the run-time system. For example, the Best Practices development tool can validate that the fields in a primary index are set to *mandatory* by querying the application model to retrieve the table field primary index properties and subsequently test them for the *mandatory* condition.

The Dynamics AX run-time environment and the portal run-time environment execute the ERP application defined by the application model elements. The Dynamics AX run-time environment has model-driven features that are required for the support of user interaction with ERP database applications. For example, specifying that a column model element on a user interface grid control requires mandatory data entry causes the Dynamics AX runtime to ensure that users enter data for a cell in that particular column.

The Dynamics AX application model also has a unique layering feature that supports very fine-grained partner and customer customizations and extensions. The MorphX development environment manages the application elements that exist in multiple layers of the model, and the run-time environment assembles the application elements from different layers so that application object instances can be created with customized and extended structure and behavior.

User and external application interactions are authenticated by the Microsoft Windows Integrated Security system before any application features can be accessed. After authentication, the Active Directory directory service associates a Microsoft Windows user with a Dynamics AX user. Dynamics AX provides role-based security for authorizing Dynamics AX user and user group access to menu items and database data.

The Dynamics AX database layer supports both Microsoft SQL Server and Oracle database systems. The portal development environments are Microsoft Windows SharePoint Services and Microsoft Visual Studio, and the Microsoft technology platform provides the communication infrastructure.

The Microsoft Windows XP and Microsoft Windows Server operating systems provide the technologies that components use to communicate. Communication technologies of importance to ERP application developers are the Microsoft remote procedure call (RPC) technology and the Microsoft ASP.NET Web service technology. Developers must understand how these technologies can affect the performance of their applications. For details about performance, see Chapter 17, "Performance." Microsoft platform communication technologies for platform services such as the file and database systems are of secondary importance to application developers.

# The Operations Environment

Dynamics AX is a three-tiered client/server application that is typically deployed in operations environments configured to meet the needs of customers. Figure 1-2 illustrates a typical deployment scenario for a company using all Dynamics AX capabilities and many Microsoft platform components.

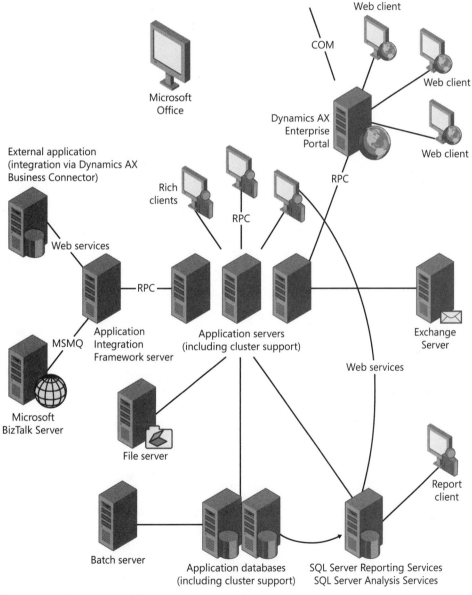

**Figure 1-2**  A Dynamics AX deployment scenario.

The Dynamics AX Application Object Server (AOS) can be hosted on one machine, but it can also scale out to many machines when more concurrent user sessions or dedicated batch servers are required. The server can also access one database or a scaled-out database cluster if the database becomes a processing bottleneck.

Dynamics AX rich clients communicate with the AOS by using the Microsoft RPC technology. For example, the Microsoft Office Excel component hosted on a rich client form communicates directly with SQL Server Analysis Services via Web services. Microsoft SQL Server Reporting Client communicates directly with Microsoft SQL Server Reporting Services via Web services. The application database servers update the SQL Server Analysis Services databases, and SQL Server Reporting Services reads data from the application databases. Dedicating one or more batch servers for batch processing jobs is common.

The Dynamics AX Enterprise Portal is typically hosted on its own machine or many scaled-out machines that also host Microsoft Internet Information Services (IIS), Microsoft Office Share-Point Portal Server, and Windows SharePoint Services. The portal communicates with the Dynamics AX server via Web services and the Dynamics AX Business Connector that communicates with the application servers by using Microsoft RPC technology.

Dynamics AX uses the Application Integration Framework (AIF) to interoperate with Microsoft BizTalk Server, Microsoft Message Queuing (MSMQ), and the file system. The AIF also hosts Web services that respond to requests for data from external applications. Dynamics AX can also interoperate with Microsoft Component Object Model (COM) components and Microsoft .NET components via the COM and Microsoft common language runtime (CLR) interoperability technologies.

Microsoft Office clients can interoperate directly with the AOS via the Dynamics AX Business Connector, and the Dynamics AX application servers can interoperate natively with Microsoft Exchange Server.

# The Application Development and Run-Time Environments

The Dynamics AX development and run-time environments support the following three ERP application configurations, as illustrated in Figure 1-3:

- Rich client application
- Web client application
- Integration client application

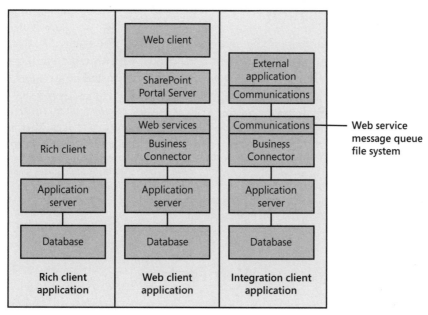

Figure 1-3   Dynamics AX application configurations.

# Rich Client Application

You develop a rich client application configuration by using only the MorphX development environment. The rich client application is hosted by the Dynamics AX runtime. Rich clients communicate with the AOS by using the Microsoft RPC communication technology.

**Caution**   All X++ business logic should be written so that it is application server–centric. This prevents duplication of business logic when business transactions must be supported on rich client, Web client, and integration client applications.

# Web Client Application

You develop a Web client application configuration by using both the MorphX development environment and the Windows SharePoint Services tools. A Web client application is hosted by the Dynamics AX runtime and the Windows SharePoint Services runtime. SharePoint components communicate via the Dynamics AX .NET Business Connector.

**Caution**   You can think of the Business Connector as a rich client without a user interface. When writing programs, remember that the potential latency in communication between client objects and business objects could affect the performance of your Web client application.

## Integration Client Application

An integration client application configuration is mostly developed using only the MorphX development environment. You might require Visual Studio with ASP.NET Web services tools in situations in which you must call from X++ to Web services hosted by an external application. Integration client applications are mostly hosted by the Dynamics AX runtime. ASP.NET Web services and IIS are required for hosting Web services.

> **Note**   The Dynamics AX application has a set of class elements whose names are table element names prefixed with *Ax*, such as *AxSalesTable*. These elements should be used by integration client applications because they allow field updates in any sequence while preserving the data default logic historically developed into rich client presentation controls. For details, see Chapter 9, "XML Document Integration."

# The Enterprise Portal and Web Parts

A portal is a Web site that provides a consolidated overview of information from many systems and serves as a starting point for locating other resources. Portals generally provide personalization capabilities that allow users to define their own views across many systems to accommodate the way they work and contribute to the business.

As the Web has become the predominant platform for electronic work, portals have taken on a significant role in business systems, and the Enterprise Portal (EP) is thus a key asset in the Web strategy for Dynamics AX. It enables customers, vendors, business partners, and employees to access relevant business information directly and conduct business transactions with Dynamics AX through personalized, role-based Web portals.

The EP is built on Windows SharePoint Services, and it brings all the rich content and collaboration functionality of an unstructured SharePoint site together with the structured business data in Dynamics AX. It provides a single touch point for users to view, share, collaborate, transact, search, and make decisions. Moreover, it serves as the platform for front-end application integration and business processes.

On an intranet, the EP could primarily target an internal information worker audience. On an extranet, it could target mobile employees, authenticated external partners, and customers. Or it could target customers on the Internet.

The EP is a complete SharePoint site. It comes with a site definition that includes hundreds of standard Web pages, content, and collaboration elements. The EP Web Parts constitute the front-end user interface elements that connect to Dynamics AX through the .NET Business Connector, and they render the HTML generated by the EP Web framework. The Web Parts are used in EP Web Part Pages together with other Windows SharePoint Services Web Parts. These pages, along with page templates and Windows SharePoint Services elements, are packaged as a SharePoint site definition. All the content and collaboration functionality comes from Windows SharePoint Services, and the EP Web Parts expose the business data from Dynamics AX.

You author Web pages by using the Windows SharePoint Services page designer tools. The pages define the layout and host the Web Parts and their properties. The Windows SharePoint Services Web Parts connect to the Windows SharePoint Services database for content and collaboration functionality. The EP Web Parts connect to Dynamics AX via the .NET Business Connector, and the EP Web framework runtime renders HTML based on the Web element defined in the AOT and pointed to by the EP Web Part and its properties. The page definition from Windows SharePoint Services Web pages is imported into the AOT so that those pages will be created at site creation time.

The Web elements in the AOT can be categorized into three groups:

- Content definition elements, including Weblets, Web forms, reports, Web reports, and Web content. They define the data source, the business logic, the UI elements, and security.

- Navigation definition elements, including the Web menu and Web menu items.

- Files and definitions used to deploy the EP site and components to the Web server.

Here is an example that describes how to display a customer list in the EP:

1. In the AOT, a Web form is created with a data source that points to the table and the user interface elements and logic defined.

2. In the AOT, Web content is created that refers to this Web form and optionally has a security key assigned.

3. In Windows SharePoint Services, a Web page is created with an EP Web Part used for rendering Web forms (in this case, the Web Form Web Part), and the property of the Web Part points to the Web content created in the preceding step.

4. In the AOT, a Web menu item is created that points to the URL of the Web page created in the preceding step, with an optional security key.

5. In the AOT, this Web menu item is included in the Web menu so that any Web page that uses it will render the new link in its navigation section.

The preceding steps define the navigation, and the elements created are placed under the navigation group of *Web* nodes (the *Web Menu Items* and *Web Menus* nodes, respectively) in the AOT. See Figure 1-4.

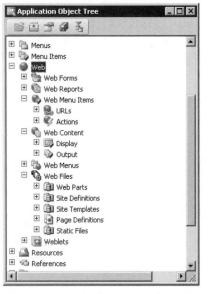

**Figure 1-4** Web elements in the AOT.

When a user browses to the URL, the Web Part connects to the Web framework through the .NET Business Connector and gets the Web content. The Web content security key setting is checked and, depending on the user's permission, the Web form generates the HTML to be rendered by the Web Part.

The EP uses Integrated Windows authentication for authorization, and it leverages Dynamics AX user groups and security models for the business data and uses SharePoint site groups for the content and collaboration data. Web content, Web menu items, and Weblets are secured with Dynamics AX security keys. Users are granted permission to these objects based on their Dynamics AX user groups. Windows SharePoint Services document libraries and lists are secured with SharePoint site groups. Users are granted permission to these objects based on their site groups.

The EP provides a common integrated search across the business data contained in Dynamics AX and Windows SharePoint Services. The Dynamics AX Data Crawler indexes application data, and Windows SharePoint Services indexes the document libraries and lists. The EP search uses both indexes to provide a combined search result.

# Application Modeling and Program Specification

The MorphX development environment provides a set of application modeling and programming tools for developing and extending Dynamics AX applications. Application modeling is a method of declaratively specifying the structure and behavior of an application that is faster, less error-prone, and more precise than programming. Specifying that data is mandatory for a field in a database record, for example, is easy in the Dynamics AX application model because the Dynamics AX runtime ensures that the condition is true in all parts of the application that manipulate data in the table. This prevents the programming effort that would otherwise be required to maintain data integrity throughout the application.

The Dynamics AX business logic is specified by the X++ programming language. X++ is an object-oriented language, much like C# and Java, that supports inheritance, encapsulation, and polymorphism. The language also includes a syntax for writing program statements much like those found in the SQL database manipulation language. The following is an X++ program specification that uses the X++ SQL syntax. The language combines the simplicity of data lookup from SQL with the expressive power of object-oriented programming. You can invoke a method call directly on an object retrieved from the database.

```
while select customer
    where customer.zipcode == campaignZipCode
{
    customer.sendEmail(campaignId);
}
```

For more details on the X++ programming language, refer to Chapter 5, "The X++ Programming Language."

# The Application Model Layering System

Application model layering is the architectural principle in Dynamics AX that allows very granular customizations and extensions to model element definitions and hence to the structure and behavior of applications. When a version of Dynamics AX is released that is not country specific or region specific, all model elements that define the application reside in the lowest layer of an element layering stack. The Dynamics AX runtime, however, does not use only these element definitions when it instantiates application objects. Rather, the runtime assembles an element definition from model elements at all levels of the element layering stack. Elements defined at higher levels of the element layering stack override elements defined at lower levels of the stack. The object that the runtime eventually instantiates is thus an instance of a dynamic type definition composed of model elements at multiple layers of the element layering stack.

Figure 1-5 illustrates the components in the model layering system. Model elements are stored in a separate file on each layer whenever they are saved from the MorphX development environment client. Element definitions are read from these files and dynamically composed by the Dynamics AX runtime. Object instances are created on either the server or the client based on the model element definition. The client can be the MorphX development environment, the rich client, or the Business Connector client.

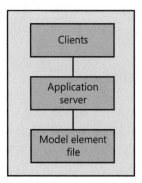

**Figure 1-5**    The application model layering system components.

Figure 1-6 shows the element layers in the application model layering system.

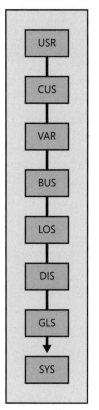

**Figure 1-6**    The model element layers.

Table 1-1 contains a description of each element layer, including ID ranges.

**Table 1-1  Layer Descriptions**

| Layer | Description | ID range |
|---|---|---|
| USR | User | 50001–60000 |
| | Individual companies or companies within an enterprise can use this layer to make customizations unique to customer installations. | |
| CUS | Customer | 40001–50000 |
| | Companies and business partners can modify their installations and add the generic company-specific modifications to this layer. | |
| | The layer is included to support the need for in-house development without jeopardizing modifications made by the business partner. | |
| VAR | Value-added reseller | 30001–40000 |
| | Business partners use this layer, which has no business restrictions, to add any development done for their customers. | |
| BUS | Business solution | 20001–30000 |
| | Business partners develop and distribute vertical and horizontal solutions to other partners and customers. Solutions in this layer can be protected with license keys with a signed agreement for the Dynamics AX Add-On Solutions program. | |
| LOS | Local solution | 18001–20000 |
| | The Dynamics AX solutions offices certify and distribute strategic local solutions developed in-house. | |
| DIS | Distributor | 16001–18000 |
| | The Dynamics AX Sustained Engineering team delivers critical hotfixes using the DIS layer. | |
| GLS | Global solution | 8001–16000 |
| | The Dynamics AX Global Development and Localization team provides a set of GLS layers that contain country-specific functionality for regions in which Dynamics AX is released. | |
| SYS | System | 1–8000 |
| | This is the lowest model element layer and the location of the standard Dynamics AX application. Only Microsoft has access to the element definitions at this layer. | |

The lowest layer is the system layer (SYS), and the highest layer is the user layer (USR). You use the client configuration utility to specify the layer at which you want to customize and extend the Dynamics AX application. When the MorphX environment is launched, it adds or modifies elements at this layer, the working layer, of the model layering system. It cannot, however, modify a model element defined at a higher model layer.

> **Note**    The Dynamics AX runtime always composes model elements starting with the user layer, regardless of the layer in which you are working.

When you modify a model element at a layer lower than the working layer, it is copied to the working model element layer. A class header or method element, for example, is copied to the working layer when it is modified. A table header, field, field group, index, or method element is copied to the working layer when modified. An entire form or report element is copied, however, if any of its members are modified. For example, if you add a button to a form, the entire form is copied to the current layer. If you delete the model element from the working layer, the model element at a lower layer is used instead. In this way, you can undo modifications and easily return to the original model element definitions. You can also compare objects from two different layers by using the MorphX Comparison tool.

Each of the model element layers shown in Figure 1-6 has an associated patch layer. Patch layers handle patches, minor updates, service packs, and hotfixes. Logically, a patch layer is placed directly above the layer that it is patching. A patch layer's name contains the first two characters of the element layer's name, postfixed with the letter *P*. For example, the first three patch layers are named SYP, GLP, and DIP. As a best practice, you should move the content of the patch layer into the main layer with each release of the application.

Most model elements have a unique identifier (ID) that is represented as an unsigned 16-bit integer. To avoid conflict, each layer has a range of available IDs, as shown in Table 1-1.

Model element IDs should never be changed. When an element is deprecated, the IDs can be reused. The IDs must not be changed because they are used as business data and in element definitions. In business data, IDs are typically used to model polymorphic relationships. In element definitions, they are used as references between elements and to relate class and table members across layers. Changing an element ID after it is deployed to an operations environment would result in data inconsistency and require model element ID scrubbing. Because this is highly undesirable, you must ensure that you use the appropriate layer when deploying application customizations and extensions to operations environments.

A model element can be moved between layers and retain its ID. This process can be used to free up a layer, but it puts limitations on the freed layer because IDs are still used, even if it is in another layer. This process can be applied if both layers can be fully controlled. For example, Microsoft successfully moved all model elements from the Microsoft Axapta 3.0 GLS layer to the Dynamics AX 4.0 SYS layer. Keeping the element IDs from the GLS layer provides consistency for business data and element definitions, but it prevents Microsoft from reusing the IDs of the moved model elements in future GLS layers.

> **Note**  Two new features in Dynamics AX 4.0 make ID management easier. A model element ID generator for version control ensures that unique IDs are allocated across multiple developer application installations. Also, new best practice rules detect whether a model element ID value has changed, providing an early warning that can help you solve potential problems before the application is deployed to operations environments.

# The Application Framework

The Dynamics AX application framework is a set of model elements that provide most of the technology requirements for ERP applications. You can incorporate these frameworks into your features so that you can focus on meeting the domain requirements. These frameworks also provide a consistent user experience across all existing and new features. Presenting all the Dynamics AX application frameworks in this book would be impossible, so only the most commonly used frameworks are described in this section.

## The RunBase Framework

The RunBase application framework runs or batches an operation. An operation is a unit of work, such as the posting of a sales order or calculation of a master schedule. The RunBase framework uses the Dialog framework to prompt a user for data input. It uses the SysLastValue framework to persist usage data and the Operation Progress framework to show operation progress.

## The Batch Framework

The Batch application framework creates batch entries in the Dynamics AX batch queue. These entries execute at time intervals specified by a user interacting with a dialog box provided by the framework. The RunBaseBatch framework extends the RunBase framework, and X++ classes that extend this framework can have their operations enlisted in the batch queue.

## The Dialog Framework

The Dialog application framework creates a dynamic dialog box that is not defined in the AOT. You can customize the dialog box by setting the caption and adding fields, field groups, menu items, text, and images. You would typically use the Dialog framework to create dialog boxes when data input is required from the user.

## The Operation Progress Framework

The Operation Progress application framework displays a dialog box that shows the progress of a processing task. You can customize the framework by setting the total number of steps in the operation and by setting the dialog box caption and animation type. You control the progress by incrementing the progress value in derived classes. Best practices include setting the total step count only if it is known (or if it can be accessed rapidly), partitioning the process task into as many steps as possible, and insuring that steps have similar durations. If you use multiple progress bars, the first bar should show overall progress. The framework automatically calculates the time remaining for an operation.

## The Number Sequence Framework

The Number Sequence application framework creates a new sequential number for uniquely identifying business transaction records in database tables. You can specify whether the numbers are sequential or allow gaps in the generated sequences. You can also specify the number format by using a specification string.

## The SysLastValue Framework

The SysLastValue application framework stores and retrieves user settings or usage data values that persist between processes. You use this framework to save, retrieve, and delete a container of usage data.

## The Application Integration Framework

The Application Integration Framework (AIF) sends business transactions to external applications and responds to requests from external applications. The framework comprises XML document classes, message queue management, Web services, and data mapping features. For details on how to use this framework to build integration applications, refer to Chapter 9.

## The Wizard Framework

The Wizard application framework helps users configure application features. You can use the Wizard Wizard to generate a set of default classes that extend the Wizard framework. (See Chapter 7, "Extending Microsoft Dynamics AX," for more information about the Wizard Wizard.) The resulting wizard provides start and finish pages and a user-defined number of empty pages in between. You customize the generated classes by populating the wizard pages with controls and controlling the page flow.

## The Infolog Framework

You use the Infolog application framework when business transaction status logging is required. The information log form control displays the logged message. The Infolog framework is also the default exception handler, so any exception not caught by application code is caught by the Infolog framework. You can extend this framework to provide customized logging features.

# Chapter Summary

This chapter provided an overview of the Dynamics AX operations environment and the components in the Dynamics AX model-based architecture. The architecture comprises client and server components that scale to support many concurrent users who integrate with external applications and interoperate with many Microsoft platform technologies. This architecture comprises a layered application model and the X++ programming language supported by the MorphX development environment and executed by the Dynamics AX run-time environment. The Dynamics AX architecture also provides an application framework that meets many of the technology requirements for business applications, allowing you to focus on meeting your ERP domain requirements for rich client, Web client, and integration applications.

# Chapter 2
# The MorphX Development Environment

The objectives of this chapter are to:

- Introduce MorphX, the Microsoft Dynamics AX 4.0 integrated development environment (IDE).

- Show how MorphX is used throughout a product's life cycle.

- Explain why MorphX is designed the way it is.

- Introduce the application model elements and their relationships.

## Introduction

This chapter provides an overview of the MorphX development environment. It introduces the designers and tools available and explains when you would typically use them when building an application with MorphX. The designers and tools are described in detail in the next two chapters.

You build an application with MorphX by using modeling. The building blocks available for modeling are commonly known as *application model elements*. This chapter introduces the different kinds of application model elements and their relationships, describes the tools necessary for working with application model elements, and explains the sequence in which to apply the tools. For a more thorough explanation of the application model elements, refer to the Microsoft Dynamics AX SDK.

## Developing with MorphX

MorphX features an extensive set of designers and tools. This section provides an overview of the tools and designers by mapping them to a typical product life cycle, shown in Figure 2-1.

Refer to Chapter 3, "The MorphX Designers," and Chapter 4, "The MorphX Development Tools," for in-depth information about how to use the designers and tools.

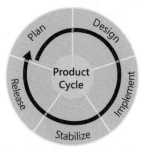

**Figure 2-1**   A product life cycle model

Figure 2-1 shows a typical product life cycle. Most software projects start with a planning phase. In this phase, you decide on the market segment, establish the vision for the product, and allocate resources. The design phase follows, in which design documents are created, design reviews are conducted, prototypes are implemented, and requirements are documented. In the next phase, implementation,  code implementation takes place. When implementation is complete, the stabilization phase begins. Here the focus is to validate the product quality: Are all requirements met? Does the product work as intended? Does the product meet performance goals? When the product stability is satisfactory, the product can be released. The release phase includes packaging, marketing, and maintenance, which might involve releasing error corrections, hotfixes, and service packs. Finally, the product life cycle starts over with the next version of the product.

You might follow this model in a strict manner, use variations, or manage your projects in a less formal manner. The purpose of this discussion is to introduce the MorphX designers and tools. Note that it is beyond the scope of this book to discuss how to run software projects optimally.

## Plan

When running a Dynamics AX project, you never start from scratch. It might be your first Dynamics AX project and you might have a lot of learning to do, practices to formulate, and partnerships to form, but you always have a code base from which to start.

In the planning phase, you investigate the existing Dynamics AX functionality and plan how to integrate with the existing functionality at a high level. Typically, this takes place at the user interface level.

It is a good idea to do this kind of investigation in demo mode. Dynamics AX automatically enters demo mode when you skip the License Information step in the installation checklist. The main benefit of investigating in demo mode is that all product functionality is available; if a license file is loaded, only the functionality purchased for that particular license is available.

When all functionality is available, you can more effectively plan how to integrate and how to avoid implementing redundant functionality. When you work in demo mode, the number of users, Application Object Servers, and companies are limited. In demo mode, MorphX is not available, the date-handling algorithm is limited, and dates after a certain threshold date cannot be used.

## Design

The first designer you will see in Dynamics AX is the Application Object Tree (AOT). This is the repository for all the elements that together constitute the existing business application.

The next designers you will use are the property sheet and the X++ editor. Most nodes in the AOT have a set of properties that can be inspected and modified by using the property sheet. Method nodes contain X++ source code. The code can be inspected and modified by using the X++ editor.

With these designers, you can, for example, see the structure of forms (by using the AOT), the properties specified on each control (by using the property sheet), and the event handler's implementation (by using the X++ editor). You will use these designers throughout the remaining phases of the product life cycle.

If you use the Version Control tool, you benefit from all elements being read-only. In read-only mode, you can investigate without the risk of modifying the existing code. If this is the first version of your project, you can also use the layering technology to provide the same safe-guard.

The designers discussed so far reveal implementation details at the element level. Three additional tools show how elements relate to each other at a higher level. The Cross-Reference tool shows you where any specific element is used. In the design phase, this tool is useful for determining where table fields are displayed, initialized, read, modified, and so on. The Find tool allows you to search any element in the AOT. In the design phase, you typically search the entire AOT. The Reverse Engineering tool raises the abstraction level. With this tool, you can generate Microsoft Visio Unified Modeling Language (UML) models. If you find yourself struggling to understand the object hierarchies or the data models, you can take advantage of a visual UML diagram by using this tool.

During the design phase, you should also consider your approach to testing. Designing for testing from the beginning makes your life easier later in the product life cycle, and it typically results in a better design. See Chapter 16, "Unit Testing," for information on implementing unit tests by using MorphX.

## Implement

When your design documents and functional specifications are complete and you are ready to start developing, you should consider setting up the Version Control tool. Version control allows you to keep track of all changes, which is particularly useful when working in large teams. You can also specify code quality criteria. Code that does not conform to the code quality that you specify is rejected in the version control check-in process, so you can always be sure that code that falls short of the quality standard is not allowed into your project.

When you are ready to start your first implementation, you should use the Project Designer to group related elements because the large number of elements in the AOT can make it hard to work efficiently otherwise. A project provides a view into the AOT, allowing you to focus on the elements that you are working with. Using a project allows you to define what you want to see and the structure in which you see it.

After you have written your first piece of source code with the X++ editor, you must compile it. The compiler generates the bytecode from your source code and presents any syntax errors. The compiler also triggers the Best Practices tool, which validates your implementation of X++ code and element definitions according to development guidelines, allowing you to automatically detect coding errors.

You can also use the Form Visual Designer and the Report Visual Designer to construct your forms and reports. If you are developing a multilingual feature, you can use the Label Editor to create localizable text resources.

You might want to refer to code examples during the implementation phase. The Find tool and the Cross-Reference tool can help you identify examples for API usage. The Cross-Reference tool is also helpful if you need to refactor your code.

If, when you are ready to run your feature, you discover that your logic is not behaving the way that you intended it to, you can use the debugger to track the problem. The debugger starts automatically when execution hits a breakpoint. You might also need to see the data that has been created by your feature. You can use the Table Browser tool to look for the data.

## Stabilize

When you have completed your implementation, you will want to find and correct any problems that you might have in your code—ideally, without introducing new problems.

You can use the debugger to find problems in your code. If a problem mandates a change of method profiles (return values or parameters), you should use the Cross-Reference tool to perform an impact analysis of your changes before you make them. If you use the Version Control tool to track changes, you can use the Compare tool to highlight differences in each revision of an element.

## Release

You might be involved in upgrading your customer from one version of an application to the next. For example, you might upgrade the customer from an earlier version of Dynamics AX, or you might upgrade the customer from one version of your functionality to the next. To detect any conflicting changes to elements, you can use the Create Upgrade Project option, available in the Upgrade Checklist, or you can access it from Tools\Development Tools\ Version Update. To resolve conflicts, the Compare tool is unmatched. It allows you to compare versions of elements, and, based on the results, upgrade elements.

# Application Model Elements

The application model dictionary in the AOT organizes application elements into element categories. Rich client forms and reports, for example, are top-level categories, and Web client forms and reports are collected under a top-level Web category. For simplicity, the rich client form category is called Forms, and the rich client reports category is called Reports.

> **Tip**   To better understand the element structure as you read, you might want to start Dynamics AX and open the AOT.

# Operational and Programming Model Elements

Operational model elements are used to model how the application should behave according to security, configuration, and licensing in an operational environment. For example, certain functionality is available only if it is enabled system wide and the user is authorized to use it. Programming model elements provide ways to reference library code, definitions, and resources. They also allow you to write small X++ scripts to experiment with the X++ language capabilities.

The following is a list of the operational model elements:

- Security keys
- Configuration keys
- License codes

These model elements change the operational characteristics of the Dynamics AX development and run-time environments.

The programming model elements encompass the following:

- **Reference elements**   Elements whose properties identify the Microsoft .NET assemblies referenced in X++ statements
- **Resource elements**   Name file resources loaded into the memory
- **Macro elements**   Libraries of X++ string replacement procedures
- **Job elements**   X++ programs primarily used for testing and debugging an executable from within the development environment.

Figure 2-2 illustrates the operational and programming element categories in the AOT.

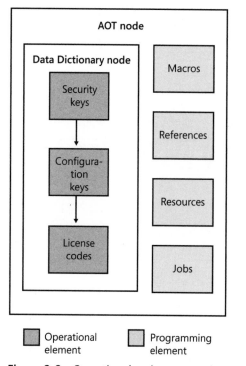

**Figure 2-2**   Operational and programming model elements.

## Operational Model Elements

You use the AOT and the property sheet to declaratively enable and disable application features by associating configuration keys with menu item elements and data elements. The MorphX development environment synchronizes table and view elements with the database schema only if they are associated with an active configuration key or if they have no configuration key. For details, see the section "Database Model Elements," later in this chapter, and the section on database synchronization in Chapter 12, "The Database Layer." The Dynamics AX runtime renders presentation controls only for menu items that are associated with an active configuration key or that have no configuration key. You can enable and disable application logic by using X++ to test for the state of a configuration key.

Dynamics AX includes all the application modules developed by Microsoft. These modules are locked with license codes that must be unlocked with license keys. An unlocked module can also be configured by using configuration keys. Dynamics AX administrators manually enable and disable configuration keys by using the check boxes in the system configuration dialog box at Administration\Setup\System\Configuration. You can manually activate configuration keys associated with license code elements only if there is a valid license key for the corresponding license code element.

Security keys are part of the Dynamics AX role-based security framework. When a user identified by a Microsoft Windows principal logs on to a Dynamics AX application, he or she is authenticated with the Microsoft Windows platform security infrastructure and then associated with a Dynamics AX application user group that denotes the application user's role. An application user role determines which user interface actions a user is authorized to perform and which data the user is authorized to view and modify.

Security keys are associated with all other model elements so that similar elements can be grouped together into a security group. Access permissions that are assigned to a security key apply to all elements that are members of the associated security group. Access permissions can also be assigned to individual elements in a security group. The security grouping provided by security keys is used to display a tree of security keys and application elements when they are displayed in the User Group Permissions dialog box. This makes it easier for an application administrator to navigate the thousands of menu item elements and data elements for which he or she needs to assign user group permissions.

## Programming Model Elements

The following list describes the programming model elements in detail:

- **Reference elements**   Reference elements hold references to Microsoft .NET assemblies for the .NET common language runtime (CLR) types to be incorporated natively into X++ source code. The X++ editor reads type data from the referenced assemblies so that IntelliSense is available for CLR namespaces, types, and type members. The MorphX compiler uses the CLR type definitions in the referenced assembly for type and member syntax validation, and the Dynamics AX runtime uses the reference elements to locate and load the referenced assembly at run time.

- **Resource elements**   Resource elements hold references to file resources that are read from the file system and stored in memory. Image and animation files used when developing Web client applications are referenced as resources. The name of the file that contains the resource also references the resource when it is stored in the database.

- **Macro elements**   Macro elements are libraries of X++ syntax replacement procedures included in the X++ source code. You should use macro libraries to provide readable names for constants. See Chapter 5, "The X++ Programming Language," for an example of a macro procedure and an example that shows how to include a macro library in X++ source code.

- **Job elements**   Job elements are X++ source code statements that are easily executed by selecting the Command\Go menu item or by pressing F5 on the keyboard while using MorphX. Job elements offer a convenient method of experimenting with features of the X++ language when they are used to write sample code. See Chapter 5 for an example of X++ code statements written in a job element. Job elements should not be used for writing application code. In fact, the Dynamics AX enterprise resource planning (ERP) application model contains no job element when it is released to customers and development partners.

# Value Type, Database, and Data Association Model Elements

Figure 2-3 illustrates the value type, database, and data association element categories that are located in the *Data Dictionary* node in the AOT. Configuration key elements can be associated with base enumeration and extended data type elements as well as with table, view, and map elements. Table, view, and map application elements can also be associated with security key elements.

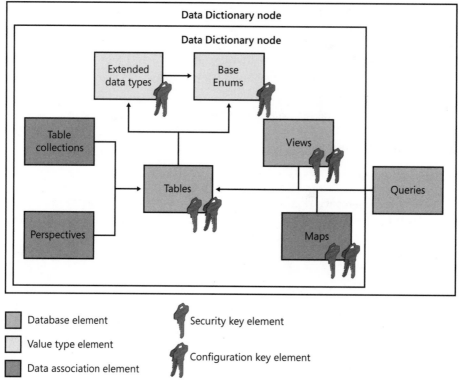

**Figure 2-3**   Value type, database, and data association model elements.

## Value Type Model Elements

A base enumeration element (sometimes shortened to "enum") defines a name for a group of symbolic constants that are used in X++ code statements. For example, an enumeration with the name *WeekDay* can be defined to name the group of symbolic constants that includes *Monday, Tuesday, Wednesday, Thursday, Friday, Saturday*, and *Sunday*.

An extended data type element can extend a base enumeration by providing a new name for a group of symbolic constants that includes the base enumeration elements and any additional symbolic constants or symbolic constraints defined in the extension. An extended data type element can also extend the *string, boolean, int, real, date, time, int64, guid,* and *container* types. An extended data type definition can also comprise a set of application parameters that define how the Dynamics AX runtime renders user interface controls. For example, an extended data type representing an account number extends a *string* value type, restricts its length to 10 characters, and sets its user interface label to "Account number."

Extended data types can also extend each other. For example, an extended data type that defines an account number can be specialized by other extended data types defining customer and vendor account numbers. The specialized extended data type inherits properties, such as string length, label, and Help text. Some of the properties can be overridden on the specialized extended data type. You constrain the possible values of an extended data type and define a database table association by adding a relationship from the extended data type to a table field element. The Dynamics AX runtime automatically ensures that the values of the extended data type are consistent with this relationship. The runtime also uses the defined relationship to navigate between rich client and Web client main table forms when a user selects the Go To The Main Table Form menu item. This menu item appears when a user right-clicks a form data grid column that is mapped to a table element field whose type is an extended data type with a defined relationship.

## Database Model Elements

Database elements are database table and view definitions that correspond to database server entities and relationships as well as query elements that define database query statements. The MorphX development environment synchronizes table and view element definitions with database schema definitions. This feature allows Dynamics AX to use both Microsoft SQL Server and the Oracle database server as application databases. MorphX synchronizes only those database elements for which there are enabled configuration keys and corresponding valid license keys.

Database element keys and indexes are used to create database entity keys and indexes, but data element interrelationships are not used to create integrity relationships in a database. Instead, they validate data entries to automatically join and select database data as a user navigates between forms, and they join data sources associated with a form. For example, a user sees confirmations only for the selected sales orders when navigating from a sales order form to a sales order confirmation form. Moreover, MorphX automatically converts between X++ programming value types such as *string*, *enum*, and *boolean* and their corresponding database data types, such as *varchar* and *int*. For example, an X++ string defined to have a maximum length of 10 characters is stored as a database *varchar* data type defined to have a maximum length of 10 characters.

A table element can also define table field groups, menu item references, table relationships, delete actions, and methods that are used by the Dynamics AX runtime when it renders data entry presentation controls and when it ensures the referential integrity of the database. The X++ editor also uses these elements to support developers with IntelliSense when they write X++ statements that create, read, update, and delete data in the database. You can also use the AOT to associate table elements with data source elements on forms, reports, queries, and views.

View elements define database table view entities and are synchronized with the application database. View elements can include a query that filters data in a table or data joined from multiple tables. View element definitions also include table field mappings and methods. Tables cannot be updated through views because they primarily provide an efficient method for reading data. View elements can be associated with form and report data sources and are instantiated in X++ variable declarations.

Query elements define a database query structure that can be executed from X++ statements, particularly X++ statements used in classes that derive from the *RunBase* class. You add tables to query element data sources and specify how they should be joined. You also specify how data is returned from the query, such as by using sort order and range specifications.

> **Note**   You do not have to use the query element as form and report data sources because these data sources have a similar built-in query specification capability.

## Data Association Model Elements

Map elements do not define database entities, so they are not synchronized with the database. They actually define X++ programming elements that wrap table objects at run time. Map elements associate common fields and methods for tables that are not in third-normal form. For example, the *CustTable* table element and the *VendTable* table element in the Dynamics AX application model are mapped to the *AddressMap* map element so that developers can use one *AddressMap* object to access common address fields and methods. The MorphX compiler validates that table variables assigned to map variables are defined as valid element mappings.

> **Note**   Maps provide a useful common interface to data entities and prevent the need to duplicate methods on denormalized tables, but you should use maps only when normalization is not an option.

Table collection elements define groups of tables that can be shared by two or more Dynamics AX companies that share virtual company accounts. An administrator creates a virtual company and then adds table collections to it. The administrator also adds the virtual company accounts to an actual Dynamics AX company's accounts. The Dynamics AX runtime uses the virtual company data area identifier instead of the actual company data area identifier when it inserts or reads data in the tables in the table collection.

> **Caution**   The tables placed in a table collection should not have foreign key relationships with tables outside the table collection unless specific extensions are written to maintain the relational integrity of the database.

Perspective elements define table collections that report views on the Dynamics AX database model. Perspectives are used to design and generate ad hoc reports by using Microsoft SQL Server Reporting Services.

# Class Model Elements

Class elements define the structure and behavior of business logic types that work on ERP reference data and business transaction data. These elements comprise object-oriented type definitions that instantiate business objects at run time. You define type declaration headers and methods by using the X++ programming language. You associate rich client and Web client menu item elements in the AOT with class element methods by using the property sheet provided by MorphX. This allows the Dynamics AX runtime to instantiate corresponding business logic objects when users select action, display, or output menu item controls on a user interface.

The Dynamics AX runtime also invokes business object methods when they overload event handlers on tables, forms, and reports. Class elements are also defined for application integration scenarios that are not driven by a user interface. Chapter 9, "XML Document Integration," describes how these elements are associated with XML document elements that read from and write to the file system, Microsoft Message Queuing, and Web services.

# Presentation Model Elements

The two types of presentation elements include rich client elements and Web client elements. The rich client element categories, Forms and Reports, are located under the *AOT root* node, and the Web client element categories, Web Forms and Web Reports, are under the *Web* node in the AOT. Presentation elements are form, report, menu, or menu item definitions for either a Microsoft Windows client application, called a rich client application, or a Microsoft Windows SharePoint Services client application, called a Web client application. Both types of clients have a control layout feature called IntelliMorph. IntelliMorph automatically lays out presentation controls based on model element property and security settings. Presentation controls are automatically supplied with database and calculated data when their data source elements are associated with database or temporary table fields.

## Rich Client Model Elements

Figure 2-4 illustrates the rich client elements and their relationships. Configuration key and security key elements can be associated with menu item elements only. This prevents users from executing application code for which there are no license keys or for which there is no active configuration key.

Table elements can also be associated with menu item elements. Each table element definition includes an optional display menu item element reference that, by convention, launches a form presentation control that renders the data from the database table in a grid control. The Dynamics AX runtime also automatically adds a Go To The Main Table Form menu item to a drop-down menu that appears when a user right-clicks a grid cell whose associated table column has a foreign key relationship with another table. The Dynamics AX runtime uses the referenced table's menu item element to launch the form that renders the data from the foreign key table in a table grid. The form is populated with all the data from the foreign key table, and the related record is displayed as the active record.

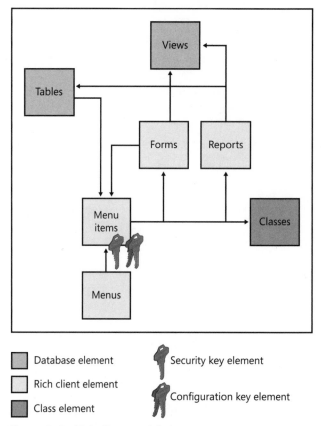

**Figure 2-4**   Rich client model elements.

Menu elements define logical menu item groupings. Menu definitions can include submenu elements and other menu elements. The menu element named *MainMenu* defines the menu entries for the Dynamics AX navigation pane.

Menu item elements define hyperlinks labeled for display, action, and output that the Dynamics AX runtime uses to instantiate and execute forms, business logic objects (defined by using class elements), and reports, respectively. When rendering forms and reports, the Dynamics AX runtime ignores menu items that are disabled by configuration keys, security keys, or role-based access permissions.

Form elements define a presentation control with which users insert, update, and read database data. A form definition includes a data source and a design element that defines the controls that must be rendered on the form, as well as their data source mappings. A form is launched when a user clicks a display menu item control, such as a button.

Report elements define a presentation control that renders database and calculated data in a page layout format. A report can be sent to the screen, a printer, an e-mail account, or the file system. A report definition includes a data source and a design element that define the output-only controls that must be rendered on the report, as well as their data source mappings. A report is launched when a user clicks an output menu item control, such as a button.

## Web Client Model Elements

Configuration key and security key elements can be associated with Web menu items and Weblet elements. This prevents users from executing Web application code for which there are no license keys or for which there is no active configuration key. Resource elements can be associated with Web form and Web report elements so that they can be incorporated into Web pages by the Dynamics AX runtime.

Figure 2-5 illustrates the Web client model elements and their relationships.

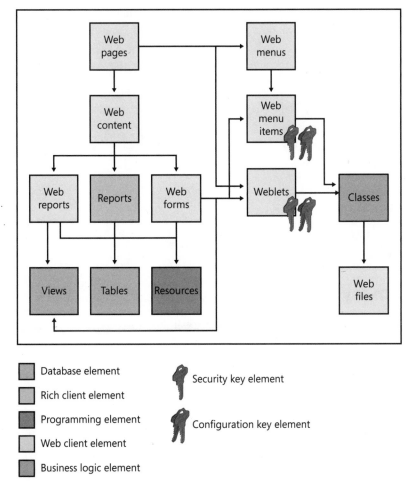

**Figure 2-5**   Web client model elements.

Web menu elements define logical Web menu item groupings. Web menu definitions can include submenu application elements and other Web menu application elements. Web menu items are rendered as hyperlinks on Web pages.

Web menu item elements define hyperlinks containing URLs and class labels that the Dynamics AX runtime uses to navigate between Web pages and to generate Web pages, respectively. Web menu items render Web form and Web menu hyperlinks and controls.

Web file elements define file references to components required by Windows SharePoint Services. These components include site definitions, templates, and Web Part installation files. The MorphX development environment saves these files to a specified Web server at deployment time.

Weblet elements define references to class application elements that extend the *Weblet* class definition. Weblet objects return HTML documents whose format is governed by input parameters.

Web form elements define Web presentation controls with which users insert, update, and read database data. A Web form definition includes a data source and a design element that defines the controls that must be rendered on the Web form, as well as their data source mappings. A Web form is generated when a Web page hosting the Web form is generated.

Web report elements define Web presentation controls that render database and calculated data in a Web format. A report definition includes a data source and a design element that define the output-only controls that must be rendered on the report, as well as their data source mappings. A Web report is generated when a Web page hosting the Web form is generated.

Web content elements define display and output elements that reference Web form, Web report, and (rich) report elements for their content.

Web page elements define the composition of an HTML document element that comprises Web content elements and Web menu elements.

# Chapter Summary

This chapter provided a brief overview of the design and operation of the tool set within the MorphX development environment, as well as an overview of all the AOT elements seen from a typical product life-cycle perspective. The next two chapters offer in-depth descriptions of how to work with each of the components in MorphX.

# Chapter 3
# The MorphX Designers

The objectives of this chapter are to:

- Provide an overview of the designers used when implementing a business application using MorphX.

- Share tips and tricks on how to use the designers efficiently.

- Demonstrate how to personalize and extend the designers.

## Introduction

The business functionality in Microsoft Dynamics AX 4.0 was built with the MorphX designers. Each feature uses the model elements described in the previous chapter. These elements contain metadata, structure, properties (key and value pairs), and X++ code. For example, a table element includes the name of the table, the properties set for the table, the fields, the indices, the relations, the methods, and so on.

The parts of the elements have different characteristics. MorphX has a set of designers that are streamlined to create, view, modify, and delete the contents of elements.

The MorphX designers include the following:

- **The Application Object Tree**   The Application Object Tree, or AOT, is the main entry point for all development activities and the repository for all elements. You can use the AOT to invoke the other designers and to browse and create elements.

- **The Project Designer**   You can group related elements into projects by using this designer.

- **The property sheet**   You can use this designer to inspect and modify properties of elements. The property sheet shows key and value pairs.

- **The X++ Editor**   You can use this text editor to inspect and write X++ source code.

- **The Label Editor**   You can create and inspect localizable strings by using this editor.

- **The Form Visual Designer and the Report Visual Designer**   You can design forms and reports in a what-you-see-is-what-you-get fashion by using these editors.

The behavior of the designers can be personalized by clicking Options on the Tools menu. Figure 3-1 shows the Options dialog box.

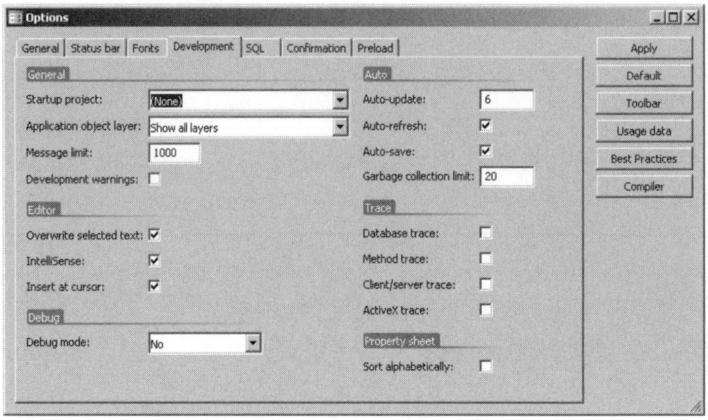

**Figure 3-1**   The dialog box in which development options are specified.

# The Application Object Tree

The AOT is the main entry point to MorphX and is the repository explorer for all metadata. You can open it by clicking its button on the toolbar or by pressing Ctrl+D.

## Navigating the AOT

As the name implies, the Application Object Tree is a tree view. The root of the AOT contains the element categories, such as Classes, Tables, and Forms. Note that some elements are grouped into subcategories to provide a better structure. For example, Tables, Maps, Views, and Extended Data Types reside under Data Dictionary, and all Web-related elements are found under Web. Figure 3-2 shows the AOT.

The AOT can be navigated by using the arrow keys on the keyboard. Pressing the right arrow expands a node if it has any children.

Elements are ordered alphabetically. Because thousands of elements exist, understanding the naming conventions and adhering to them is important to effectively use the AOT.

**Figure 3-2**   The Application Object Tree.

All element names in the AOT follow this structure:

*<Business area name>* + *<Business area description>* + *<Action performed or type of contents>*

In this naming convention, similar elements are placed next to each other. The business area name is also often referred to as the prefix. The prefixes are commonly used to indicate the team responsible for an element.

Table 3-1 contains a list of the most common prefixes and their descriptions.

**Table 3-1   Common Prefixes**

| Prefix | Description |
| --- | --- |
| Ax | Dynamics AX typed data source |
| Axd | Dynamics AX business document |
| BOM | Bill of material |
| COS | Cost accounting |
| Cust | Customer |
| HRM | Human resource management |
| Invent | Inventory management |
| JMG | Shop floor control |
| KM | Knowledge management |
| Ledger | General ledger |
| PBA | Product builder |
| Prod | Production |
| Proj | Project |

Table 3-1    **Common Prefixes**

| Prefix | Description |
|--------|-------------|
| Purch | Purchase |
| Req | Requirements |
| Sales | Sales |
| SMA | Service management |
| SMM | Sales and marketing management |
| Sys | Application frameworks and development tools |
| Tax | Tax engine |
| Vend | Vendor |
| Web | Web framework |
| WMS | Warehouse management |

When creating new elements, make sure to follow the recommended naming conventions. This will make future development and maintenance much easier.

An alternative view of the information organized by the AOT is provided by the Project Designer. The Project Designer is described in detail later in this chapter.

## Creating New Elements

You can create new elements in the AOT by right-clicking the element category node and selecting New <*Element Name*>, as shown in Figure 3-3.

Figure 3-3    Creating a new element in the AOT.

Objects are given automatically generated names when they are created. However, the default names should be replaced with new names in accordance with the naming convention.

## Modifying Elements

Each node in the AOT has a set of properties and either subnodes or X++ code. The property sheet (shown in Figure 3-9) can be used to inspect or modify properties, and the X++ editor (shown in Figure 3-12) can be used to inspect or modify X++ code.

The order of the subnodes may play a role in the semantics of the element. For example, the tabs on a form display in the order in which they are listed in the AOT. The order of nodes can be changed by selecting a node and pressing the Alt key while pressing the Up or Down arrow key on the keyboard.

A red vertical line next to an element name marks it as modified and unsaved, or *dirty*, as shown in Figure 3-4.

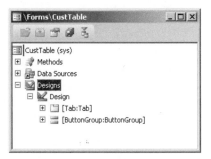

**Figure 3-4**   A dirty element in the AOT, indicated by a vertical line next to CustTable (sys).

A dirty element is saved when:

- The element is executed.

- The Save or Save All actions are explicitly invoked by the developer.

- Auto-save takes place. The frequency of this is specified in the Options dialog box accessible from the Tools  menu.

## Refreshing Elements

If several developers make modifications to elements simultaneously in the same installation of Dynamics AX, each developer's local elements could become out of sync with the latest version. To ensure that the local versions of remotely changed elements are updated, an auto-refresh thread runs in the background. This auto-refresh functionality will eventually update all changes, but you might want to explicitly force a refresh. You do this by right-clicking the element that you want to restore and then selecting Restore. This action refreshes both the on-disk and in-memory versions of the element. The following is a less elegant way of ensuring that the latest elements are used:

1.   Close the Dynamics AX client to clear in-memory elements.

2.   Close the Dynamics Server service on the AOS to clear in-memory elements.

3.   Delete the application object cache files (*.auc) from the Local Application Data folder (located in Documents and Settings\<*User*>\Local Settings\Application Data) to remove the on-disk elements.

> **Note**   In earlier versions of Dynamics AX, the application object cache was stored in .aoc files. To support Unicode, the file extension has been changed to .auc in Dynamics AX 4.0.

## Element Actions

Each node in the AOT contains a set of available actions. These actions are accessed from the context menu, which can be opened by right-clicking the node in question.

Note that:

■   The actions available depend on the type of node selected.

■   You may select multiple nodes and perform actions simultaneously on all of the nodes selected.

A frequently used action is Open New Window, which is available for all nodes. It opens a new AOT window with the current nodes as the root. This action was used when creating the screen capture of the *CustTable* element shown in Figure 3-4, and it can be very useful when dragging and dropping elements.

The list of available actions on the context menu is extendable. You may create custom actions for any element in the AOT by using the features provided by MorphX. In fact, all actions listed on the Add-Ins submenu are implemented in MorphX by using X++ and the MorphX designers.

You can enlist a class as a new add-in by following this procedure:

1.   Create a new menu item and give it a meaningful name, a label, and Help text.

2.   Set the menu item's *Object Type* property to Class.

3.   Set the menu item's *Object* property to the name of the class to be invoked by the add-in.

4.   Drag the menu item to the *SysContextMenu* menu.

5.   If the action will be available only for certain nodes, the *verifyItem()* method on the *SysContextMenu* class must be modified.

## Element Layers

When an element from a lower layer is modified, a copy of the element is placed in the current layer. All elements in the current layer appear in bold type (as shown in Figure 3-5), which makes it easy to recognize changes. For a description of the layer technology, see the section "The Application Model Layering System" in Chapter 1, "Architectural Overview."

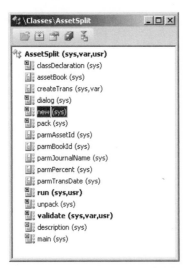

**Figure 3-5**   An element in the AOT that exists in several layers.

The Application Object Layer setting in the Options dialog box can be used to personalize the layer information shown in the AOT. Figure 3-5 shows a class with the option set to All Layers. As you can see, each method is suffixed with information about the layers in which it is defined, such as sys, var, and usr. If an element exists in several layers, you can right-click it and select Layers to access the versions of an element from lower layers. The All Layers setting is highly recommended during code upgrade because it provides a visual representation of the layer dimension directly in the AOT.

# The Project Designer

For a fully customizable overview of the elements, you can use *projects*. In a project, elements can be grouped and structured according to the developer's preference. This is a powerful alternative to the AOT because all the elements needed for a feature can be collected in one project.

## Creating a New Project

The Project Designer is opened by clicking the Project button on the toolbar. Figure 3-6 shows the Project Designer.

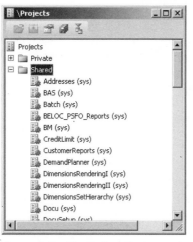

**Figure 3-6**   The Project Designer, showing available private and shared projects.

Except for its structure, the Project Designer behaves exactly like the AOT. Every element in a project is also present in the AOT.

When you create a new project, you must decide whether it should be private or shared among all developers. You cannot set access requirements on shared projects. A shared project can be made private (and a private project can be shared) by dragging it from the shared category into the private category.

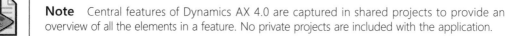

> **Note**   Central features of Dynamics AX 4.0 are captured in shared projects to provide an overview of all the elements in a feature. No private projects are included with the application.

A startup project may be specified in the Options dialog box. If specified, the chosen project automatically opens when Dynamics AX is started.

## Automatically Generated Projects

Projects can be automatically generated in several ways to make working with them easier.

### Group Masks

Groups are folders in a project. When you create a group, the contents of the group can be automatically generated by setting the *ProjectGroupType* property (All is an option) and a regular expression as the *GroupMask* property. The contents of the group are created automatically and kept up to date as elements are created, deleted, and renamed. This ensures that the project is always current, even when elements are created directly in the AOT.

Figure 3-7 shows the *ProjectGroupType* property set to Tables and the *GroupMask* property set to <xref on a project group. All table names starting with *xref* (the prefix for the Cross-Reference tool) will be included in the project group.

**Figure 3-7**   The property sheet specifying settings for *ProjectGroupType* and *GroupMask*.

Figure 3-8 shows the resulting project when using the settings from Figure 3-7.

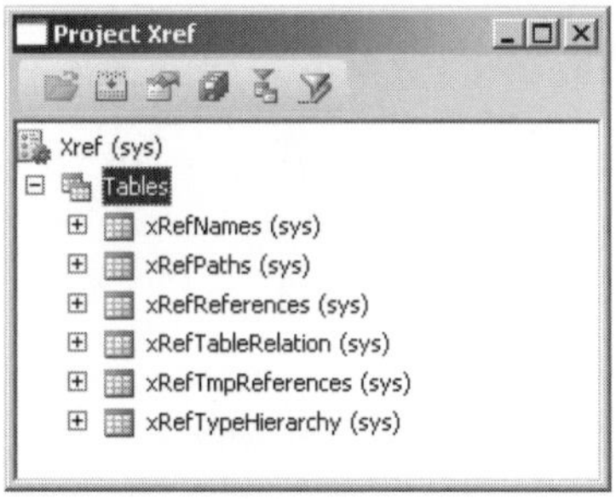

**Figure 3-8**   A project created by using group masks.

## Filters

You can also generate a project based on a filter. Because all elements in the AOT persist in a database format, you can use a query to filter elements and have the results presented in a project. A project filter is created by clicking the Filter button on the project's toolbar. Depending on the complexity of the query, project generation can take several minutes.

This feature allows you to create a project containing:

- Elements created or modified within the last month.
- Elements created or modified by a named user.
- Elements from a particular layer.

## Development Tools

Several development tools, such as the Wizard Wizard, produce projects containing the elements created by the wizard. The result of running the Wizard Wizard is a new project that contains a form, a class, and a menu item—all the elements you need to run the wizard.

Several other wizards also create projects, such as the Report Wizard and the Class Wizard. You can access the wizards by clicking Tools\Development Tools\Wizards.

## Layer Comparison

You can compare all elements in one layer with elements in another layer, called the reference layer. If an element exists in both layers, and the definitions of the element are different or the element does not exist in the reference layer, the element will be added to the resulting project. You can compare layers by clicking Tools\Development Tools\Version Update\ Compare Layers.

## Upgrade Projects

When you upgrade from one version of Dynamics AX to another or install a new service pack, new elements are introduced and existing elements are modified. These changes might conflict with customizations implemented in a higher layer.

The upgrade project feature makes a three-way comparison to establish whether an element has an upgrade conflict. It compares the original version with both the customized version and the updated version. If a conflict is detected, the element is added to the project.

The resulting project provides a list of elements to update based on upgrade conflicts between versions. You can use the Compare tool described in Chapter 4, "The MorphX Development Tools," to see the conflicts in each element. Together, these features provide a cost-effective toolbox to use when upgrading.

You can create an upgrade project by clicking Tools \Development Tools \Version Update\ Create Upgrade Project.

# Project Types

When you create a new project, you can specify a project type. So far, the discussions in this chapter have been limited to standard projects. Two specialized project types are also provided:

- **Test project**    Project used to group a set of classes for unit testing
- **Help Book project**    Project used for the table of contents in the online Help system

You can create a custom specialized project by creating a new class that extends the *ProjectNode* class. Specialized projects allow you to control the structure, icons, and actions available to the project.

# The Property Sheet

Properties are an important part of the metadata system..Each property is a key and value pair. The property sheet allows you to inspect and modify properties of elements.

Open the property sheet by pressing Alt+Enter or by clicking the Properties button. The property sheet automatically updates itself to show properties for any element selected in the AOT.

You do not have to manually open the property sheet for each element; you can simply leave it open and browse the elements. Figure 3-9 shows the property sheet for a class. The two columns are the key and value pairs for each property.

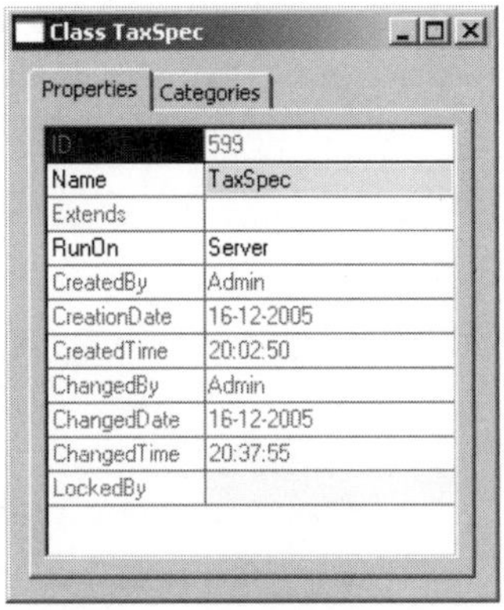

**Class TaxSpec**

Properties | Categories

| ID | 599 |
| Name | TaxSpec |
| Extends | |
| RunOn | Server |
| CreatedBy | Admin |
| CreationDate | 16-12-2005 |
| CreatedTime | 20:02:50 |
| ChangedBy | Admin |
| ChangedDate | 16-12-2005 |
| ChangedTime | 20:37:55 |
| LockedBy | |

**Figure 3-9**   The property sheet for an object in the AOT.

Figure 3-10 shows the Categories tab for the class shown in Figure 3-9. Here, related properties are categorized. For elements with many properties, this view can make it easier to find the right property.

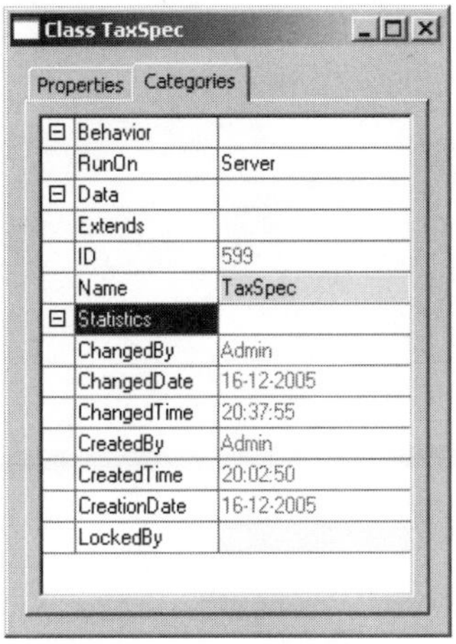

**Class TaxSpec**

Properties | Categories

| ⊟ Behavior | |
| RunOn | Server |
| ⊟ Data | |
| Extends | |
| ID | 599 |
| Name | TaxSpec |
| ⊟ Statistics | |
| ChangedBy | Admin |
| ChangedDate | 16-12-2005 |
| ChangedTime | 20:37:55 |
| CreatedBy | Admin |
| CreatedTime | 20:02:50 |
| CreationDate | 16-12-2005 |
| LockedBy | |

**Figure 3-10**   The Categories tab on the property sheet for an element in the AOT.

Read-only properties appear in gray. Just like files in the file system, elements contain information about who created them and when they were modified. The Microsoft build process ensures that all elements that ship from Microsoft have the same time and user stamp.

The default sort order places related properties near each other. Categories were introduced in an earlier version of Dynamics AX to make finding properties easier, but properties can also be sorted alphabetically by setting a parameter in the Options dialog box. (Thanks to

Erik Damgaard, founder of Damgaard Data.)The default sorting order is retained in the current version for developers familiar with the layout of properties.

The property sheet can be docked on either side of the screen by right-clicking the title bar. Docking ensures that the property sheet is never hidden behind another designer.

The property sheet can also be used as a designer component in custom application code by using the *DynamicPropertyManager* class, which provides an application programming interface (API) to the property sheet. The API supports default values, callbacks when properties are changed, categories, read-only properties, and so on.

The following sample code shows how you can create the custom property sheet shown in Figure 3-11. The property sheet automatically updates itself depending on which element has focus. To update without giving an element focus, you can execute the code sample through a menu item or a button on a form. Otherwise, the property sheet will flash your properties for a split second before focus returns to an element and the property sheet is updated with the element's properties.

```
DynamicPropertyManager dynamicPropertyManager =
    new  DynamicPropertyManager();
Struct propertyStruct =
    new Struct("int Property1; int Property2; str Property3");

propertyStruct.value("Property1", 100);
propertyStruct.value("Property2", 200);
propertyStruct.value("Property3", "Hello World!");
dynamicPropertyManager.setProperties(1,
    "My Property Sheet", propertyStruct);
```

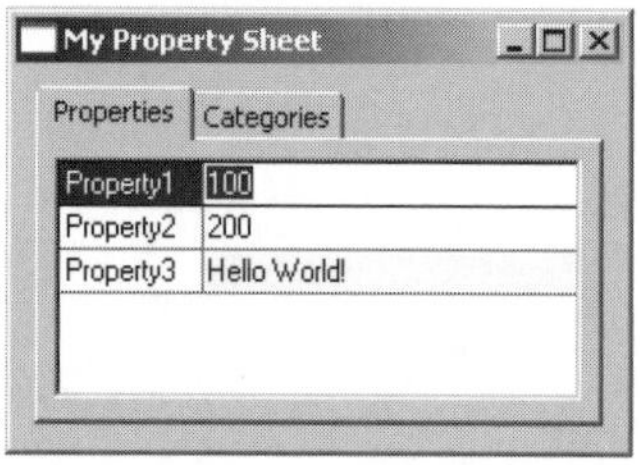

**Figure 3-11**    A custom property sheet showing three custom properties.

# The X++ Editor

All X++ code is written with the X++ editor. You open the editor by selecting a node in the AOT and pressing Enter. The editor contains two panes. The left pane shows the methods available, and the right pane shows the X++ code for the selected method, as shown in Figure 3-12.

**Figure 3-12**    The X++ editor.

The X++ editor is a basic text editor that supports color coding and IntelliSense, a Microsoft program that provides lookup capability for context-sensitive information as the developer types.

## Shortcut Keys

Navigation and editing in the X++ editor follow standard shortcuts, as described in Table 3-2.

**Table 3-2    X++ Editor Shortcut Keys**

| Action | Shortcut keys | Description |
| --- | --- | --- |
| Show Help window | F1 | Opens context-sensitive Help for the type or method currently selected in the editor. |
| Go to next error message | F4 | Opens the editor and positions the cursor at the next compilation error, based on the contents of the compiler output window. |
| Execute current element | F5 | Starts the current form, report, or class. |
| Compile | F7 | Compiles the current method. |
| Toggle a breakpoint | F9 | Sets or removes a breakpoint. |
| List enumerations | F11 | Provides a drop-down list of all enumerations available in the system. |
| List reserved words | Shift+F2 | Provides a drop-down list of all reserved words in X++. |
| List built-in functions | Shift+F4 | Provides a drop-down list of all built-in functions available in X++. |
| Run an editor script | Alt+M | Lists all available editor scripts and lets you select one to execute (such as Send to mail recipient). |
| Open the Label Editor | Ctrl+Alt+Spacebar | Opens the Label Editor and searches for the selected text. |

**Table 3-2   X++ Editor Shortcut Keys**

| Action | Shortcut keys | Description |
|---|---|---|
| Show parameter information or IntelliSense list members | Ctrl+Spacebar | Shows parameter information as a ScreenTip or shows members in a drop-down list. |
| Go to implementation (drill down in code) | Ctrl+Shift+Spacebar | Goes to the implementation of the selected method. Highly useful for fast navigation. |
| Go to the next method | Ctrl+Tab | Sets focus on the next method in the editor. |
| Go to the previous method | Ctrl+Shift+Tab | Sets focus on the previous method in the editor. |
| Enable block selection | Ctrl+O | Enables block selection, instead of the default line selection. |

## Editor Scripts

The X++ editor contains a set of editor scripts that can be invoked by clicking the Editor Scripts button on the toolbar. Editor scripts provide functionality such as the following:

■ Send to mail recipient

■ Send to file

■ Comment or un-comment code

■ Check out element, if version control is enabled

■ Generate code for standard code patterns

■ Open the AOT for the element that owns the method

> **Note**   Code generation allows you, in a matter of minutes, to create a new class with the right constructor method and the right encapsulation of member variables by using parm methods. Parm methods (*parm* is short for parameter) are used as simple property getters/setters on classes. Naturally, code generation is carried out in accordance with X++ best practices.

The list of editor scripts is extendable. You can create your own scripts by adding new methods to the *EditorScripts* class.

## The Label Editor

The term *label* in Dynamics AX simply refers to a localizable text resource. Text resources are used throughout the product as messages to the user, form control labels, column headers, Help text in the status bar, captions on forms, and text on Web forms, to name just a few places. Labels are localizable, meaning that they can be translated into any language. Because the space requirement for displaying text resources typically depends on the language, you might fear that the actual user interface must be manually localized as well. However, with IntelliMorph technology, the user interface is dynamically rendered and honors any space requirements imposed by localization.

The technology behind the label system is simple. All text resources are kept in a Unicode-based label file that must have a three-letter identifier. The label file is located in the application folder (Documents and Settings\All Users\Application Data\Microsoft\Axapta 4.0\ Axapta Application\Appl\Standard) and follows this naming convention:

Ax<*Label file identifier*><*Locale*>.ALD

The following are two examples:

Axsysen-us.ALD

Axtstda.ALD

Each text resource in the label file has a 32-bit integer label ID, label text, and an optional label description. The structure of the label file is very simple:

@<*Label file identifier*><*Label ID*> <*Label text*>

[*Label description*]

Figure 3-13 shows an example.

**Figure 3-13**   A label file opened in Microsoft Notepad showing a few labels from the en-us label file.

This simple structure allows for localization outside Dynamics AX using third-party tools.

After the localized label files are in place, the end user can choose a language in the Options dialog box. When the language is changed, the user must close and restart the Dynamics AX client.

You can create new label files by using the Label File Wizard, which is accessed by clicking Tools\Development Tool\Wizards\Label File Wizard. The wizard guides you through the steps for adding a new label file or a new language to an existing label file. After you run the wizard, the label file is ready to use.

**Note**   Any combination of three letters can be used when naming a label file, and any label file can be used from any layer. A common misunderstanding is that the label file identifier must be the same as the layer in which it is used. This misunderstanding is caused by the Microsoft label file identifiers. Dynamics AX ships with a SYS layer and a label file named SYS; service packs contain a SYP layer and a label file named SYP. This naming standard was chosen because it is simple, easy to remember, and easy to understand. Dynamics AX does not impose any limitations on the label file name.

The following are tips for working with label files:

- When naming a label file, you should choose a three-letter ID that has a high chance of being unique, such as your company's initials. Do not choose the name of the layer, such as VAR or USR. It is likely that you will eventually merge two separately developed features into the same installation, a task that will be more difficult if the label files collide.

- Feel free to reference labels in the Microsoft-provided label files, but avoid making changes to labels in these label files, because they are updated with each new version of Dynamics AX.

## Creating a New Label

The Label Editor is used to create new labels. It can be started by using any of the following procedures:

- Clicking Tools\Development Tools\Label\Label Editor.
- Clicking the Label Lookup/Text button on the X++ editor toolbar.
- Clicking the lookup button on text properties in the property sheet.

The Label Editor (shown in Figure 3-14) allows you to find existing labels. It is often preferable to reuse a label rather than create a new label. You can create a new label by pressing Ctrl+N or by clicking the New button.

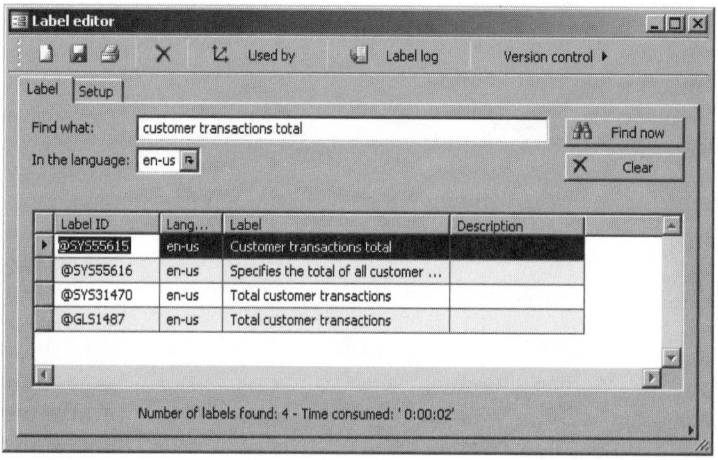

**Figure 3-14**   The Label Editor.

In addition to finding and creating new labels, the Label Editor can also show where a label is used. You can also see a log of changes to each label.

The following are tips to consider when creating and reusing labels:

- When reusing a label, make sure that the label meaning is what you intend it to be in all languages. Some words have a dual meaning in certain languages and translate into two different words. For example, the English word *can* is both a verb and a noun. The description column describes the intended meaning of the label.

■ When creating new labels, make sure to use complete sentences or other standalone words or phrases in each label. Do not construct complete sentences by concatenating labels with one or few words because the order of words in a sentence differs from one language to another.

## Referencing Labels from X++

In the MorphX design environment, labels are referenced in the format *@<LabelFileIdentifier><LabelID>*. If you do not want a label reference to automatically convert to the label text, you can use the *literalStr* function. When a placeholder is needed to display the value of a variable, the *strFmt* function and a string containing *%n*, where *n*>=1, can be used. Placeholders can also be used within labels. The following code shows a few examples.

```
// prints: Time transactions
print "@SYS1";

// prints: @SYS1
print literalStr("@SYS1");

// prints: Microsoft Dynamics is a Microsoft brand
print strFmt("%1 is a %2 brand", "Microsoft Dynamics", "Microsoft");
```

The following are some best practices to consider when referencing labels from X++:

■ You should always create user interface text by using a label. When referencing labels from X++ code, use double quotation marks.

■ You should never create system text such as file names by using a label. When referencing system text from X++ code, use single quotation marks. You can place system text in macros to make it reusable.

Using single and double quotation marks to differentiate between system text and user interface text allows the Best Practice tool to find and report any hard-coded user interface text. The Best Practice tool is described in Chapter 4.

# The Form Visual Designer and Report Visual Designer

MorphX has two visual designers, one for forms and one for reports, that allow you to drag controls on the design surface in a what-you-see-is-what-you-get fashion. The actual position of the controls is determined by IntelliMorph, so precise placement of controls is not possible. These layout restrictions can be overridden by changing property values, such as Top, Left, Height, and Width, from Auto to a fixed value, allowing the controls to be laid out entirely with the visual designers. However, doing so interferes with the automated layout attempted by IntelliMorph. This means that there is no guarantee that your forms and reports will display well when translated, configured, secured, and personalized. For this reason, it is a best practice to let IntelliMorph control all the layout. You will find more detailed information about IntelliMorph in Chapter 11, "Configuration and Security." Most forms and reports that ship with Dynamics AX are designed by using the AOT. When the visual designer is opened, a tree structure of the design is displayed, and adding new controls to the design is quite simple. You can do so by either dragging fields or field groups from the data source to the design or right-clicking the design and choosing New Control.

> **Note**    IntelliMorph and MorphX treat form and report designs as hierarchical structures. A control can be next to another control or inside a group control. This makes a lot of sense for business applications. If you require controls to be on top of one another, you must use absolute pixel positions. The order of the controls in the AOT mandates the z-order—that is, the order in which controls are virtually stacked in the display.

You can use a report wizard, located in Tools\Development Tools\Wizards, to help you create reports. The wizard guides you through the process step by step, allowing you to specify data sources, sorting, grouping, layout, and other settings before producing a report in the AOT.

## The Form Visual Designer

The designers can be helpful tools for learning how the IntelliMorph layout scheme works. If you have the Form Visual Designer open when you start designing a form, you immediately see what the form will look like, even when it is modified in the AOT. In fact, after creating a few forms, you will probably feel so confident of the power of IntelliMorph and the effectiveness of designing forms in the AOT that you will only rarely use the Form Visual Designer.

The Form Visual Designer is opened by right-clicking a form's design in the AOT and selecting Edit. The designer is shown in design mode in Figure 3-15. Next to the form is a toolbar with all the available controls, which can be dragged onto the form's surface. You can also see the property sheet showing the selected control's properties.

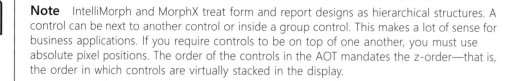

Figure 3-15    The Form Visual Designer.

One interesting form that overrides IntelliMorph is the form *tutorial_Form_freeform*. Figure 3-16 shows how a scanned bitmap of a payment form is used as a background image for the form, and the controls are positioned where data entry is needed.

**Figure 3-16**   A somewhat non-standard form that uses a bitmap background.

# The Report Visual Designer

The majority of reports fall into two categories—internal reports and external reports. Requirements for reports used internally in a company are often more relaxed than requirements for external reports. Often external reports are part of the company's face to the outside world. An invoice report is a classic example of an external report.

Leveraging the features of IntelliMorph, internal reports typically use an autodesign that allows the consumer of the report to add and remove columns from the report and control report orientation, font, and font size.

External reports typically use a generated design, which effectively overrides IntelliMorph. So for external reports, the Report Visual Designer is a clear winner. Often, external reports are printed on pre-printed paper, so the ability to easily control the exact position of each control is essential.

A generated design is created from an autodesign by right-clicking a design node of a report in the AOT and selecting Generate Design. The Report Visual Designer can be opened by right-clicking a generated design and selecting Edit. As shown in Figure 3-17, each control can be moved freely, and new controls can be added.

Notice the zoom setting in the lower right corner. This setting allows you to get a close-up view of the report and, with a steady hand, position each control exactly where you want it.

The rendering subsystem of the report engine can print only generated designs because it requires all controls to have fixed positions. If a report has only an autodesign, the report engine will generate a design in memory before printing.

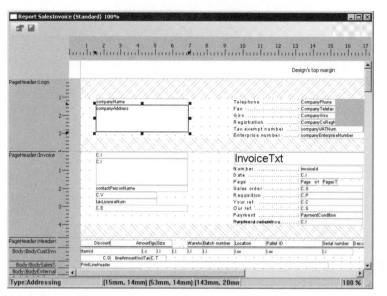

**Figure 3-17** The Report Visual Designer.

# Chapter Summary

This chapter introduced you to the many designers in MorphX and described what you can expect when using MorphX. However, the only way to truly understand how the designers work is to use them. Part II, "Developing with Microsoft Dynamics AX," discusses a scenario in which many aspects of the Dynamics AX application are changed by using the designers introduced in this chapter and the tools described in the following chapter.

Chapter 4

# The MorphX Development Tools

The objectives of this chapter are to:

- Provide an overview of the most useful development tools in MorphX.
- Demonstrate how to use the tools proficiently and productively.
- Explain how the tools are designed and how some of them can be extended to suit individual preferences and development standards.

## Introduction

The business functionality in Microsoft Dynamics AX 4.0 was built with the MorphX designers described in Chapter 3, "The MorphX Designers." A toolbox helps you work efficiently with the designers. Chapter 2, "The MorphX Development Environment," explained how the designers and tools fit into a product's life cycle.

This chapter describes the following commonly used tools:

- **Compiler**  This tool is used to compile X++ code into an executable format.
- **MorphX SDK**  The MorphX software developer kit contains valuable developer documentation.

- **Best Practice tool**   This is a static code analysis tool that can automatically detect defects in both your code and your elements.

- **Debugger**   The X++ debugger helps you find bugs in your X++ code.

- **Reverse Engineering tool**   You can generate Microsoft Office Visio Unified Modeling Language (UML) diagrams from elements by using the Reverse Engineering tool.

- **Table Browser tool**   This tool allows you to view the contents of a table directly from the table elements.

- **Find tool**   The Find tool allows you to search for code or metadata patterns in the Application Object Tree (AOT).

- **Compare tool**   Use this tool to see a line-by-line comparison of two versions of the same element.

- **Cross-Reference tool**   The Cross-Reference tool allows you to determine where an element is used.

- **Version Control tool**   You can track all changes to elements and see a full revision log by using the Version Control tool.

You access all of these development tools from one of two places:

- The Development Tools submenu on the Tools menu

- The context menu on elements in the AOT

# The Compiler

Whenever you make a change to X++ code, you must recompile, just as you would in any other development language. You start the recompile by pressing F7 in the X++ editor. Your code also recompiles whenever you close the editor or save a dirty element.

The compiler also produces a list of the following information:

- **Compiler errors**   These prevent code from compiling and should be fixed as soon as possible.

- **Compiler warnings**   These typically indicate that something is wrong in the implementation. See Table 4-1, later in this section, for a list of compiler warnings. Compiler warnings can and should be addressed. Check-in attempts with compiler warnings are rejected.

- **Tasks (also known as to-dos)**   The compiler picks up single-line comments that start with TODO. These comments can be useful during development for adding reminders, but they should be used only in cases in which implementation cannot be completed. For example, you might use a to-do comment when you are waiting for a check-in from another developer. You should avoid using to-do comments to postpone work that can readily be completed, to ensure that the work is not overlooked. For a developer, there is nothing worse than debugging an issue at a customer site and finding a to-do comment indicating that the issue was already known.

> **Note**   Unlike other languages, X++ requires that you only compile code that you have modified. This is because the intermediate language produced by the compiler is persisted along with the X++ code and metadata. Of course, your changes can require consumers of your code to be changed and recompiled if, for example, you rename a method or modify its parameters. If the consumers are not recompiled, a run-time error is thrown when they are invoked. This means that you can execute your business application even when compile errors exist, as long as the code that cannot compile is not used. You should always compile the entire AOT when you consider your changes complete and fix any compilation errors found.

- **Best practice deviations**   More complex validations are carried out by the Best Practices tool. See the section entitled "The Best Practices Tool," later in this chapter, for more information.

The Compiler Output dialog box provides access to everything reported during compilation, as shown in Figure 4-1. Each category of findings has a dedicated tab. Each tab contains the same information for each issue that the compiler detects: a description of the issue and where it was found. The Status tab shows a count of the detected issues.

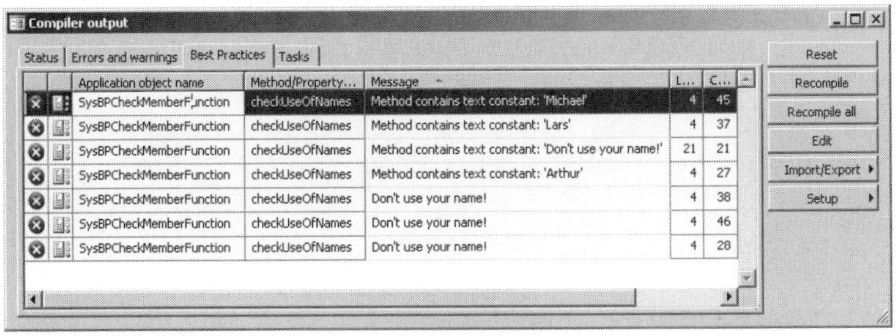

**Figure 4-1**   The Compiler Output dialog box.

Compile results can be exported. This is useful if you want to share the list of issues with team members. The exported file is an HTML file that can be viewed in Microsoft Internet Explorer or re-imported into the Compiler Output dialog box in another Dynamics AX 4.0 session.

In the Compiler Output dialog box, click Setup and then click Compiler to define the types of issues that the compiler should report. Compiler warnings are grouped into four levels, as shown in Table 4-1.

**Table 4-1    Compiler Warnings**

| Warning message | Level |
|---|---|
| Break statement found outside legal context | 1 |
| The new method of a derived class does not call super() | 1 |
| The new method of a derived class may not call super() | 1 |
| Function never returns a value | 1 |
| Not all paths return a value | 1 |
| Assignment/Comparison loses precision | 1 |
| Unreachable code | 2 |
| Empty compound statement | 3 |
| Class names should start with an uppercase letter | 4 |
| Member names should start with a lowercase letter | 4 |

# The MorphX SDK

Constructing quality software has become a daunting task during the last decade. Many new competencies are expected of the developer, and mastering them fully and at all times is nearly impossible. Today you must write code that conforms to many requirements, including security, localization, internationalization, customization, performance, accessibility, reliability, scalability, compatibility, supportability, interoperability, and so on. The list seems to grow with each revision, and keeping up with all of these competencies is increasingly difficult.

Dynamics AX 4.0 includes a software development kit (SDK) that explains how to satisfy these requirements when using MorphX. You access the SDK from the application Help menu under Developer Help. The Developer Help section of the SDK includes an important discussion on conforming to best practices in Dynamics AX. Reading the Developer Help section is highly recommended—not just for novices, but also for experienced developers who will find that the content has been extensively revised for version 4.0.

The motivation for conforming to best practices should be obvious to anyone. Constructing code that follows proven standards and patterns cannot guarantee a project's success, but it certainly minimizes the risk of failure. To ensure your project's success, you should learn, conform to, and advocate best practices within your group.

The following are a few benefits of following best practices:

■ You will avoid less-than-obvious pitfalls. Following best practices helps you avoid many obstacles, even those that surface only in border scenarios that would otherwise be difficult and time-consuming to detect and test. Using best practices allows you to leverage the combined experiences of Dynamics AX expert developers.

■ The learning curve is flattened. When similar tasks are performed in a standard way, you are more comfortable in an unknown area of the application. This makes it more cost-efficient to add new resources to a project and enables downstream consumers of the code to make changes more readily.

- You will be making a long-term investment. Code that conforms to standards is less likely to require rework during an upgrade process. This is true for upgrading to Dynamics AX 4.0, installing any service packs, and upgrading to future releases.

- You are more likely to ship on time. Most of the problems that you will face when implementing a solution in Dynamics AX have been solved at least once before. Choosing a proven solution will result in faster implementation and less regression. You can find solutions to known problems in both the Developer Help section of the SDK and the code base.

# The Best Practices Tool

A powerful supplement to the best practices discussion in the SDK is the Best Practices tool. This tool is the MorphX version of a static code analysis tool, similar to FxCop for the Microsoft .NET Framework and PREfix and PREfast for C and C++. The Best Practices tool is embedded in the compiler, and the result is located on the Best Practices tab of the Compiler Output dialog box.

The purpose of static code analysis is to automatically detect defects in the code. The longer a defect exists, the more costly it becomes—a bug found in the design phase is much cheaper to correct than a bug in shipped code running at several customer sites. The Best Practices tool allows any developer to run an analysis of his or her code to ensure that it conforms to a set of predefined rules. Developers can run analysis during development, and they should always do so before implementations are tested.

The Best Practices tool displays deviations from the best practice rules, as shown in Figure 4-1. Double-clicking a line on the Best Practices tab opens the X++ editor on the violating line of X++ code.

## Understanding Rules

The Best Practices tool includes about 300 rules, a small subset of the best practices mentioned in the SDK. Clicking Setup and then Best Practices opens the Best Practice Parameters dialog box, which allows you to define the best practice rules that you want to run.

> **Note**   The compiler error level must be set to 4 if best practice rule violations are to be reported. To turn off the Best Practices tool, click Tools\Options\Compiler, and then set the diagnostic level to less than 4.

The best practice rules are divided into categories. By default, all categories are turned on, as shown in Figure 4-2.

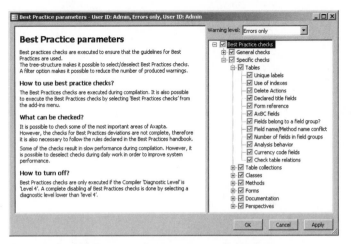

**Figure 4-2**   The Best Practice Parameters dialog box.

The best practices rules are divided into three levels of severity:

- **Errors**   The majority of the rules focus on errors. Any check-in attempt with a best practice error is rejected. All errors must be taken seriously and fixed as soon as possible.

- **Warnings**   A 95/5 rule should be followed for warnings. This means that 95 percent of all warnings should be treated as errors; the remaining 5 percent constitute exceptions to the rule. Valid explanations should be provided in the design document for all warnings that are not fixed.

- **Information**   In some situations, your implementation might have a side effect that is not obvious to you or the user. These are typically reported as information messages.

Dynamics AX 4.0 introduces a notion of suppressible errors and warnings. A suppressed best practice deviation is reported as information. This gives you a way to identify the deviation as reviewed and accepted. To identify a suppressed error or warning, place a line containing the following text just before the deviation.

```
//BP Deviation Documented
```

Only a small subset of the best practice rules can be suppressed. The following guidelines should be used for selecting rules to suppress:

- Where exceptions exist that are impossible to detect automatically, you should examine each error to ensure the right implementation. APIs are a typical example of this. A dangerous API is an API that can compromise the system's security when used incorrectly. If a dangerous API is used, a suppressible error will be reported. Using a dangerous API is allowed when certain precautions are taken, such as using code access security. You can suppress the error after applying the appropriate mitigations.

- About 5 percent of all warnings are false positives and can be suppressed. Note that only warnings caused by actual code can be suppressed, not warnings caused by metadata.

After you set up the best practices, the compiler will automatically run the best practices check whenever an element is compiled. The results are displayed on the Best Practices tab in the Compiler Output dialog box.

## Adding Custom Rules

The X++ Best Practices tool allows you to create your own set of rules. The classes used to check for rules are named SysBPCheck<*ElementKind*>. The *init, check,* and *dispose* methods are called once for each node in the AOT for the element being compiled.

One of the most interesting classes is *SysBPCheckMemberFunction*, which is called for each piece of X++ code whether it is a class method, form method, macro, or other method. For example, if you do not want your developers to include their names in the source code, you can implement a best practice check by creating the following method on the *SysBPCheck-MemberFunction* class.

```
protected void checkUseOfNames()
{
    #Define.MyErrorCode(50000)
    container devNames = ["Arthur", "Lars", "Michael"];
    int i;
    int j;
    int pos;
    str line;
    int lineLen;

    for (i=scanner.lines(); i; i--)
    {
        line = scanner.sourceLine(i);
        lineLen = strlen(line);
        for (j=conlen(devNames); j; j--)
        {
            pos = strscan(line, conpeek(devNames, j), 1, lineLen);
            if (pos)
            {
                sysBPCheck.addError(#MyErrorCode, i, pos,
                    "Don't use your name!");
            }
        }
    }
}
```

To enlist the rule, make sure to call the preceding method from the *check* method. Compiling this sample code results in the best practice errors shown in Table 4-2.

Table 4-2    **Best Practice Errors in** *checkUseOfNames*

| Message | Line | Column |
| --- | --- | --- |
| Method contains text constant: 'Arthur' | 4 | 27 |
| Don't use your name! | 4 | 28 |
| Method contains text constant: 'Lars' | 4 | 37 |
| Don't use your name! | 4 | 38 |
| Method contains text constant: 'Michael' | 4 | 45 |
| Don't use your name! | 4 | 46 |
| Method contains text constant: 'Don't use your name!' | 20 | 59 |

In a real-world implementation, names of developers would probably be read from a file. Make sure to cache the names to prevent the compiler from going to the disk to read the names for each method being compiled.

# The Debugger

Like most development environments, MorphX features a debugger. The debugger is a stand-alone application, not part of the Dynamics AX shell like the rest of the tools mentioned in this chapter. As a stand-alone application, the debugger allows you to debug X++ in any of the Dynamics AX components in the following list:

- Windows Client
- Application Object Server
- Enterprise Portal
- Business Connector

## Using the Debugger

For the Debugger to start, a breakpoint must be hit during execution of X++ code. You set breakpoints by using the X++ editor in the Windows Client. The debugger starts automatically when any component hits a breakpoint.

You must enable debugging for each component as follows:

- In the Windows Client, click Tools\Options. On the Development tab, select When Breakpoint in the Debug Mode list.
- For the Application Object Server, open the Microsoft Dynamics AX Server Configuration Utility under Start\Administrative Tools. Create a new configuration (if necessary) and select the check box labeled Enable Breakpoints To Debug X++ Code Running On This Server.
- For the Enterprise Portal and Business Connector, open the Microsoft Dynamics AX Configuration Utility under Start\Administrative Tools. Select one of two check boxes

on the Developer tab: Enable User Breakpoints For Debugging Code Running In The Business Connector or Enable Global Breakpoints For Debugging Code Running In The Business Connector Or Client. The latter is useful for debugging incoming Web requests.

**Caution**   In a live environment, enabling any of the debugging capabilities is not recommended. Execution will stop when it hits a breakpoint, and users will experience a hanging client.

The debugger allows you to set and remove breakpoints by pressing F9. You can set a breakpoint on any line that you want. However, if you set a breakpoint on a line without an X++ statement, the breakpoint will be triggered on the next X++ statement in the method. A breakpoint on the last brace will never be hit.

You can enable or disable a breakpoint by pressing Ctrl+F9. For a list of all of your breakpoints, press Shift+F9.

Breakpoints are persistent in the *SysBreakpoints* database table. Each developer has his or her own set of breakpoints. This means that your breakpoints are not cleared when you close Dynamics AX and that other Dynamics AX components can access them and break where you want them to.

## The Debugger Interface

The main window in the debugger initially shows the point in the code where a breakpoint was hit. Execution can be controlled one step at a time while variables and other aspects are inspected. Figure 4-3 shows the debugger opened to a breakpoint with all of the windows enabled.

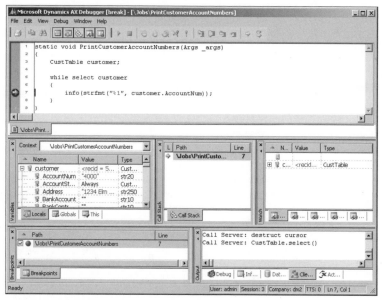

**Figure 4-3**   The debugger with all windows enabled.

The debugger windows include the following:

## Main window

The main debugger window shows you the current X++ code. Each variable has a ScreenTip that reveals its value. You can drag the next-statement pointer in the left margin. This is particularly useful if the execution path is not what you expected or if you want to repeat a step.

## Variables

In this window, local, global, and member variables can be inspected. Local variables are variables in scope at the current execution point. Global variables are the global classes that are always instantiated: *Appl*, *Infolog*, *Classfactory*, and *VersionControl*. Member variables make sense only on classes and show the class member variables.

The Variables window shows the name, value, and type of the variables. If a variable is changed during execution stepping, it is marked in red. Each variable is shown associated with a client or server icon. You can modify the value of a variable by double-clicking the value.

> **Tip**   As a developer, you might want to provide more information than what is provided by default in the value field. For a class, the defaults are New and Null. You can change the defaults by overriding the *toString()* method. If your class does not explicitly extend *object* (the base class of all classes), you must add a new method named *toString*, returning *str* and taking no parameters, to implement this functionality.

## Call Stack

The Call Stack window shows the code path visited to arrive at this execution point. Clicking a line in the Call Stack window opens the code in the Code window and updates the local Variables window. A client or server icon indicates the tier on which the code is executed.

## Watch

In the Watch window, you can inspect variables without the scope limitations of the Variables window. You can drag a variable here from the code window or from the Variables window.

The Watch window shows the name, value, and type of the variables. Five different Watch windows are available. You can use these to group the variables you are watching in the way that you prefer.

## Breakpoints

The Breakpoints window lists all of your breakpoints. You can delete, enable, and disable your breakpoints.

## Output

The Output window shows the traces that are enabled and the output to the Infolog, the information log framework introduced in Chapter 1, "Architectural Overview." The Output window includes the following pages:

- **Debug**   You can instrument your X++ code to trace to this page by using the *printDebug* static method on the *Debug* class.

- **Infolog**   This page contains messages in the queue for the Infolog.

- **Database, Client/server, and ActiveX Trace**   Any traces enabled on the Development tab in the Options dialog box will appear on these pages.

## Status Bar

The status bar at the bottom of the debugger is also worth some attention. It offers the following important context information:

- **Current user**   The ID of the user who is logged in to the system. This information is especially useful when debugging incoming Web requests.

- **Current session**   The ID of the session on the Application Object Server (AOS).

- **Current company accounts**   The ID of the current company accounts.

- **Transaction level**   The current transaction level. When reaching zero, the transaction will be committed.

## Debugger Shortcut Keys

Table 4-3 shows the most important shortcut keys available in the debugger.

**Table 4-3   Debugger Shortcut Keys**

| Action | Shortcut | Description |
| --- | --- | --- |
| Run | F5 | Continue execution |
| Stop debugging | Shift+F5 | Break execution |
| Step over | F10 | Step over next statement |
| Run to cursor | Ctrl+F10 | Continue execution, but break at the cursor's position |
| Step into | F11 | Step into next statement |
| Step out | Shift+F11 | Step out of method |
| Toggle breakpoint | Shift+F9 | Insert or remove breakpoint |
| Variables window | Ctrl+Alt+V | Open or close Variables window |
| Call Stack window | Ctrl+Alt+C | Open or close Call Stack window |
| Watch window | Ctrl+Alt+W | Open or close Watch window |
| Breakpoints window | Ctrl+Alt+B | Open or close Breakpoints window |
| Output window | Ctrl+Alt+O | Open or close Output window |

# The Visio Reverse Engineering Tool

Dynamics AX 4.0 allows you to generate Office Visio UML models from existing metadata. Considering the amount of metadata available in Dynamics AX 4.0 (more than 30,000 elements and more than 5 million lines of text when exported), it is practically impossible to get a clear view of how the elements relate to each other by using the AOT. The Visio Reverse Engineering tool is a great aid when you need visualization of metadata.

> **Note**    You must have Microsoft Office Visio 2003 installed to use the Visio Reverse Engineering tool. The Reverse Engineering tool replaces the Visual MorphXplorer from the previous version of Dynamics AX.

The Reverse Engineering tool can generate either a UML data model or a UML object model, including all elements from a private or shared project. To open the tool, right-click a project, point to Add-Ins, and then click Reverse Engineer. In the dialog box shown in Figure 4-4, you must specify a file name and model type.

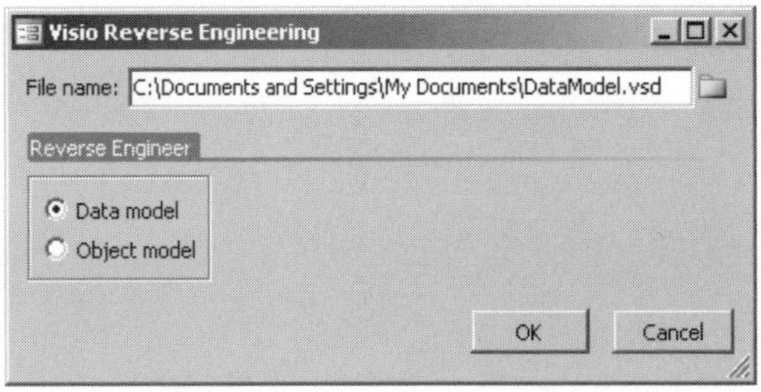

**Figure 4-4**    The Visio Reverse Engineering dialog box.

When you click OK, the tool uses the metadata for all elements in the project to generate an Office Visio document that opens automatically in Visio. You can drag elements from the Visio Model Explorer onto the drawing surface, which is initially blank. Any relationship between two elements is automatically shown.

## Data Model

When generating a UML data model, the Reverse Engineering tool looks for tables in the project. The UML model will contain a class for each table in the project and its attributes and associations. Figure 4-5 shows a class diagram with the *CustTable* (Customers), *InventTable* (Inventory Items), *SalesTable* (Sales Order Header), and *SalesLine* (Sales Order Line) tables. To simplify the view, some attributes have been removed.

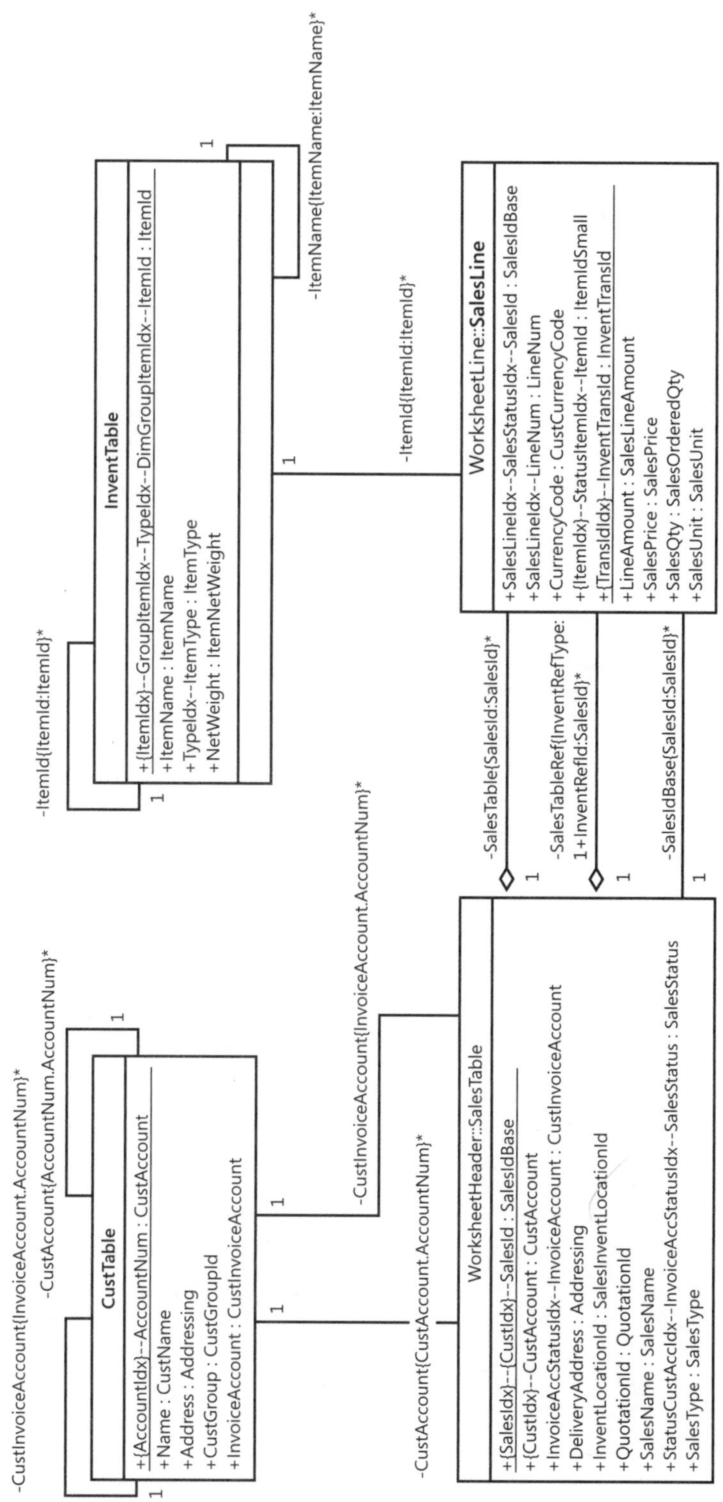

**Figure 4-5**   A UML data model diagram.

The UML model also contains referenced tables and all extended data types, base enumerations, and X++ data types. This allows you to include these in your diagrams without having to run the Reverse Engineering tool again.

Fields in Dynamics AX are generated as UML attributes. All attributes are marked as public because of the nature of fields in Dynamics AX. Each attribute also shows the type. The primary key field is underlined. If a field is a part of one or more indexes, the names of the indexes are prefixed to the field name; if the index is unique, the index name is noted in brackets.

Relationships in Dynamics AX are generated as UML associations. The aggregation property of the association is set based on two conditions in metadata:

- If the relationship is validating (the validate property is set to Yes), the aggregation property is set to shared. This is also known as UML aggregation, visualized by a white diamond.

- If a cascading delete action exists between the two tables, a composite association is added to the model. A cascading delete action ties the life span of two or more tables and is visualized by a black diamond.

The end name on associations is the name of the Dynamics AX relationship, and the names and types of all fields in the relationship appear in brackets.

## Object Model

When generating an object model, the Reverse Engineering tool looks for Dynamics AX classes, tables, and interfaces in the project. The UML model will contain a class for each Dynamics AX table and class in the project and an interface for each Dynamics AX interface. The UML model will also contain attributes and operations including return types, parameters, and the parameters' types. Figure 4-6 shows an object model of the most important *RunBase* and *Batch* classes and interfaces in Dynamics AX. To simplify the view, some attributes and operations have been removed, and operation parameters are suppressed.

The UML model also contains referenced tables, classes and tables, and all extended data types, base enumerations, and X++ data types. This allows you to include these in your diagrams without having to run the Reverse Engineering tool again.

Fields and member variables in Dynamics AX are generated as UML attributes. All fields are generated as public attributes, whereas member variables are generated as protected attributes. Each attribute also shows the type. Methods are generated as UML operations, including return type and parameters, and the parameters' types.

The Reverse Engineering tool also picks up any generalizations (classes extending other classes), realizations (classes implementing interfaces), and associations (classes using each other). The associations are limited to references in member variables.

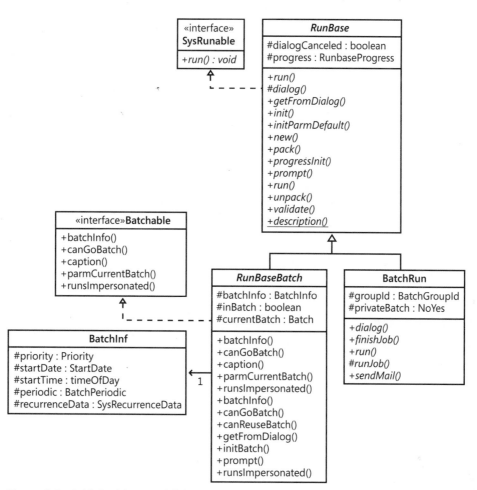

**Figure 4-6**   A UML object model diagram.

**Note**   To get the names of operation parameters, you must reverse engineer in debug mode. The names are only read from metadata and placed into the stack when in debug mode. You can enable debug mode on the Development tab in the Options dialog box by selecting When Breakpoint in the Debug Mode list.

# The Table Browser Tool

The usage scenarios of this small, helpful tool are numerous. The Table Browser tool lets you see the records in a table without requiring you to build any user interface. This is useful when debugging, validating data models, and modifying or cleaning up data, to name just a few uses.

The table browser can be accessed from the Add-Ins submenu in the AOT on:

- Tables.

- Tables listed as data sources in Forms, Reports, Web Forms, and Web Reports.

- System tables listed in the AOT under System Documentation\Tables.

> **Note**   The Table Browser tool is implemented in X++. You can find it in the AOT under the name *SysTableBrowser*. It is a good example of how to bind the data source to a table at run time.

Figure 4-7 shows the Table Browser tool started from the *CustTable* table. In addition to the querying, sorting, and filtering capabilities provided by the grid control, the Table Browser tool allows you to type an SQL SELECT statement directly into the form using the X++ language syntax and see a visual display of the result set. This is great for trying out complex SELECT statements. The tool fully supports grouping, sorting, aggregation, and field lists.

| AccountNum | Name | Address | Phone |
|---|---|---|---|
| 4000 | Light and Design | 1234 Elm Street Los Angeles, CA ... | 213 555 0100 |
| 4001 | The Glass Bulb | 2345 Oak Street Fargo, ND 5812... | 701 5550102 |
| 4002 | The Radiant Idea | 678 25th Street Orlando, FL 3285... | 407 555 0105 |
| 4003 | Office Lights Inc. | 4567 Evergreen Road Lakeside, ... | 619 555 0107 |
| 4004 | The Lighting Specialist | 34 Old Forrest Road Kent, WA 9... | 206 555 0110 |
| 4005 | Office Supplies Inc. | 4567 Clover Street Chicago, IL 6... | 312 555 0112 |
| 4006 | Desk World | 101 High Street Des Moines, IA 5... | 515 555 0115 |
| 4007 | Style and Design Inc. | 4567 Water Street Ohio City, OH ... | 419 555 0117 |
| 4008 | City Power and Light | 123 Harbor Street New York, NY ... | 212 555 0120 |

```
SELECT * FROM CustTable
```
Show fields
- All fields
- Autoreport

**Figure 4-7**   The Table Browser tool, showing *CustTable* from demo data.

The Table Browser tool also allows you to choose to see only the fields from the auto-report field group. These fields will be printed in a report when the user clicks Print in a form with this table as a data source. Typically, these fields hold the most interesting information. This option can make it easier to find the values that you are looking for in tables with many fields.

> **Note**   The Table Browser tool is just a normal form that uses IntelliMorph. This means that it cannot display fields for which the *visible* property is set to No or fields that the current user does not have access to.

# The Find Tool

Search is everything! The size of the Dynamics AX application calls for a powerful and effective search tool. The scenarios demanding search are numerous, but here are just a few:

- A new developer is looking for the right place to implement changes.

- A developer is searching for an example of how to use an API. He would like to find real examples to complement the examples in the documentation.

- An experienced developer is scanning the source code or metadata properties for deviations from best practices.

The Find tool, shown in Figure 4-8, can be started from any node in the AOT by pressing Ctrl+F or by clicking Find on the context menu. Note that the Find tool supports multiple selections in the AOT.

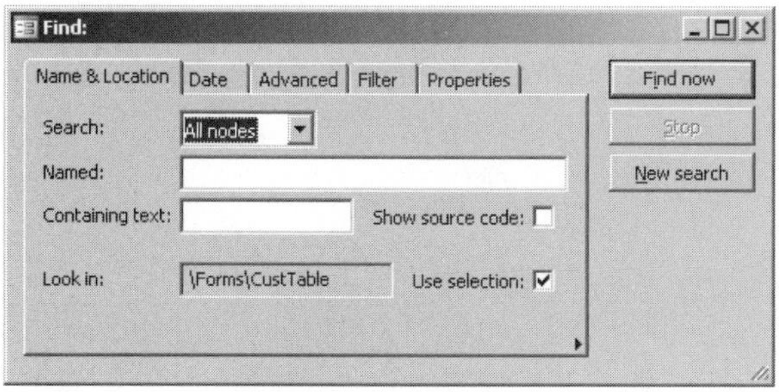

**Figure 4-8**   The Find tool.

The Name & Location tab defines what you are searching for and where to look:

- **Search**   Menu options are Methods and All Nodes. When All Nodes is chosen, the Properties tab appears.

- **Named**   This text box limits the search to nodes with the name specified. This option is rarely used.

- **Containing Text**   Use this box to specify the text to look for in the method expressed as a regular expression.

- **Show Source Code**   When this check box is selected, results include a snippet of source code containing the match. This makes it easier to browse the results.

- **Look In and Use Selection**   By default, the Find tool searches the node selected in the AOT (and its sub-nodes). If focus is changed in the AOT while the Find tool is open, the Look In value is updated. This is quite powerful if several nodes should be searched with the same criterion. This behavior can be disabled by clearing the Use Selection check box.

The Date tab lets you specify additional ranges for your search, such as Modified Date and Modified By.

On the Advanced tab, you can specify more advanced settings for your search, such as the layer to search, the size range of elements, the type of element, and the tier on which the element is set to run.

The Filter tab, shown in Figure 4-9, allows you to write a more complex query by using X++ and type libraries. The code written in the Source text box will be the body of a method with the following profile:

```
boolean FilterMethod(str _treeNodeName,
                     str _treeNodeSource,
                     XRefPath _path,
                     ClassRunMode _runMode)
```

The example in Figure 4-9 uses the class *SysScannerClass* to find any occurrence of the *TTSAbort* X++ keyword. The scanner is primarily used to pass tokens into the parser during compilation. Here, however, it detects use of a special keyword. This is more accurate (and slower) than using a regular expression, because X++ comments do not produce tokens.

**Figure 4-9**    Filtering in the Find tool.

The Properties tab appears when All Nodes is selected in the Search menu. A search range can be specified for any property. Leaving the range blank for a property is a powerful setting when inspecting properties: It matches all nodes, and the property value is added as a column in the results, as shown in Figure 4-10. The search begins when you click Find Now. The results appear at the bottom of the dialog box as they are found. Searching all methods in the AOT takes about three minutes when you search only for text patterns.

Double-clicking any line in the result set opens the X++ editor with focus on the matched code snippet. When you right-click the lines in the result set, a context menu containing the Add-Ins menu opens.

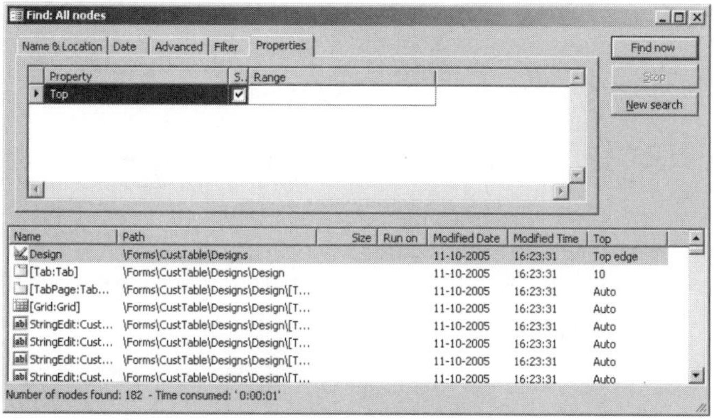

**Figure 4-10**   Search results in the Find tool.

# The Compare Tool

Several versions of the same element typically exist. These versions might emanate from various layers or revisions in version control, or they could be modified versions that exit in-memory. Dynamics AX has a built-in Compare tool that highlights any differences between two versions of an element.

The comparison shows changes to elements, which can be modified in three ways:

- A metadata property can be changed.
- X++ code can be changed.
- The order of sub-nodes can be changed, such as the order of tabs on a form.

## Starting the Compare Tool

You open the Compare tool by right-clicking an element and then clicking Compare on the Add-Ins submenu. A dialog box allows you to select the versions of the element that you want to compare, as shown in Figure 4-11.

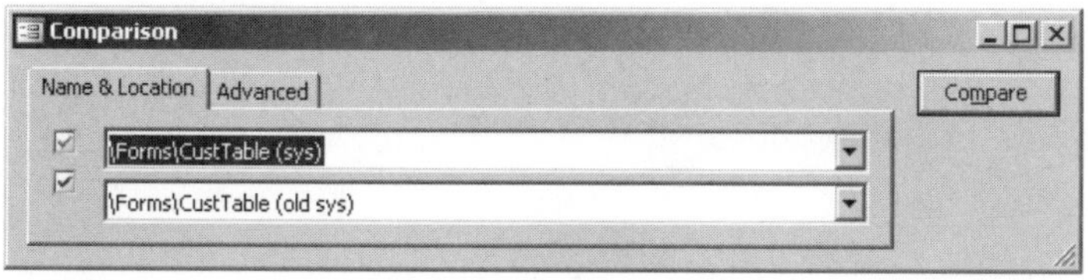

**Figure 4-11**   The Comparison dialog box.

The versions to choose from come from many sources. The following is a list of all possible types of versions:

- **Standard layered version types**   (sys, syp, gls, glp, dis, dip, los, lop, bus, bup, var, vap, cus, cup, usr, usp)

- **Old layered version types (old sys, old syp, and so on)**    If .aod files are present in the Old Application folder (located in Program Files\Microsoft Dynamics AX\40\Application \Appl\Standard\Old), elements from the files are available here. This allows you to compare an older version of an element with a 4.0 version of the element. See Chapter 1, "Architectural Overview," for more information on layers. In Chapter 1, Figure 1-5 illustrates the components in the model layering system.

- **Version control revisions (Version 1, Version 2, and so on)**    Any revision of an element from the version control system can be retrieved individually and used for comparison. The version control system is explained later in this chapter.

- **Best practice washed version (Washed)**    A few simple best practice issues can be resolved automatically by a best practice "wash." Selecting the washed version shows you how your implementation differs from best practices. To get the full benefit of this, select the Case Sensitive check box on the Advanced tab.

- **Export/import file (XPO)**    Before you import elements, these can be compared with existing elements (which they will overwrite during import). The Compare tool can be used during the import process (Command\Import) by selecting the Show Details check box in the Import dialog box and right-clicking any elements that appear in boldface. Boldface objects already exist in the application and objects that are not boldface do not.

- **Upgraded version (Upgraded)**    MorphX can automatically create a proposal for how a class should be upgraded. The requirement for upgrading a class arises during a version upgrade. The Create Upgrade Project step in the Upgrade Checklist automatically detects customized classes conflicting with new versions of the class. A class is conflicting when you have changed the original version of the class, and the original version has also been changed by the publisher of the class. MorphX constructs the proposal by merging your changes and the publisher's changes to the class. MorphX requires access to all three versions of the class—the original version in the Old Application folder, a version with your changes in the current layer in the Old Application folder, and a version with the publisher's changes in the same layer as the original. The installation program ensures that the right versions are available in the right places during an upgrade. The conflict resolution is shown in Figure 4-12.

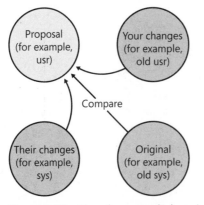

**Figure 4-12**    How the upgraded version proposal is created.

> **Note**   Two different elements can also be compared. To do this, select two elements in the AOT, right-click, point to Add-Ins, and then click Compare.

Figure 4-13 shows the Advanced tab, on which you can specify comparison options.

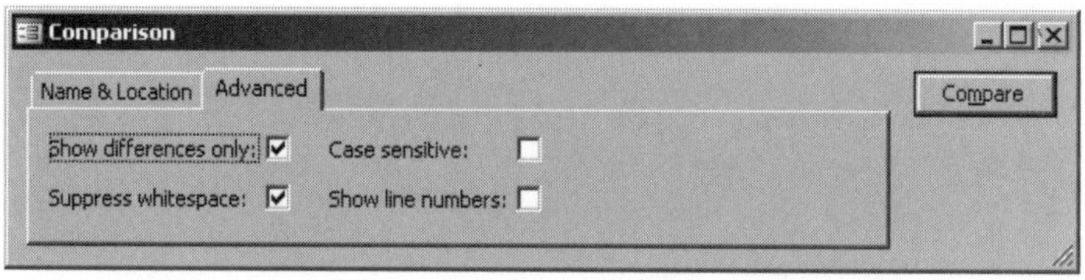

**Figure 4-13**   Comparison options on the Advanced tab.

Table 4-4 describes the comparison options.

**Table 4-4   Comparison Options**

| Option | Description |
| --- | --- |
| Show Differences Only | All equal nodes are suppressed from the view, making it easier to find the changed nodes. This option is selected by default. |
| Suppress Whitespace | White space, such as spaces and tabs, is suppressed into a single space when comparing. The Compare tool can ignore the amount of white space, just as the compiler does. This option is selected by default. |
| Case Sensitive | Because X++ is not case-sensitive, the Compare tool is also not case-sensitive by default. In certain scenarios, case sensitivity is required and must be enabled, such as when you are using the best practice wash feature mentioned earlier in this section. This option is not selected by default. |
| Show Line Numbers | The Compare tool can add line numbers to all displayed X++ code. This can be useful during an upgrade of larger chunks of code. This option is not selected by default. |

## Using the Compare Tool

After you choose elements and set parameters, you can start the comparison by clicking Compare. Results are displayed in a three-pane dialog box, as shown in Figure 4-14. The top pane is the element selection, the left pane is a tree structure resembling the AOT, and the right pane shows details of the tree selection.

The icons in the tree structure indicate how each node is changed. A red or blue check mark indicates that the node exists only in a red or blue element. Red corresponds to the sys layer, and blue corresponds to the old sys layer. A gray check mark indicates that the nodes are identical but one or more sub-nodes are different. A not equal symbol (≠) on a red and blue background indicates that the nodes are different in the two versions.

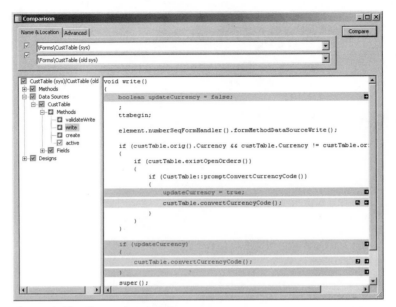

**Figure 4-14**  Comparison results.

> **Note**   Each node in the tree view has a context menu that provides access to the Add-Ins submenu and the Open New Window option. The Open New Window option provides an AOT view on any element, including old layer elements.

Details of the differences are shown in the right pane. Color coding is also used in this pane to highlight differences. If an element is editable, small action icons appear. These icons allow you to make changes to source, metadata, and nodes, which can save you time when performing an upgrade. A right or left arrow will remove or add the difference, and a bent arrow will move the difference to another position. These arrows always come in pairs, so you can see where the difference will be moved to and from. An element is editable if it is from the current layer and checked out if a version control system is used.

## Compare APIs

Although Dynamics AX uses the comparison functionality for development purposes only, the general comparison functionality can be used more widely. The available APIs allow you to compare and present differences in the tree structure or text representation of any type of entity.

The *Tutorial_CompareContextProvider* class shows how simple it is to compare business data by using these APIs and present it by using the Compare tool. The tutorial consists of two parts:

■   *Tutorial_Comparable*   This class implements the *SysComparable* interface. Basically, it creates a text representation of a customer.

■ *Tutorial_CompareContextProvider*   This class implements the *SysCompareContext-Provider* interface. It provides the context for comparison. For example, it lists a *tutorial_Comparable* class for each customer, sets the default comparison options, and handles context menus.

Figure 4-15 shows a comparison of two customers, the result of running the tutorial.

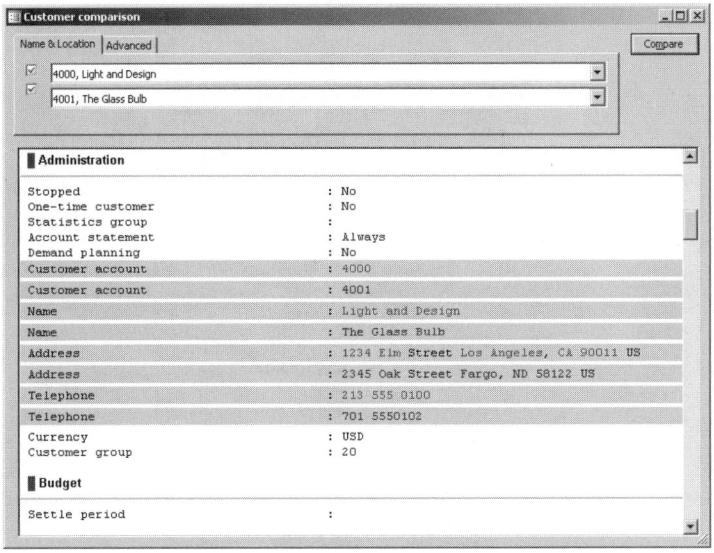

**Figure 4-15**   Result of comparing two customers using the Compare API.

The line-by-line comparison functionality can also be used directly in X++. The static *run* method on the *SysCompareText* class, shown in the following code, takes two strings as parameters and returns a container that highlights differences in the two strings. A set of optional parameters can also be used to control the comparison.

```
public static container run(str _t1,
                str _t2,
                boolean _caseSensitive      = false,
                boolean _suppressWhiteSpace = true,
                boolean _lineNumbers        = false,
                boolean _singleLine         = false,
                boolean _alternateLines     = false)
```

Refer to the Microsoft Dynamics AX SDK for documentation of the classes.

# The Cross-Reference Tool

The concept of cross-references in Dynamics AX is simple. If an element uses another element, the reference is recorded. Cross-references allow you to determine which elements a particular element uses, as well as which elements are being used by other elements. Dynamics AX provides the Cross-Reference tool to access and manage cross-reference information.

The Cross-Reference tool must be updated regularly for accuracy. The update typically takes several hours. The footprint in your database is about 1 gigabyte for the standard application.

You can update the Cross-Reference tool from Tools\Development Tools\Cross-Reference \Periodic\Update. Updating the Cross-Reference tool also compiles the entire AOT, because cross-reference information is emitted by the compiler.

> **Tip**    Keeping the Cross-Reference tool updated is important if you want to rely on its information. If you work in a shared development environment, you share cross-reference information with your team members. Updating the Cross-Reference tool nightly is a good approach for a shared environment. If you work in a local development environment, you can keep the Cross-Reference tool updated by enabling cross-referencing when compiling. This will, however, slow down the compilation. Another option is to manually update cross-references for the elements in a project. You can do so by right-clicking the project, pointing to Add-Ins, pointing to Cross-Reference, and then clicking Update.

In addition to the main cross-reference information, two smaller cross-reference subsystems exist:

- **Data model**    This cross-reference subsystem stores information about relationships between tables. It is primarily used by the query form and the Reverse Engineering tool.

- **Type hierarchy**    This cross-reference subsystem stores information about class and data type inheritance. It is used in the Application Hierarchy Tree only. The Application Hierarchy Tree is available in Tools\Development Tools\Application Hierarchy Tree.

Further discussion of these tools is beyond the scope of this book. Refer to the Microsoft Dynamics AX SDK for more information on these subsystems and the tools relying on them.

The cross-reference information collected is quite complete. Table 4-5 shows a list of the kinds of elements included in the cross-reference tool, as documented in the AOT under System Documentation\Enums\xRefKind.

**Table 4-5    Kinds of Cross-Referenced Element**

| | |
|---|---|
| BasicType | Class |
| ClassInstanceMethod | ClassStaticMethod |
| ClrType (new in version 4.0) | ClrTypeMethod (new in version 4.0) |
| ConfigurationKey | Enum |
| Enumerator | ExtendedType |
| Label | LicenseCode |
| Map | MapField |
| MapInstanceMethod | MapStaticMethod |

**Table 4-5   Kinds of Cross-Referenced Element**

| | |
|---|---|
| MenuItemAction (new in version 4.0) | MenuItemDisplay (new in version 4.0) |
| MenuItemOutput (new in version 4.0) | Predefined (predefined functions) |
| SecurityKey | Table |
| TableField | TableIndex |
| TableInstanceMethod | TableStaticMethod |
| WebActionItem (new in version 4.0) | WebDisplayContentItem (new in version 4.0) |
| WebOutputContentItem (new in version 4.0) | WebUrlItem (new in version 4.0) |

When the Cross-Reference tool is updated, it scans all metadata and X++ code for references to elements of the kinds listed in Table 4-5.

> **Tip**   It is a good idea to use intrinsic functions when referring to elements in X++ code. An intrinsic function can evaluate to either an element name or an ID. The intrinsic functions are named <*ElementKind*>Str or <*ElementKind*>Num, respectively. Using intrinsic functions provides two benefits: You have compile-time verification that the element you reference actually exists, and the reference is picked up by the Cross-Reference tool. Also, there is no run-time overhead. Here is an example:
>
> ```
> print classNum(myClass);   //Prints ID of myClass, such as 50001
> print classStr(myClass);   //Prints "MyClass"
> print "MyClass";           //No compile check or cross-reference;
> ```
>
> See Chapter 14, "Reflection," for more information about intrinsic functions.

The primary function of the Cross-Reference tool is to determine where a particular element is being used. Here are a couple of scenarios:

- You want to find usage examples. If the product documentation does not help you, you can use the Cross-Reference tool to find real implementation examples.

- You need to perform an impact analysis. If you are changing an element, you need to know which other elements are affected by your change.

To access usage information, right-click any element in the AOT, point to Add-Ins, point to Cross-Reference, and then click Used By. If the option is not available, the element is not used or that cross-reference has not been updated.

Figure 4-16 shows where the *prompt* method is used on the *RunBaseBatch* class.

When you view cross-references for a class method, the Application Hierarchy Tree is visible, allowing you to see whether the same method is used on a parent or sub-class. For types that do not support inheritance, such as tables, table methods, and table fields, the Application Hierarchy Tree is hidden.

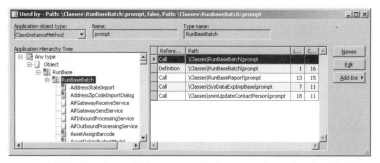

**Figure 4-16**    The Cross-Reference tool, showing where *RunBaseBatch.prompt()* is used.

# The Version Control Tool

The Version Control tool is a new feature in Dynamics AX 4.0 that makes it possible to use a version control system, such as Microsoft Visual SourceSafe 6.0, to keep track of changes to elements in the AOT. The tool is accessible from Tools\Development Tools\Version Control and from the context menu on elements in the AOT.

The benefits of using a version control system include:

- **Revision history of all elements**    All changes are captured along with a description of the change, making it possible to consult change logs and retrieve old versions of an element.

- **Code quality enforcement**    The implementation of version control in Dynamics AX 4.0 enables a fully configurable quality bar for all check-ins. With the quality bar, all changes are verified according to coding practices. If the change does not meet the criteria, it is rejected. The quality bar is used at Microsoft for all check-ins, which has helped raise the quality level of X++ code to an unprecedented level. Microsoft developers may not check in code with compiler errors, compile warnings, or best practice errors. In the final stages of development, tasks in code (to-dos) are also prohibited.

- **Local development environment**    Each developer must have a local installation and make all modifications locally. When modifications are ready, they can be checked in and made available to consumers of the build. This allows a developer to rewrite fundamental areas of the system without causing any instability issues for others. It also makes developers immune to any downtime of a centralized development server.

Using a version control system when developing is optional, and it is perfectly possible and recommended to develop without using a version control system for smaller development projects. Because using a version control system adds overhead to the entire process, smaller projects do not usually warrant the extra cost.

The elements persisted in the version control server are file representations of the elements in the AOT. The file format used is the standard Dynamics AX export format (.xpo). Each .xpo file contains only one element.

The .xpo file format has changed slightly from the previous version of Dynamics AX to better fit the purpose of a version control system. Properties set to their default values are not exported, and the timestamp inside the file is removed.

Figure 4-17 shows a typical deployment, in which each developer locally hosts the AOS and the database. Each developer also needs a copy of all .xpo files. When a developer communicates with the version control server, the .xpo files are transmitted. When he or she creates a new element or label, a unique ID is required. An ID Server, implemented as a Microsoft .NET Web service, is required to ensure uniqueness of IDs across all the local developers' environments. The ID Server is a component available with Dynamics AX.

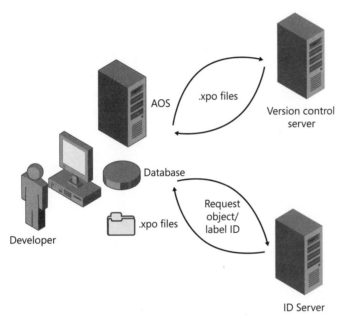

**Figure 4-17**   A typical deployment using version control.

# Element Life Cycle

Figure 4-18 shows the element life cycle in a version control system. When the element is in a state marked with a green color, it can be edited; otherwise it is read-only.

You can create a new element in one of two ways:

- Create a completely new element.
- Customize an existing element, resulting in an overlayered version of the element. Because elements are stored per layer in the version control system, customizing an element effectively creates a new element.

After an element is created, it must be added to the version control system. First give it a proper name in accordance with naming conventions, and then click Create on the context menu. After the element is created, it must be checked in.

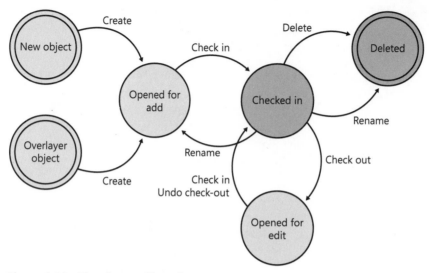

**Figure 4-18** The element life cycle.

An element that is checked in can be renamed. Renaming an element deletes the element with the old name and adds an element with the new name.

## Check-out

To modify an element, you must check it out. Checking out an element locks it so that others cannot modify it while you are working.

By clicking Tools\Development Tools\Version Control\Pending Objects, you can see which elements you currently have checked out. The elements that you have checked out (or that you have created and not yet checked in), appear in blue, rather than black, in the AOT.

## Undo Check-out

If you decide that you do not want to modify an element that you checked out, you can undo the check-out. This releases your lock on the element and imports the server version of the element to undo your changes.

## Check-in

When you have finalized your modifications, elements must be checked in to be part of the next build. When you click Check-In on the context menu, the dialog box shown in Figure 4-19 appears, displaying all of the elements that you currently have checked out. The Check In dialog box shows all open elements by default; any elements not required in the check-in can be removed from the list by pressing Alt+F9.

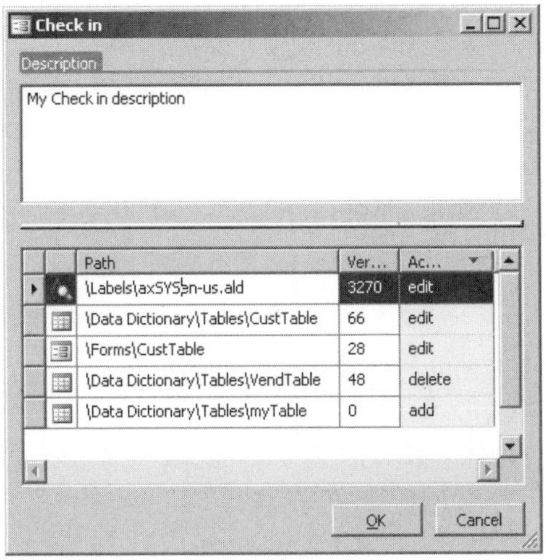

**Figure 4-19**   The Check In dialog box.

The following is the recommended check-in procedure.

1. Perform synchronization to update all elements in your environment to the latest version.

2. Verify that everything is still working as intended. Compilation is not enough!

3. Check in the elements.

## Quality Checks

Before a check-in is accepted by the version control system, the elements being checked in may be subject to quality checks. You define what will be accepted in a check-in when you set up the version control system. The following checks are supported:

- Compiler errors
- Compiler warnings
- Compiler tasks
- Best practice errors

When a check is enabled, it will be carried out when you do a check-in. If the check fails, the check-in stops. You must address the issue and restart the check-in.

## Updating Source Code Casing

Before elements are checked in, the Source Code Titlecase Update tool, available on the Add-Ins submenu, can be automatically executed to ensure a uniform casing in variable and parameter declarations and references. You can specify this parameter when setting up the version control system by selecting the Run Title Case Update check box.

# Creating New Elements

When using version control, you create new elements just as you normally would in the MorphX environment without a version control system. These elements will not be part of your check-in until you click Create on the context menu.

You may also create all element types except those listed in System Settings (Tools\Development Tools\Version Control\Setup\System Settings). By default, jobs and private projects are not accepted.

New elements should follow Dynamics AX naming conventions. The best practice naming conventions are enforced by default, so you cannot check in elements with names such as *aaaElement*, *Del_Element*, *element1*, or *element2*. (The only *Del* elements allowed are those required for version upgrade purposes.) Naming requirements can be changed in System Settings.

# Renaming Elements

An element must be in the checked-in state to be renamed. Because all references in .xpo files are strictly name based (and not ID based), all references to renamed elements must be updated. For example, when a table field is renamed, any form or report that uses that field must be updated. Most references in metadata in the AOT are ID based, and they are not affected when an element is renamed; in most cases, it is enough to simply check out the form or report and include it in the check-in to update the .xpo file. The cross-reference functionality can be leveraged to identify references. References in X++ code are name based. You can use the compiler to find affected references.

Revision history of the element is kept intact when elements are renamed. No tracking information in the version control system is lost as a result of a rename.

# Deleting Elements

You delete an element as you normally would in Dynamics AX. An element must be in the checked-in state to be deleted. The deletion occurs when the element is checked in. You can see pending deletions in the Pending Objects dialog box.

# Labels

Working with labels is very similar to working with elements. To change, delete, or add a label, you must check out the label file containing the label. You can check out the label file from the Label Editor dialog box.

The main difference between checking out elements and checking out label files is that simultaneous check-outs are allowed for label files. This means that others can change labels while you have a label file checked out.

When you check in a label file, your changes are automatically merged into the latest version of the file. If you modify or delete a label that another person has also modified or deleted, your changes will be lost. Lost changes are shown in the Infolog.

Label IDs are guaranteed to be unique by the ID Server; adding labels will not generate conflicts.

## Get Latest

If someone else has checked in a new version of an element, the Get Latest option on the context menu allows you to get the version of the element that was most recently checked in. This option is not available when you have the element checked out yourself.

## Synchronization

Synchronization allows you to get the latest version of all elements. This is a required step that must be performed before checking in. It can be started from Tools\Development Tools\Version Control\Periodic\Synchronize.

Synchronization is divided into three operations that happen automatically in the following sequence:

1. Copy the latest files from the Version Control Server to the local disk.
2. Import the files into the AOT.
3. Compile the imported files.

Synchronization should be used to get your system up-to-date. Synchronization will not affect any new elements that you have created or any elements that you have checked out.

Figure 4-20 shows the Synchronization dialog box.

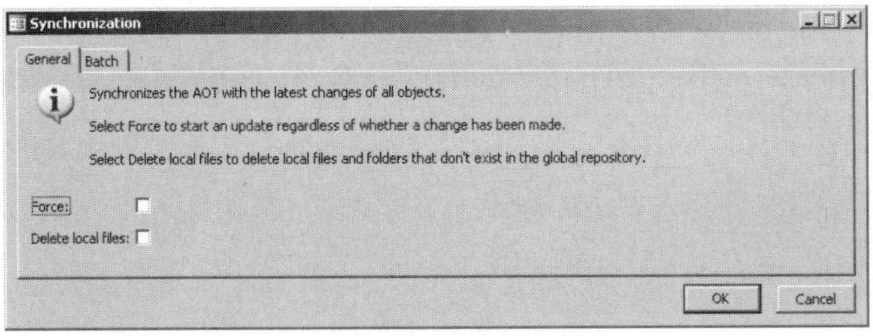

**Figure 4-20**   The Synchronization dialog box.

Selecting the Force check box gets the latest version of all files, whether they have changed or not, and then imports every single file.

## Synchronization Log

How you keep track of versions on the client depends on the version control system. Visual SourceSafe requires that Dynamics AX keep track of itself. When you synchronize the latest version, it is copied to the local repository folder from the version control system. Each file must be imported into Dynamics AX to be reflected in the AOT. To minimize the risk of partial synchronization, a log entry is created for each file. When all files are copied locally, the log is processed, and the files are automatically imported into Dynamics AX.

When synchronization fails, the import operation is usually the cause of problems. Synchronization failure leaves your system in a partially synchronized state. To complete the synchronization, you must restart Dynamics AX and restart the import. You use the synchronization log to restart the import, which is accessed from Tools\Development Tools\Version Control\Inquiries\Synchronization Log.

The Synchronization Log dialog box, shown in Figure 4-21, displays each batch of files, and you can restart the import by clicking Process. If the Processed check box is not selected, the import has failed and should be restarted.

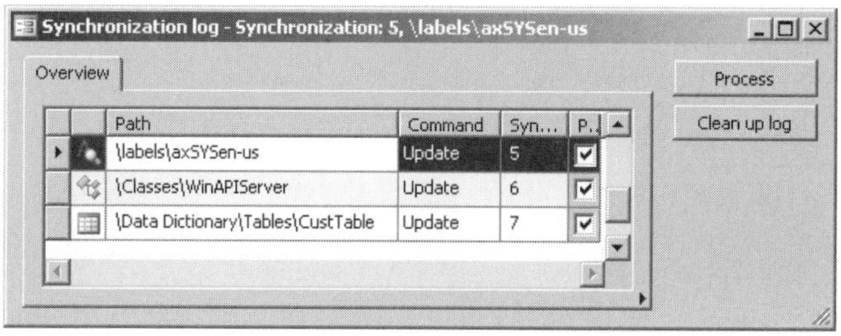

**Figure 4-21**    The Synchronization Log dialog box.

## Show History

One of the biggest advantages of a versioning system is the ability to track changes to elements. Selecting Show History on an element's context menu displays a list of all changes to an element, as shown in Figure 4-22.

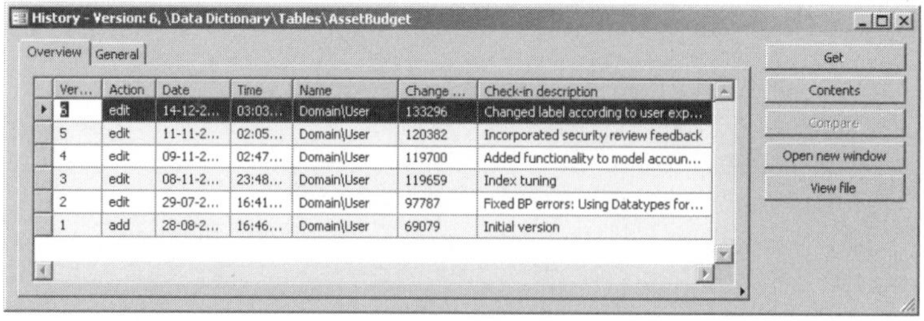

**Figure 4-22**    Revision history of an element.

This dialog box shows the version number, the action performed, the time the action was performed, and who performed the action. You can also see the change number and the change description.

A set of buttons in the revision history dialog box allows further investigation of each version. Clicking Contents opens a form that shows other elements included in the same change. Clicking Compare opens the Compare dialog box, which allows you to do a line-by-line comparison of two versions of the element. The Open New Window button opens an AOT window that shows the selected version of the element, which is useful for investigating properties because it allows you to use the standard MorphX toolbox. Clicking View File opens the .xpo file for the selected version in Microsoft Notepad.

## Revision Comparison

Comparison is the key to harvesting the benefits of a version control system. You can start a comparison from several places, including the Compare option on the Add-Ins submenu. Figure 4-23 shows the Comparison dialog box where two revisions of the table *AssetBudget* are selected.

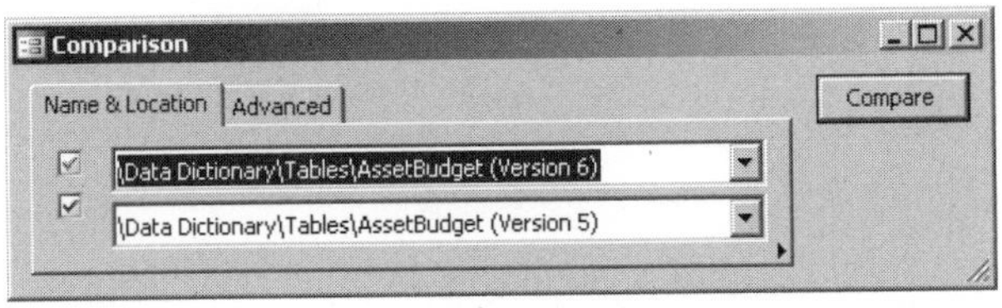

**Figure 4-23**  Comparing element revisions from version control.

Note that a comparison contains a list of all checked-in versions, in addition to the layer element versions.

## Pending Elements

When you are working on a project, it is easy to lose track of which elements have been opened for editing. The Pending Objects dialog box in Figure 4-24 shows a list of elements that are currently checked out in the version control system. Notice the column containing the action performed on the element. Deleted elements are available only in this dialog box; they are no longer shown in the AOT.

You can access the Pending Objects dialog box from Tools\Development Tools\Version Control\Pending Objects.

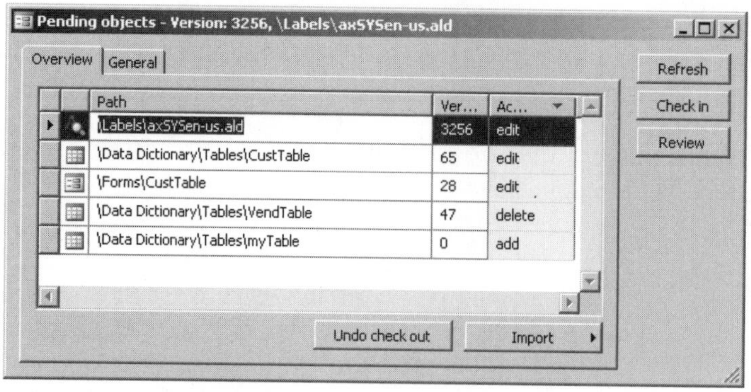

**Figure 4-24** Pending elements.

# Build

Because the version control system contains .xpo files, and not an .aod file, a build process is required to generate an .aod file from the .xpo files. The following procedure is a high-level overview of the build process.

1. Use the CombineXPOs command-line utility to create one .xpo file by combining all .xpo files. The purpose of this step is to make the .xpo file consumable by Dynamics AX. Dynamics AX requires all referenced elements to be present in the .xpo file or already exist in the AOT to maintain the references during import.

2. Import the new .xpo file by using the command-line parameter  -AOTIMPORT-FILE=<*FileName*.xpo> to Ax32.exe. This step imports the .xpo file and compiles everything. After it is complete, the new .aod file is ready.

These steps must be followed for each layer being built. The steps are described in detail in the SDK.

# Integration with Other Version Control Systems

The implementation of the version control system in Dynamics AX is fully pluggable. This means that any version control system can be integrated with Dynamics AX.

Figure 4-25 shows a simplified UML class diagram of the implementation.

The *xVersionControl* class is a system class. It is the integration point with MorphX. The kernel implementation in this class instructs MorphX to behave as if there were no version control system. MorphX calls methods on this class when the developer navigates the AOT. The *VersionControl* application class derives from *xVersionControl* and acts as factory and dispatcher. It creates an instance of *SysVersionControlSystem* and dispatches all MorphX events to this class. An instance of the *VersionControl* class is always available with the same name.

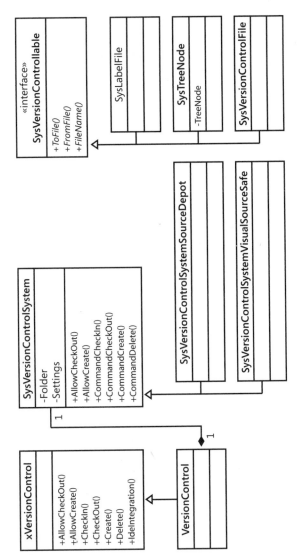

**Figure 4-25**   A UML class diagram of the version control system implementation.

*SysVersionControlSystem* is the base class for integration with any version control system. The Visual SourceSafe specializations derive from this class.

Classes implementing *SysVersionControllable* can be passed to the command methods on *SysVersionControlSystem*. Three classes are required to do this: one to handle label files, one to handle tree nodes, and one to handle all other files.

Integrating with another version control system requires a new specialized *SysVersionControl-System* class that implements the command methods by communicating with the version control system. For example, the check-in and check-out commands must be implemented to interface correctly with the version control system.

# Chapter Summary

This chapter showed you how to use and leverage some of the many tools available in MorphX. Some of these tools can be extended, such as the Best Practices tool, or used from your own code, such as the Compare tool.

Much of this chapter focused on the Version Control tool. From a development perspective, this tool is the most exciting addition to version 4.0. Understanding and using it can have a very positive impact on your organization.

# Chapter 5
# The X++ Programming Language

The objectives of this chapter are to:

- Provide an introduction to the X++ programming language.

- Introduce job model elements, which are useful for executing X++ samples.

- Describe the Microsoft Dynamics AX 4.0 runtime type system that supports value types, reference types, and type hierarchies.

- Explain the syntax of the X++ programming language and provide examples of variable declarations, expressions, statements, macros, and comments.

- Describe the syntax of class and interface definitions.

## Introduction

The X++ language is an object-oriented, application-aware, and data-aware programming language. The language is object-oriented because it supports object abstractions, abstraction hierarchies, polymorphism, and encapsulation. The language is application-aware because it includes keywords such as *client*, *server*, *changecompany*, and *display* that are useful for writing client-server enterprise resource planning (ERP) applications. The language is data-aware because it includes keywords such as *firstFast*, *forceSelectOrder*, and *forUpdate*, as well as a database query syntax, that are useful for programming database applications.

You use the Dynamics AX designers and tools to edit the structure of application types. You specify the behavior of application types by writing X++ source code using the X++ editor. The X++ compiler compiles this source code into bytecode intermediate format. Model data, X++ source code, and intermediate bytecode are stored in the .aod files. The Dynamics AX runtime dynamically composes object types by loading overridden bytecode from the highest level definition in the model layering stack. (For more information about the layering technology, see Chapter 1, "Architectural Overview.") Objects are instantiated from these dynamic types.

This chapter describes the Dynamics AX runtime type system and the essential features of the X++ language used to write ERP applications. This introduction to the language will help you understand the examples provided in this book. It will also help you avoid common programming pitfalls that stem from the language implementation. For an in-depth discussion of the type system and the X++ language, refer to the Microsoft Dynamics AX SDK.

# Jobs

Jobs are model elements that you create by using the Application Object Tree (AOT). The following X++ compilation unit provides an example of a job model element that prints the "Hello World" string to an automatically generated window. The *pause* statement stops program execution and waits for user input from a dialog box.

```
static void myJob(Args _args)
{
    print "Hello World";
    pause;
}
```

Jobs are globally defined functions that execute in the rich client run-time environment. Jobs are frequently used because they are easily executed from within the MorphX development environment by pressing F5 or selecting Go on the command menu. Applications should not use jobs as part of their core design. No jobs are distributed with the Dynamics AX application code. The examples provided in this chapter can be run as jobs.

# The Type System

The Dynamics AX runtime manages the storage of value type data on the call stack and reference type objects on the memory heap. The call stack is the memory structure that holds data about the active methods called during program execution. The memory heap is the memory area that allocates storage for objects that are destroyed automatically by the Dynamics AX runtime.

# Value Types

Value types include the built-in primitive types, extended data types, enumeration types, and built-in collection types:

- The primitive types are *boolean*, *int*, *int64*, *real*, *date*, *timeofday*, *str*, and *guid*.

- The extended data types are specialized primitive types and specialized base enumerations. User-defined extended data types are dynamically composed from application model layers.

- The enumeration types are base enumerations and extended data types. User-defined enumeration types are dynamically composed from application model layers. Dynamics AX runtime enumeration types are exposed in the system API.

- The collection types are the built-in array and container types.

By default, variables declared as value types are assigned their zero value by the Dynamics AX runtime. These variables cannot be assigned to null. Variable values are copied when variables are used to invoke methods and when they are used in assignment statements. Therefore, two value type variables cannot reference the same value.

## Reference Types

Reference types include the record types, class types, and interface types.

- The record types are *table*, *map*, and *view*. User-defined record types are dynamically composed from application model layers. Dynamics AX runtime record types are exposed in the system API.

> **Note**   Although they are not visible in the AOT, all record types implement the methods that are members of the system *xRecord* type, a Dynamics AX runtime class type.

- User-defined class types are dynamically composed from application model layers and Dynamics AX runtime class types exposed in the system API.

- Interface types are type specifications and cannot be instantiated in the Dynamics AX runtime. Class types can, however, implement interfaces.

Variables declared as reference types contain references to objects that the Dynamics AX runtime instantiates from dynamically composed types defined in the application model layering system and from types exposed in the system API. The Dynamics AX runtime also performs memory de-allocation (garbage collection) for these objects when they go out of scope and there are no longer any references to them. Reference variables declared as record types reference objects that are automatically instantiated by the Dynamics AX runtime. Class type objects are programmatically instantiated using the *new* operator. Copies of object references are passed as reference parameters in method calls and are assigned to reference variables, so two variables could reference the same object.

> **More Info**   Not all nodes in the AOT name a type declaration. Some class type declarations are merely *syntactic sugar*—convenient, human-readable expressions. For example, the class header definition for all rich client forms declares a *FormRun* class type, the class header definition for all rich client reports declares a *ReportRun* class type, and the class header definition for a Web client form declares a *WebFormRun* class type. *FormRun*, *ReportRun*, and *WebFormRun* are also, however, class types in the system API. Allowing their declarations is syntactic sugar because it is technically illegal to have two types with the same name in the Dynamics AX class type hierarchy.

# Type Hierarchies

The X++ language supports the definition of type hierarchies that specify generalization and specialization relationships between class types. For example, a check payment method is a type of payment method. A type hierarchy allows code reuse. Reusable code is defined on base types defined higher in a type hierarchy as they are inherited, or reused, by derived types defined lower in a type hierarchy. This section introduces the base types provided by the Dynamics AX runtime and describes how they are extended in type hierarchies.

> **Caution**    The Dynamics AX type system is known as a weak type system because the X++ language accepts certain type assignments that are clearly erroneous and lead to run-time errors. Be aware of the caveats outlined in the following sections, and try to avoid weak type constructs when writing X++ code.

## The *anytype* Type

There is no strict type hierarchy with a concrete base type for all types in the Dynamics AX type system. The *anytype* type therefore imitates a base type for all types. Variables of the *anytype* type behave like value types when they are assigned a value type variable and like reference types when they are assigned a reference type variable. The *SysAnyType* class can be used to explicitly box all types, including value types, and make them behave like reference types.

The *anytype* type, shown in the following code sample, is syntactic sugar that allows methods to accept any type as a parameter or allows a method to return different types.

```
static str queryRange(anytype _from, anytype _to)
{
    return SysQuery::range(_from,_to);
}
```

You can declare variables by using *anytype*. However, the *anytype* type locks its primitive type at first assignment and cannot be changed later, as shown here.

```
anytype a = 1;
print strfmt("%1 = %2", typeof(a), a); //Integer = 1
a = "text";
print strfmt("%1 = %2", typeof(a), a); //Integer = 0
pause;
```

## The *common* Type

The *common* type is the base type of all record types. Like the *anytype* type, record types are context-dependent types whose variables can be used as though they reference single records or a record cursor that can iterate over a set of database records.

Using the *common* type allows you to cast one record type to another (possibly incompatible) record type, as shown in this example.

```
//customer = vendor; //Compile error
common = customer;
vendor = common;      //Accepted
```

Table maps defined in the AOT are a more type-safe method of capturing commonalities between record types and should be used to prevent incompatible record assignments. A table map defines fields and methods that safely operate on one or more record types.

Note that method calls on the *common* type are validated by the compiler. The following method invocation, for example, is accepted by the compiler, even though the method does not exist.

```
common.nonExistingMethod();
```

For this reason, you should use reflection to confirm that the method on the *common* type exists before it is invoked.

## The *object* Type

The built-in *object* type is a weak reference type whose variables reference objects that are instances of class or interface types in the Dynamics AX class hierarchy.

The type system allows programmers to implicitly cast base type objects to derived type objects and to cast derived type objects to base type objects, as shown here.

```
baseClass = derivedClass;
derivedClass = baseClass;
```

Note that the *object* type allows you to use the assignment operator and cast one class type to another incompatible class type, as shown in the following code. This will, however, probably result in a run-time exception when your code encounters an object of an unexpected type.

```
//textIO = binaryIO; //Compile error
Object = textIO;
binaryIO = object;    //Accepted
```

Use the *SysDictClass* class instead of the assignment operator to prevent these incompatible type casts. The *SysDictClass* class provides *is()* methods to safely cast derived types of base types and the *as()* method to safely cast base types to derived types.

Note that method calls on the *object* type are not validated by the compiler. The following method invocation is accepted by the compiler, even though the method does not exist.

```
object.nonExistingMethod();
```

### Extended Data Types

You use the AOT to create extended data types that model concrete data values and data hierarchies. For example, the *Name* data type is a string, and the *CustName* and *VendName* data types extend the *Name* data type.

The X++ language supports extended data types but does not offer any type checking according to the hierarchy of extended data types. X++ treats any extended data type as its primitive type; therefore, code such as the following is allowed.

```
CustName customerName;
FileName fileName = customerName;
```

When used properly, however, extended data types improve readability of X++ code; it is easier to understand the intended use of a *CustName* data type than a *string* data type, even if they are both used to declare string variables.

## Syntax

The X++ language belongs to the "curly brace" family of programming languages (those that use curly braces to delimit syntax blocks), such as C, C++, C#, and Java. If you are familiar with any of these languages, you will have no problem reading and understanding the X++ syntax.

In contrast to many other programming languages, the X++ language is not case-sensitive. However, using camel casing (camelCasing) for class names and Pascal casing (PascalCasing) for variable names is considered a best practice. (More best practices for writing X++ code are available in the Microsoft Dynamics AX SDK.) You can use the Source Code Titlecase Update tool (accessed from the Add-Ins submenu in the AOT) to automatically apply casing in X++ code to match the best practice recommendation.

CLR types, which are case-sensitive, are one important exception to the casing guidelines. This is explained later in this chapter.

## Variable Declarations

Variable declarations must be placed at the beginning of methods. Table 5-1 provides examples of value type and reference type variable declarations, as well as example variable initializations. Parameter declaration examples are provided in the "Classes and Interfaces" section later in this chapter.

**Table 5-1   X++ Variable Declaration Examples**

| Type | Examples |
| --- | --- |
| *anytype* | `anytype type = null;`<br>`anytype type = 1;` |
| record types | `common record = null;`<br>`CustTable custTable = null;` |
| object types | `object obj = null;`<br>`ClrObject dt = new ClrObject("System.DateTime");`<br>`MyClass myClass = new MyClass();` |
| *boolean* | `boolean b = true;` |
| *int* | `int i = -5;`<br>`int h = 0xAB;` |
| *int64* | `int64 i = -5;`<br>`int64 h = 0xAB;`<br>`int64 u = 0xA0000000u;` |
| *real* | `real r1 = 3.14;`<br>`real r2 = 1.0e3;` |
| *date* | `date d = 12\12\2004` |
| *timeofday* | `timeofday time = 43200;` |
| *str* | `str s1 = "a string";`<br>`str s2 = 'a string';`<br>`str 40 s40 = "string 40";`<br>`str right sr = "justified";` |
| *guid* | `guid g = newguid();` |
| *container* | `container c1 = ["a string", 123];`<br>`container c2 = connull();` |
| base enumeration types | `NoYes theAnswer = NoYes::Yes;` |
| extended data types | `Name name = "name";` |

Declaring variables with the same name as their type is a common practice. At first glance, this might be confusing. Consider this class and its getter/setter method to its field.

```
Class Person
{
    Name name;
```

```
public Name Name(Name _name = name)
{
    ;
    name = _name;
    return name;
}
}
```

Because X++ is not case-sensitive, the word *name* is used in eight places in the preceding code. Three refer to the extended data type, four refer to the field, and one refers to the method ("*_name*" is used twice). To improve readability, you could rename the variable to something more specific, such as *personName*. However, using a more specific variable name implies that a more specific type should be used (and created if it does not already exist). Changing both the type name and the variable name to *PersonName* would not improve readability. The benefit of this practice is that if you know the name of a variable, you also know its type.

Because X++ allows you to define variables with the same name as their type, variable names become ambiguous. The X++ compiler expects methods to start with variable declarations. To denote a variable with an ambiguous name and not a type, you must add a hanging semicolon, as shown in the preceding example, to signify the end of variable declarations. Including the hanging semicolon is considered a best practice because it allows your code to accommodate new types easily. Variable names could become ambiguous when new extended data types are created, causing compilation errors.

# Expressions

X++ expressions are sequences of operators, operands, values, and variables that yield a result. Table 5-2 summarizes the types of expressions allowed in X++ and includes examples of their use.

**Table 5-2   X++ Expression Examples**

| Category | Examples | |
|----------|----------|---|
| Object creation operators | `new MyClass()`<br>`new System.DateTime()` | `//X++ object creation`<br>`//CLR object wrapper and`<br>`//CLR object creation` |
| Values and variables | `"string"`<br>`myVariable` | |
| Access operators | `this`<br>`element`<br>`<datasource>_ds`<br>`x.y`<br>`E::e`<br>`a[x]`<br>`Table.Field`<br>`Table.(FieldId)`<br>`(select statement).Field`<br>`System.Type` | `//Instance member access`<br>`//Form member access`<br>`//Form data source access`<br>`//Instance member access`<br>`//Enum access`<br>`//Array access`<br>`//Table field access`<br>`//Table field access`<br>`//Select result access`<br>`//CLR namespace type access` |

**Table 5-2   X++ Expression Examples**

| Category | Examples |
|---|---|
| Method invocations | `super()`                    //Base member invocation<br>`MyClass::m()`             //Static member invocation<br>`myObject.m()`            //Instance member invocation<br>`this.m()`                    //This instance member invocation<br>`myTable.MyMap::m();`//Map instance member invocation<br>`f()`                              //Built-in function call |
| Arithmetic operators | `+  -  *  /   div  mod` |
| Shift operators | `<<  >>` |
| Relational operators | `<  >  <=  >= ==  != like` |
| Logical operators | `!  &&  ||` |
| Bitwise operators | `~  ^  &  |` |
| Conditional operators | `x ? y : z` |
| String concatenation | `"Hello" + "World"` |
| Parentheses | `(x)` |

# Statements

X++ statements specify object state and object behavior. Table 5-3 provides examples of X++ language statements that are commonly found in many programming languages. In-depth descriptions of each statement are beyond the scope of this book.

**Table 5-3   X++ Statement Examples**

| Statement | Example |
|---|---|
| assignment statement | `int i;`<br>`;`<br>`i = 1;`<br>`i++;`<br>`++i;`<br>`i--;`<br>`--i;`<br>`i += 1;`<br>`i -= 1;` |
| compound statement | `int i;`<br>`{`<br>`    i = 3;`<br>`    i++;`<br>`}` |
| *print* statement | `int i = 0;`<br>`;`<br>`prin  print i;`<br>`prin  print "Hello World";`<br>`print 5.2;` |

Table 5-3   X++ Statement Examples

| Statement | Example |
|---|---|
| *if* statement | ```
boolean b = true;
int i = 0;
;
if ( b == true )
{
    i++;
}
else
{
    i--;
}
``` |
| *break* statement | ```
int i;
;
for ( i = 0; i < 100; i++ )
{
        if ( i > 50 )
    {
        break;
    }
}
``` |
| *continue* statement | ```
int i;
int    j = 0;
;
for    for( i = 0; i < 100; i++ )

{
    if ( i < 50 )
    {
        continue;
    }
    j++;
}
}
``` |
| *while* statement | ```
int i = 4;
;
while ( i <= 100 )
{
    i++;
}
``` |
| *do while* statement | ```
int i = 4;
;
do
{
    i++;
}
while ( i <= 100 );
``` |
```

**Table 5-3   X++ Statement Examples**

| Statement | Example |
|---|---|
| *for* statement | ```
int i;
;
for ( i = 0; i < 42; i++ )
{
    print i;
}
``` |
| *switch* statement | ```
str s = "test";
;
switch ( s )
{
    case "test" :
        print s;
        break;
    default :
        print "fail";
}
``` |
| *pause* statement | ```
print "Hello World";
pause;
``` |
| *window* statement | ```
window 100, 10 at 100,10;
print "Hello World";
pause;
``` |
| *breakpoint* statement | ```
breakpoint;
``` |
| *return* statement | ```
static void myJob(Args _args)
{
    return;
}
``` |
| *throw* statement | ```
throw error("Error text");
``` |
| *try* statement | ```
try
{
    throw error("Force exception");
}
catc  catch( exception::Error )
{
    print "Error";
    pause;
}
``` |
| *retry* statement | ```
try
{
    throw error("Force exception");
}
catch( exception::Error )
{
    retry;
}
``` |
```

**Table 5-3   X++ Statement Examples**

| Statement | Example |
|---|---|
| .NET CLR interoperability statement | ```str s;```<br>```System.Guid g = System.Guid::NewGuid();```<br>```;```<br>```s = g.ToString();```<br>```print s;```<br>```pause;``` |
| *inner* function | ```static void myJob(Args _args)```<br>```{```<br>```    str myLocalFunction()```<br>```    {```<br>```        return "Hello World";```<br>```    }```<br>```    ;```<br>```    print myLocalFunction();```<br>```    pause;```<br>```}``` |
| *system* function | ```guid g = newguid();```<br>```;```<br>```print abs(-1);``` |
| *flush* statement | ```MyTable myTable;```<br>```;```<br>```flush myTable;``` |
| *changecompany* statement | ```MyTable myTable;```<br>```;```<br>```while select myTable```<br>```{```<br>```    Print myTable.myField;```<br>```}```<br>```changecompany("ZZZ")```<br>```{```<br>```    while select myTable```<br>```    {```<br>```        print myTable.myField;```<br>```    }```<br>```}``` |

## Data-Aware Statements

The X++ language has built-in support for querying and manipulating database data. The syntax for database statements is similar to Structured Query Language (SQL), and this section assumes that you are familiar with SQL. The following code shows how a *select* statement is used to return only the first selected record from the MyTable database table and how the data in the record's *myField* field is printed.

```
static void myJob(Args _args)
{
    MyTable myTable;
    ;
    select firstOnly * from myTable where myTable.myField1=='value';
    print myTable.myField2;
    pause;
}
```

Note that the "* from" part of the *select* statement in the example is optional. The asterisk (*) character can be replaced by a comma-separated field list, such as *myField2, myField3*. All fields must, however, be defined on the selection table model element, and only one selection table is allowed after the *from* keyword. The *where* expression in the *select* statement can comprise any number of logical and relational operators. The *firstOnly* keyword is optional and can be replaced by one or more of the optional keywords. Table 5-4 describes all the possible keywords.

**Table 5-4   Keyword Options for *select* Statements**

| Keyword | Description |
| --- | --- |
| *firstfast* | Fetches the first selected record faster than the remaining selected records. |
| *firstonly* | Returns only the first selected record. |
| *forupdate* | Selects records for updating. |
| *nofetch* | Specifies that the Dynamics AX runtime should not execute the statement immediately because the records are required only by some other operation. |
| *forceplaceholders* | Forces the Dynamics AX runtime to generate a query with placeholder field constraints. For example, the query generated for the preceding code example looks like this: *select * from myTable where myField1=?*. Database query plans are reused when this option is specified. This is the default option for *select* statements that do not join table records. This keyword cannot be used with the *forceliterals* keyword. |
| *forceliterals* | Forces the Dynamics AX runtime to generate a query with the specified field constraints. For example, the query generated for the preceding code example looks like this: *select * from myTable where myField1='value'*. Database query plans are not reused when this option is specified. This keyword cannot be used with the *forceplaceholders* keyword. |
| *forceselectorder* | Forces the Microsoft SQL Server query processor to access tables in the order in which they are specified in the query. (No effect on Oracle.) |
| *forcenestedloop* | Forces the SQL Server query processor to use a nested-loop algorithm for table join operations. Other join algorithms, such as hash-join and merge-join algorithms, are therefore not considered by the query processor. |
| *reverse* | Returns records in reverse of the *select* order. |

The following code example demonstrates how a table index clause is used to suggest the index that a database server should use when querying tables. The Dynamics AX runtime appends an *order by* clause and the *index* fields to the first *select* statement's database query. Records are thus ordered by the index. The Dynamics AX runtime inserts an optional query hint into the second *select* statement's database query.

```
static void myJob(Args _args)
{
    MyTable1 myTable1;
    MyTable2 myTable2;
    ;
    while select myTable1
        index myIndex1
    {
        print myTable1.myField2;
    }

    while select myTable2
        index hint myIndex2
    {
        print myTable2.myField2;
    }
    pause;
}
```

The following code example demonstrates how the results from a *select* query can be ordered and grouped. The first *select* statement specifies that the resulting records must be sorted in ascending order based on *myField1* values and then descending order based on *myField2* values. The second *select* statement specifies that the resulting records must be grouped by *myField1* values and sorted in descending order.

```
static void myJob(Args _args)
{
    MyTable myTable;
    ;
    while select myTable
        order by Field1 asc, Field2 desc
    {
        print myTable.myField;
    }
    while select myTable
        group by Field1 desc
    {
        print myTable.Field1;
    }
    pause;
}
```

The following code demonstrates use of the *avg* and *count* aggregate functions in *select* statements. The first *select* statement averages the values in the *myField* column and assigns the result to the *myField* field. The second *select* statement counts the number of records returned by the selection and assigns the result to the *myField* field.

```
static void myJob(Args _args)
{
    MyTable myTable;
    ;
    select avg(myField) from myTable;
    print myTable.myField;

    select count(myField) from myTable;
    print myTable.myField;
    pause;
}
```

**Caution**   The compiler does not verify that aggregate function parameter types are numeric, so the result returned by the function could be assigned to a field of type *string*. The compiler also performs rounding if, for example, the *average* function calculates a value of 1.5 and the type of *myField* is an integer.

Table 5-5 describes the aggregate functions supported in X++ *select* statements.

**Table 5-5   Aggregate Functions**

| Function | Description |
|---|---|
| *avg* | Returns the average of the non-null field values in the records returned by the selection. |
| *count* | Returns the number of non-null field values in the records returned by the selection. |
| *sum* | Returns the sum of the non-null field values in the records returned by the selection. |
| *minof* | Returns the minimum of the non-null field values in the records returned by the selection. |
| *maxof* | Returns the maximum of the non-null field values in the records returned by the selection. |

The following code example demonstrates how tables are joined with *join* conditions. The first *select* statement joins two tables by using an equality *join* condition between fields in the tables. The second *select* statement joins three tables to illustrate how *join* conditions can be nested and how an *exists* operator can be used as an existence test with a *join* condition. The second *select* statement also demonstrates how a *group by* sort can be used in *join* conditions. In fact, the *join* condition can comprise multiple nested *join* conditions because the syntax of the *join* condition is the same as the body of a *select* statement.

```
static void myJob(Args _args)
{
    MyTable1 myTable1;
    MyTable2 myTable2;
    MyTable3 myTable3;
    ;
    select myField from myTable1
        join myTable2
            where myTable1.myField1=myTable2.myField1;
    print myTable1.myField;

    select myField from myTable1
        join myTable2
            group by myTable2.myField1
            where myTable1.myField1=myTable2.myField1;
                exists join myTable3
                    where myTable1.myField1=myTable3.mField2
    print myTable1.myField;
    pause;
}
```

Table 5-6 describes the *exists* operator and the other *join* operators that can be used in place of the *exists* operator in the previous example.

**Table 5-6   Join Operators**

| Operator | Description |
| --- | --- |
| *exists* | Returns true if any records are in the result set after executing the join clause. Returns false otherwise. |
| *notexists* | Returns false if any records are in the result set after executing the join clause. Returns true otherwise. |
| *outer* | Returns the left outer join of the first and second tables. |

The following example demonstrates use of the *while select* statement that increments the *myTable* variable's record cursor on each loop.

```
static void myJob(Args _args)
{
    MyTable myTable;
    ;
    while select myTable
    {
        Print myTable.myField;
    }
}
```

The *ttsbegin*, *ttscommit*, and *ttsabort* transaction statements must be used for updating records in tables and inserting records into tables. The *ttsbegin* statement marks the beginning of a database transaction block; *ttsbegin-ttscommit* transaction blocks can be nested, and the outermost block commits all database inserts and updates performed since the first *ttsbegin* statement to the database. The *ttsabort* statement rolls back all the database inserts and updates performed since the *ttsbegin* statement. Table 5-7 provides examples of these transaction statements for single records and operations and for set-based (multiple-record) operations.

**Table 5-7   Transaction Statement Examples**

| Statement type | Example |
| --- | --- |
| *ttsbegin*<br>*ttscommit*<br>*ttsabort* | ```boolean b = true;
;
ttsbegin;
if ( b == true )
    ttscommit;
else
    ttsabort;``` |
| *select forupdate* | ```MyTable myTable;
;
ttsbegin;
select forupdate myTable;
myTable.myField = "new value";
myTable.update();
ttscommit;``` |
| *insert* method | ```MyTable myTable;
;
ttsbegin;
myTable.id = "new id";
myTable.myField = "new value";
myTable.insert();
ttscommit;``` |
| *update_recordset* | ```MyTable myTable;
;
ttsbegin;
update_recordset myTable setting
    myField1 = "value1",
    myField2 = "value2"
    where myTable.id == "001";
ttscommit;``` |
| *insert_recordset* | ```MyTable1 myTable1;
MyTable2 myTable2;
;
ttsbegin;
insert_recordset myTable2 ( myField1, myField2 )
    select myField1, myField2 from myTable1;
ttscommit;``` |

## Exception Handling

It is a best practice to use the X++ exception handling framework instead of programmatically halting a transaction by using the *ttsabort* statement. This is because an exception (other than the update conflict exception) thrown inside a transaction block halts execution of the block, and all the inserts and updates performed since the first *ttsbegin* statement are rolled back. Throwing an exception has the additional advantage of providing a way to recover object state and maintain database transaction consistency. The following example demonstrates throwing an exception inside a database transaction block.

```
static void myJob(Args _args)
{
    MyTable myTable;
    boolean state = true;
    ;
    try
    {
        ttsbegin;
        state = false;
        update_recordset myTable setting
            myField = "value"
            where myTable.id == "001";
        if(state==false)
        {
            throw error("Error text");
        }
        ttscommit;
    }
    catch(Exception::Error)
    {
        state = true;
        retry;
    }
    catch
    {
        print "Unhandled Exception";
        pause;
    }
}
```

The *throw* statement throws an exception that causes the database transaction to halt and roll back. Code execution cannot continue inside the scope of the transaction, so the runtime ignores *try* and *catch* statements when inside a transaction. This means that an exception thrown inside a transaction can be caught only outside the transaction, as shown here.

```
static void myJob(Args _args)
{
    try
    {
        ttsbegin;
```

```
    try
    {
        ...
        throw error("Error text");
    }
    catch  //Will never catch anything
    {
    }
    ttscommit;
}
catch
{
    print "Got it";
    pause;
}
}
```

Although a *throw* statement takes the exception enumeration as a parameter, using the *error* method to throw errors is the best practice. The *try* statement's catch list can contain more than one *catch* block. The first *catch* block in the preceding example catches error exceptions and resets the *state* variable. The *retry* statement performs a jump to the first statement in the *try* block. The second *catch* block catches all exceptions not caught by *catch* blocks earlier in the *try* statement's catch list. Table 5-8 describes the Dynamics AX system *Exception* data type enumerations that can be used in try-catch statements.

**Table 5-8   *Exception* Data Type Enumerations**

| Element | Description |
| --- | --- |
| *Deadlock* | Thrown when a database transaction has deadlocked. |
| *Error* | Thrown when an unrecoverable application error occurs. A *catch* block should assume that all database transactions in a transaction block have been halted and rolled back. |
| *Internal* | Thrown when an unrecoverable internal error occurs. |
| *Break* | Thrown when a user presses the Break key or Ctrl+C. |
| *DDEerror* | Thrown when an error occurs in the use of a DDE system class. |
| *Sequence* | Thrown by the Dynamics AX kernel if a database error or database operation error occurs. |
| *Numeric* | Thrown when an unrecoverable error occurs in the *str2int*, *str2int64*, or *str2num* system functions. |
| *CLRError* | Thrown when an unrecoverable error occurs in a CLR process. |
| *CodeAccessSecurity* | Thrown when an unrecoverable error occurs in the *demand* method on a *CodeAccessPermission* object. |
| *UpdateConflict* | Thrown when an update conflict error occurs in a transaction block using optimistic concurrency control. The *catch* block should use a *retry* statement to attempt to commit the halted transaction. |
| *UpdateConflictNot-Recovered* | Thrown when an unrecoverable error occurs in a transaction block using optimistic concurrency control. The *catch* block should not use a *retry* statement to attempt to commit the halted transaction. |

> **Caution**   The error method in the preceding table is a static method on the global
> X++ class for which the X++ compiler allows an abbreviated syntax. The expression
> *Global::error("Error text")* is equivalent to the error expression in the examples. These global
> methods are X++ methods that should not be confused with system functions that are
> Dynamics AX system API methods, such as *newguid()*.

## Interoperability

The X++ language has statements that allow interoperability (interop) with Microsoft .NET
CLR assemblies and Microsoft COM components. Interoperability with both technologies is
obtained by wrapping external objects in Dynamics AX object wrappers and by dispatching
method calls from the Dynamics AX object to the wrapped object.

## CLR Interoperability

You can write X++ statements for CLR interoperability in one of two ways. The first is to use
Dynamics AX system types as shown in the following example, which demonstrates CLR
interoperability with the XML document type in the .NET XML assembly. This example
assumes that the .NET *System.Xml* assembly has been added to the AOT references node. (See
Chapter 4, "The MorphX Development Tools," for a description of the Cross-Reference tool.)
CLR types must be identified by their fully qualified name; for example, the expression
*System.Xml.XmlDocument* is the fully qualified type name for the Microsoft .NET Framework
XML document type. The programs are somewhat verbose, because the compiler does not
support operator expressions more than one deep.

```
static void myJob(Args _args)
{
    ClrObject doc = new ClrObject("System.Xml.XmlDocument");
    ClrObject docStr;
    ClrObject rootElement;
    ClrObject headElement;
    ClrObject docElement;
    ClrObject xml;
    ;
    docStr = ClrInterop::getObjectForAnyType("Document");
    rootElement = doc.CreateElement(docStr);
    doc.AppendChild(rootElement);
    headElement = doc.CreateElement("Head");
    docElement = doc.get_DocumentElement();
    docElement.AppendChild(headElement);
    xml = doc.get_OuterXml();
    print ClrInterop::getAnyTypeForObject(xml);
    pause;
}
```

The first statement in the preceding example demonstrates the use of a static method to
convert between X++ primitive types and CLR objects. The *print* statement shows the reverse,

converting CLR value types to X++ primitive types. Table 5-9 lists the value type conversions that Dynamics AX supports.

**Table 5-9   Type Conversions**

| CLR type to Dynamics AX type | |
| --- | --- |
| *Byte, SByte, Int16, UInt16, Int32* | *int* |
| *Byte, Sbyte, Int16, UInt16, Int32, Uint32, Int64* | *int64* |
| *Double, Single* | *real* |
| *Guid* | *guid* |
| *String* | *str* |
| **Dynamics AX type to CLR type** | |
| *int* | *Int32, Int64* |
| *int64* | *Int64* |
| *real* | *Single, Double* |
| *guid* | *Guid* |
| *str* | *String* |

The preceding code example also demonstrates the X++ method syntax used to access CLR object properties, such as get_DocumentElement. CLR supports several operators that are not supported in X++. Table 5-10 lists the supported CLR operators and the alternative method syntax.

**Table 5-10   CLR Operators and Methods**

| CLR operators | CLR methods |
| --- | --- |
| Property operators | *get_<property>, set_<property>* |
| Index operators | *get_Item; set_Item* |
| Math operators | *op_<operation>;(arguments)* |

The following features of CLR cannot be used with X++:

- Public fields (These can be accessed by using CLR reflection classes.)
- Events and delegates
- The *ref* parameter modifier
- The *out* parameter modifier
- Generics
- Inner classes
- The *Container* composite type
- The *Array* composite type
- Namespace declarations

The second method of writing X++ statements for CLR, shown in the following example, uses CLR types that perform the same steps performed in the previous example. In this case, however, the MorphX support for Microsoft IntelliSense can provide token lookahead, which makes it easier to write CLR interoperability statements. Fully qualified type names must still be used because X++ does not support namespace importing.

> **Caution**   X++ is case-sensitive when referring to CLR types!

The following example demonstrates implicit type conversions from Dynamics AX strings to CLR strings in the string assignment statements, as well as how CLR exceptions are caught in X++.

```
static void myJob(Args _args)
{
    System.Xml.XmlDocument doc = new System.Xml.XmlDocument();
    System.Xml.XmlElement rootElement;
    System.Xml.XmlElement headElement;
    System.Xml.XmlElement docElement;
    System.String xml;
    System.String docStr = "Document";
    System.String headStr = "Head";
    System.Exception ex;
    str errorMessage;
    ;
    try
    {
        rootElement = doc.CreateElement(docStr);
        doc.AppendChild(rootElement);
        headElement = doc.CreateElement(headStr);
        docElement = doc.get_DocumentElement();
        docElement.AppendChild(headElement);
        xml = doc.get_OuterXml();
        print ClrInterop::getAnyTypeForObject(xml);
        pause;
    }
    catch(Exception::CLRError)
    {
        ex = ClrInterop::getLastException();
        if( ex )
        {
            errorMessage = ex.get_Message();
            info( errorMessage );
        }
    }
}
```

X++ does not support enumeration literals natively. The next code example demonstrates how X++ uses CLR enumerations.

```
static void myJob(Args _args)
{
    System.Uri uri;
    System.String scheme;
    System.UriComponents uriComponents;
    System.UriFormat uriFormat;
    ;
    uri = new System.Uri("http://localhost");
    uriComponents = ClrInterop::parseClrEnum("System.UriComponents","Scheme");
    uriFormat = ClrInterop::parseClrEnum("System.UriFormat","UriEscaped");
    scheme = uri.GetComponents(uriComponents, uriFormat);
    print ClrInterop::getAnyTypeForObject(scheme);
    pause;
}
```

The following example illustrates how static CLR methods are invoked by using the X++ static method accessor operator ::.

```
static void myJob(Args _args)
{
    System.Guid g = System.Guid::NewGuid();
    ;
}
```

## COM Interoperability

The following code example demonstrates COM interoperability with the XML document type in the Microsoft XML Core Services (MSXML) 6.0 COM component. The example assumes that the MSXML COM component is installed. The MSXML document is first instantiated and wrapped in a Dynamics AX COM object wrapper. A COM variant wrapper is created for a COM string. The direction of the variant is into the COM component. The root element and head element variables are declared as COM objects. The example shows how to fill a string variant with an X++ string and then use the variant as an argument to a COM method, the *loadXml* method. The statement that creates the head element demonstrates how the Dynamics AX runtime automatically converts Dynamics AX primitive objects into COM variants.

```
static void Job2(Args _args)
{
    COM doc = new COM("Msxml2.DomDocument.6.0");
    COMVariant rootXml = new COMVariant(COMVariantInOut::In,COMVariantType::VT_BSTR);
    COM rootElement;
    COM headElement;
    ;
    rootXml.bStr("<Root></Root>");
    doc.loadXml(rootXml);
    rootElement = doc.documentElement();
```

```
        headElement = doc.createElement("Head");
        rootElement.appendChild(headElement);
        print doc.xml();
        pause;
    }
```

## Macros

A macro is an X++ string replacement procedure that can improve the readability of source code. A macro comprises successive logical expressions that are evaluated by the X++ pre-processor. The result of an evaluation is an X++ value, expression, or statement that is included in the source code when it is passed on to the X++ compiler. X++ supports three kinds of macro directives: macro libraries, stand-alone macros, and local macros that are defined inside method definitions. The following is an example of a local macro.

```
void myMethod()
{
#localmacro.HelloWorld
{
    print "Hello World";
    pause;
}#endmacro;
;
    #HelloWorld
}
```

A macro library is created with the AOT. The library is included in a class declaration header or class method, as shown in the following example.

```
class myClass
{
    #MyMacroLibrary1
}
public void myMethod()
{
    #MyMacroLibrary2
    ;
    #MacroFromMyMacroLibrary1
    #MacroFromMyMacroLibrary2
}
```

## Comments

X++ allows single-line and multiple-line comments. Single-line comments start with // and end at the end of the line. Multiple-line comments start with /* and ended with */. You cannot nest multiple-line comments.

You can add reminders to yourself in comments that will be picked up by the compiler and presented to you as tasks in the compiler output window. You do this by starting a single-line comment with the word *TODO* (all uppercase). Be aware that tasks occurring inside multiple-line comments are treated as commented out, and thus are not picked up by the compiler.

Here is a code example with comments reminding the developer to add a new procedure, while disabling an existing procedure in the meantime.

```
public void myMethod()
{
    //Declare variables
    int value;

//TODO Validate if calculation is really required
/*
    //Perform calculation
    value = this.calc();
*/
    ...
}
```

## Classes and Interfaces

You define types and the structure of types in the AOT, not in the X++ language as you would in other programming languages that support type declarations. This is because Dynamics AX supports an object layering feature that accepts X++ source code customizations to type declaration parts that comprise variable declarations and method declarations. Each part of a type declaration is managed as a separate compilation unit, and model data is used to manage, persist, and reconstitute dynamic types whose parts can comprise compilation units from many object layers.

You use the X++ language to define logic, including method profiles (return value, method name, and parameter type and name). The X++ editor allows you to add new methods to the AOT, so you can continue to use the X++ editor while constructing types.

X++ class declarations are used to declare protected instance variable fields that are members of application logic and framework reference types. You cannot declare private or public variable fields. Classes can be declared abstract if they are incomplete type specifications that cannot be instantiated. They can also be declared final if they are complete specifications that cannot be further specialized. The following code provides an example of an abstract class declaration header.

```
abstract class MyClass
{
}
```

Classes can also be structured into single-inheritance generalization or specialization hierarchies in which derived classes inherit and override members of base classes. The following code shows an example of a derived class declaration header that specifies that *MyDerived-Class* extends the abstract base class *MyClass*. It also specifies that *MyDerivedClass* is final and cannot be further specialized by another class. Derived classes can extend only one base class because X++ does not support multiple inheritance.

```
final class MyDerivedClass extends MyClass
{
}
```

The X++ language also supports interface type specifications that specify method signatures but do not define their implementation. Classes can implement more than one interface, but the class and its derived classes should together provide definitions for the methods declared in all the interfaces. If it fails to provide the method definitions, the class itself is marked as abstract. The following code provides an example of an interface declaration header and a class declaration header that implements the interface.

```
interface MyInterface
{
    void myMethod();
}
class MyClass implements MyInterface
{
    void myMethod()
    {
    }
}
```

# Fields

A field is a class member that represents a variable and its type. Fields are declared in class declaration headers as shown in the following code example. Fields are accessible only to code statements that are part of the class declaration or derived class declarations. Assignment statements are not allowed in class declaration headers. The following example demonstrates how variables are initialized with assignment statements in a *new* method.

```
class MyClass
{
    str s;
    int i;
    MyClass1 myClass1;
```

```
    public void new()
    {
        i = 0;
        myClass1 = new MyClass1();
    }
}
```

# Methods

A class method is a member that defines the behavior of an object by using statements. An interface method is a member that declares an expected behavior of an object. The following code provides an example of a method declaration on an interface and an implementation of the method on a class that implements the interface.

```
interface MyInterface
{
    public str myMethod()
    {
    }
}
class myClass implements MyInterface
{
    public str myMethod();
    {
        return "Hello World";
    }
}
```

Methods are defined with public, private, or protected access modifiers. Methods are publicly accessible by default. Additional method modifiers supported by X++ are provided in Table 5-11.

**Table 5-11   Method Modifiers Supported by X++**

| Modifier | Description |
| --- | --- |
| *static* | Static methods are accessed via class declarations. Fields cannot be accessed from within a static method. |
| *final* | Final methods cannot be overridden by methods with the same name in derived classes. |
| *abstract* | Abstract methods have no implementation. Derived classes must provide definitions for abstract methods. |
| *server* | Server methods can execute only on an Application Object Server. The *server* modifier is allowed only on static methods. |
| *client* | Client methods can execute only on a MorphX client. The *client* modifiers are allowed only on static methods. |

**Table 5-11    Method Modifiers Supported by X++**

| Modifier | Description |
| --- | --- |
| *display* | Display methods are invoked each time a form or report is redrawn. The *display* modifier is allowed only on table, form, form data, report, and report design methods. |
| *edit* | The *edit* method is invoked each time a form is redrawn or a user provides input through a form control. The *edit* modifier is allowed only on table, form, and form data source methods. |

Method parameters may have default values that are created when parameters are omitted from method invocations. The following code sample prints "Hello World" when the *myMethod* method is invoked with no parameters.

```
public void myMethod( str s = "Hello World" )
{
    print s;
    pause;
}

public void myMethod1();
{
    myMethod();
}
```

A constructor is a special instance method that is invoked to initialize an object when the *new* operator is executed by the Dynamics AX runtime. Constructors cannot be called directly from X++ code. The following sample provides an example of a class declaration header and an instance constructor method that takes one parameter as an argument.

```
class myClass
{
    int i;

    public void new( int _i )
    {
        i = _i;
    }
}
```

# Chapter Summary

This chapter introduced the Dynamics AX runtime type system, as well as X++ expressions, jobs, statements, classes, interfaces, tables, maps, views, and macros. This chapter also provided details on the unique data-aware features of X++, exception handling, and interoperability with the .NET CLR system and COM technology.

# Part II
# Developing with Microsoft Dynamics AX

# Customizing Microsoft Dynamics AX

The objectives of this chapter are to:

- Describe how to customize Microsoft Dynamics AX 4.0 inventory tables and classes to implement new inventory dimensions.

- Explain how to customize Dynamics AX forms.

- Describe how to customize Dynamics AX reports.

- Explain how to customize the Dynamics AX number sequence classes to implement a new number sequence.

## Introduction

Dynamics AX allows you to customize the application by changing or adding new metadata or modifying the application source code in almost any way. The unique layering feature ensures that you can always return to the point at which you began to make modifications and restore the original metadata and X++ code.

The next section of this chapter describes how to customize Dynamics AX to include a set of new inventory dimensions by customizing a set of tables and classes. The new dimensions automatically appear in forms and reports without requiring changes to the original code or metadata of any of these elements.

The chapter also describes form and report customizations. The sales order form is modified to include a product image, and the sales invoice report is modified to include promotional text.

The last section of the chapter explains how to customize the number sequence classes to enable the use of a new number sequence, which is useful for creating invoice numbers, voucher numbers, and so on.

# Table and Class Customization

By default, Dynamics AX 4.0 supports up to eight inventory dimensions. (Additional inventory dimensions can be defined by the user.) Dimensions describe the characteristics of items or item lots. Item dimensions might include characteristics such as configuration, model, and size. Item lots might have storage dimensions, such as warehouse, location, or pallet, or they might be identified by a serial number and batch number.

The following customization scenario describes how to customize tables and classes used by the inventory dimension feature to implement two new item dimensions that describe a specific bicycle configuration: frame size and wheel size. This description is not an exhaustive list of elements that must be changed; instead, it offers guidelines on how to find the elements necessary to customize the full implementation of a new inventory dimension.

## Creating New Dimension Types

When implementing new inventory dimensions, your first task is to create extended data types for each of the dimensions. Doing so provides the following benefits:

- To apply the inventory dimensions to multiple tables, you define the type just once and then apply it to each table.

- The *Label* property, the *HelpText* property, and a few constraints can be defined on the data type, ensuring consistent behavior and appearance of fields of the same type.

- If the type is declared as a parameter or a return type for a method, you can declare variables of the type in X++ code to optimize IntelliSense responsiveness and to improve the readability of the code.

This scenario defines a table in which a field of the specific type is part of the primary key. You can define the relationship to this table on the extended data type and subsequently instruct the application runtime to provide lookups and Go To The Main Table Form support.

In this example, you enter the Data Dictionary in the Application Object Tree (AOT) and create a *BikeFrameSize* extended data type and a *BikeWheelSize* extended data type. Table 6-1 lists the property settings that deviate from the default settings.

Figure 6-1 shows the property sheet for the *BikeFrameSize* extended data type, accessible by clicking Properties on the context menu for the type.

**Table 6-1** *BikeFrameSize* and *BikeWheelSize* Property Settings

| Property | *BikeFrameSize* | *BikeWheelSize* |
|---|---|---|
| Type | Real | Real |
| Label | Frame size | Wheel size |
| HelpText | Frame size in inches | Wheel size in inches |
| AllowNegative | No | No |
| ShowZero | No | No |
| NoOfDecimals | 0 | 0 |

**Figure 6-1**  The *BikeFrameSize* extended data type property sheet.

> **Best Practices**  Creating labels for text in the *Label* and *HelpText* properties is, of course, a best practice, but the text in this example is written as a literal (as opposed to referencing a label) to improve readability.

Next, create two tables, named *BikeFrameSizeTable* and *BikeWheelSizeTable*, in which the frame and wheel sizes for each item can be stored. In addition to the specific inventory dimension types, the tables also contain an *ItemId* field and a *Name* field. The *ItemId* and dimension in each table constitute the table's primary index.

Table 6-2 lists the *BikeFrameSizeTable* property settings that deviate from the default settings. (The property settings for *BikeWheelSizeTable* are identical except for the *BikeWheelSize* field and its extended property type.)

**Table 6-2   Field Property Settings**

| Property | ItemId | BikeFrameSize | Name |
|---|---|---|---|
| Type | String | Real | String |
| ExtendedDataType | ItemId | BikeFrameSize | Name |
| Mandatory | Yes | Yes | No (default) |
| AllowEdit | No | No | Yes (default) |

Create a unique index on both tables. For *BikeFrameSizeTable*, name the index *FrameIdx* and make it contain the *ItemId* field and the *BikeFrameSize* field. For *BikeWheelSizeTable*, name the index *WheelIdx* and make it contain the *ItemId* field and the *BikeWheelSize* field. Declare the indexes as the *PrimaryIndex* on the respective tables. In the AOT, the fields and the index appear as shown in Figure 6-2.

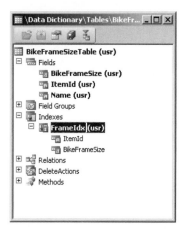

**Figure 6-2**   The *BikeFrameSizeTable* definition.

In addition to the fields and index shown in Figure 6-2, you should also set properties in the tables for caching, form references, and so on, and the table should contain field groups and methods for checking the validity of the fields. However, it is beyond the scope of this chapter to describe these enhancements. The Microsoft Dynamics AX SDK contains guidelines and best practices for creating tables.

After you define the tables, you should update the extended data types to reflect their relationship to the individual tables, as shown in Figure 6-3.

**Figure 6-3**   The *BikeFrameSize* extended data type relation.

This relationship instructs the Dynamics AX runtime to provide lookup and Go To The Main Table Form functionality when fields of these types appear on forms. The application runtime uses the related table as the data source for the lookup form and also to find the main table form from the *FormRef* property on the table. You must therefore create forms for the *BikeFrameSizeTable* and *BikeWheelSizeTable* tables and menu items to open the forms. These menu items are added to the *FormRef* properties on the corresponding tables. You could design the forms to mirror the form shown in Figure 6-4, but this is also beyond the scope of this chapter.

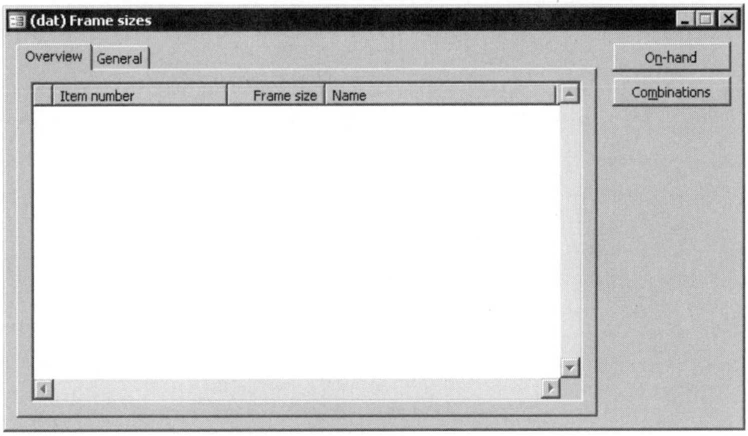

**Figure 6-4**   The Frame Sizes form.

# Adding New Dimensions to a Table

To store transactions with the new inventory dimensions, the dimensions must be added to the *InventDim* table. You do this by creating two new fields, *BikeFrameSize* and *BikeWheelSize*, of the corresponding type on the *InventDim* table. You should also add these fields to the unique *DimIdx* index, because any combination of inventory dimensions may exist only once in the *InventDim* table.

The display of inventory dimensions in almost any form in the Dynamics AX application is based on field groups and where the content of the field group in the form is built at run time. The forms runtime in Dynamics AX builds the group from the list of fields in the associated field group defined on the *InventDim* table. Therefore, by adding the new fields to the *InventoryDimensions* field group on the *InventDim* table, you make the two new fields available in almost any form that displays inventory dimensions. Position the fields in the field group based on where you want them to appear relative to the other dimensions, as shown in Figure 6-5.

Figure 6-5 shows "usr" flags on the *AutoReport* and *ItemDimensions* field groups, indicating that the custom fields have been added to these groups as well. The *AutoReport* group is modified so that it will print the new dimensions if you create an auto-report by clicking Print on a form; the *ItemDimensions* group is modified because the new dimensions are considered to be item dimensions.

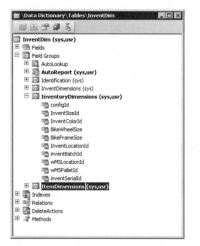

**Figure 6-5**    The *InventDim* table with customized *InventoryDimensions* field group.

Although the inventory dimensions are now available in any form because of the interpretation of the field groups by the Dynamics AX forms runtime, the fields are still not visible or editable, because they are not enabled in any inventory dimension group. Moreover, the two new inventory dimensions automatically appear in the Dimension Groups form, because the inventory dimension feature also interprets the *InventoryDimensions* field group on the *Invent-Dim* table to find all the currently available inventory dimensions. To make the form work with the new dimensions, you merely state whether the new dimensions are item dimensions. You do this by adding the new dimensions to the *isFieldItemDim* method on the *InventDim* table, as shown in the following X++ code. The added lines are shown in bold.

```
static public boolean isFieldIdItemDim(fieldId dimFieldId)
{
    ;
    #InventDimDevelop

    switch (dimFieldId)
    {
        case (fieldnum(InventDim,ConfigId))         :
        case (fieldnum(InventDim,InventSizeId))     :
        case (fieldnum(InventDim,InventColorId))    :
        case (fieldnum(InventDim,BikeFrameSize))    : // Frame size added
        case (fieldnum(inventDim,BikeWheelSize))    : // Wheel size added
            return true;

        case (fieldnum(InventDim,InventLocationId)) :
        case (fieldnum(InventDim,InventBatchId))    :
        case (fieldnum(InventDim,wMSLocationId))    :
        case (fieldnum(InventDim,wMSPalletId))      :
        case (fieldnum(InventDim,InventSerialId))   :
            return false;
    }
    throw error("@SYS70108");
}
```

The new dimensions will be available for setup in the Dimension Groups form, which is reached through the Navigation Pane under Inventory Management\Setup\Dimensions \Dimension Groups. The dimensions are located in the Item Dimensions grid, as shown in Figure 6-6.

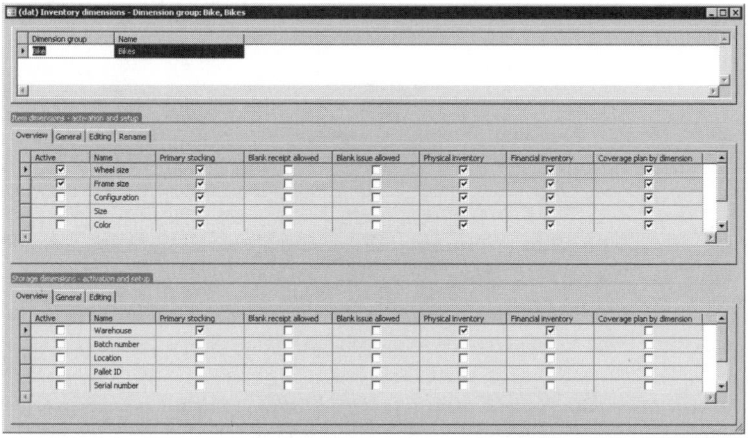

**Figure 6-6**   The Dimension Groups form with new item dimensions.

> **Important**   You might have to restart the Application Object Server (AOS) after adding fields to the *InventoryDimensions* field group, because the list of fields in the group is cached in memory on both the client tier and the server tier.

## Enabling New Dimensions in Forms

The new dimensions can be enabled by setting up dimension groups, but the dimensions are not yet visible in the forms. The inventory dimension feature uses a temporary table called *InventDimParm* to carry certain information, such as whether a dimension:

- Is enabled.

- Is an item dimension.

- Is a primary stocking dimension.

- Is visible.

- Serves as a filter-by term.

- Serves as a group-by term.

- Serves as an order-by term.

This is done by reflecting each inventory dimension as a Boolean flag field on the *InventDimParm* table and then matching the corresponding fields in the X++ code. For example, when a dimension group is queried to determine which dimensions are active, an *InventDimParm* record is returned where the corresponding flag field is set to true for the active dimensions. The remaining flags are set to false. You must therefore add a frame-size flag and a wheel-size flag to the *InventDimParm* table, as shown in Table 6-3.

**Table 6-3**   *BikeFrameSizeFlag* and *BikeWheelSizeFlag* **Property Settings**

| Property | BikeFrameSizeFlag | BikeWheelSizeFlag |
| --- | --- | --- |
| Type | Enum | Enum |
| Label | Frame size | Wheel size |
| HelpText | View by frame size | View by wheel size |
| ExtendedDataType | NoYesId | NoYesId |
| Enum | NoYes | NoYes |

The new fields should also be added to the *FixedView* and *View* field groups defined on the *InventDimParm* table, because they are used in forms from which it is possible to specify whether a dimension should be visible.

When you add fields to the table and field groups, the new fields on the *InventDim* table must be mapped to the corresponding fields on the *InventDimParm* table in the X++ code. To do this, you modify the *dim2DimParm* method on the *InventDim* table, as shown in the following X++ code. The added mappings of *BikeFrameSize* and *BikeWheelSize* appear in bold.

```
static public fieldId dim2dimParm(fieldId dimField)
{
    ;
    #InventDimDevelop

    switch (dimField)
    {
        case (fieldnum(InventDim,ConfigId))         :
            return fieldnum(InventDimParm,ConfigIdFlag);
        case (fieldnum(InventDim,InventSizeId))      :
            return fieldnum(InventDimParm,InventSizeIdFlag);
        case (fieldnum(InventDim,InventColorId))     :
            return fieldnum(InventDimParm,InventColorIdFlag);
        case (fieldnum(InventDim,InventLocationId)) :
            return fieldnum(InventDimParm,InventLocationIdFlag);
        case (fieldnum(InventDim,InventBatchId))     :
            return fieldnum(InventDimParm,InventBatchIdFlag);
        case (fieldnum(InventDim,wMSLocationId))     :
            return fieldnum(InventDimParm,WMSLocationIdFlag);
        case (fieldnum(InventDim,wMSPalletId))       :
            return fieldnum(InventDimParm,WMSPalletIdFlag);
        case (fieldnum(InventDim,InventSerialId))    :
            return fieldnum(InventDimParm,InventSerialIdFlag);
        case (fieldnum(InventDim,BikeFrameSize))     : // Add mapping
            return fieldnum(InventDimParm,BikeFrameSizeFlag);
        case (fieldnum(InventDim,BikeWheelSize))     : // Add mapping
            return fieldnum(InventDimParm,BikeWheelSizeFlag);
    }
```

```
      throw error(strfmt("@SYS54431",funcname()));
}
```

The same modification must be made to the *dimParm2Dim* method on the same table to map *InventDimParm* fields to *InventDim* fields.

## Customizing Other Tables

The customizations made so far allow the new dimensions to be enabled on dimension groups and presented in forms. However, you should also consider customizing the following additional tables by adding inventory dimensions to them:

- *InventDimCombination*
- *InventSumDeltaDim*
- *InventStatusReportTmp*
- *PBATreeInventDim*
- *PriceDiscTmpPrintout*
- *InterCompanyInventDim*

Whether and how these tables should be customized depends on the functionality you are implementing. You should therefore examine how the inventory dimensions are implemented and used for each of the tables.

## Adding Dimensions to Queries

Because of the generic implementation of the inventory dimension concept using the *InventDim* and *InventDimParm* tables, a substantial number of queries written in X++ use just a few patterns to select, join, and filter the inventory dimensions. So that you do not have to repeatedly copy and paste the same X++ code, these patterns exist as macros that you can apply in your code. To modify these queries, you simply customize the macros, and then recompile the entire application to update the X++ code with the new dimensions.

You should customize the following macros:

- *InventDimExistsJoin*
- *InventDimGroupAllFields*
- *InventDimJoin*
- *InventDimSelect*

The bold text in the following X++ code shows the changes that you must make to the *InventDimExistsJoin* macro to enable the two new dimensions for all *exists* joins written as statements involving the *InventDim* table.

```
/* %1  InventDimId        */
/* %2  InventDim          */
/* %3  InventDimCriteria  */
/* %4  InventDimParm      */
/* %5  Index hint         */

exists join tableId from %2
    where
    (%2.InventDimId      == %1) &&
    (%2.ConfigId         == %3.ConfigId         || ! %4.ConfigIdFlag)        &&
    (%2.InventSizeId     == %3.InventSizeId     || ! %4.InventSizeIdFlag)    &&
    (%2.InventColorId    == %3.InventColorId    || ! %4.InventColorIdFlag)   &&
    (%2.BikeFrameSize    == %3.BikeFrameSize    || ! %4.BikeFrameSizeFlag)   &&
    (%2.BikeWheelSize    == %3.BikeWheelSize    || ! %4.BikeWheelSizeFlag)   &&
    (%2.InventLocationId == %3.InventLocationId || ! %4.InventLocationIdFlag) &&
    (%2.InventBatchId    == %3.InventBatchId    || ! %4.InventBatchIdFlag)   &&
    (%2.WMSLocationId    == %3.WMSLocationId    || ! %4.WMSLocationIdFlag)   &&
    (%2.WMSPalletId      == %3.WMSPalletId      || ! %4.WMSPalletIdFlag)     &&
    (%2.InventSerialId   == %3.InventSerialId   || ! %4.InventSerialIdFlag)

#InventDimDevelop
```

The three remaining macros are just as easy to modify. Just remember to recompile the entire application after you make your changes.

## Adding Lookup, Validation, and Defaulting X++ Code

In addition to macro customizations and the customizations to the previously mentioned methods on the *InventDim* table, you must also implement and customize lookup, validation, and defaulting methods. These include methods such as the *InventDim::findDim* lookup method, the *InventDim.validateWriteItemDim* validation method, and the *InventDim.initFrom-InventDimCombination* defaulting method. The necessary changes in the *InventDim::findDim* lookup method for the new inventory dimensions are shown in bold in the following X++ code.

```
server static public InventDim findDim(InventDim _inventDim,
                                       boolean    _forupdate = false)
{
    InventDim    inventDim;
    ;
    if (_forupdate)
        inventDim.selectForUpdate(_forupdate);

    select firstonly inventDim
        index hint DimIdx
        where inventDim.ConfigId        == _inventDim.ConfigId        &&
              inventDim.InventSizeId     == _inventDim.InventSizeId    &&
              inventDim.InventColorId    == _inventDim.InventColorId   &&
              inventDim.BikeFrameSize    == _inventDim.BikeFrameSize   &&
```

```
        inventDim.BikeWheelSize      == _inventDim.BikeWheelSize      &&
        inventDim.InventLocationId == _inventDim.InventLocationId   &&
        inventDim.InventBatchId      == _inventDim.InventBatchId      &&
        inventDim.wMSLocationId      == _inventDim.wMSLocationId      &&
        inventDim.wMSPalletId        == _inventDim.wMSPalletId        &&
        inventDim.InventSerialId     == _inventDim.InventSerialId;

    #inventDimDevelop

    return inventDim;
}
```

Notice the use of the *inventDimDevelop* macro in the preceding method. The *inventDim-Develop* macro is merely a macro that contains the following comment.

```
/* used to locate code with direct dimension references */
```

Performing a global search for use of the *inventDimDevelop* macro should be sufficient to find all the X++ code that must be considered when implementing a new dimension. This search returns all the methods that require further investigation. Figure 6-7 shows results of a search for the use of the macro on all tables.

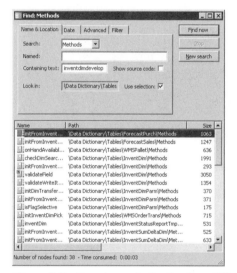

**Figure 6-7**   Search results for the *inventDimDevelop* macro.

**Best Practices**   Inserting the *inventDimDevelop* macro in X++ code when it makes a direct reference to an inventory dimension is considered a best practice. Doing so makes implementing new dimensions easier.

Most of the methods you will find when searching for the macro will be lookup, validation, and defaulting methods, but you will also see other methods that do not fall under these categories. Such methods would include those that modify the *Query* object, such as the *InventDim::queryAddHintFromCaller* method, and methods that describe dimensions, such as the *InventDimParm.isFlagSelective* method. You should also review these methods when investigating the X++ code.

> **Tip**    Although the inventory dimension feature is implemented with the *inventDimDevelop* macro to direct developers to the methods that they need to change, you might encounter methods with no macro included, or tables, forms, or reports for which the inventory dimensions are not used generically. You are therefore advised to use the cross-reference system on an existing dimension that has the same behavior as the new dimension to determine its use and review it appropriately. You should also investigate whether the new dimension is or should be available in the same element.

# Form Customization

Like most of the elements in the AOT, forms can be customized to include additional information and actions, such as fields and buttons, and to fulfill end user requirements. The design and behavior of a form is generally a combination of how a table used as a data source for the form is designed and how the form itself is designed. All necessary customizations can be implemented by modifying just the form. However, this is not the recommended approach. As a best practice, some customizations should be implemented at the table level.

The best practice for implementing forms is to keep most of the business logic and design decisions at the table level, and focus only on the positioning of fields and menu items when designing the form. This approach has several advantages:

- X++ code in forms is executed on the client tier only; X++ code in table methods can be executed on the server tier for optimal performance.

- Customizations made to a form are restricted to that form; customizations made to a table apply to all forms that use the table as a data source. This results in a consistent user experience wherever the table is used.

- Customization of a form copies the entire form to the current layer; customizations to tables are more granular. Customization of fields, field groups, and methods results in a copy of the specific element to the current layer only. This makes upgrading to service packs and new versions easier.

- X++ customizations to the validate, default, and database trigger methods on forms, such as *validate*, *modified*, and *write*, affect records only, which are modified through the user interface. If records are modified through the business logic in X++ code, the customized X++ code will not execute, because the business logic only executes the corresponding methods on the table.

The following actions can be implemented only by customizing the form:

- Enable and disable fields
- Hide and show fields
- Enable and disable menu items

However, you should consider having a table method determine the business logic on the form. An example of this is shown in the following lines of X++ code from the *InventTable* form, in which a method on the table determines whether a field can be edited.

```
void setItemDimEnabled()
{
    boolean     configActive    = inventTable.configActive();

    inventTable_ds.object(
            fieldnum(InventTable,StandardConfigId)).allowEdit(configActive);
    inventTable_ds.object(
            fieldnum(InventTable, StandardConfigId)).skip(!configActive);

}
```

By moving these decision-making methods to the table, you make them available to other forms that manipulate the same table.

## Displaying an Image

The following example illustrates how to customize the sales order form to allow a user to upload and display an image of a custom order. In this example, a customer must be able to place an order for a bike through the enterprise portal and upload a sketch of the bike at the same time. An example of a customer-supplied bike image is shown in Figure 6-8.

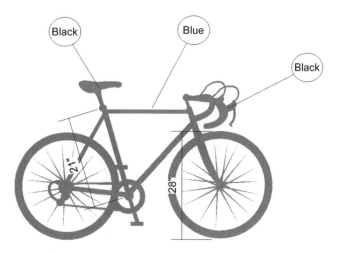

**Figure 6-8**   An uploaded bike image.

This image must be stored in the database and attached to the sales order line. Sales order lines are stored in the *SalesLine* table. You could add a new field to the *SalesLine* table of type *container* and store the image in this field, but this example uses the document management functionality in Dynamics AX. The image is therefore stored in the *DocuValue* table with a reference to a record in the *DocuRef* table from the image record in *DocuValue* to the *SalesLine* record. The relationship and multiplicity between the three tables is shown in Figure 6-9.

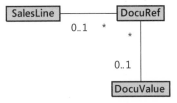

**Figure 6-9** The relationship between the *SalesLine*, *DocuRef*, and *DocuValue* tables.

> **Caution**  In general, adding *container* type fields to existing tables is not considered a best practice, because the *container* type fields in Microsoft SQL Server 2000 are stored separately from the remaining fields on disk, and extra reads are required to retrieve the value in the *container* field. This causes performance degradation in scenarios in which the entire record is fetched but the value in the *container* field is not needed. The same applies to fields of type *memo*.

In this example, a new document type named Image stores the attached file in the database. The Image document type is shown in Figure 6-10. The Document Type form is located in the Navigation Pane, Basic\Setup\Document Management\Document Types.

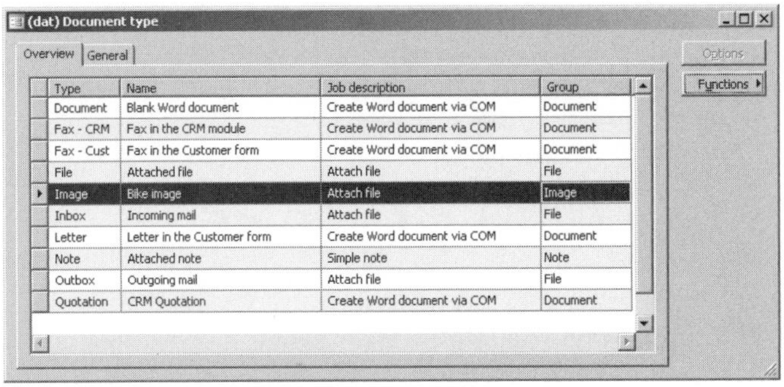

![The Image document type form showing Document type overview with columns Type, Name, Job description, and Group. Rows include: Document / Blank Word document / Create Word document via COM / Document; Fax - CRM / Fax in the CRM module / Create Word document via COM / Document; Fax - Cust / Fax in the Customer form / Create Word document via COM / Document; File / Attached file / Attach file / File; Image / Bike image / Attach file / Image (selected); Inbox / Incoming mail / Attach file / File; Letter / Letter in the Customer form / Create Word document via COM / Document; Note / Attached note / Simple note / Note; Outbox / Outgoing mail / Attach file / File; Quotation / CRM Quotation / Create Word document via COM / Document.]

**Figure 6-10** The Image document type.

Any uploaded image is therefore stored in the document management system; a user can view the image by either clicking the Document Handling icon on the status bar or choosing Document Handling on the Command menu. The user sees the dialog box shown in Figure 6-11, in which the image can be viewed, modified, or deleted, and additional notes or documents can be attached.

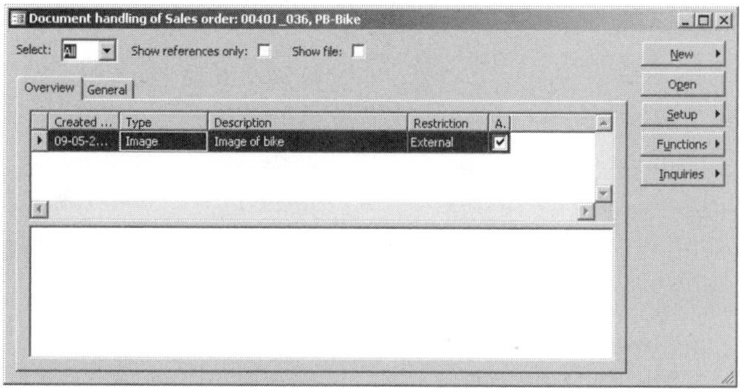

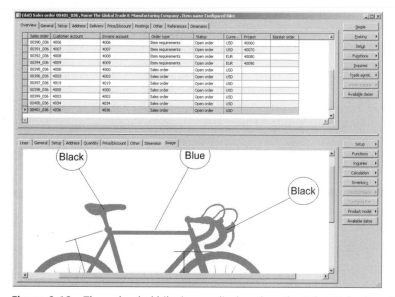

**Figure 6-11**   Storage of the uploaded bike image in the document management system.

## Displaying an Image on a Form

You can display the image directly by placing it on a separate Image tab on the sales order form. Figure 6-12 shows an order for a bike with a frame size of 21 inches and a wheel size of 28 inches. The user can click the Image tab to view the uploaded bike image and confirm that it matches the ordered item before confirming the sales order. The Sales Order form is located in the Navigation Pane, Accounts Receivable\Sales Order.

**Figure 6-12**   The uploaded bike image displayed on the Sales Order form Image tab.

The following two example implementations describe how to use the document management tables as data sources in the form and how to create a separate method on the *SalesLine* table. These examples demonstrate customization of the *SalesTable* sales order form and the *SalesLine* table.

## Displaying an Image by Using Joined Data Sources

One way to display the image is to apply the *DocuRef* and *DocuValue* tables as data sources for the *SalesTable* form. The following example creates a *DocuRef* data source based on the relationship between the *SalesLine*, *DocuRef*, and *DocuValue* tables shown in Figure 6-9. The *DocuRef* data source relates to the *DocuRef* table and will be joined to the *SalesLine* data source. Additionally, a *DocuValue* data source will be created to connect to the *DocuRef* data source. Table 6-4 shows additional properties of the data sources.

**Table 6-4    *DocuRef* and *DocuValue* Property Settings**

| Property | DocuRef | DocuValue |
| --- | --- | --- |
| Table | DocuRef | DocuValue |
| AllowEdit | No | No |
| AllowCreate | No | No |
| AllowDelete | No | No |
| JoinSource | SalesLine | DocuRef |
| LinkType | Active | Active |

The properties *JoinSource* and *LinkType* allow the *DocuRef* and *DocuValue* records to be fetched when the user moves from one line to another. The remaining properties disable editing of the records.

You can attach multiple files, documents, and notes to a *SalesLine* record by using the document management feature, but the goal of this example is to display an image from a linked document named Image. You can limit the retrieved records from the *DocuRef* table by adding a range to the query used by the *DocuRef* data source. You do this by customizing the *init* method on the *DocuRef* data source, as shown here.

```
public void init()
{
    super();

    docuRef_ds.query().dataSourceTable(
                    tableNum(DocuRef)).addRange(
                    fieldNum(DocuRef,TypeId)).value(queryValue('Image'));
}
```

This X++ code limits the query so that it retrieves only records from the *DocuRef* table in which the *TypeId* field is equal to the value 'Image'.

**Note**    The use of a constant such as the word *Image* is not a best practice. The value must be retrieved from a configuration table so that the user can decide the naming. 'Image' is hard-coded in the preceding example only to improve the readability and limit the scope of the example.

The image is displayed by using a window control, which is placed in a tab control, as shown in Figure 6-13.

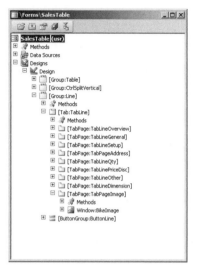

**Figure 6-13**    Tab and window controls in the *SalesTable* form.

Although the image is stored in the *File* field on the *DocuValue* table, to display the image you cannot simply link the field as a *DataField* value on the window control Properties sheet. The image must be parsed to the control by using a method on the control in X++ that uses the *FormWindowControl* object. The *AutoDeclaration* property on the *FormWindowControl* object is therefore set to *Yes* so that the forms designer automatically declares an object handle with the same name. This handle can be used in X++ and manipulated at run time because the form application runtime automatically ensures that it is a handle to the *FormWindowControl* object. Moreover, the *Width* and *Height* properties are set to *Column Width* and *Column Height* so that the image takes up all the space on the tab.

The last step is to parse the retrieved image from the *DocuValue* table to the *BikeImage Form-WindowControl* object. You can do this when a *DocuValue* record buffer is present. This record must contain an image that is stored in the database, and the X++ code should be placed in the *active* method on the *DocuValue* data source and look like the following.

```
public int active()
{
    Image    image;
    int      ret;
    ret = super();
    if (docuValue.File)
    {
        image = new Image();
        image.setData(docuValue.File);
        bikeImage.image(image);
    }
```

```
    else
    {
        bikeImage.imageResource(0);
    }
    return ret;
}
```

This code determines whether a value exists in the *File* field and, if so, instantiates an image object and parses the *File* field value to the image object. This object is then parsed by using the *image* method to the *FormWindowControl* object that will display the image. If the *File* field does not contain a value, the *imageResource* method on the *FormWindowControl* object is called with a value of zero to clear the control of any previous content. The *active* method is executed only if a *DocuValue* record has been retrieved. However, if a user moves from an order line with an image to an order line without an image, the image is not cleared because the *active* method is not executed. If you add the following line to the *active* method on the *SalesLine* data source, the image is cleared when a new order line becomes active and before the *DocuRef* and *DocuValue* records are retrieved.

```
    docuBikeImage.imageResource(0);
```

The customizations described in this section make it possible to display the image on the Image tab. This solution has one downside, however. Whenever a user moves from one order line to another or a line is created or saved, calls are made from the client to the server and lookups are made in the database for the *DocuRef* and *DocuValue* data sources. You can see this by turning on the client/server or SQL trace option in the Options dialog box which is accessed from the Tools menu. The next section addresses this issue and offers a solution—decreasing the number of client/server calls and lookups in the database.

## Displaying an Image when Activating the Image Tab

The following example implements a solution similar to the previous example, but it results in calls to the server and the database only when the image is actually displayed.

The *TabPage* control must be added to the *SalesTable* form and contain a *FormWindowControl* with property settings similar to those in the preceding example. The *DocuRef* and *DocuValue* tables are not, however, added as data sources for the form. Instead, this example retrieves the image—the only element shown on the Image tab—from the database only when the user chooses to display the content of the Image tab. You configure this by adding the following X++ code to the *pageActivated* method on the *TabPage* control.

```
public void pageActivated()
{
    Image           image;
    DocuValueFile   docuValueFile;
    ;
```

```
        docuValueFile = salesLine.bikeImage();
        if (docuValueFile)
        {
            image = new Image();
            image.setData(docuValueFile);
            bikeImage.image(image);
        }
        else
        {
            bikeImage.imageResource(0);
        }

        super();
    }
```

This code is very similar to the code added to the *DocuValue active* method, but in this case the value is retrieved from a *bikeImage* method on the *SalesLine* table. The *bikeImage* method is a new method created on the *SalesLine* table with the following content.

```
server public DocuValueFile bikeImage()
{
    DocuRef       docuref;
    DocuValue     docuValue;
    ;
    select forceplaceholders firstonly tableid from docuRef
        where docuRef.RefCompanyId   == this.DataAreaId   &&
              docuRef.RefTableId      == this.TableId       &&
              docuRef.RefRecId        == this.RecId         &&
              docuRef.TypeId          == 'Image'
    join file from docuValue
        where docuValue.RecId    == docuRef.ValueRecId;

    return docuValue.File;
}
```

The *select* statement in the *bikeImage* method is a combination of the two lookups in the database produced by the runtime shown in the first sample implementation, which used data sources. However, the statements in this method are joined. The *bikeImage* method could simply be implemented in the *SalesTable* form, but implementing it on the *SalesLine* table allows it to be reused in other forms or reports and executed on the server tier, if required.

The advantage of this implementation method is that both database lookups and calls from the client to the server are reduced by half. And because calls are made only when the Image tab is activated, they are not made when a user simply moves through the order lines without viewing the content of the Image tab. The disadvantage, however, is that the user cannot personalize the form or move the display of the image to another tab, because retrieval of the image is dependent on activation of the Image tab.

# Report Customization

Reports, like forms, can be customized to include and exclude information, and you can modify their design and layout. As with forms, the design and layout of a report depend on settings on the table and on the report itself. The best practice is, once again, to keep as much of the business logic as possible with the table methods or metadata. The X++ code in reports must deal with the functionality for the specific report. All other X++ code must generally be implemented on the table to be reused by other areas in the application. Advantages to such an approach include:

- Customizations made to a report are isolated; customizations made to a table affect all reports using that table, resulting in a consistent user experience wherever the table is used.
- Customization of a report copies the entire report to the current layer; customizations made to tables are more granular, because customization of fields, field groups, and methods results in a copy of the specific element to the current layer only. This makes upgrading to service packs and new versions easier.
- Methods in reports always execute on the tier where the report is generated; methods on tables can be targeted to execute on the server tier. Where a report is generated is controlled by the *RunOn* property on the menu item that starts the report. The property can be set to *Client*, *Server*, or *Called From*.

## Creating Promotional Materials

The example in this section demonstrates how to customize the sales order invoice report named *SalesInvoice*. The invoice is customized to include promotions based on items listed on the invoice. The promotion appears below each item on the invoice associated with a promotion. Figure 6-14 shows an example of an invoice that displays a promotion for a water bottle.

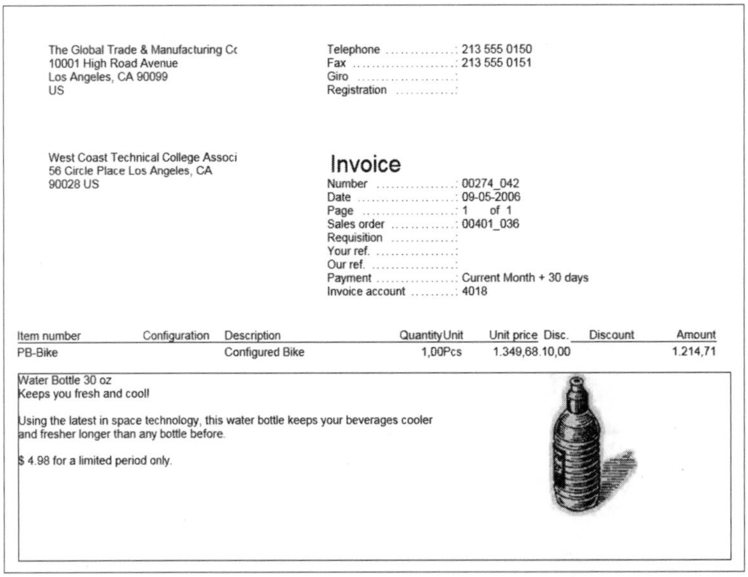

The Global Trade & Manufacturing Cc
10001 High Road Avenue
Los Angeles, CA 90099
US

Telephone: 213 555 0150
Fax: 213 555 0151
Giro:
Registration:

West Coast Technical College Associ
56 Circle Place Los Angeles, CA
90028 US

Invoice

Number: 00274_042
Date: 09-05-2006
Page: 1 of 1
Sales order: 00401_036
Requisition:
Your ref.:
Our ref.:
Payment: Current Month + 30 days
Invoice account: 4018

| Item number | Configuration | Description | Quantity | Unit | Unit price | Disc. | Discount | Amount |
|---|---|---|---|---|---|---|---|---|
| PB-Bike | | Configured Bike | 1,00 | Pcs | 1.349,68 | 10,00 | | 1.214,71 |

Water Bottle 30 oz
Keeps you fresh and cool!

Using the latest in space technology, this water bottle keeps your beverages cooler and fresher longer than any bottle before.

$ 4.98 for a limited period only.

**Figure 6-14** A promotion on an invoice.

Like the forms example, this example uses the document management feature in Dynamics AX. You use document handling to store the text and image in the database. The information is attached to the item table as two different types of document information, named *PromoText* and *PromoImage*, for storing the text and image. Figure 6-15 shows the new document types.

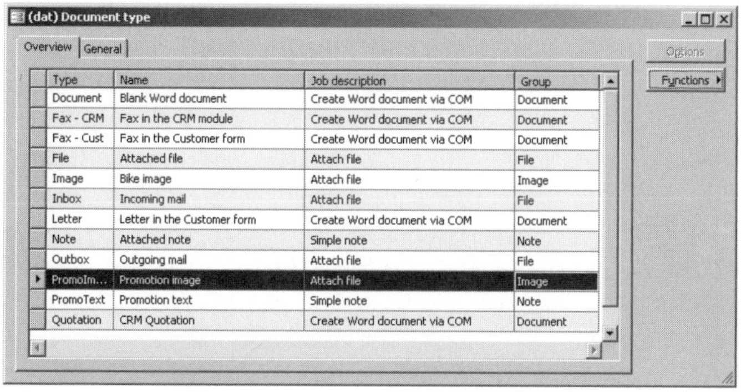

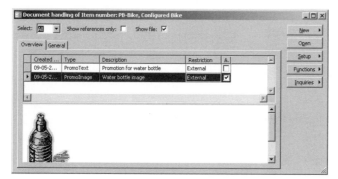

**Figure 6-15**   The *PromoText* and *PromoImage* document types.

Figure 6-16 shows the text and image attached to an item named PB-Bike.

**Figure 6-16**   Text and image attached to an item.

The X++ code used to display the promotions on the invoice looks up the item in the *InventTable* table and searches the document handling for documents of type *PromoText* and *PromoImage* to print on the invoice. If neither type is attached to the item, no promotion information prints.

## Adding Promotional Materials to an Invoice Report

Before you customize the *SalesInvoice* report for this example, you must decide where in the design of the report to place the printing of the promotion. The printed information should be printed for each invoiced item, so you must place it under the *CustInvoiceTrans* section group because the *CustInvoiceTrans* table contains the invoiced items. The *CustInvoiceTrans* section group contains a reference body section that can print other pieces of reference information, such as from inventory dimensions or the packing slip lines posted when the invoiced item is shipped. The promotion resembles this kind of information in terms of when and how it is printed.

This example, therefore, creates a new section group within the reference body section below the existing three groups. The new section group must reference a table type so that it can be invoked when a record buffer of the same type is sent to the report by using the *element.send* method. The *DocuRef* table stores the promotion text, and the *DocuValue* table stores the promotion image with an association created in the *DocuRef* table.

Although the storage of the text and image results in the creation of *DocuRef* records, the choice of *DocuRef* as the reference table type for the new section group is not an optimal solution. First, the information is stored as two records in the *DocuRef* table, but the text and image should be printed side by side for this example. The *element.send* method should be called only once, parsing in only a single record buffer. Also, two other section groups already use *DocuRef* as the table type, so using this type might result in the other section groups getting invoked as well when the promotion prints. You could prevent this by introducing a variable to control which section group to invoke, but then you would have to customize even more of the report, making it harder to upgrade the report when a new version or service pack is installed.

Both of the *DocuRef* records are, however, related to the same *InventTable* record, so this table is used as the type for the section group, and an *InventTable* record buffer is sent to the report to print the promotion text and image. Figure 6-17 shows the new section group, named *InventTable*, and its positioning within the report.

**Figure 6-17**   The *InventTable* section group in the *SalesInvoice* report.

## Implementing Promotional Methods

When the promotion text and image print, an *InventTable* record buffer is sent to the report. For this reason, this example implements two methods to return the text and image by using an *InventTable* record buffer. The methods can be implemented directly in the report, but because the methods are not report-specific—and therefore can be reused in other reports, or even forms—the methods are implemented as instance methods on *InventTable*. The following code shows the new methods. The *PromotionImage* method is implemented like the *BikeImage* method in the forms example discussed earlier. However, the *PromotionImage* method must only look in the *DocuRef* table to find the text.

```
display server public DocuValueFile PromotionImage()
{
    DocuRef     docuref;
    DocuValue   docuValue;
    ;
    select forceplaceholders firstonly tableid from docuRef
        where docuRef.RefCompanyId   == this.DataAreaId    &&
              docuRef.RefTableId      == this.TableId       &&
              docuRef.RefRecId        == this.RecId         &&
              docuRef.TypeId          == 'PromoImage'
    join file from docuValue
        where docuValue.RecId   == docuRef.ValueRecId;

    return docuValue.File;
}
```

```
display server public Notes PromotionText()
{
    DocuRef     docuref;
    ;
    select firstonly notes from docuRef
        where docuRef.RefCompanyId   == this.DataAreaId    &&
              docuRef.RefTableId      == this.TableId       &&
              docuRef.RefRecId        == this.RecId         &&
              docuRef.TypeId          == 'PromoText';

    return docuRef.Notes;
}
```

Both methods are implemented as display methods to allow them to bind directly to report controls and to print the information.

## Binding Display Methods to Report Controls

The next step is to bind the methods to report controls. A new body section called *Body-InventTable* is created in the *InventTable* section group with several altered properties, as shown in Table 6-5.

**Table 6-5**   *BodyInventTable* Property Settings

| Property | Settings |
|---|---|
| NoOfHeadingLines | 0 |
| LineAbove | Solid |
| LineBelow | Solid |
| LineLeft | Solid |
| LineRight | Solid |

The *NoOfHeadingLines* property must be set to zero because the text and image must not include any headers when printed. The *Line* property settings create a border around the promotion.

In the body section, a string control, named *PromotionText*, and a bitmap control, named *PromotionImage*, are added and bound to the two new *InventTable* methods. The properties shown in Table 6-6 are changed on the two controls.

**Table 6-6**   *PromotionText* and *PromotionImage* Property Settings

| Property | PromotionText | PromotionImage |
|---|---|---|
| Left | | Auto (right) |
| Width | 70.00 char | 2.0 inch |
| Height | | 2.0 inch |
| DynamicHeight | Yes | |
| ShowLabel | No | No |
| Table | InventTable | InventTable |
| DataMethod | PromotionText | PromotionImage |

The *ShowLabel* properties are set to No because no headers should be printed. The *Promotion-Text* control is set to a fixed width of 70 characters with a dynamic height so that the text will not be truncated. The *PromotionImage* has a fixed size of 2 inches by 2 inches and is right-justified on the page.

The last step is to look up an *InventTable* record buffer based on the invoiced item, and then send the buffer to the report. You do this with the following new method on the *BodyReference* body section.

```
void printInventTable()
{
    InventTable inventTable = custInvoiceTrans.inventTable();
    if (inventTable.RecId)
    {
        element.send(inventTable);
    }
}
```

The method uses the *InventTable* lookup method on the *CustInvoiceTrans* table, which returns a record buffer for the invoiced item, which the method subsequently sends to the report.

The preceding method should be called from the *executionSection* method on the same body section. The following method is therefore customized by including the call to the *printInventTable* method.

```
void  executeSection()
{;
    this.printCustPackingSlipTrans();
    this.printDimHistory();
    this.printInventTable();
}
```

The positioning of the body section, report control, and report methods is shown in Figure 6-18.

**Figure 6-18**   The position of the new sections, control, and methods in the *SalesInvoice* report.

After the completion of all the customizations to the *SalesInvoice* report and the addition of new methods to *InventTable*, the report prints the promotion below each invoiced item on the report, as shown in Figure 6-14.

## Preventing Printing of an Empty Body Section

The solution thus far has one flaw: It prints an empty *BodyInventTable* body section if there is no document reference for the *PromoText* and *PromoImage* document types, which causes an empty box to appear below each item on the invoice. You could easily fix this by altering the *printInventTable* method to include a check for text or images, as shown in the following change to the *printInventTable* method.

```
void printInventTable()
{
    InventTable inventTable = custInvoiceTrans.inventTable();
    if (inventTable.RecId &&
        (inventTable.PromotionText() || inventTable.PromotionImage()))
    {
        element.send(inventTable);
    }
}
```

This code ensures that the *InventTable* record buffer is sent to the report only if the *Promotion-Text* method or the *PromotionImage* method returns a value.

In terms of performance, this change is not optimal because methods may be executed twice if a promotion is added to the *InventTable* record. This could result in as many as five round trips to the database for each printed invoiced item: two from the *printInventTable* method, two when printing the values, and one when the report runtime determines the height of the *PromotionText* control.

A better solution is to cache the returned values from the *PromotionText* and *PromotionImage* methods when they are called in the *printInventTable* method, and then use the cached values instead of retrieving them from the database when printing the *PromotionText* and *Promotion-Image* controls.

The cache variables must be added to the *classDeclaration* of the report, so the following lines are inserted there.

```
DocuValueFile          promotionImage;
Notes                  promotionText;
```

The *printInventTable* method is modified to store the returned values from the *PromotionText* and *PromotionImage* methods on the *InventTable* record buffer in the newly created variables, as shown in the following copy of the method.

```
void printInventTable()
{
    InventTable inventTable = custInvoiceTrans.inventTable();
    ;
    promotionImage  = inventTable.PromotionImage();
    promotionText   = inventTable.PromotionText();

    if (inventTable.RecId &&
        (promotionText || promotionImage))
    {
        element.send(inventTable);
    }
}
```

In addition to these two new display methods, *PromotionText* and *PromotionImage* are created to return the values of the variables. The following code samples show these methods, implemented in the *BodyInventTable* body section.

```
display Notes PromotionText()
{
    return promotionText;
}
```

```
display DocuValueFile PromotionImage()
{
    return promotionImage;
}
```

With these two methods named similarly to the *InventTable* methods, you must only remove the value in the *Table* property on the *PromotionImage* and *PromotionText* report controls to enable the report to retrieve the value from the local report methods instead of the *InventTable* methods. You can even remove the display method modifiers from the two *InventTable* methods, because they are no longer used as display methods.

When you print the report again, empty *BodyInventTable* body sections do not appear and the printing of this specific section is optimized. The report will never result in more than two round trips to the database for each invoiced item. The only disadvantages are that return types of the methods on the *InventTable* and the equivalent methods on the report should be kept synchronized, and these return types should again be kept synchronized with the types of the cache variables. This was not necessary earlier in the example, before the values in the report were cached.

# Number Sequence Customization

In Chapter 7, "Extending Microsoft Dynamics AX," the sample X++ code shows that a service order feature must have a number sequence to generate a unique identification number. To achieve this, you must customize the number sequence class, setting up the relationship between a module and a number sequence reference, and also associating the number sequence reference with the extended data type in which you want to store a number from the sequence.

When you want to create a new number sequence, you must first create an extended data type. The ID of the type is used as the identifier for the number sequence reference, so it must be unique. Figure 6-19 shows a string data type named *BikeServiceOrderId*.

**Figure 6-19**    The *BikeServiceOrderId* extended data type.

The properties on the extended data type are set to create a type with a maximum length of 20 characters, as shown in Table 6-7.

**Table 6-7    *BikeServiceOrderId* Property Settings**

| Property | Settings |
| --- | --- |
| *Type* | String |
| *Label* | Service order |
| *HelpText* | Service order ID |
| *StringSize* | 20 |

To implement a number sequence reference for service orders and assign it a specific service order number sequence, you must make changes to a *NumberSeqReference* class. To implement the reference in the Accounts Receivable module, among other references used by the sales order functionality, you add the following lines of X++ code to the *loadModule* method on the *NumberSeqReference_SalesOrder* class.

```
numRef.DataTypeId           = typeId2ExtendedTypeId(
                              typeid(BikeServiceOrderId));
numRef.ReferenceHelp        = "Unique key for the service order table, "+
                              "used when identification of a service "+
                              "order is allocated automatically.";
numRef.WizardContinuous     = false;
numRef.WizardManual         = NoYes::No;
numRef.WizardAllowChangeDown = NoYes::No;
numRef.WizardAllowChangeUp  = NoYes::No;
numRef.SortField            = 100;
this.create(numRef);
```

These are the only modifications necessary to set up a new number sequence reference. The reference is available in the Accounts Receivable parameter form, and a number sequence can be created automatically by using the Number Sequence Wizard. You start the Number Sequence Wizard by clicking the Wizard button in the Number Sequences form located in the Navigation Pane under Basic\Setup\Number Sequences\Number Sequences.

The *numRef* table buffer in the preceding example is of a *NumberSequenceReference* table type. This table contains several fields that can be set depending on the reference you are about to create. These fields are described in Table 6-8.

**Table 6-8** *NumberSequenceReference* **Field Explanations**

| Field | Explanation |
|---|---|
| *DataTypeId* | The ID for the reference. Use the ID of the extended data type. |
| *ConfigurationKeyId* | The configuration key that must be enabled for the reference to display. The configuration key should be set only if it is different from the key associated with the extended data type. |
| *ReferenceLabel* | The number sequence reference label should be set only if it is different from the label on the extended data type. |
| *ReferenceHelp* | The number sequence reference user interface help field should be set only if the help text is different from text in the *HelpText* property on the extended data type. |
| *DataTypeSameAsId* | Indicates that the reference can use the number from another number sequence. To make this possible, set the ID for the reference to the listed number sequence. Usually this setting is applied to voucher references that use the ID of the journal as the voucher number. |
| *GroupEnabled* | Indicates that the reference is enabled for use with number sequence groups. This setting should be specified only if the reference can be set up for each number sequence group. |
| *SortField* | The position of the reference in the list. Use a sufficiently high number to avoid conflict with other or future references within the same module. |
| *WizardLowest* | The default value for the Smallest field when creating the number sequence with the Number Sequence Wizard. |
| *WizardHighest* | The default value for the Largest field when creating the number sequence with the Number Sequence Wizard. |
| *WizardManual* | The default value for the Manual field when creating the number sequence with the Number Sequence Wizard. |
| *WizardContinuous* | The default value for the Continuous field when creating the number sequence with the Number Sequence Wizard. |
| *WizardAllowChangeDown* | The default value for the To A Lower Number field when creating the number sequence with the Number Sequence Wizard. |
| *WizardAllowChangeUp* | The default value for the To A Higher Number field when creating the number sequence with the Number Sequence Wizard. |
| *WizardFetchAheadQty* | The default value for the Quantity Of Numbers pre-allocation field when creating the number sequence with the Number Sequence Wizard. This field also enables the pre-allocation number sequence feature, but it cannot be used in combination with a sequence marked Continuous. |

Finally, the following method is implemented on the *SalesParameters* table. The method returns the new number sequence reference and should be used in the X++ code that requires numbers from the number sequence.

```
static client server NumberSequenceReference  numRefBikeServiceOrderId()
{
    return NumberSeqReference::findReference(
                        typeId2ExtendedTypeId(typeid(BikeServiceOrderId)));
}
```

# Chapter Summary

Customizing the Dynamics AX application is easy, but customizing it in the right manner is much more difficult. Dynamics AX is designed, according to best practice guidelines, to operate as optimally as possible in a production environment. When customizing the application, you are advised to follow the guidelines in the Microsoft Dynamics AX SDK. Customizing an application is harder than implementing an extension, because customization requires that you consider the ramifications of upgrades to the Dynamics AX application. This chapter focused on issues that you should consider when customizing tables, classes, forms, or reports, but it barely scratches the surface of what is possible in Dynamics AX.

# Chapter 7
# Extending Microsoft Dynamics AX

The objectives of this chapter are to:

- Explain how to create new wizards with the same look and feel as the standard Microsoft Dynamics AX 4.0 wizards.

- Demonstrate how to use the RunBase application framework to implement new business transaction jobs.

## Introduction

A wizard is a special form of user assistance that automates a single task or set of tasks. A wizard presents users with a series of dialog boxes to collect information necessary to complete a task. Wizards are especially useful for complex or infrequent tasks that the user might have difficulty learning or doing and for tedious, frequently performed tasks. The first part of this chapter shows how to build a simple wizard to create new inventory items.

The second part of the chapter examines the RunBase framework. The RunBase framework supports business transaction jobs, such as exchange rate adjustment or inventory closing. The framework helps developers write new business transaction jobs by supplying all the programming infrastructure so that the developer can focus solely on the business logic. This chapter implements a sample RunBase class that sends bike-tuning service offers to customers via e-mail.

## Wizard Framework Extension

The wizard framework supplies the programming infrastructure to create wizards with a consistent look and feel. When developing wizards, you should follow some simple guidelines to ensure that all wizards have the same look and feel and are as helpful to the user as possible.

For example, all wizards should state a clear purpose on the first page and present a very limited set of choices and controls. Figure 7-1 shows a sample first page.

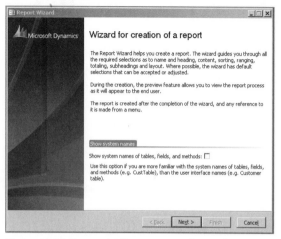

**Figure 7-1**    A sample first page, stating a clear purpose.

You should provide extensive instructions to users to make the concepts implemented by the wizard easy to understand. Consider the use of instructions with graphics, as shown in Figure 7-2, if you want to explain very complex concepts.

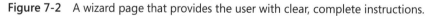

**Figure 7-2**    A wizard page that provides the user with clear, complete instructions.

The user should be able to finish the entire task within the wizard itself. Do not confuse users by redirecting them to other forms to complete the wizard. Include default values or settings (as shown in Figure 7-3) wherever possible. If possible, enable the Finish button as soon as the wizard has collected enough information to skip the rest of the wizard pages. Try to minimize the number of decisions that the user must make.

**Figure 7-3**    A wizard page showing default values for Label, Labelfile ID, and Enumerated Value.

Make sure that the wizard clearly states the actions it will take and how the user can proceed when the wizard has been completed. You can present this information on the last page of the wizard as fixed text with a summary of the selected values and settings, as shown in Figure 7-4.

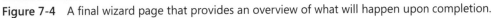

**Figure 7-4**    A final wizard page that provides an overview of what will happen upon completion.

# Creating a New Wizard

The Wizard Wizard is a special wizard in Dynamics AX that helps you create wizards that have the same look and feel as the standard Dynamics AX wizards. You open the Wizard Wizard, shown in Figure 7-5, from the Dynamics AX menu bar: click Tools\Development Tools\Wizards\Wizard Wizard.

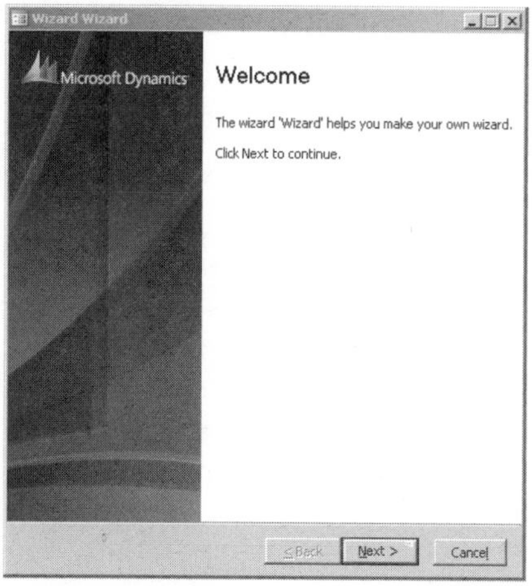

**Figure 7-5**   The Wizard Wizard welcome page.

As shown in Figure 7-6, the wizard asks you to choose between two types of wizards: a Standard Wizard, for any kind of job, and a Default Data Wizard, especially designed to help the user create basic default data in the system. This section demonstrates creation of a standard wizard that will be available from the Navigation Pane and the main menu of Dynamics AX.

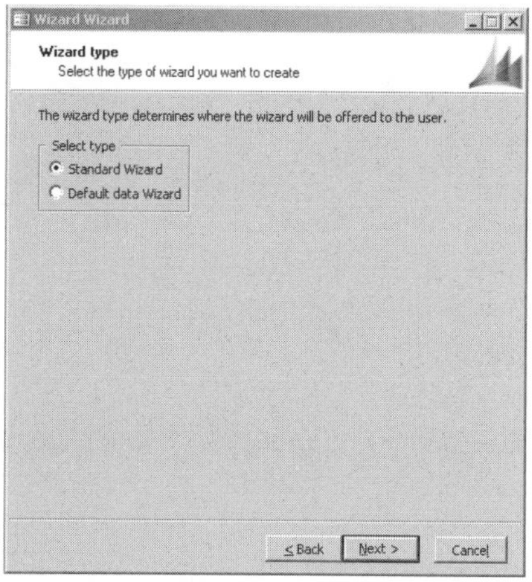

**Figure 7-6**   The Wizard Type page.

When you enter a name for your wizard on the next screen (shown in Figure 7-7), you can see how the names of the elements that will be created in the Application Object Tree (AOT) are suffixed with either *Wizard* or *DefaultDataWizard*, depending on the type of wizard.

In the last step, you enter the number of steps that you want in your wizard, as shown in Figure 7-8. This number includes the welcome page and the summary page. If you change your mind about the number of steps after completing the wizard, you can change the elements generated by the wizard in the AOT.

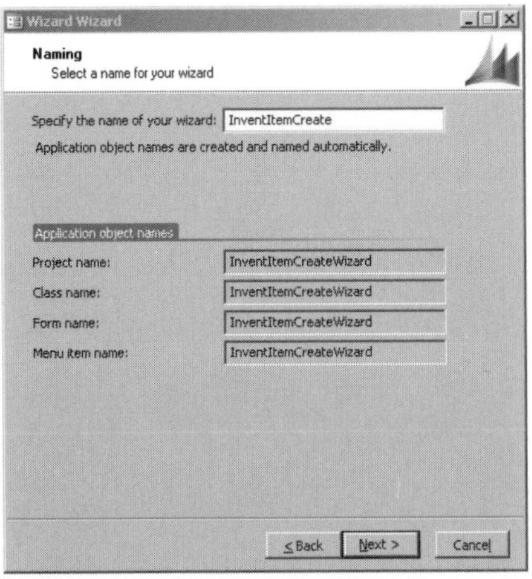

**Figure 7-7**    The Naming page.

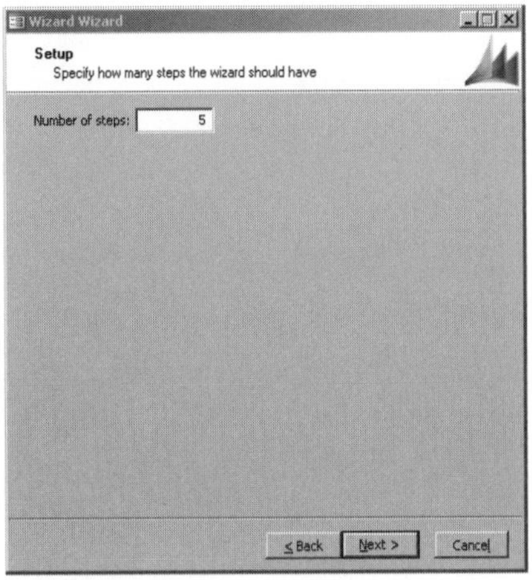

**Figure 7-8**    The Setup page.

Because this sample wizard does not include any complicated selections, the summary page, shown in Figure 7-9, is rather short.

The Wizard Wizard creates a private project, shown in Figure 7-10, that contains three new elements, described from top to bottom:

- A *class* for holding the business logic of the wizard and the logic for running the wizard in the framework. The class extends either *SysWizard* or *SysDefaultDataWizard*, depending on the type of wizard.

- A *form* with the user interface of the wizard.

- A *display menu item* to start the wizard. The menu item starts the class that starts the form.

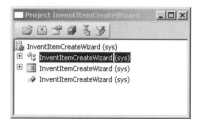

**Figure 7-9**    The summary page.

**Figure 7-10**    The elements of a new wizard collected in a private project.

> **Note**    The Wizard Wizard does not add the new elements to the version control system if version control is enabled. You must do this manually.

## Creating Labels

After creating the basic frame for the new wizard, the next step is to add labels. To open the Label Editor, click Tools\Development Tools\Label\Label Editor. The Label Editor is shown in Figure 7-11.

The Label Editor creates labels in your default language. The Setup tab allows you to set the default language and displays the default label file in which new labels are stored. (If there is no default label file, you must create one with the Label File Wizard, located in Tools\ Development Tools\Label, and then select it as the default on the Setup tab.) You may change these default settings.

Labels are identified with an ID consisting of the label file name and a counter. The label IDs displayed depend on any existing labels and your choice of label file. In the following table, a default label file–USR–results in the label IDs @USR1, @USR2, @USR3, and so on.

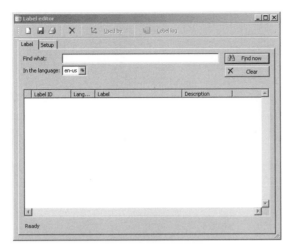

**Figure 7-11**   The Label Editor.

Press Ctrl+N to create the new labels shown in Table 7-1. The label ID is generated automatically when you provide text in the Label field; the additional Description field is optional.

**Table 7-1   Label IDs and Labels**

| Label ID | Label |
| --- | --- |
| @USR1 | Create inventory item wizard. |
| @USR2 | This wizard helps you create a new inventory item. |
| @USR3 | Item identification. |
| @USR4 | Item number and description. |
| @USR5 | Select proper group relationships for the item. |
| @USR6 | Create inventory item. |
| @USR7 | This is all the wizard needs to know to create the inventory item. |
| @USR8 | Click Finish to create and save the item. |

Take note of the label numbers you are given so that you can use them in your code if you have label numbers other than those listed in the table. You may also use the Label Editor to search for previously created labels based on their content.

## Adding Content to the Wizard

Next, you will add selection fields to the wizard you created earlier and write the logic to create the inventory item. You edit the wizard form by using the AOT. In the AOT, scroll to the name of the wizard form you want to design and right-click it. Select Properties, and then set the *Caption* property of the form design to @USR1.

Right-click TabPage:Step1, select Properties, and then change the *Caption* property from "Step 1 Title" to @USR1. Add a *StaticText* control to TabPage:Step1 by right-clicking it and selecting New Control\Static Text. A *Text* Property appears in the properties list; set it to @USR2.

On TabPage:Step2, change the *Caption* property from "Step 2 Title" to @USR3. Set the *HelpText* property to @USR4.

Now you may begin adding input fields. In this example, the user must be able to enter an item ID, item name, and item description. Start by investigating the type of item IDs. The table in which items are stored is called *InventTable*. Look up the item ID on the table, open the properties, and note that the extended data type of the field is *ItemId*. Using this extended data type directly in the wizard will cause a problem, because the extended data type has a relationship with *InventTable*; the drop-down list for the extended data type displays existing item IDs associated with the field. You must find the name of the parent of the extended data type for use in the new wizard.

Locate the extended data type in the AOT and examine the properties. You can see that the type extends the *ItemIdBase* extended data type; because this type does not have any database relationships, you can safely use it in the wizard. In other situations, if you cannot find a suitable extended data type, you can either create one or change the *LookupButton* property of the form control to *Never*.

Right-click TabPage:Step2, point to New Control, and then click StringEdit. Open the properties of the new field and change the *Name* property to *ItemId*, change the *ExtendedDataType* property to *ItemIdBase*, and change the *AutoDeclaration* property to *Yes*. (Setting the *AutoDeclaration* property to *Yes* allows you to easily address the control by using X++ code later; the runtime automatically creates an object handle, which allows access to the control.)

Repeat this procedure to add a field for the *ItemName* of *InventTable*. The *ExtendedDataType* type should be *Name*. Remember to set the *AutoDeclaration* property to *Yes*.

Finally, add the inventory description field. Give it the name ItemDescription. The inventory item description field is in the *InventTxt* table, not in *InventTable* as in the previous case, so you must open *InventTxt* to determine the extended data type. As you can see from the *Txt* field on the table, the extended data type is *ItemFreeTxt*. Supply this type in the *ExtendedData Type* property. Remember to set the *AutoDeclaration* property to *Yes*.

On the third page of the wizard, the user should be able to link the item to the mandatory item group, inventory model group, and dimension group. To make this possible, open the properties list for TabPage:Step3 and change the *Caption* property from "Step 3 Title" to @SYS1177, reading "Groups," and change the *HelpText* property to @USR5. Using the procedure described earlier, add three fields to the page with the following extended data types: *ItemGroupId*, *InventModelGroupId*, and *InventDimGroupId*. Give the fields names that match the extended data type name, and remember to set the *AutoDeclaration* property to *Yes*.

The fourth page of the wizard is dedicated to prices. For this example, you will add a sales price field. Change the *Caption* property of the fourth tab from "Step 4 Title" to @SYS73780, reading "Pricing," and change the *HelpText* property to @SYS87796, reading "Set up sales prices." Add a *RealEdit* control with the extended data type *Price* to the tab. Change the *Name* property to *Price* and remember to set the *AutoDeclaration* property to *Yes*.

On the fifth and final page, you will add a short summary that describes what the wizard does when the user clicks Finish. Change the *Caption* property of the tab from "Step 5 Title" to @USR6. Add a *StaticText* control to the tab. Change the *Name* property to *TxtFinish*, change the *AutoDeclaration* property to *Yes*, change the *Width* property to *Column Width*, change the *Height* property to *Column Height*, and remove the text value from the *Text* property. Because this summary text will be composed of several sentences with more than one label, you will write X++ code to set the text. The code must be added to the *setTexts* method on the form, as shown here.

```
void setTexts()
{
;

    txtFinish.text("@USR7" + '\n\n' +
                   "@USR8" + '\n'   +
                   "@SYS68351");
}
```

Next, you will set up the navigation for the wizard. You will implement three simple rules:

- The Next button must not be enabled on the Item Identification page if an item ID has not been entered.

- The Next button must not be enabled on the Groups page unless all three fields have a value.

- The Finish button must be enabled as soon as the Groups page is filled in. It is not mandatory for the user to enter a price, so the step in which the user can enter the price can safely be skipped.

Start in the class declaration of the *InventItemCreateWizard* class by defining macro variables so that you can address the tabs by name rather than by number, as shown in this example.

```
public class InventItemCreateWizard extends SysWizard
{
    #define.Welcome(1)
    #define.Id(2)
    #define.Groups(3)
    #define.Prices(4)
    #define.Finish(5)
}
```

To make the Finish button available before the last page, override the *hasFinishButton* method by right-clicking the *InventItemCreateWizard* class, clicking Override Method, and choosing *hasFinishButton*. Set the return value to *true*, as shown here.

```
boolean hasFinishButton()
{
;
    return true;
}
```

The *setupNavigation* method describes the initial navigation settings that apply when the wizard is opened. Override this method as shown in the following code.

```
void setupNavigation()
{
;
    nextEnabled[#Welcome]    = true;
    backEnabled[#Welcome]    = false;
    finishEnabled[#Welcome]  = false;

    nextEnabled[#Id]         = false;
    backEnabled[#Id]         = true;
    finishEnabled[#Id]       = false;

    nextEnabled[#Groups]     = false;
    backEnabled[#Groups]     = true;
    finishEnabled[#Groups]   = false;

    nextEnabled[#Prices]     = true;
    backEnabled[#Prices]     = true;
    finishEnabled[#Prices]   = true;

    nextEnabled[#Finish]     = false;
    backEnabled[#Finish]     = true;
    finishEnabled[#Finish]   = true;
}
```

To enable the Next button when an item ID has been entered, find the *ItemId* control on the form and override the *textChange* method with the following code.

```
public void textChange()
{
;
    super();

    if (this.text())
    {
        if (!sysWizard.isNextEnabled())
        {
            sysWizard.nextEnabled(true, sysWizard.curTab(), false);
        }
    }
    else
    {
        if (sysWizard.isNextEnabled())
```

```
        {
            sysWizard.nextEnabled(false, sysWizard.curTab(), false);
        }
    }
}
```

On the Groups page, all three fields must be filled in before the Next button is enabled. Create a single method on the form, in the Methods section directly under the form name node, to control the values *Next* and *Finish*, as shown here.

```
void enableNextOnGroups()
{
;
    if (itemGroupId.text()             &&
        inventModelGroupId.text()      &&
        inventDimGroupId.text())
    {
        if (!sysWizard.isNextEnabled())
        {
            sysWizard.nextEnabled(true, sysWizard.curTab(), false);
        }

        if (!sysWizard.isFinishEnabled())
        {
            sysWizard.finishEnabled(true, sysWizard.curTab(), false);
        }
    }
    else
    {
        if (sysWizard.isNextEnabled())
        {
            sysWizard.nextEnabled(false, sysWizard.curTab(), false);
        }

        if (sysWizard.isFinishEnabled())
        {
            sysWizard.finishEnabled(false, sysWizard.curTab(), false);
        }
    }
}
```

Override the *textChange* method of each of the three controls on the Groups page as follows.

```
public void textChange()
{
;
    super();

    element.enableNextOnGroups();
}
```

Also override the *modified* method of each of the three controls as follows.

```
public boolean modified()
{
    boolean ret;
    ;
    ret = super();

    element.enableNextOnGroups();

    return ret;
}
```

Before you can write the business logic to create the inventory item, you must create methods on the form to return the selected values from the controls that you have added, as shown in the following code.

```
public ItemId itemId()
{
    ;
        return itemId.text();
}

public ItemName itemName()
{
    ;
    return itemName.text();
}

public ItemFreeTxt itemDescription()
{
    ;
        return itemDescription.text();
}

public itemGroupId itemGroupId()
{
    ;
        return itemGroupId.text();
}

public InventModelGroupId inventModelGroupId()
{
    ;
        return inventModelGroupId.text();
}

public InventDimGroupId inventDimGroupId()
{
    ;
        return inventDimGroupId.text();
}
```

```
public Price price()
{
;
    return price.realValue();
}
```

You may now write the X++ code that uses the selections made in the wizard and creates the inventory item. The following code is inserted in the *run* method of the *wizard* class.

```
void run()
{
    InventTable          inventTable;
    InventTxt            inventTxt;
    InventTableModule    inventTableModule;
    InventItemLocation   inventItemLocation;
    ;

    ttsBegin;

    inventTable.initValue();
    inventTable.ItemId      = formRun.itemId();
    inventTable.ItemName    = formRun.itemName();
    inventTable.ItemGroupId = formRun.itemGroupId();
    inventTable.ModelGroupId= formRun.inventModelGroupId();
    inventTable.DimGroupId  = formRun.inventDimGroupId();
    inventTable.insert();

    inventTxt.initValue();
    inventTxt.ItemId        = formRun.itemId();
    inventTxt.LanguageId    = CompanyInfo::find().LanguageId;
    inventTxt.Txt           = formRun.itemDescription();
    inventTxt.insert();

    inventTableModule.initValue();
    inventTableModule.ItemId       = formRun.itemId();
    inventTableModule.ModuleType   = ModuleInventPurchSales::Invent;
    inventTableModule.insert();

    inventTableModule.ItemId       = formRun.itemId();
    inventTableModule.ModuleType   = ModuleInventPurchSales::Purch;
    inventTableModule.insert();

    inventTableModule.ItemId       = formRun.itemId();
    inventTableModule.ModuleType   = ModuleInventPurchSales::Sales;
    inventTableModule.Price        = formRun.price();
    inventTableModule.insert();

    inventItemLocation.initValue();
    inventItemLocation.ItemId      = formRun.itemId();
    inventItemLocation.InventDimId = InventDim::inventDimIdBlank();
    inventItemLocation.insert();

    ttsCommit;
}
```

You could include calls to *validateWrite* of the tables to ensure that it is impossible to create items with the wizard that cannot be created with the normal form.

## Adding the Wizard to the Navigation Pane and Main Menu

To make the wizard available from the Dynamics AX main menu and the Navigation Pane, you must add the menu item to the main menu. First, you must associate the menu item with a configuration key and a security key.

Open properties for the menu item and change the *ConfigurationKey* property to *LogisticsBasic*. The *SecurityKey* property must match the position of the menu item on the main menu or Navigation Pane, so set *SecurityKey* to *InventPeriodic*. Because the wizard adds data to the system, you must also change the *NeededAccessLevel* property to *Add*. Finally, change the *Label* property of the menu item to @USR1 and the *HelpText* property to @USR2.

Now the menu item can be added to the main menu. The main menu consists of several submenus; you will add the wizard menu item to the Inventory Management submenu. In the AOT, expand Menus, right-click Invent, point to New, and then click Menu Item. Right-click the new menu item, and then select Properties. Make sure that *MenuItemType* is set to *Display*, and set *MenuItemName* to *InventItemCreateWizard*. Then drag the menu item to the Periodic folder. Save the menu, and then restart the Dynamics AX client to make the new menu item appear in the Navigation Pane and the Dynamics AX main menu. When the menu item is saved in the main menu, it is also visible in the Navigation Pane, which is another view of the main menu.

> **Tip**   You could also add the menu item to the menu by simply dragging it from the Menu Items node and dropping it on the MainMenu node in the AOT.

## Creating a Default Data Wizard

Default data wizards are targeted especially for creating base data in the system. An example is the Unit Creation Wizard available from Basic\Setup\Units\Units\Functions. A default data wizard has one step more than the standard wizard. In this additional step, you must choose from two types of default data wizards:

- Set up several groups of tables.
- Set up one group of tables.

If you select the first type of default data wizard, a grid on the second tab allows the user to select the areas in which to run the wizard. You typically use the second type of default data wizard for complex wizards that will operate on only a few tables. This kind of wizard is typically started from the main form for the table for which it creates data, and not from the menu.

> **Note**   Dynamics AX includes a sample default data wizard called TutorialDefaultData Wizard.

# RunBase Framework Extension

Use the RunBase framework throughout Dynamics AX whenever you must execute a business transaction job. Extending the RunBase framework allows you to implement business operations that do not have default support in the Dynamics AX application. The RunBase framework supplies many features, including dialog boxes, query windows, validation-before-execution windows, the progress bar, client/server optimization, pack-unpack with versioning, and optional scheduled batch execution at a given date and time.

## Inheritance in the RunBase Framework

Classes that use the RunBase framework must inherit from either the *RunBase* class or the *RunBaseBatch* class. If the class extends *RunBaseBatch*, it can be enabled for scheduled execution in batch mode.

In a good inheritance model, each class has a public construction mechanism, unless the class is abstract. If initialization of the class is not required, use a static construct method. Because X++ does not support method name overloading, you should use a static *new* method if the class must be initialized further upon instantiation. Static *new* methods have the following characteristics:

- They are public and static.

- Their names are prefixed with *new*.

- They are named logically or with the arguments that they take. Examples include *newInventTrans* and *newInventMovement*.

- They usually take non-default parameters only.

- They always return a valid object of the class type, instantiated and initialized, or throw an error.

> **Note**   A class can have several *new* methods with different parameter profiles. The *NumberSeq* class is an example of a class with multiple *new* methods.

The default constructor (the *new* method) should be protected to force users of the class to instantiate and initialize it with the static construct or *new* method. If *new* has some extra initialization logic that is always executed, you should place it in a separate *init* method.

To ease the task of writing customizations, the best practice is to add construction functionality for new subclasses (in higher layers) without mixing code with the construct method in the original layer.

# The Property Method Pattern

To allow other business operations to run your new business operation, you might want to run it without presenting the user with any dialog boxes. If you do this, you will need an alternative to dialog box to set the values of the necessary member variables of your business operation class.

In Dynamics AX classes, member variables are always protected. In other words, they cannot be accessed outside of the class; they can be accessed only from within objects of the class itself or its subclasses. To access member variables from outside of the class, you must write accessor methods. The accessor methods can get, set, or both get and set member variable values.

A Dynamics AX best practice is to not use separate get and set accessor methods. The accessor methods are combined into a single accessor method, handling both get and set, in a pattern called the property method pattern. Accessor methods should have the same name as the member variable that they access, prefixed with *parm*.

The following is an example of what a method implementing the property method pattern could look like.

```
public NoYesId parmCreateServiceOrders(NoYesId _createServiceOrders =
createServiceOrders)
{
;
    createServiceOrders = _createServiceOrders;

    return createServiceOrders;
}
```

If you want the method to work only as a *get* method, change it to something such as this.

```
 public NoYesId parmCreateServiceOrders()
{
;
    return createServiceOrders;
}
```

And if you want the method to work only as a *set* method, change it to this.

```
public void parmCreateServiceOrders(NoYesId _createServiceOrders =
createServiceOrders)
{
;
    createServiceOrders = _createServiceOrders;
}
```

When member variables contain huge amounts of data (such as large containers or memo fields), the technique in the following example is recommended. This technique determines whether the parameter is changed. The disadvantage of using this technique in all cases is the overhead of an additional method call.

```
public container parmCode(container _code = conNull())
{
;
    if (!prmIsDefault(_code)
    {
        code = _code;
    }

    return code;
}
```

**Tip**   From the X++ editor window, you can access a template script to help you create *parm* methods. Right-click the editor window, point to Scripts, point to Template, point to Method, and then click Parm. A dialog box appears in which you must enter the variable type and name of the member variable that you want the *parm* method to give access to. You can also access the script by pressing Shift+F10 in the editor window and then selecting Scripts.

## The Pack-Unpack Pattern

When you want to save the state of an object with the option to reinstantiate the same object later, you must use the pack-unpack pattern. The RunBase framework requires that you implement this pattern to switch the class between client and server (for client/server optimization) and to present the user with a dialog box that states the choices made at the last execution of the class.

The pattern consists of a *pack* method and an *unpack* method. These methods are used by the SysLastValue framework, which stores and retrieves user settings or usage data values that persist between processes.

**Note**   A reinstantiated object is not the same object as the saved object. It is a copy of the object with the same values as the packed and unpacked member variables.

### The *pack* and *unpack* Methods

The *pack* method must be able to read the state of the object and return it in a container. Reading the state of the object involves reading the values of the variables needed to hydrate and dehydrate the object. Variables used at execution time that are declared as member variables do not have to be included in the *pack* method. The first entry in the container must be a version number that identifies the version of the saved structure. The following is an example of the *pack* method.

```
container pack()
{
;
    return [#CurrentVersion, #CurrentList];
}
```

The macros must be defined in the class declaration. *CurrentList* is a macro defined in the ClassDeclaration holding a list of the member variables to pack. If the variables in the *CurrentList* macro are changed, the version number should also be changed to allow safe and versioned unpacking. The *unpack* method can support unpacking previous versions of the class, as shown in the following example.

```
class InventCostClosing extends RunBaseBatch
{
    #define.maxCommitCount(25)

    // Parameters

    TransDate                     transDate;
    InventAdjustmentSpec          specification;
    NoYes                         prodJournal;
    NoYes                         updateLedger;
    NoYes                         cancelRecalculation;
    NoYes                         runRecalculation;
    FreeTxt                       freeTxt;
    Integer                       maxIterations;
    CostAmount                    minTransferValue;
    InventAdjustmentType          adjustmentType;
    InventCostMinSettlePct        minSettlePct;
    InventCostMinSettleValue      minSettleValue;
    ...

    #DEFINE.CurrentVersion(2)
    #LOCALMACRO.CurrentList
        TransDate,
        Specification,
        ProdJournal,
        UpdateLedger,
        FreeTxt,
        MaxIterations,
        MinTransferValue,
        adjustmentType,
        minSettlePct,
        minSettleValue,
        cancelRecalculation,
        runRecalculation,
```

```
            collapseGroups
    #ENDMACRO


}
public boolean unpack(container packedClass)
{
    #LOCALMACRO.Version1List
        TransDate,
        Specification,
        ProdJournal,
        UpdateLedger,
        FreeTxt,
        MaxIterations,
        MinTransferValue,
        adjustmentType,
        minSettlePct,
        minSettleValue
    #ENDMACRO


    boolean        _ret;
    Integer        _version    = conpeek(packedClass,1);

    switch (_version)
    {
        case #CurrentVersion:
            [_version, #CurrentList] = packedClass;
            _ret = true;
            break;

        case 1:
            [_version, #Version1List] = packedClass;
            cancelRecalculation      = NoYes::Yes;
            runRecalculation         = NoYes::No;
            _ret = true;
            break;

        default:
            _ret = false;
    }
    return _ret;
}
```

If any member variable is not packable, the class cannot be packed and reinstantiated to the same state. If any of the members are other classes, records, cursors, or temporary tables, they must also be made packable. Other classes that do not extend *RunBase* may implement the *pack* and *unpack* methods by implementing the *SysPackable* interface.

When the object is reinstantiated, it must be possible to call the *unpack* method, which reads the saved state and reapplies the values of the member variables. The *unpack* method can reapply the correct set of member variables according to the saved version number, as shown in this example.

```
public boolean unpack(container _packedClass)
{
    Version     version = conpeek(_packedClass, 1);
    ;
    switch (version)
    {
        case #CurrentVersion:
            [version, #CurrentList] = _packedClass;
            break;

        default:
            return false;
    }
    return true;
}
```

The *unpack* method returns a Boolean value that indicates whether the initialization was a success.

# Bike-Tuning Service Offers Example

In this section, you will create an extension of the *RunBase* class to send bike-tuning service offers to customers via e-mail. Each bike-tuning offer could result in the creation of a service order transaction. To follow this example, you must have created an extended data type and a number sequence for bike-tuning service orders, as described in Chapter 6, "Customizing Microsoft Dynamics AX."

> **Note**   To send e-mail messages, you must first set up the e-mail parameters in Dynamics AX. You access the e-mail parameters from Administration\Setup\E-Mail Parameters. To run the example without sending e-mail messages, omit the bits that use the *SysMailer* class.

## Creating the Labels

Start by creating the labels that you need. Open the Label Editor from Tools\Development Tools\Label\Label Editor. The label numbers that appear in the Label Editor depend on your existing labels and the choice of label file. This example refers to the labels as @USR9, @USR10, and @USR11. Press Ctrl+N to create the  labels shown in Table 7-2.

**Table 7-2   Bike-Tuning Label Numbers and Text**

| Label number | Text |
| --- | --- |
| @USR9 | Bike-tuning offers. |
| @USR10 | Create bike-tuning offers |
| @USR11 | Send bike-tuning offers to existing customers via e-mail. |

Take note of the label numbers you are given so that you can use them in your code if you have label numbers other than those listed in the table.

## Creating the Table

To store information about the generated service orders, a simple table with only two fields must be created. If you are not confident in your ability to create new tables, the Microsoft Dynamics AX SDK offers detailed table creation information.

The table must be created with the following properties.

| Name | BikeServiceOrderTable |
|------|-----------------------|
| *Label* | @SYS79051  The label reads "Service Orders." |

Add two fields to identify the service order and the customer. The fields must have the following properties.

| Name | CustAccount |
|------|-------------|
| *ExtendedDataType* | CustAccount |

| Name | BikeServiceOrderId |
|------|--------------------|
| *ExtendedDataType* | BikeServiceOrderId |

Finally, add an index with the following properties to the table.

| Name | ServiceOrderIdx |
|------|-----------------|
| *AllowDuplicates* | No |
| *DataField* | BikeServiceOrderId |

## Creating the Class

Now you can begin to create the business transaction class itself. Create a new class that extends the *RunBase* class, as shown in this example.

```
public class BikeTuningOffers extends RunBase
{
}
```

Implement the two abstract *pack* and *unpack* methods of *RunBase*. For now, you will make a very simple implementation to be able to compile the class. You will make the final implementation with the correct class members later. Insert to-do comments in the code, as shown in the following example, so that compile log messages will remind you to revisit the methods.

```
public container pack()
{
;
    //TODO Make the final implementation.
    return conNull();
}

public boolean unpack(container _packedClass)
{
;
    //TODO Make the final implementation.
    return true;
}
```

To enable the example for execution, you must implement the *run* method. Because it is too early to add the business operation, you will implement an empty method, as shown here.

```
public void run()
{

}
```

## Implementing the Class Description

You must implement a static method that returns a description of what the class does. This method sets the title of the dialog box, and it can also be used for different kinds of user interface presentations on the class. The description method must effectively be executed on the tier from which it is called, so define it as *client server*. Use one of the labels created earlier, as shown in this example.

```
client server static ClassDescription description()
{
;
    return "@USR9";
}
```

## Implementing Constructors

Next, you create a custom static constructor as shown here.

```
public static BikeTuningOffers construct()
{
    BikeTuningOffers    bikeTuningOffers;
    ;
```

```
      bikeTuningOffers = new BikeTuningOffers();

   return bikeTuningOffers;
}
```

To force users of the class to use your constructor, rather than the default constructor (*new*), make the default constructor protected. Right-click the class, point to Override Method, click *new*, and change the method as shown here.

```
protected void new()
{
;
    super();
}
```

To enable your job to run from a menu item, you must create the static constructor that is called by the menu item that you will eventually create. This is the method with the name *main*, and it should look like this.

```
public static void main(Args args)
{
    BikeTuningOffers     bikeTuningOffers;
    ;

    bikeTuningOffers = BikeTuningOffers::construct();

    if (bikeTuningOffers.prompt())
    {
        bikeTuningOffers.run();
    }
}
```

In the *main* method, you call the *prompt* method of the framework. This method opens the user dialog box. It returns *true* if the user clicks OK and the values entered are free of errors. The *run* method of the framework starts the actual job.

## Implementing a User Dialog Box

The user dialog box should allow the user to choose whether to create service orders automatically for each bike-tuning offer sent to customers via e-mail. To make this option available, you must have two global member variables in the class declaration. One is the dialog box field object shown in the dialog box, and the other is a variable used to store the value entered in the dialog box field. The changed class declaration looks like this.

```
public class BikeTuningOffers extends RunBase
{
    DialogField dialogCreateServiceOrders;

    NoYesId      createServiceOrders;
}
```

The RunBase framework sets up the basic dialog box by using the dialog framework, so you must add your dialog box field to the dialog box by overriding the *dialog* method. The following code sample displays what the system gives you when you override the *dialog* method.

```
protected Object dialog(DialogRunbase dialog, boolean forceOnClient)
{
    Object ret;

    ret = super(dialog, forceOnClient);

    return ret;
}
```

Rewrite this code as shown here so that it is more readable and follows the general pattern for the method.

```
protected Object dialog()
{
    DialogRunBase    dialog;
    ;

    dialog = super();

    return dialog;
}
```

Now add your field to the dialog box, as shown in the following code. Dialog box fields are objects of the *DialogField* class.

```
protected Object dialog()
{
    DialogRunBase    dialog;
    ;

    dialog = super();

    dialogCreateServiceOrders = dialog.addField(typeId(NoYesId), "@SYS79091", "@SYS84386");

    return dialog;
}
```

To use the values entered in the dialog box, you must retrieve them from the dialog box fields and store them in member variables. When the user clicks OK or Cancel, the framework calls the *getFromDialog* method to retrieve and save the values. Implement an override of this method as follows.

```
public boolean getFromDialog()
{
    boolean ret;
    ;
    ret = super();

    createServiceOrders = dialogCreateServiceOrders.value();

    return ret;
}
```

When the user clicks OK, the framework calls the *validate* method. Although further validation is not necessary for this example, the following code shows how to implement an override that prevents the user from running the job without selecting the Create Service Orders check box.

```
public boolean validate()
{
    boolean ret;
    ;
    ret = super();

    if (ret && createServiceOrders == NoYes::No)
    {
        ret = checkFailed("You cannot run the job without creating service orders.");
    }

    return ret;
}
```

You can view the user dialog box, shown in Figure 7-12, by opening the class. Right-click the class in the AOT, and then click Open.

**Figure 7-12**   The Create Bike-Tuning Offers dialog box.

## Implementing the *run* Method

You can now write the *sendOffers* method that contains your business operation as follows.

```
private void sendOffers()
{
    CustTable              custTable;
    BikeServiceOrderId     bikeServiceOrderId;
    BikeServiceOrderTable  bikeServiceOrderTable;
    SysMailer              sysMailer;
    ;

    sysMailer = new SysMailer();

    ttsBegin;

    while select custTable
    {
        if (createServiceOrders)
        {
            bikeServiceOrderId =
NumberSeq::newGetNum(SalesParameters::numRefBikeServiceOrderId()).num();
            bikeServiceOrderTable.BikeServiceOrderId  = bikeServiceOrderId;
            bikeServiceOrderTable.CustAccount         = custTable.AccountNum;
            bikeServiceOrderTable.insert();
        }

        sysMailer.quickSend(CompanyInfo::find().Email,
                            custTable.Email,
                            "Tune your bike",
                            strFmt("Hi %1,\n\nIt's time to tune your
bike...", custTable.name));
    }

    ttsCommit;
}
```

To call the method, you must add it to the *run* method, which, as you might remember, is called from the value *main* if the user clicks OK in the dialog box and the values pass validation. The *run* method follows a specific pattern, as shown here.

```
public void run()
{
    #OCCRetryCount
    ;
    if (! this.validate())
        throw error("");

    try
    {
        ttsbegin;
```

```
        // Place the code that carries out the actual business transaction here.

        ttscommit;
    }
    catch (Exception::Deadlock)
    {
        retry;
    }
    catch (Exception::UpdateConflict)
    {
        if (appl.ttsLevel() == 0)
        {
            if (xSession::currentRetryCount() >= #RetryNum)
            {
                throw Exception::UpdateConflictNotRecovered;
            }
            else
            {
                retry;
            }
        }
        else
        {
            throw Exception::UpdateConflict;
        }
    }
}
```

This pattern ensures that the transaction is carried out within the scope of a database transaction and that the execution can recover from a deadlock or update conflict in the database. The *run* method calls validation again because someone may call *run* without showing the dialog box. In *run*, an error is thrown to completely stop the execution if validation fails. (Using the class without showing the dialog box is discussed later in this section.) When you add the call to the *sendOffers* method that holds your business operation, the *run* method looks like this.

```
public void run()
{
    #OCCRetryCount
    ;
    if (! this.validate())
        throw error("");

    try
    {
        ttsbegin;

        this.sendOffers();

        ttscommit;
    }
    catch (Exception::Deadlock)
    {
```

```
          retry;
    }
    catch (Exception::UpdateConflict)
    {
        if (appl.ttsLevel() == 0)
        {
            if (xSession::currentRetryCount() >= #RetryNum)
            {
                throw Exception::UpdateConflictNotRecovered;
            }
            else
            {
                retry;
            }
        }
        else
        {
            throw Exception::UpdateConflict;
        }
    }
}
```

## Implementing the *pack* and *unpack Methods*

Now is a good time to revisit the *pack* and *unpack* methods. Start in the class declaration by setting up the member variables that you want to store. In this example, you store the *createServiceOrders* variable. State the version number of the current set of member variables. The version number allows you to add new member variables later and still retrieve the old settings from the last execution of the operation. Also, you can specify the version number to be treated as the first version of the member variable list in the #Version1 declaration. This allows you to treat another version as the first version, which you might choose to do if you simply want to ignore a range of older versions. The first version is typically version 1.

```
public class BikeTuningOffers extends RunBase
{
    DialogField dialogCreateServiceOrders;

    NoYesId     createServiceOrders;

    #define.CurrentVersion(1)
    #define.version1(1)
    #localmacro.CurrentList
        createServiceOrders
    #endmacro
}
```

When more variables are stored in the *#CurrentList* macro, separate each variable by a comma.

The *pack* method must be changed to follow this specific pattern.

```
public container pack()
{
;
    return [#CurrentVersion, #CurrentList];
}
```

The *unpack* method must be changed to follow this pattern.

```
public boolean unpack(container _packedClass)
{
    Version version = runbase::getVersion(_packedClass);
    ;

    switch (version)
    {
        case #CurrentVersion:
            [version, #CurrentList] = _packedClass;
            break;

        default:
            return false;
    }

    return true;
}
```

You must also make the following change to your implementation of the *dialog* method to show the old values in the dialog box fields.

```
protected Object dialog()
{
    DialogRunBase    dialog;
    ;

    dialog = super();

    dialogCreateServiceOrders = dialog.addFieldValue(typeId(NoYesId),
createServiceOrders, "@SYS79091", "@SYS84386");

    return dialog;
}
```

Notice that you call the *addFieldValue* method rather than the *addField* method. The *addField-Value* method allows you to pass a default value to the dialog box field. The RunBase framework ensures that the variable is set to the value saved in the SysLastValue framework at this point in time.

## Creating a Menu Item

To make the operation available from the main menu and the Navigation Pane, you must create a menu item for the operation. The menu item must be attached to a configuration key and a security key.

To create a new configuration key, open the AOT and expand Data Dictionary, right-click Configuration Keys, and then select New Configuration Key. Right-click the new configuration key and select Properties to open the property sheet. Change the name to BikeTuningOffers, and add the label number @USR9 to the *Label* field. The label should read "Bike-tuning offers." If you want to make the configuration dependent on another configuration key, you should fill in the *ParentKey* property. For this example, make the configuration key dependent on the *Quotation* configuration key by entering *QuotationBasic* in the *ParentKey* property field.

The security key property for the menu item should be chosen from the existing security keys. The chosen security key must match the position of the menu item on the main menu or in the Navigation Pane. For example, if you wanted to put your menu item under Accounts Receivable\Periodic, the security key must be *CustPeriodic*.

With the configuration and security keys in place, you are ready to create the menu item. In the AOT, expand Menu Items, right-click Action, and then select New Menu Item. Right-click the new menu item, and then select Properties. Fill out the properties as described in the Table 7-3.

**Table 7-3   Bike-Tuning Menu Item Properties**

| Property | Value | Explanation |
| --- | --- | --- |
| *Name* | *BikeTuningOffers* | This is the name of the menu item as it appears in the AOT. |
| *Label* | @USR10 | The label should read, "Create bike-tuning offers." |
| *HelpText* | @USR11 | The label should read, "Send bike-tuning offers to existing customers via e-mail." |
| *ObjectType* | *Class* | This is the type of object opened by the menu item. |
| *Object* | *BikeTuningOffers* | This is the name of the object opened by the object. |
| *RunOn* | *Server* | Execute the job on the server tier. |
| *ConfigurationKey* | *BikeTuningOffers* | This is the new configuration key that you just created. |
| *SecurityKey* | *CustPeriodic* | This is the security key chosen according to the position of the menu item on the main menu or in the Navigation Pane. |

> **Tip**   You can drag the class node in the AOT onto the Action node under Menu Items to create a new menu item with the same name as the class and the *ObjectType* and *Object* properties already defined.

Now add the menu item to the Accounts Receivable submenu. In the AOT, expand Menus, right-click Cust, point to New, and then click Menu Item. Right-click the new menu item, and then select the Properties tab. Change *Name* to BikeTuningOffers. Change *MenuItemType* to Action and *MenuItemName* to BikeTuningOffers. Finally, move the menu item to the Periodic folder of the menu. Save the menu, and then restart the Dynamics AX client to make the new menu item appear in the Navigation Pane and on the Dynamics AX main menu.

## Adding Property Methods

Suppose that you want to run the Bike-Tuning Offers business operation directly from another piece of code without presenting the user with a dialog box. To do so, you must implement property methods according to the property method pattern. This pattern allows you to set and get the properties that would otherwise be inaccessible because member variables in Dynamics AX are protected.

Start by writing a *parm* method for the property as follows.

```
public NoYesId parmCreateServiceOrders(NoYesId _createServiceOrders =
createServiceOrders)
{
    ;
    createServiceOrders = _createServiceOrders;

    return createServiceOrders;
}
```

This job demonstrates how you can run the operation without showing the dialog box.

```
static void createBikeTuningOffersJob(Args _args)
{
    BikeTuningOffers     bikeTuningOffers;
    ;

    bikeTuningOffers = BikeTuningOffers::construct();
    bikeTuningOffers.parmCreateServiceOrders(NoYes::Yes);

    bikeTuningOffers.run();
}
```

# Adding Constructors

As mentioned earlier in this chapter, X++ does not support method name overloading, and you should avoid using default parameters on constructors. You must create individually named *new* methods with different parameter profiles instead.

In the preceding example, you created an instance of the class and set the necessary parameters. Imagine that there is one more parameter in your class that indicates a certain customer account number for creating bike offers. Add a new member variable to the class declaration, and then add the new parameter method, like this.

```
public class BikeTuningOffers extends RunBase
{
    DialogField dialogCreateServiceOrders;

    NoYesId      createServiceOrders;
    CustAccount custAccount;

    #define.CurrentVersion(1)
    #define.version1(1)
    #localmacro.CurrentList
        createServiceOrders
    #endmacro
}

public CustAccount parmCustAccount(CustAccount _custAccount = custAccount)
{
    ;
    custAccount = _custAccount;

    return custAccount;
}
```

Suppose that the customer record contained information about the option to create service orders with bike offers. For example, imagine that offers are not sent to the customer if the customer has been stopped for new transactions. Because you want to avoid using default parameters in the construct method, you must call both of these *parm* methods when you create an instance based on a customer record.

Running the business operation from a job with a specific customer would look like this.

```
server static void createBikeTuningOffersJobCustomer(Args _args)
{
    CustTable           custTable = CustTable::find('4001');
    BikeTuningOffers    bikeTuningOffers;
    ;

    bikeTuningOffers = BikeTuningOffers::construct();
    bikeTuningOffers.initParmDefault();
```

```
        bikeTuningOffers.parmCustAccount(custTable.accountNum);
        bikeTuningOffers.parmCreateServiceOrders(custTable.blocked == CustVendorBlocked::No);

        bikeTuningOffers.run();
    }
```

This code is a good candidate for the static *new* pattern, so implement a static *newCustTable* method on the *BikeTuningOffers* class to create an instance based on a customer record, as shown here.

```
server static public BikeTuningOffers newCustTable(CustTable  _custTable)
{
    BikeTuningOffers      bikeTuningOffers;
    ;

    bikeTuningOffers = BikeTuningOffers::construct();
    bikeTuningOffers.initParmDefault();
    bikeTuningOffers.parmCustAccount(_custTable.accountNum);
    bikeTuningOffers.parmCreateServiceOrders(_custTable.blocked == CustVendorBlocked::
No);

    return biketuningOffers;
}
```

Now change your job to a simpler version to be assured that the class gets properly instantiated and initialized.

```
server static void createBikeTuningOffersJobCustomer(Args _args)
{
    CustTable           custTable = CustTable::find('4001');
    BikeTuningOffers    bikeTuningOffers;
    ;

    bikeTuningOffers = BikeTuningOffers::newCustTable(custTable);

    bikeTuningOffers.run();
}
```

# Adding a Query

Adding a query to the business operation class allows the user to select a range of targets to apply the operation to, such as sending bike-tuning offers to selected customers. To use the query, you must be able to create an instance of *QueryRun*. Start by adding *QueryRun* as a member variable, as shown here.

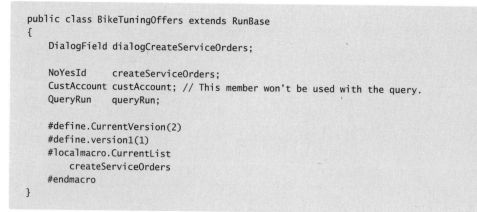

```
public class BikeTuningOffers extends RunBase
{
    DialogField dialogCreateServiceOrders;

    NoYesId     createServiceOrders;
    CustAccount custAccount; // This member won't be used with the query.
    QueryRun    queryRun;

    #define.CurrentVersion(2)
    #define.version1(1)
    #localmacro.CurrentList
        createServiceOrders
    #endmacro
}
```

To initialize the *QueryRun* object, override the *initParmDefault* method, as shown in the following code. This method is called by the RunBase framework if no saved object state is found by the SysLastValue framework via the *unpack* method.

```
public void initParmDefault()
{
    Query   query;
    ;

    super();

    query = new Query();
    query.addDataSource(tableNum(CustTable));

    queryRun = new QueryRun(query);
}
```

You must modify the *pack* method, as shown in the following example, so that you can save the state of the *QueryRun* object.

```
public container pack()
{
    ;
    return [#CurrentVersion, #CurrentList, queryRun.pack()];
}
```

Consequently, you must also modify the *unpack* method to reinstantiate the *QueryRun* object, as shown here.

```
public boolean unpack(container _packedClass)
{
    Version     version = runbase::getVersion(_packedClass);
```

```
    Container   packedQuery;
    ;

    switch (version)
    {
        case #CurrentVersion:
            [version, #CurrentList, packedQuery] = _packedClass;

            if (packedQuery)
                queryRun = new QueryRun(packedQuery);

            break;

        default:
            return false;
    }

    return true;
}
```

To make the *QueryRun* object available for presentation in the dialog box, override the *queryRun* method to return your *QueryRun* object, as shown in the following code.

```
public QueryRun queryRun()
{
    ;
    return queryRun;
}
```

To actually show the query in the dialog box, you must override the *showQueryValues* method to return the value *true*, as follows.

```
boolean showQueryValues()
{
    ;
    return true;
}
```

If you open the class now, you can see that the query is embedded in the dialog box, as shown in Figure 7-13.

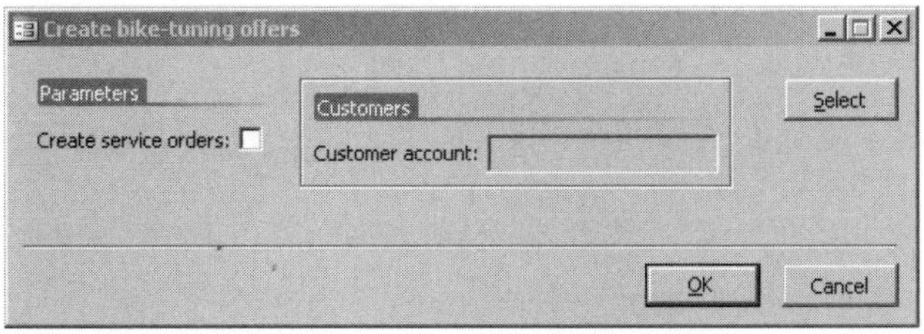

**Figure 7-13**   The Create Bike-Tuning Offers dialog box with an embedded query.

Finally, you must change your business logic method, *sendOffers*, so that it uses the *QueryRun* object, as shown here.

```
private void sendOffers()
{
    CustTable              custTable;
    BikeServiceOrderId     bikeServiceOrderId;
    BikeServiceOrderTable  bikeServiceOrderTable;
    SysMailer              sysMailer;
    ;

    sysMailer = new SysMailer();

    ttsBegin;

    while (queryRun.next())
    {
        custTable = queryRun.get(tableNum(CustTable));

        if (createServiceOrders)
        {
            bikeServiceOrderId = NumberSeq::newGetNum(SalesParameters::
numRefBikeServiceOrderId()).num();
            bikeServiceOrderTable.BikeServiceOrderId  = bikeServiceOrderId;
            bikeServiceOrderTable.CustAccount         = custTable.AccountNum;
            bikeServiceOrderTable.insert();
        }

        sysMailer.quickSend(CompanyInfo::find().Email,
                            custTable.Email,
                            "Tune your bike",
                            strFmt("Hi %1,\n\nIt's time to tune your bike...",
custTable.name));
    }

    ttsCommit;
}
```

# Client/Server Considerations

Typically, you will want to execute business operation jobs on the server tier, because these jobs almost always involve several database transactions. However, you want the user dialog box to be executed on the client to minimize client/server calls from the server tier. Fortunately, the RunBase framework can help you run the dialog box on the client and the business operation on the server tier.

To run the business operation job on the server and push the dialog box to the client, you should be aware of two settings. On the menu item that calls the job, ypou must set the *RunOn* property to Server; on the class, you must set the *RunOn* property to Called from. Figure 7-14 shows where to set the *RunOn* property of a class.

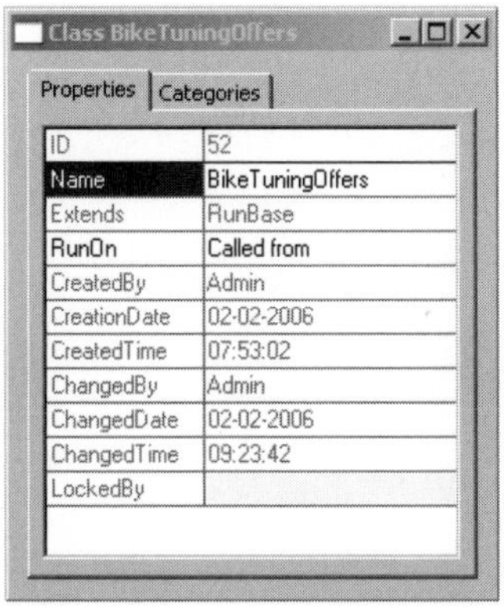

**Figure 7-14**   The execution tier of the class set to Called from.

When the job is initiated, it starts on the server, and the RunBase framework packs the internal member variables and creates a new instance on the client, which then unpacks the internal member variables and runs the dialog box. When the user clicks OK in the dialog box, RunBase packs the internal member variables of the client instance and unpacks them again in the server instance.

## Chapter Summary

This chapter has introduced you to wizard development and RunBase-controlled business operation transaction classes. To fully understand these concepts, you should, of course, try to create some new wizards and *RunBase* classes yourself. You should also look at some of the existing wizards and *RunBase* classes.

# Chapter 8
# The Business Connector

The objectives of this chapter are to:

■ Describe the two components of the Business Connector, what they do, and how they relate to other integration components in Microsoft Dynamics AX 4.0.

■ Provide example scenarios that use the Business Connector.

■ Explain how to use the new .NET Business Connector to build managed applications that integrate with Dynamics AX 4.0.

■ Illustrate the differences between the COM Business Connector and the .NET Business Connector.

## Introduction

The Business Connector is a versatile platform component that you can use to build software applications that interact deeply with both the data and the business logic residing in Dynamics AX 4.0. The Business Connector consists of two components: the COM Business Connector and the .NET Business Connector. This chapter focuses mainly on the .NET Business Connector because it is new in Dynamics AX 4.0 and will be of interest to anyone who wants to develop managed solutions with Dynamics AX without using COM.

This chapter compares the Business Connector with other integration components included with Dynamics AX 4.0. It also explains the Business Connector architecture to help you understand how it functions. Several example scenarios demonstrate the variety of potential uses for the Business Connector. The .NET Business Connector managed classes are described and code examples are provided to illustrate their use. This chapter also describes how to port applications built with the COM Business Connector in earlier versions of Dynamics AX to the .NET Business Connector, and it highlights the differences between the two Business Connector components.

# Integration Technologies

Integration of enterprise resource planning (ERP) systems with other systems within and beyond an organization is now a common requirement, and Dynamics AX provides a variety of ways to implement such integration. Figure 8-1 shows all the integration components in Dynamics AX 4.0.

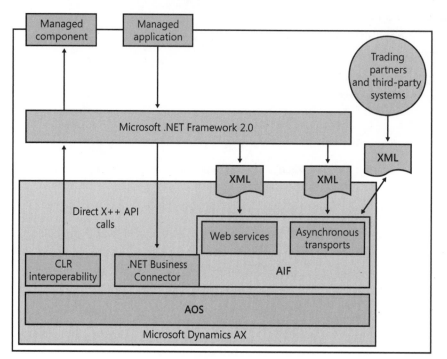

**Figure 8-1**   The integration components in Dynamics AX 4.0.

All the integration components interact with Dynamics AX through the Application Object Server (AOS). Dynamics AX 4.0 supports only a three-tier architecture (earlier versions supported both a two-tier and a three-tier architecture), which means that the integration components, like the database, can interact with Dynamics AX only through the AOS. The majority of the integration components use Microsoft .NET Framework 2.0 in some way, which is a reflection of the goal to make it easier for the development community to use the .NET platform for solutions development.

The .NET Business Connector enables development of managed applications, using the .NET Framework and a common language runtime (CLR)–compatible language to integrate with Dynamics AX. In Figure 8-1, the arrow from the .NET Framework to the .NET Business

Connector shows that the managed applications interact with Dynamics AX through the .NET Business Connector, in contrast to how CLR interoperability works. The .NET Business Connector is the most general-purpose integration component in Dynamics AX and is particularly appropriate for developing custom applications that require a large degree of flexibility and control over implementation.

CLR interoperability enables external managed components to be instantiated and executed from the X++ code. In Figure 8-1, the arrow from CLR interoperability to the .NET Framework represents the flow from the X++ code to the Microsoft .NET CLR, mirroring the flow into Dynamics AX via the .NET Business Connector. CLR interoperability is built into the Dynamics AX kernel and can therefore be used wherever the kernel runs. Like the .NET Business Connector, CLR interoperability is a general-purpose feature, and it is in many ways complementary to the type of integration that the .NET Business Connector provides.

The Application Integration Framework (AIF) is a comprehensive, feature-rich, standards-based integration infrastructure that provides the ability to implement loosely coupled, XML-based document integration scenarios with Dynamics AX. AIF comprises both synchronous Web services, which internally use the .NET Business Connector, and a more traditional integration component that supports a variety of asynchronous transports. These capabilities allow interaction with third-party systems and external trading partners. AIF is the recommended solution for business-to-business, application-to-application, and enterprise application integrations. See Chapter 9, "XML Document Integration," for details.

# Inside the Business Connector

As stated earlier, the Business Connector is a versatile platform component. The Business Connector itself comprises two components: one that provides Microsoft COM interoperability, and another that provides interoperability with the .NET Framework. You should choose the component that is appropriate to the environment in which you are working. Both Business Connector components contain the Dynamics AX kernel and provide a run-time environment for executing X++ code and interacting with other elements in the AOT. This is because virtually the entire Dynamics AX development and run-time environment is based on X++, and the kernel is responsible for interpreting and executing this code.

Table 8-1 summarizes the primary characteristics of the two types of Business Connector.

**Table 8-1   Business Connector Characteristics**

| Characteristic | COM Business Connector | .NET Business Connector |
|---|---|---|
| Single-user with single-session or multi-session  support (desktop PC deployment) | Yes | Yes |
| Multi-user and multi-session support (Web or other server deployment) | Yes | Yes |

Table 8-1    **Business Connector Characteristics**

| Characteristic | COM Business Connector | .NET Business Connector |
|---|---|---|
| Microsoft COM–based interface | Yes | No |
| .NET Framework 2.0 managed classes | No | Yes |
| Integration with the managed HTTP context (for enabling Web applications) | No<br><br>The COM Business Connector in the previous version supported the unmanaged HTTP context, but Dynamics AX 4.0 does not. | Yes |
| CLR interoperability available | Yes | Yes |

As you can see, the Business Connector versions are largely similar, differentiated only by managed HTTP context integration and the programming environment for which each is intended.

# The Logical Component Stack

If you divide the .NET Business Connector into its constituent parts, you will see that the following three logic components (illustrated in Figure 8-2) interoperate to deliver functionality:

- Managed classes
- Transition layer
- Interpreter

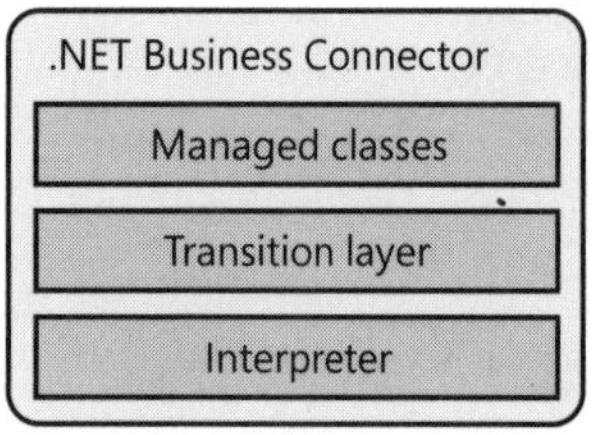

Figure 8-2    The logical component stack in the .NET Business Connector.

## Managed Classes

The managed classes component is a set of .NET Framework–based classes that expose functionality that can be accessed through the .NET Business Connector. It includes the following classes: *Axapta, AxaptaBuffer, AxaptaContainer, AxaptaObject,* and *AxaptaRecord.* The purpose of each of these classes is described later in this chapter, in the section called "Working with the .NET Business Connector." If you used the COM Business Connector in the previous version of the application, you will find that the functionality of the managed classes in Dynamics AX 4.0 is mostly equivalent.

### The Transition Layer

The transition layer is where the mapping occurs between .NET Framework objects and types and their Dynamics AX equivalents, as part of both request and response processing associated with the use of the Business Connector.

### The Interpreter

The interpreter consists of the kernel. Dynamics AX allows code to be executed locally in the Business Connector AX kernel or remotely in the AX kernel of the AOS. The interpreter manages local and remote code execution. It also manages connectivity to the AOS and other infrastructure, such as session management and security.

# Run Time

At run time, both types of Business Connector interact with the AOS because the two-tier model is not supported in Dynamics AX 4.0. The diagram in Figure 8-3 depicts the run-time interaction.

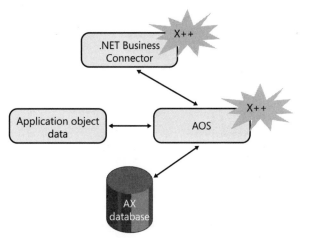

**Figure 8-3**   The Business Connector run-time interactions.

The important interactions among the Business Connector, the AOS, and the AX database are as follows:

- The Business Connector authenticates against the AOS when the *Axapta.Logon()* method is called. The credentials passed to the AOS by the Business Connector must correspond to an existing Dynamics AX user, who must be enabled and have the appropriate rights, granted through security keys, to use the Business Connector.

- The AOS completes the authentication and establishes a session for the Dynamics AX user.

■ Other Business Connector classes and methods are invoked as needed. Data in Dynamics AX can be selected, inserted, updated, and deleted by using the Business Connector through the AOS. In addition, the X++ business logic that resides in the Dynamics AX metadata store, the Application Object Directory (AOD), can be invoked and executed either on the AOS or in the Business Connector itself.

# Web Interoperability

The Dynamics AX development environment includes a feature known as the Web framework. This is covered in more detail in Chapter 10, "The Enterprise Portal." The Web framework is used to develop the Web-based functionality in X++, which is then exposed in the Dynamics AX Enterprise Portal (EP). However, Web applications generally must interact with the HTTP context data, which typically includes the request, response, view state, and so forth. The Dynamics AX EP uses the .NET Business Connector to integrate with Dynamics AX, and the .NET Business Connector can interoperate with Internet Information Services (IIS) and Microsoft ASP.NET to provide access to the HTTP context information necessary to enable Web-based functionality. Note that in earlier versions of Dynamics AX, the COM Business Connector integrated with the unmanaged HTTP context as part of the interoperability with Active Server Pages (ASP). This is no longer supported.

The diagram in Figure 8-4 illustrates how Web interoperability works.

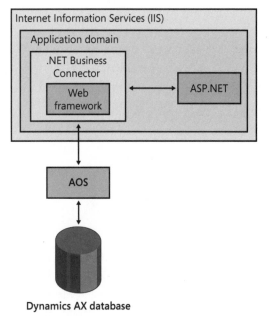

**Figure 8-4**   .NET Business Connector Web interoperability.

Managed Web applications, including the Dynamics AX EP, execute in IIS within an application domain. Upon initialization, the application domain loads and instantiates the

.NET Business Connector. The managed application then uses the .NET Business Connector to invoke Dynamics AX Web framework elements, such as Web menu items, Web forms, and Web reports. The X++ code stored in the AOD that defines these elements accesses the HTTP context as needed through the following classes (located in the AOT under System Documentation\Classes):

- *IISApplicationObject*
- *IISContextObject*
- *IISPostedFile*
- *IISReadCookie*
- *IISRequest*
- *IISRequestDictionary*
- *IISResponse*
- *IISServer*
- *IISSessionObject*
- *IISStringList*
- *IISVariantDictionary*
- *IISViewState*
- *IISWriteCookie*

For example, you could write an X++ class to retrieve a variable from the HTTP context, which you could then use in another X++ class. In the following code example, the method takes a parameter, which is the name of the HTTP context variable, the value of which will be obtained using IISRequest().

```
str getIISServerVariable(str 80 var)
{
    IISRequest request;
    str res;

    request = new IISRequest();
    res = request.serverVariables().itemTxt(var);
    return res;
}
```

If you want to develop a new, custom Web-enabled application that integrates with Dynamics AX and can access managed HTTP context information, you can use both ASP.NET and the .NET Business Connector. The interoperability among IIS, ASP.NET, and the .NET Business Connector allows you to access HTTP context information from X++ code that is part of your application.

> **Important**   Existing applications developed with the previous version of the COM Business Connector and ASP that accessed the unmanaged HTTP context must be migrated to ASP.NET to successfully run with Dynamics AX 4.0.

# Security

A significant amount of effort has been expended on enhancing security within Dynamics AX 4.0. This section highlights the security mechanisms in place for the Business Connector.

## Authentication

Microsoft Windows authentication is implemented throughout Dynamics AX 4.0, and this change is reflected in both types of Business Connector. The COM interface (COM Business Connector) and the managed classes (.NET Business Connector) have been refactored to accommodate parameters that are specific to Windows authentication.

## Authorization

The Business Connector has an associated set of Dynamics AX security keys that control access to different parts of the Business Connector functionality. Table 8-2 describes these security keys.

**Table 8-2   Dynamics AX Security Keys**

| Security key | Description |
| --- | --- |
| SysCom | Enables or disables the use of either type of Business Connector |
| SysComData | Controls the level of access that users have to data |
| SysComExecution | Controls access to execution rights of classes and jobs in the Business Connector |
| SysComIIS | Controls whether the Business Connector is accessible to users when running in the context of IIS |

These keys can be browsed in the Data Dictionary under Security Keys. You can control the use of the Business Connector in different user groups in Dynamics AX by configuring these security keys.

## Code Access Security

Code Access Security (CAS) is a new feature in Dynamics AX 4.0. CAS is a mechanism intended to help Dynamics AX developers write code that invokes protected X++ APIs in a manner that minimizes the potential for malicious exploitation of these APIs. A protected API is an X++ API method that has been secured by using CAS. It also ensures that the protected APIs are executed only on the AOS, not on the Dynamics AX client or the Business Connector. CAS therefore restricts the X++ APIs that can be executed locally in the Business Connector. If such an attempt is made, a CAS exception is returned.

# Usage Scenarios

This section provides several scenarios to demonstrate how the Business Connector might be used in real-world situations. The usage scenarios described here fall into the following categories:

- Client
- Web
- Server

# Client

In client-based scenarios, the Business Connector and the application that uses it are installed on a user's desktop computer. To make this easier to set up, Dynamics AX 4.0 allows the installation of just the COM or .NET Business Connector, instead of the entire Dynamics AX rich client (which was required in the previous version of Dynamics AX).

## Office Excel Integration Example

Microsoft Office Excel integration is probably the best illustration of client-based use of the COM Business Connector, because it is a commonly used tool and particularly appropriate for viewing and manipulating data sets from ERP systems such as Dynamics AX.

You can extend Office Excel by developing add-ins that load when Excel launches. Office Excel exposes a menu that can be accessed by users working on a spreadsheet. Here are the requirements for this type of integration:

- It must be possible for the current Windows user to be authenticated in Dynamics AX.
- It must be possible to retrieve data from Dynamics AX into a range within a workbook in Office Excel.
- It must be possible to update data in Dynamics AX that corresponds to the retrieved data.

Figure 8-5 illustrates the topology of this integration.

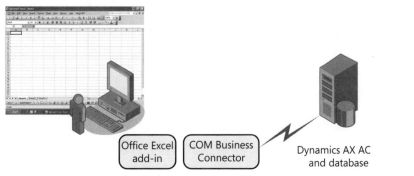

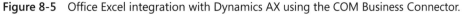

**Figure 8-5**   Office Excel integration with Dynamics AX using the COM Business Connector.

The following actions are associated with the use of the COM Business Connector from the Office Excel add-in:

1. The COM Business Connector is invoked initially to authenticate the current Windows domain user and to establish a session with Dynamics AX.

2. An Office Excel user clicks a menu option to retrieve data from Dynamics AX. This executes code in the add-in to query data (through the Business Connector). Data retrieved from Dynamics AX is then passed back to the worksheet via the Business Connector.

3. After the data appears in the worksheet, the user manipulates it.

4. When the data is ready to be saved back to Dynamics AX, the user clicks a menu option, which causes the Business Connector to execute code in the add-in to persist the data. Note that any business logic attached to the destination table in Dynamics AX is executed when the Business Connector processes the updates, and exceptions are passed back to the calling application, which in this case is the Office Excel add-in.

This scenario illustrates the concept of developing an add-in to a popular Microsoft Office program using the COM Business Connector. In fact, this concept was used to develop several snap-ins for the previous version of the application, which are published here: *http://www.gotdotnet.com/codegallery/codegallery.aspx?id=b44f8ee7-4d2b-4e39-9bfb-1119fffbe018*. Search the page for "Snap-ins for Microsoft Dynamics AX 3.0." Note that you must register to see the snap-ins. As of this writing, there are three such snap-ins:

- **Business Data Lookup**    Provides the ability to access Dynamics AX data from Microsoft Office applications by using the task pane

- **Time Sheet Management**    Enables time sheet data to be entered and submitted from Office Outlook

- **Vacation Scheduler**    Allows users to submit time-off requests from Office Outlook

Each of these snap-ins uses the COM Business Connector to access Dynamics AX business logic and data. You can download the source code to see how the Business Connector is used in each one.

## PDA Synchronization Example

A potential client-based use of the .NET Business Connector is for PDA synchronization. For example, you could develop an application that allows a PDA to collect information that can be uploaded to Dynamics AX. PDAs generally rely on some kind of synchronization manager; if this synchronization program is customizable, you can extend it to integrate with Dynamics AX.

The specific requirements for this type of integration are as follows:

- It must be possible to verify that the current Windows user matches the identity of the device owner.

- It must be possible to retrieve the data to be uploaded from the PDA, or from the local file system if downloaded from the PDA.

- It must be possible to validate and insert the downloaded data into the corresponding Dynamics AX tables.

The diagram in Figure 8-6 illustrates the topology of this integration.

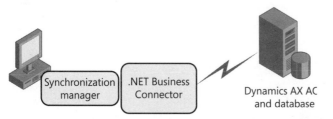

**Figure 8-6**   PDA synchronization using the .NET Business Connector.

The following actions are associated with the use of the .NET Business Connector during PDA synchronization:

1. The synchronization manager downloads data from the PDA and recognizes that it needs to be uploaded to Dynamics AX.

2. The synchronization manager authenticates the current user's credentials with the Business Connector and establishes a Dynamics AX session.

3. Data read from the PDA is uploaded to Dynamics AX through the Business Connector. The data is validated using X++ business logic defined in Dynamics AX. Exceptions are reported as errors in the synchronization manager.

4. Validated data is persisted in the Dynamics AX database.

This usage scenario shows how the Business Connector might be incorporated into the synchronization mechanism for a PDA, and how data entered on the PDA can be transferred to Dynamics AX.

# Web

Earlier in this chapter, we explained how the .NET Business Connector interacts with the managed HTTP context, thus enabling Web applications, including the Dynamics AX EP, to access and use this context information. One of the primary processes in the EP is page processing, which is a good example of how you can use a Business Connector to enable a Web application. Refer to Chapter 10 for a detailed description of page processing and the role of the Business Connector.

# Server

A final usage scenario uses the .NET Business Connector on the server that hosts the AOS and the Dynamics AX database, as shown in Figure 8-7.

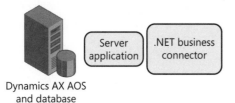

Dynamics AX AOS
and database

**Figure 8-7**  Server-based use of the .NET Business Connector.

In this scenario, a non-Web-based managed application uses the .NET Business Connector to integrate with Dynamics AX. This approach can be used for a variety of purposes, but one example is offline processing. Typically, a Dynamics AX user must be logged on to a computer to authenticate in Dynamics AX. In some cases, this is not possible. For example, the asynchronous integration offered by the AIF does not require the originating user to be logged on to the machine where data is processed and inserted into Dynamics AX. However, this task must be executed using the correct user identity.

The solution is to use the .NET Business Connector to impersonate a Dynamics AX user. You can do this in one of three ways:

1. Use the *Logon()* API method and supply the original user's credentials, assuming they are known and maintained securely.

2. Use the *LogonAs()* API method and supply the credentials of the Dynamics AX Business Connector Proxy user. The Business Connector Proxy user is a specifically nominated domain account used within the user impersonation mechanism in both types of Business Connector. For more details about this, review the documentation supplied with the application.

3. Execute the Business Connector in a Windows process owned by the Dynamics AX Business Connector Proxy user, and then call the *LogonAs()* API method.

If you use one of these methods to log on to the Business Connector, you can develop server-based applications that can process data using the correct Dynamics AX user identity.

# Working with the .NET Business Connector

This section takes a closer look at building applications with the .NET Business Connector, including the following topics:

- Data types and mappings
- Managed classes
- Request and response processing
- Exception handling

# Data Types and Mappings

The .NET Business Connector makes it easier to develop managed applications that integrate with Dynamics AX by bridging two programming environments: the managed .NET Framework environment and the unmanaged Dynamics AX X++ environment. Inevitably, some form of translation is required when passing objects and data between these two environments. Table 8-3 maps equivalent data types between .NET and Dynamics AX.

**Table 8-3   Data Type Mappings**

| Dynamics AX data type | .NET Framework data type |
|---|---|
| String, RString, VarString | System.String |
| Integer | System.Int32 |
| Real | System.Double |
| Enums | System.Enum <br> The Business Connector uses integers for enumerations. |
| Time | System.Int <br> You must convert this value to Dynamics AX time format. |
| Date | System.Date <br> You need only use the date portion, because time is stored separately in Dynamic AX. |
| Container | AxaptaContainer |
| Boolean (enumeration) | System.Boolean <br> Dynamics AX uses integers to represent Boolean values of true and false. |
| GUID | System.GUID <br> This data type is new in Dynamics AX 4.0 (but it is not supported in the COM Business Connector). |
| Int64 | System.Int64 <br> This data type is new in Dynamics AX 4.0. |

The Business Connector managed class methods explicitly support specific data types for parameters and return values. Refer to the Microsoft Dynamics AX SDK for more information.

# Managed Classes

This section provides an overview of the managed classes in the .NET Business Connector. You develop applications with the .NET Business Connector by instantiating and using the public managed classes described in Table 8-4.

Table 8-4   .NET Business Connector Managed Classes

| Class name | Description |
| --- | --- |
| *Axapta* | The *Axapta* class provides methods for connecting to a Dynamics AX system, creating Dynamics AX objects (class objects, record objects, container objects, and buffer objects), and executing transactions. |
| *AxaptaBuffer* | The *AxaptaBuffer* class represents an array of bytes and provides methods for manipulating the buffer contents. *AxaptaBuffer* objects can be added to *AxaptaContainer* objects. |
| *AxaptaContainer* | The *AxaptaContainer* class provides methods for reading and modifying containers. In Dynamics AX 4.0, this class is implemented by using the *IList* and *ICollection* interfaces in the .NET Framework. *AxaptaContainer* contains the methods defined by these interfaces, so behavioral similarities exist between *AxaptaContainer* and these interfaces. |
| *AxaptaObject* | The *AxaptaObject* class provides a single method for invoking X++ class methods. |
| *AxaptaRecord* | The *AxaptaRecord* class provides methods for reading and manipulating *AxaptaRecord* objects (tables in the Dynamics AX database). |

Examples of how these classes are used in an application are provided in the following sections.

# Request and Response Processing

Much like any integration component, the Business Connector processes requests and returns responses associated with the use of the managed classes by applications across all the established Business Connector user sessions. The steps described in the following section traverse the logical component stack presented in Figure 8-2.

## Request Processing

The diagram shown in Figure 8-8 depicts the processing steps associated with a request made through the managed classes.

1. A request is initiated by invoking a managed class.

2. The request is received and marshaled across the transition layer (where .NET objects and data are converted from .NET to X++).

3. The transition layer dispatches the request to the interpreter in the .NET Business Connector.

4. If the request involves executing X++ code, this code is run either locally or remotely on the AOS, depending on the directive associated with the code.

5. After the request is processed, a response is generated.

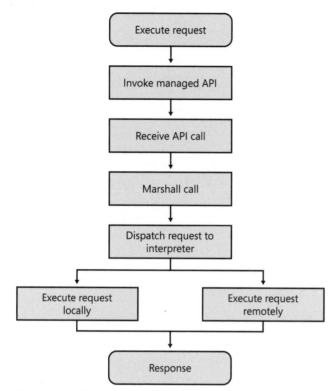

**Figure 8-8**   Request processing in the .NET Business Connector.

## Response Processing

The diagram shown in Figure 8-9 depicts the processing steps associated with generating a response.

1.  The active request processed by the .NET Business Connector completes, successfully or unsuccessfully.

2.  The response is instantiated and dispatched by the interpreter to the transition layer.

3.  The transition layer marshals the response to the managed classes (converting objects and data from X++ to .NET).

4.  The response is returned to the caller, which is the application that initially invoked the Business Connector.

The main variation in the request and response cycle is the location where the X++ code being invoked is executed. This is controlled by the declaration associated with the X++ code. By default, the X++ code runs where called—that is, from the interpreter where it is invoked. If the *client* keyword is used, this forces execution on either the Business Connector or the Dynamics AX client. If the *server* keyword is used, the code is executed by the AOS.

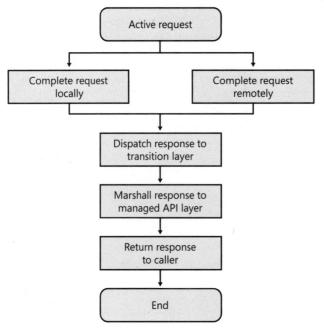

**Figure 8-9**    Response processing in the .NET Business Connector.

## Exception Handling

The .NET Business Connector has a large set of managed exceptions that can be raised at run time. Although it was originally based on the errors in the COM Business Connector, this set of managed exceptions has been extended in Dynamics AX 4.0 to provide improved granularity, and therefore more flexibility, in handling those exceptions. Most notable is the addition of several remote procedure call (RPC)–related exceptions, which you can use to control error handling associated with the connectivity between the Business Connector and the AOS. As a general rule, unhandled exceptions (such as *OutOfMemoryException*) are not caught by the Business Connector. This type of exception is simply propagated to the calling application and prevents such unhandled exceptions from being masked or hidden by the Business Connector.

A new exception has been added in Dynamics AX 4.0 that provides a consistent way to manage AOS failures. If the AOS to which the .NET Business Connector currently has affinity becomes inaccessible, a *BusinessConnectorInstanceInvalidException* exception is raised for every call to a method in the managed classes thereafter. This exception can then be used to take other actions, such as terminating the process so it can be restarted.

Refer to the Microsoft Dynamics AX SDK for more information on the data types, managed classes, and managed exceptions referenced in this section.

# HelloWorld Example

How do you write C# code that uses the .NET Business Connector? The simple example that follows (the Business Connector equivalent of "Hello World") demonstrates logging on to Dynamics AX. To use the following code, you must be able to log on successfully using the AX client. Also, the .NET Business Connector must be installed from wherever you will execute the code. Create a new project in Microsoft Visual Studio. In the New Project dialog box, select Console Application under Visual C#. This creates the project file structure and files and presents you with a program called Program.cs. Paste the code in the following example between the curly brackets associated with the Main method. In Solution Explorer, right-click References and choose Add Reference. In the Add Reference dialog box, click the Browse tab. Use the file controls to navigate to the Dynamics AX Client\Bin folder. Select Microsoft.Dynamics.BusinessConnectorNet.dll, and then click OK. This makes the .NET Business Connector accessible to the C# application. Now you can build and run the solution.

```
Axapta ax;

// Log on.
ax = new Axapta();

try {
    ax.Logon(null, null, null, null);
}
catch (Exception)
{
    Console.WriteLine("Exception occurred");
}
Console.WriteLine("Hello World!");
ax.Logoff();
```

First, you must instantiate the *Axapta* class to authenticate, using one of the methods within the *Axapta* class. Authentication is accomplished by using the *Logon()* method. If you do not provide any explicit parameter values, the following values, which can be overridden as needed, are used:

- The current Windows user
- The default Dynamics AX company for the user
- The default language for the user
- The default active configuration

A message appears on the console, and the Dynamics AX session is terminated using the *Logoff()* method.

## Accessing Data

To access data in Dynamics AX, you must use the *AxaptaRecord* class. The following example shows how to retrieve a list of bike-related inventory items that are classified as "raw material."

```csharp
using System;
using Microsoft.Dynamics.BusinessConnectorNet;

namespace ListInvItemRecords
{
    // ListInvItemRecords
    // Shows how to retrieve and iterate through a list of Dynamics AX records
    class ListInvItemRecords
    {
        public static void Run()
        {
            Axapta ax;
            String invItemNameField = "ItemName";
            Object invItemName;
            String invItemIdField = "ItemId";
            Object invItemId;

            // Log on.
            ax = new Axapta();

            try
            {
                ax.Logon(null, null, null, null);
            }
            catch (Exception)
            {
                Console.WriteLine("Exception occurred");
            }

            Console.WriteLine("*** List inventory item records");

            // Instantiate the Dynamics AX record.
            AxaptaRecord axRecord = ax.CreateAxaptaRecord("InventTable");

            // Execute a query.
            axRecord.ExecuteStmt("select * from %1
            where %1.ItemGroupId == 'RawMat'");

            // Loop through matching Dynamics AX records.
            while (axRecord.Found)
            {
                invItemName = axRecord.get_Field(invItemNameField);
                invItemId = axRecord.get_Field(invItemIdField);
                Console.WriteLine(invItemId + "\t" + invItemName);
```

```
            axRecord.Next();
        }

        axRecord.Dispose();

        // Log off of Dynamics AX.
        ax.Logoff();
        }
    }
}
```

Here are the important aspects of the code example:

- Variables are declared to store the Dynamics AX record data that you will retrieve and to hold the field names used.

- Authentication is the same as in the HelloWorld example.

- To begin working with a specific type of Dynamics AX record, you must first instantiate an *AxaptaRecord* object, and you must provide the name or ID of the record as an argument.

- A query is executed against the Dynamics AX record using *ExecuteStmt*, which parses the query syntax and replaces the substitution variable (%1) with the name of the record. The query syntax is of a generic form. Dynamics AX executes the query with the exact syntax appropriate for the database being used, whether it is Microsoft SQL Server or Oracle.

- A *while* loop cycles through the records returned from Dynamics AX, which uses another method on *AxaptaRecord* called *Found* to determine that matching records exist.

- For each record, *get_Field()* retrieves each of the field values and assigns a value to the appropriate variable declared earlier.

- To proceed to the next record, the *Next()* method is called.

- The *AxaptaRecord* object instance is disposed of to release any unmanaged resources associated with it, and *Logoff()* is called to terminate the session.

You can also invoke X++ business logic directly from the .NET Business Connector, as shown in the following section.

## Invoking Business Logic

In addition to accessing data, you can also invoke business logic defined in Dynamics AX directly from the .NET Business Connector. In this example, you call a method in an X++ class to update inventory item details in Dynamics AX based on data from a separate inventory management system. To do this, you use the *CallStaticClassMethod* method in the *Axapta* managed class, as shown in this code.

```
try {
    returnValue = ax.CallStaticClassMethod("InventoryManager",
        "updateInventoryQty");

    if((Boolean)returnValue)
        Console.WriteLine("Inventory quantity updated successfully");
    else
        Console.WriteLine("Inventory quantity update failed");
}
catch (Exception)
{
    Console.WriteLine("Exception occurred");
}
```

The X++ class returns a Boolean result in this case, which is then used to determine the next action in the application.

As you can see from these examples, developing applications that integrate with Dynamics AX using the .NET Business Connector is relatively straightforward. Although real applications would use the managed classes more extensively, the approach to accessing data and invoking business logic remains the same.

# CLR Interoperability

As explained in Chapter 5, "The X++ Programming Language," you can invoke external managed components from Dynamics AX by using CLR interoperability. CLR interoperability can be used from any Dynamics AX kernel, so you can use it from either type of Business Connector included with Dynamics AX 4.0. Why should you consider using CLR interoperability? You might need to invoke functionality provided by an externally managed program during some processing activity in the Business Connector, and rather than invoke the managed program on the AOS, you could choose to exploit the processing capacity of the Business Connector, especially if it is located on a separate machine.

The diagram in Figure 8-10 shows how CLR interoperability works from the .NET Business Connector.

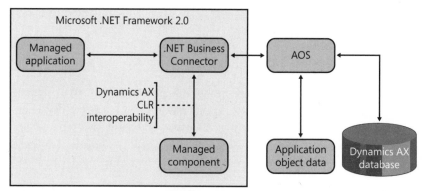

**Figure 8-10** Invoking externally managed components from the .NET Business Connector using CLR interoperability.

In this scenario, a bicycle distributor has purchased a third-party managed component, called *ThirdPartyUtilities*, that contains the business logic necessary to validate an account number. The managed component must be integrated into the Dynamics AX application, which processes account information by using the Business Connector.

The following steps illustrate the use of CLR interoperability from within the .NET Business Connector for enabling the *ThirdPartyUtilities* managed component:

1. Create a reference in the AOT under the References node so that Dynamics AX recognizes the third-party component. You can do this by adding a new reference item in the AOT, opening it, and browsing for the .dll file. Save the reference after the required information has been provided.

2. Create an X++ class, called *ProcessingManager*, that invokes a method in the managed component by using the CLR interoperability feature. This requires you to instantiate the class that you will use in the *ThirdPartyUtilities* component, called *ValidationManager*, and then invoke the appropriate method, called *validateAccNum*, in that class with a parameter that represents the data to be validated, called *inboundAccNum*, and return the result, as shown here.

```
static boolean validateAccNum(inboundAccNum)
{
    ThirdPartyUtilities.ValidationManager valMgr = new
        ThirdPartyUtilities.ValidationManager();
    boolean validationResult;
    ;
    validationResult = valMgr.validateAccNum(inboundAccNum);

    return validationResult;
}
```

3. In the managed application, add code in the appropriate place to invoke the X++ method in *ProcessingManager* and provide the account number to validate, as shown here.

```
returnValue = ax.CallStaticClassMethod("ProcessingManager",
                        "validateAccNum",
                        inboundAccNum);
```

At run time, the managed application invokes the *validateAccNum* X++ method in the *ProcessingManager* class, which then instantiates the CLR object from the Business Connector and returns a Boolean result. By default, the X++ methods execute from the location where they are called, which in this case is the Business Connector. Therefore, the processing associated with this request is performed in the interpreter within the Business Connector, rather than in the AOS.

# Migrating Applications

This section explains how to migrate existing applications to use the COM Business Connector included with Dynamics AX 4.0. If you developed applications with the COM Business Connector in the previous version of Dynamics AX, you should be aware of a few changes to ensure that your application works with Dynamics AX 4.0:

- Interface names have changed: *IAxapta* is now *IAxapta3*, and *IAxapta2* has been integrated with *IAxapta3*. You must update the application code to reference the correct name, and you must also recompile your application. The other interfaces are the same as in the previous version.

- Both types of Business Connector use Integrated Windows authentication. The *Logon()* method is still used to connect to Dynamics AX, but it attempts to authenticate the current Windows domain user because there is no longer any concept of Dynamics AX application users. A new method called *LogonAs()* allows user impersonation in the .NET Business Connector and the COM Business Connector.

- Web-related X++ classes interoperate only with the managed HTTP context, rather than with the unmanaged HTTP context as in the previous version of Dynamics AX. Therefore, existing applications that use the Web-related X++ classes must be updated to work with the managed HTTP context.

- The COM Business Connector is installed as a standard COM application. There are no longer any options in the Dynamics AX Client Configuration Utility for registering by using COM+ or DCOM. However, you can accomplish the COM+ registration manually, if necessary.

To take advantage of the capabilities of the .NET Framework, you might consider migrating applications built with the COM Business Connector to its .NET-based successor. You should consider the following when doing this:

- The *IAxaptaParameterList* interface has been removed; you can now supply arrays to methods that contain parameters.

- Similar methods have been combined into a single method call with multiple signatures. For example, *AxaptaObject.Call* and *AxaptaObject.CallEx* have been consolidated into *AxaptaObject.Call*.

- The following methods have been removed because they do not have any use in managed applications:
  *IAxapta3::CreateReference*
  *IAxapta3::GetReference*
  *IAxapta3::ReleaseReference*
  *IAxapta3::Stop* You must refactor your code to remove the use of these methods.

- *AxaptaContainer* has been completely re-implemented to use *IList* and *ICollection* from the .NET Framework. If you developed managed applications using these classes, you will be familiar with how they work in Dynamics AX 4.0.

- The Business Connector uses Windows Integrated authentication for connections to Dynamics AX 4.0. Supported authentication methods include *Logon* and *LogonAs*. Review your application code to determine which type of authentication is needed.

- Errors are thrown as managed exceptions. In Dynamics AX 4.0, you can catch a large number of exceptions, which enables greater control of the Business Connector application at run time.

## Chapter Summary

This chapter explained the role of the Dynamics AX Business Connector in developing applications that integrate with Dynamics AX, and it described specific scenarios in which the Business Connector can be used. It also described managed classes and provided code examples to illustrate how applications that use the .NET Business Connector are written. The chapter highlighted the use of CLR interoperability to demonstrate the flexibility of the Dynamics AX kernel in providing a way to invoke reusable third-party managed components. Finally, this chapter presented important information on the changes to the COM Business Connector in Dynamics AX 4.0 and explained how to migrate applications to the .NET Business Connector.

# Chapter 9
# XML Document Integration

The objectives of this chapter are to:

- Describe the *AxdBase* and *AxInternalBase* class hierarchies.

- Introduce the Axd Wizard.

- Describe how to customize a Microsoft Dynamics AX 4.0 XML document.

- Explain how to send XML documents to partners who are not known at coding time by using the send framework.

- Discuss the security implications associated with transmitting XML documents in and out of Dynamics AX.

## Introduction

The Application Integration Framework (AIF) has replaced Commerce Gateway in Dynamics AX 4.0 as the conduit for exchanging electronic business documents. To provide broad support for business-to-business collaboration scenarios, the AIF enables interaction with application integration platforms such as Microsoft BizTalk Server 2006. It also enables enterprise application integration scenarios via a variety of communication channels, including Microsoft Message Queuing (MSMQ) and Web services.

The AIF depends on the XML document framework to provide an XML document interface to Dynamics AX. The XML document framework consists of two X++ class hierarchies:

■ Dynamics AX document classes (referred to as *Axd* classes) present data as electronic documents. They protect the user from the complexity of the underlying table structures and associated business logic and elevate error handling from individual database tables and fields to the document level. In addition, the *Axd* classes provide methods for serializing instances to XML and deserializing document class instances from XML while performing value mapping and data filtering. The *Axd* classes can also automatically generate an XML schema that describes the equivalent XML document based on the associated query in the Application Object Tree (AOT).

■ *Ax<Table>* classes have a 1:1 relationship with the database tables in Dynamics AX and protect the user from the underlying table-specific business logic and the complexities of default settings. The *Ax<Table>* classes eliminate the need for the calling application to set database fields in a specific order and replicate any table-specific business logic. For this reason, the *Axd* classes always use *Ax<Table>* classes to manipulate the underlying Dynamics AX database tables.

# AIF Architectural Overview

The overall AIF architecture, shown in Figure 9-1, consists of two major components: transport and business logic exposure. This chapter focuses primarily on business logic exposure, which is what you will modify as you implement new documents or modify default solutions.

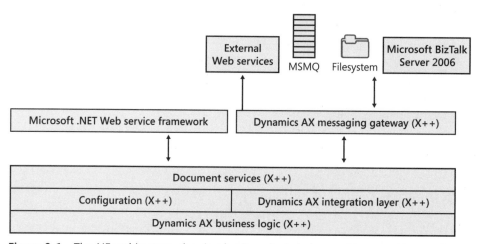

**Figure 9-1**    The AIF architecture, showing business logic below and transport layers above.

The design of the Dynamics AX business logic encompasses two primary type hierarchies: *AxInternalBase* and *AxdBase*. You can think of the *AxInternalBase* class hierarchy as an extension of the table functionality. Your custom classes inherit the table properties and settings, and you must subsequently apply any additional business logic and validation to suit your needs. The children classes of *AxInternalBase* in Dynamics AX 4.0 primarily implement validation, value substitution, and value defaulting.

New XML documents inherit the *AxdBase* class. This class allows you to serialize and deserialize XML from and to Dynamics AX; it is also the single point of entry to Dynamics AX whether you want to query, read, or create documents. The *AxdBase* class implements the *AifServiceable* interface, which enables the derived classes to be externally available through either Web services or the transport layers in the AIF. Figure 9-2 illustrates the interaction between the Dynamics AX core business functionality and the XML application programming interface (API), as well as the interaction between the XML API and the transport layers of the AIF.

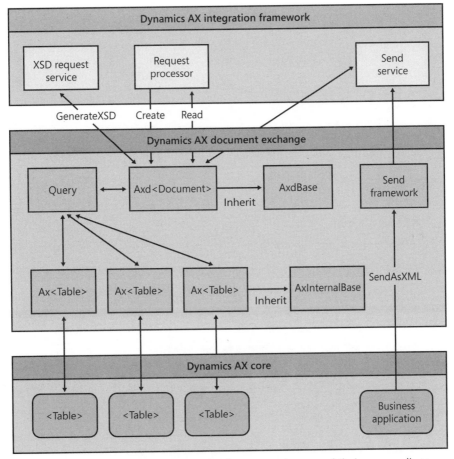

**Figure 9-2**   The interaction between the document classes and their surroundings.

# The XML Structure

The primary goal for the Dynamics AX XML document feature was a reduction in implementation time for new XML documents. Because most systems integrating with Dynamics AX need mapping columns regardless of the schema, the product team decided to implement the Dynamics AX internal schema as the API. This way, only one mapping per integration endpoint is needed, and most Dynamics AX developers are already familiar with the internal schema.

It was clear that this should be expressed using AOT queries. The data sources for the AOT query directly associate with tables, and these tables carry fields which in the XML translate into properties. Benefiting from the extended data type definitions in the AOT, the XML schema definition (XSD) can be constrained using the available metadata describing data type, field sizes, and so on.

The widely adopted approach in the XML community regarding properties appearing in a fixed sort order in the documents is supported by the query structure, in which tables are addressed in the order of appearance in the query. The XML document framework automatically addresses the fields in alphabetical order; individual documents therefore require no manual development. Note that if the same table will be referenced in several nodes in the query, XML schema restrictions require that the name be unique. The table fields, when referenced in the XML, are referenced with their field names from the table, but the table names are the name under which they are identified on the query.

The limitations are that only one root table per query is allowed, and the unique entity key of an XML document can be associated with this root table. When constructing the queries, you should outer-join the child data sources to uphold 1:*n* relationships. If 1:1 relationships are to be enforced, you should choose an inner join.

Figure 9-3 illustrates the mapping between the query in the AOT, which is referenced by the *Axd*<Document> class, and the XML document structure.

**Figure 9-3**  Correlation between the AOT query and the XML document structure.

# The *AxdBase* API

The *AxdBase* class offers an API that allows you to implement new XML documents with a minimal amount of work. As mentioned earlier, the basic operations enabled with this framework are create XML, read XML, and generate XSD. In this context, Dynamics AX does not support delete and update operations. When you use this XML document interface, you can only read documents or create new ones in Dynamics AX.

Table 9-1 lists the methods implemented by *AxdBase*, along with a short description of the provided functionality.

**Table 9-1**   *AxdBase* **Method Descriptions**

| Method | Description |
| --- | --- |
| *read* | Reads a posted transaction from the database and returns it in an XML string. |
| *readList* | Reads posted transactions from the database and returns them in an XML string. |
| *create* | Creates the document in the XML string as a transaction in the database tables and returns the primary key of the created transaction. |
| *createList* | Behaves like *create*, except that it accepts more than just one document in the XML string. |
| *findList* | Returns posted transactions from the database and writes them to an XML string. |
| *getSchema* | Returns the XSD of the Dynamics AX XML document. |
| *getActionList* | Returns a list of all available actions for the Dynamics AX XML document specified. |
| *getLabel* | Returns the label that corresponds to the localized document name. |
| *getName* | Returns a fixed string that contains the name of the document. |
| *getQueryName* | Returns the name of the query to be used—that is, the query that corresponds to the Dynamics AX XML document. |
| *setTableFieldAsMandatory* | Sets a field as mandatory. To specify additional mandatory fields, the *Axd* class must extend the *initMandatoryFieldsMap* method. If a field should be mandatory, but not mandatory in the data model, this method must call either *setParmMethodAsMandatory* or *setTableFieldAsMandatory* to indicate that the field must be mandatory. |
| *prepareForSave* | Prepares an *Ax*<Table> class for saving. |
| *prepareForQuery* | Abstract method that may be overridden by derived classes if the corresponding query needs preparation before execution. Temporary tables, for example, must be populated with data before they can be queried. |

**Table 9-1**   *AxdBase* **Method Descriptions**

| Method | Description |
|---|---|
| *updateNow* | Abstract method that may be overridden by derived classes to implement document-specific updates (for example, posting the document or running some business logic). The method is called as the very last step when processing an inbound document. |
| *validateDocument* | Abstract method that may be overridden by derived classes to implement document-wide business logic. This method is called immediately after processing an inbound document and right before the transaction is persisted to the database. |

For improved productivity, the framework enables all implemented operations by default. This means that if, for example, you do not want to support *create*, you must override it in your derived document class and throw an exception explaining that the operation is not supported. The following example of an unsupported *create* action is from the actual implementation in the *AxdASN* class, which is included with Dynamics AX.

```
public AifEntityKey create(XML _xML,
                           AifEndpointActionPolicyInfo _actionPolicyInfo,
                           AifConstraintList _constraintList)
{
    ;
    throw error(strfmt("@SYS94924", this.getName(), 'create'));
}
```

When you create a completely new document, you must override the following methods:

- *getActionList*
- *getConstraintList*
- *getLabel*

When you include more tables in the query, and the field values in one query rely on field values in, for example, the parent tables, you must also override the *prepareForSave* method. This is necessary only if you intend to support *create* or *createList* actions. In the following example, using the *prepareForSave* method of the *AxdChartOfAccount* class, the foreign key is populated with the values from the primary fields in the parent table. Pay particular attention to the lines in bold, which set up the association.

```
public boolean prepareForSave(AxdStack _axdStack, str _dataSourceName)
{
    AxLedgerTable              axLedgerTable;
    AxledgerTableInterval      axledgerTableInterval;
    ;
    switch (classidget(_axdStack.top()))
    {
```

```
        case classnum(AxLedgerTable) :
            axLedgerTable = _axdStack.top();
            return true;

        case classnum(AxledgerTableInterval) :
            axledgerTableInterval = _axdStack.top();
            if(classidget(axledgerTableInterval.parentAx<Table>()) ==
classnum(AxLedgerTable))
            {
                axLedgerTable = axledgerTableInterval.parentAx<Table>();
                axledgerTableInterval.parmAccountTableId(axLedgerTable
.currentRecord().TableId);
                axledgerTableInterval.parmAccountRecID(axLedgerTable.currentRecord()
.RecId);
                return true;
            }
            else
                error(strfmt("@SYS97762"));
            return false;
        default :
            error(strfmt("@SYS88979", classId2Name(classidget(_axdStack.top()))));
            return false;

    }
    return false;
}
```

# The *AxInternalBase* API

The goal for creating *Ax*<Table> classes was to have an API available when creating and updating records in Dynamics AX tables. The design goals of the *AxInternalBase* API were as follows:

- The API must be easy to use.

- The API must handle related fields. The default value should apply when a field is updated. For example, when you update the customer account field on the sales order, the address fields should be populated with default values when you copy the address fields from the customer record to the sales order record.

- The API must handle the sequence of field updating. For example, the invoice account field is a related field, which should revert to the default value when the customer account field is updated.

- Field value defaulting might not always provide the expected end result. Consider an example: If the invoice account field is updated first and related fields' values are defaulted, and then the customer account field is updated and its related fields' values are defaulted, the defaulted value would then overwrite the explicitly provided value in the invoice account field.

■ The API must handle fetching numbers or identifiers from number sequences. For example, when you create a sales order, a sales order number must be fetched from a sales order number sequence. The business logic that handles this is implemented in these classes.

New *Ax<Table>* classes must inherit from the base class *AxInternalBase*. The *AxInternalBase* class keeps track of which methods have been executed to set a table field to a specific value. You can implement this tracking either externally or internally. Externally, for example, you can call the *parmCustAccount* method on the *AxSalesTable* class with a specific value. Internally, you can call the *parmInvoiceAccount* method on the *AxSalesTable*, because it is a related field that should revert to the default value when the *parmCustAccount* method is executed. By monitoring the methods that have been executed, the *AxInternalBase* class ensures that a value set externally is not overwritten.

The class declaration on the *AxBC* class must declare a record variable of the table type that the *AxBC* class relates to. The *AxSalesTable* class declaration therefore has the following declaration.

```
class AxSalesTable extends AxInternalBase
{
    SalesTable      salesTable;
}
```

On an *Ax<Table>* class, you should create an instance method for each field on the related table. The method name must be the same as the field name, prefixed with the word *parm*, and it must use the following template.

```
public DataType parmFieldName(DataType _fieldName = literal)
{
    if (!prmisdefault(_fieldName))
    {
        this.setField(fieldNum(TableName, FieldName), _fieldName);
    }
    return tableName.fieldName;
}
```

If the instance method is executed without a parameter, the value of the field is returned. If the method is executed with a parameter, the *setField* method is executed with the field ID of the table field as well as the passed parameter.

The *setField* instance method on the *AxInternalBase* class determines whether the field has already been set to a specific value, and it assigns the value if not already set. At the same time, a list of fields with assigned values is updated. The *setField* method uses the logic shown in Figure 9-4.

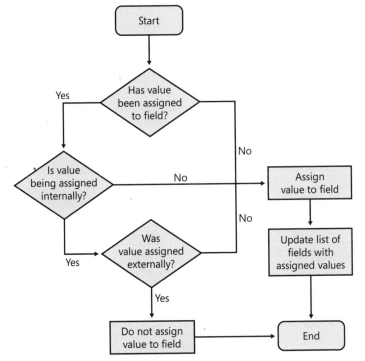

**Figure 9-4**    The *setField* method logical flow.

You can see an actual implementation of the *setField* method in the following declaration of the *parmCustAccount* method on the *AxSalesTable* class.

```
public CustAccount parmCustAccount(CustAccount _custAccount = '')
{
    if (!prmisdefault(_custAccount))
    {
        this.setField(fieldNum(SalesTable, custAccount), _custAccount);
    }
    return salesTable.custAccount;
}
```

When you must solve intra-table field relations in which a table field will default to a specific value when the value of another table field changes, you must create an instance method for both fields. The method name must be the same as the field name, including a set prefix, and it must apply the following template. The bold text is subject to modification of current table and field names.

```
protected void setFieldName()
{
    if (this.isMethodExecuted(funcName(), fieldNum(TableName, FieldName)))
```

```
    {
        return;
    }
// Additional code goes here.
}
```

Because the method may be executed several times, the *isMethodExecuted* method determines whether the method has already been executed and whether the field has already been assigned a value. The *isMethodExecuted* method uses the logic shown in Figure 9-5.

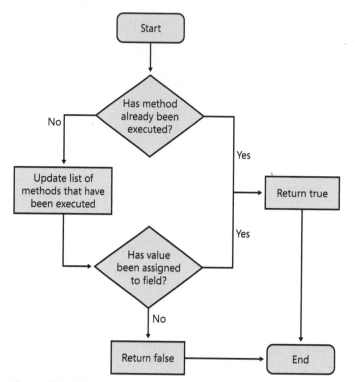

**Figure 9-5** The *isMethodExecuted* method logical flow.

Dependencies on other fields must be programmed like this.

```
this.setAnotherFieldName();

if (this.isFieldSet(fieldNum(TableName, AnotherFieldName)))
{
    this.fieldName(newValue);
}
```

First, you should execute the set method of the field for which the current field has dependencies to get a value assigned to this field if any of its dependencies have changed. Then you should determine whether the dependent field has been assigned a new value. If it has, assign a new value to the current field. You can see an implementation in the following declaration of the *setPaymMode* method on the *AxSalesTable* class.

```
protected void setPaymMode()
{
    if (this.isMethodExecuted(funcName(), fieldNum(SalesTable, paymMode)))
    {
        return;
    }

    this.setInvoiceAccount();

    if (this.isFieldSet(fieldNum(SalesTable, invoiceAccount)))
    {
        this.parmPaymMode(this.invoiceAccount_CustTableRecord().paymMode);
    }
}
```

To set and get the current record, the instance of the *currentRecord* method in *AxSalesTable* must be overridden. The override must apply the following template.

```
protected TableName currentRecord(TableName _tableName = tableName)
{
    if (!prmisdefault(_tableName))
    {
        super(_tableName);
        tableName = _tableName;
    }
    else
    {
        super();
    }

    return tableName;
}
```

The *super* call in *currentRecord* executes the *currentRecord* instance method on the *AxInternal-Base* class. The *currentRecord* instance method uses the logic shown in Figure 9-6.

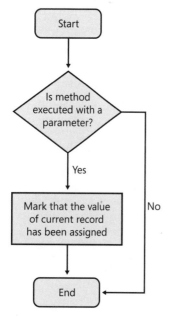

**Figure 9-6** The *currentRecord* method logical flow.

You can see an implementation in the following declaration of the *currentRecord* method on the *AxSalesTable* class.

```
protected SalesTable currentRecord(SalesTable _salesTable = salesTable)
{
    if (!prmisdefault(_salesTable))
    {
        super(_salesTable);
        salesTable = _salesTable;
    }
    else
    {
        super();
    }
    return salesTable;
}
```

To update fields on an existing record, the record must be passed to an *Ax<Table>* object via a table record instance method. The method name must be the same as the table name, and it must apply the following template.

```
public TableName tableName(TableName _tableName = tableName)
{
    if (!prmisdefault(_tableName))
    {
        this.setCurrentRecordFromExternal(_tableName);
```

```
        }
        return this.currentRecord();
    }
```

The *setCurrentRecordFromExternal* instance method executes the *currentRecord* methods and clears all internal variables to prepare the object for changes to the new record.

To ensure that all defaulting methods are called before inserting or updating a record, you must override the *setTableFields* method on the *AxInternalBase* class. The method should include a call to all defaulting methods. You can see part of the implementation in the following declaration of the *setTableFields* method on the *AxSalesTable* class.

```
protected void setTableFields()
{
    SalesTableLinks     salesTableLinks;
    ;
    super();

    useMapPolicy = false;

    this.setCashDisc();
    this.setCommissionGroup();
    this.setContactPersonId();
    this.setCurrencyCode();
    this.setCustAccount();
    this.setCustGroup();
    this.setDeliveryAddress();
    this.setDeliveryCity();
// And so on…
```

# The Query

An important feature of the *Axd* classes is their ability to serialize and deserialize the class instance objects of Dynamics AX–specific XML documents. The schemas for these documents are generated by iterating the query, defining the schemas, and using the names of the *Ax<Table>* classes and their properties to name the XML elements.

A *<table>* element is created for each table in the query. Each of these *<table>* elements contains a list of all the properties of the corresponding *Ax<Table>* class for which there is a *parm<Fieldname>* get/set method. You must adhere to naming conventions, because you cannot assign attributes to X++ class field names and methods to indicate whether you should be able to serialize the field values. After the elements representing properties, still embedded within the *<table>* element, is a series of *<child-table>* elements that represent the children of the *<table>* element as defined in the query. If a *<table>* element in the query has no children, it contains only elements representing the *parm<Fieldname>* properties of the corresponding *Ax<Table>* class.

> **Note** The query can hold only one root table. Having more than one root table will cause the framework to throw an error and stop the execution.

To implement a 1:*n* relationship, you must set the *Join* mode property on the query equal to *outerJoin*. You are advised to do this whenever there is no particular reason for keeping a 1:1 relationship. In most documents included with Dynamics AX, this approach is enforced; only queries involving the *InventDim* table have an inner join clause.

# The Axd Wizard

The purpose of the Axd Wizard is to simplify and automate the development and maintenance of *Axd* and *Ax<Table>* classes and reduce the risk of errors caused by *Ax<Table>* classes that are out of sync with the underlying Dynamics AX tables. The wizard helps you identify manual analysis and coding tasks by removing the mechanical part of the development and allowing you to concentrate on the business logic. The wizard interaction is illustrated in Figure 9-7.

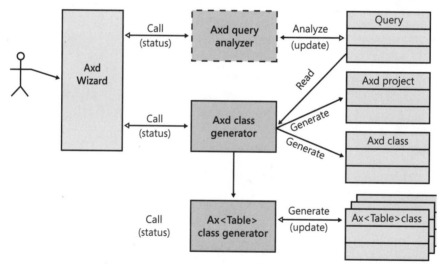

**Figure 9-7** The Axd Wizard.

You must provide an existing query as input, state the name and label for the *Axd* class, and select the actions to be generated (*read, readList, create, createList, findEntityKeys, findList*). An *Axd* class is generated. The wizard generates all methods from templates with to-do comments inserted where manual action is needed. If only outbound actions (*read, readList, findEntityKeys, findList*) are selected, you will have an opportunity to choose whether *Ax<Table>* classes should be generated.

If the *Ax<Table>* class is new, the basic skeleton is generated containing *parm<Fieldname>* methods with the correct parameter types and return types for every field on the underlying

Dynamics AX tables that is marked as visible and is neither a system field nor marked for deletion (that is, prefixed with DEL). For existing *Ax*<Table> classes, the *Ax*<Table> class generator adds any missing *parm*<Field> methods, verifies the signature of existing *parm*<Field> methods, and optionally fixes any discrepancies in the method signatures. The *Ax*<Table> class generator will not delete any existing *parm*<Fieldname> methods from an existing *Ax*<Table> class, even if the corresponding field has been removed from the underlying table. It is not necessary to issue any to-do comments in the case of deleted elements; if you do so, the *Ax*<Table> class will not compile and an error will automatically be issued.

The *Ax*<Table> class generator provides the following services:

- Adds to-dos to the generated *Ax*<Table> class skeleton, highlighting any manual analysis or coding tasks required by you.

- Identifies write references for each field. This means that you must use the Dynamics AX Cross-Reference tool to identify all places in the application source code where the field is assigned a value or the value is updated. This information is needed to reverse-engineer the defaulting and validating logic for each field. The generated skeleton includes clickable links to all the code fragments updating the field value. The *Ax*<Table> class generator logs a warning if the cross-reference information is not current.

- Identifies value mapping for each field. It determines whether the extended data type of the field is a specialization of one of the extended data types for which the *Ax*<Table> classes must perform value mapping; if it is, it updates the signature of the *parm*<Field> method.

In addition to the output mentioned previously, the Axd Wizard generates a job that will generate the XML schema for the newly generated *Axd* class.

## Customizing an Existing XML Document

For an example of how to customize an XML document, assume that a new table containing several illustrations per inventory item is implemented in one of your customer-specific solutions. Now you want to include the illustrations with all purchase orders sent out as XML documents. The custom table layout for this example appears as shown in Figure 9-8.

**Figure 9-8**   Custom table layout.

The first step is to modify the query *AxdPurchaseRequisition* to also include the *ItemIllustration* table, the new table in the example custom solution. Figure 9-9 shows how the query looks when the new table is added. The boxed area must be added to the query that ships with Dynamics AX 4.0.

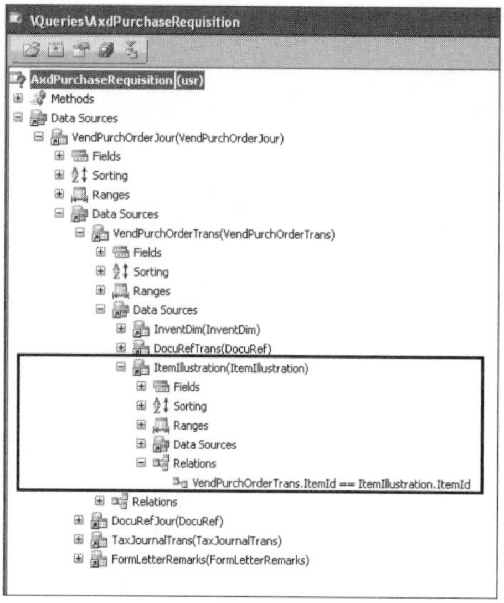

**Figure 9-9**   The query after adding the *ItemIllustration* table.

The second step in the process of customizing your XML document is to run the query through the Axd Wizard. The second page of the wizard prompts you for the query name on which you want to base your solution. In this example, the query name is *AxdPurchaseRequisition*. On the next page of the wizard, shown in Figure 9-10, you state the class name, which has the same value as the query name by default.

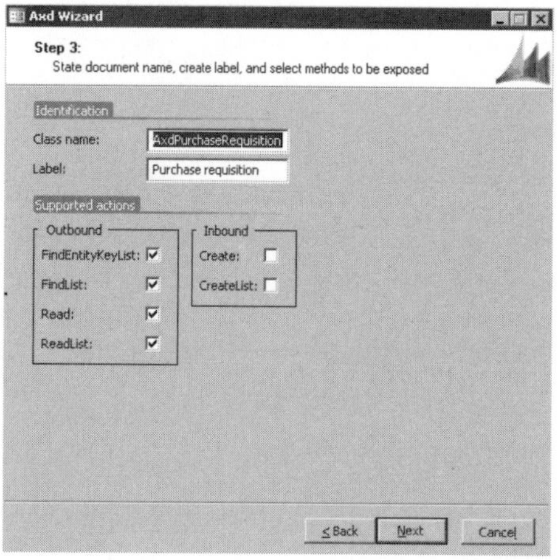

**Figure 9-10**   The wizard page on which you choose the actions that the XML document should support.

The remaining fields are indifferent to the processing, because no modifications will be made to existing *Axd<Document>* classes. If you carefully created the relationships in the query, the wizard can construct all required code in the *prepareForSave* method.

On the next page, select the first check box to generate new *Ax<Table>* classes. The second check box, which is optional, updates existing *Ax<Table>* classes, which will probably be current already.

After you complete the wizard, you must fix potential compilation errors and all the to-dos that the Axd Wizard produces. First, you remove the caching if it is not needed. You do this by removing the two methods called *CacheObject* and *CacheRecordRecord*. When removing these classes, you must also remove the two static variables from the class declarations *cacheRecordIdx* and *cacheObjectIdx*. Assume that *InventDim* is not influencing the Illustration; then you simply remove the optional parameter so that the *parmItemId* method looks like this.

```
public str parmItemId(str _itemId = '')
{
    DictField    dictField;
    ;
    if (!prmisdefault(_itemId))
    {
        dictField = new DictField(tablenum(ItemIllustration),fieldnum(ItemIllustration,
ItemId));
        this.validateInboundItemIdString(_itemId,dictField);
        if(this.valueMappingInbound())
        {
            item = _itemId;
        }

        this.setField(fieldNum(ItemIllustration, ItemId), _itemId);
    }

    if (this.valueMappingOutbound())
    {
        return conpeek(this.axSalesItemId('', itemIllustration.ItemId),1);
    }
    else
    {
        return itemIllustration.ItemId;
    }
}
```

This concludes the implementation of the new table, and you can re-register the *AxdPurchase-Requisition* query from Basic\Setup\Application Integration Framework\Action to publish the new XML schema.

# The Entity Key Class

The *AifEntityKey* class is used for all operations that require one or more specific records and also as a return value from all *create* and *createList* operations. An *AifEntityKey* instance uniquely identifies a transaction in a Dynamics AX database. It consists of a table ID, the field IDs for a unique index of that table, and the values of the respective fields. In addition, it holds the record ID of the retrieved records. The following code shows a partial implementation from the *AxdBaseCreate* class.

```
protected void setEntityKey()
{
    Map      keyData;
    ;
    keyData = SysDictTable::getKeyData(axBcStack.top().currentRecord());

    entityKey = AifEntityKey::construct();
    entityKey.parmTableId(axBcStack.top().currentRecord().TableId);
    entityKey.parmRecId(axBcStack.top().currentRecord().RecId);
    entityKey.parmKeyDataMap(keyData);

// More code lines go here.

}
```

# The Send Framework

The send framework, implemented in the *AxdSend* API, provides the functionality to send documents that are associated with no specific endpoint and have no unique entity key used to scope the document. The exact range of records, such as a range of ledger accounts, is selected by the user. Dynamics AX includes several default documents that use this feature, such as *AxdChartOfAccounts* and *AxdPricelist.*

The send framework provides default dialog boxes for selecting endpoints and ranges for a document and enabling generation of XML documents with multiple records. The framework allows you to provide specific dialog boxes for documents that need more user input than the default dialog box provides. The framework is not intended for documents that can be identified by a publicly known unique entity key and have inherent endpoints associated with them.

The default dialog box includes an endpoint drop-down list and, optionally, a Select button to open the standard query form. The query is retrieved from the *Axd<Document name>* class specified by the caller. Many endpoints can potentially be configured in the AIF, but only a few are allowed to receive the current document. The lookup shows only the endpoints that are valid for the document, honoring the constraint set up for the *read* and *readList* actions for the current document.

The framework requires minimal coding to support a new document. If a document requires you to simply select an endpoint and fill out a query range, most of the functionality will come from the framework without additional coding.

The framework implements a standard dialog box, as shown in Figure 9-11.

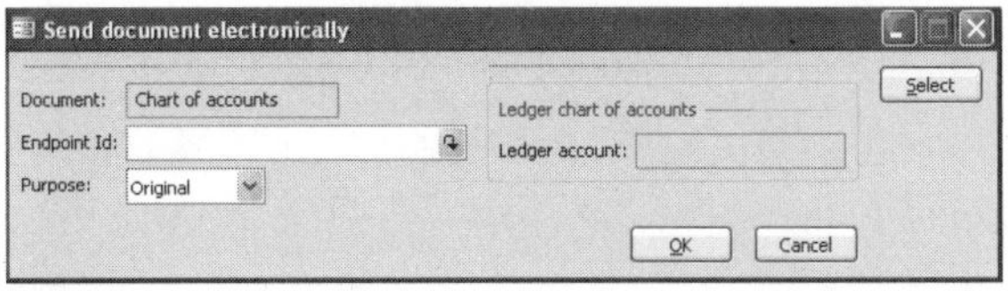

**Figure 9-11**   The Send Document Electronically dialog box for the Chart Of Accounts XML document.

If a document requires a more specific dialog box, you simply inherit the *AxdSend* class and provide the necessary user interface interaction to the dialog box method. In the following code example, an extra field has been added to the dialog box . You simply add one line of code (shown in bold in the following code sample from the *AxdSendChartOfAccounts* class) to implement *parmShowDocPurpose* from the *AxdSend* class and to make this field appear on the dialog box.

```
static public void main(Args args)
{
    AxdSendChartofAccounts        axdSendChartofAccounts ;
    AifConstraintList             aifConstraintList;
    AifConstraint                 aifConstraint;
    ;
    axdSendChartofAccounts        = new  AxdSendChartofAccounts();
    aifConstraintList             = new AifConstraintList();
    aifConstraint                 = new AifConstraint();

    aifConstraint.parmType(AifConstraintType::NoConstraint);
    aifConstraintList.addConstraint(aifConstraint);

    axdSendChartofAccounts.parmShowDocPurpose(true) ;

      axdSendChartofAccounts.sendMultipleDocuments(classnum(AxdChartOfAccounts),A
ifSendMode::Async,aifConstraintList) ;

}
```

Sorting is not supported in the send framework, and the query structure is locked to ensure that the resulting query will match the query defined by the XML document framework, which is why these sorting and structure limitations are enforced by the *AxdSend* class. The query dialog box shows only the fields on the top-level tables because of the mechanics of queries with an outer join predicate. The result set will very likely be different from what would be expected from an end-user perspective. For example, restrictions on inner data sources will only filter these data sources, and not the data sources that contain them. The restrictions are imposed on the user interface to match the restrictions on the query when using the *findList* method on the document.

# Security

By default, record-level and column-level security are applied to all data retrieval. However, in some cases it is crucial that record-level and column-level security be ignored, such as when transmitting invoices. In such a case, it is essential that the customer be presented with the same data as actually posted, regardless of the security settings for the person invoking the document. The following example shows how to override the default behavior.

```
protected void unpackPropertyBag(AifPropertyBag _aifPropertyBag)
{
    AxdSendContext  axdSendContext = AxdSendContext::create(_aifPropertyBag);
    ;
    // Get send context properties.
    ...
    this.security(axdSendContext.parmSecurity());
    ...
}
```

To prevent spoofing, you can implement the notion of constraints. Constraints essentially filter the endpoints that are potential legal recipients of an XML document. An example of a constraint is a customer associated with specific endpoints configured in the AIF. Immediately before transmission, the framework verifies that all constraints in the XML to be sent are legal for the endpoint chosen.

The *getConstraintList* method populates the list of *AifConstraint* objects present in the parameter list with the constraint type and the constraint ID. This helps prevent spoofing. The method is abstract in the *AxdBase* class and must be implemented by all derived classes. The following is an example of an overridden *getConstraintList* method.

```
protected void getConstraintList(Common _curRec,
                                 AifConstraintList _constraintList)
{
    AifConstraint   aifConstraint = new AifConstraint();
    SalesTable      salesTable;
    ;
    if (_curRec.TableId != tablenum(SalesTable))
    {
        throw error(strfmt("@SYS23396",funcname()));
    }
    salesTable = _curRec;
    aifConstraint.parmId(salesTable.CustAccount);
    aifConstraint.parmType(AIFConstraintType::Customer);
    _constraintList.addConstraint(aifConstraint);
}
```

# Chapter Summary

This chapter introduced the XML document framework and explained its environment, which resides between the ordinary business logic and the actual transports in and out of Dynamics AX. The chapter also explained that the structure of the XML mirrors the internal data structure. When you create documents, the primary tasks are creating the relevant AOT query, running the Axd Wizard, and then verifying the code of the generated classes and, in some cases, also implementing business logic to address value validation, value mapping, and value defaulting.

This chapter also explained why little work is necessary to modify existing XML documents. In many cases, you must only update the AOT query and run the Axd Wizard.

Finally, the send framework was covered. The chapter explained that not all documents have a native recipient. Such documents must have a form in which the end user can choose the desired endpoint at run time.

# Part III
# Under the Hood

# Chapter 10
# The Enterprise Portal

The objectives of this chapter are to:

- Introduce the Enterprise Portal.

- Provide insight into the Web framework design and run-time components.

- Illustrate Application Object Tree and Microsoft Windows SharePoint Services integration.

- Describe the steps necessary to develop and customize Web applications on the Enterprise Portal.

- Explain content management and search integration.

- Offer a detailed look at Enterprise Portal security.

## Introduction

The Enterprise Portal (or EP) is the Web platform for Microsoft Dynamics AX 4.0 that is used to Web-enable and customize existing or new applications in Dynamics AX. The Dynamics AX EP enables customers, vendors, business partners, and employees to directly access relevant business information and collaborate and conduct business transactions with Dynamics AX through personalized, role-based Web portals.

Users access the EP through a Web browser remotely or from within a corporate intranet, depending on how the EP is configured and deployed. The EP contains a set of default Web pages and user roles that can be used as-is or modified to meet the customer's unique business needs. Roles are designed for casual users of the system, to be used in a self-service manner to fulfill business requirements. The EP serves as the central place for users to access any data, structured or unstructured, such as transactional data, reports, charts, key performance indicators (KPIs), documents, and alerts, from anywhere and collaborate. Figure 10-1 shows the home page of an example EP site.

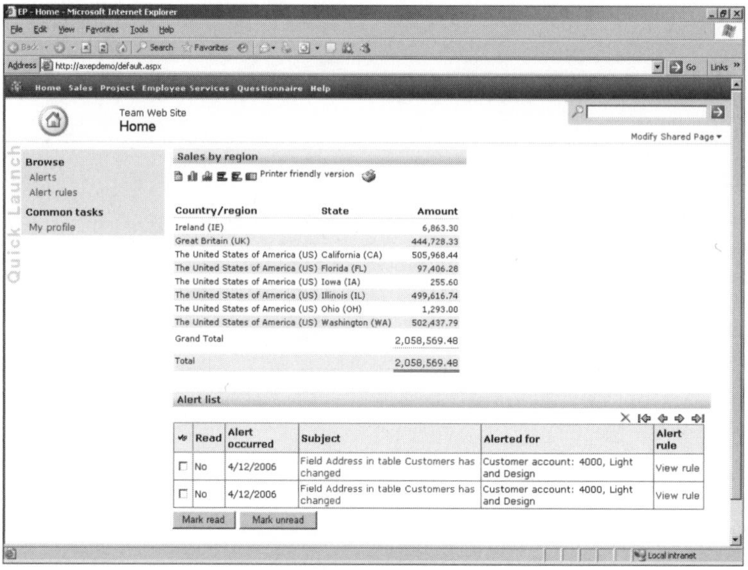

**Figure 10-1**    An example of an EP home page.

# Inside the Enterprise Portal

The EP is built on Windows SharePoint Services, and it combines all the rich content and collaboration functionality in Windows SharePoint Services with structured business data in Dynamics AX.

The EP Web pages use EP Web Parts and other Windows SharePoint Services Web Parts. The EP Web Parts present information and expose functionality from Dynamics AX and are implemented with Windows SharePoint Services Web Part technology. EP Web Parts connect to Weblets in the EP Web framework through the Dynamics AX .NET Business Connector and render the HTML generated by the EP Web framework. Windows Share-Point Services Web Parts fulfill content and collaboration needs. Figure 10-2 shows the high-level components of the EP.

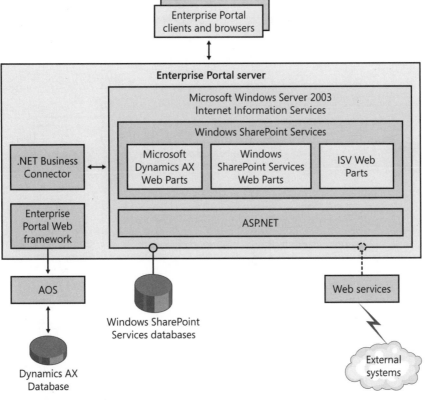

**Figure 10-2**   The EP components.

# Page Processing

The first step in developing or customizing an application on the EP is to understand the interactions between the user's browser on the client and the EP on the server when the user accesses the EP. Figure 10-3 shows a simplified version of the page request process.

The following is the sequence of interactions that occurs when a user accesses the EP:

1. The user opens the browser on his or her machine and navigates to the EP URL.

2. The browser establishes a connection with the Internet Information Services (IIS) Web server.

3. Based on the authentication mode enabled, IIS authenticates the user.

4. After the user is authenticated, the Windows SharePoint Services Internet Server Application Programming Interface (ISAPI) filter intercepts the page request and checks the user's right to access the site.

5. After the user is authorized by Windows SharePoint Services, the Web page routes to a custom Microsoft ASP.NET page handler object of Windows SharePoint Services.

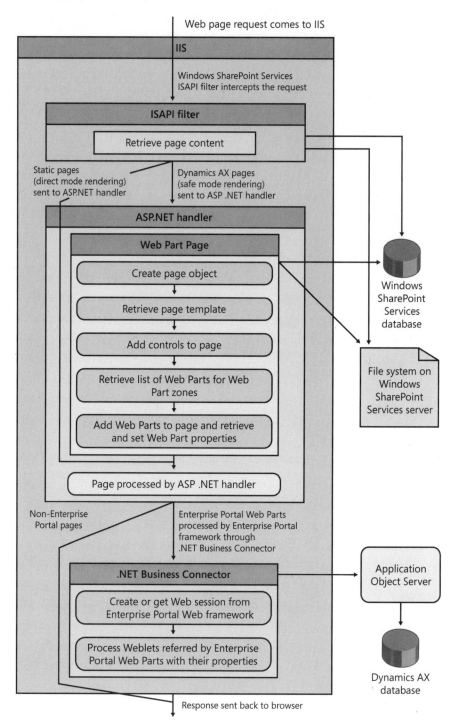

**Figure 10-3**   The EP page request flow.

6. The page handler pulls the Web Part Page data from the Windows SharePoint Services content database. This data contains information such as the page template ID, the Web Parts used and their properties, and the page template stored on the file system on the Web server. Windows SharePoint Services then processes the page and creates and initializes the Web Parts on the page with properties and personalization data, if any.

7. When initialing the Web Parts, the EP initializes a Web session with the EP Web framework through the .NET Business Connector.

8. The Web framework checks for Dynamics AX authorization, and then calls the appropriate Web handlers in the Web framework to process the EP objects that the Web Part points to.

9. The framework runs the business logic and returns the processed HTML to the Web Part.

10. The Web page assembles all the HTML returned by all the Web Parts and renders the page to the user's browser.

11. The EP Web session ends.

As you can see in this sequence, all the business logic, data retrieval, and user interface elements are defined in the MorphX development environment and stored in the Application Object Tree (AOT), and Windows SharePoint Services handles the overall page layout and personalization. Figure 10-4 shows a sample EP topology.

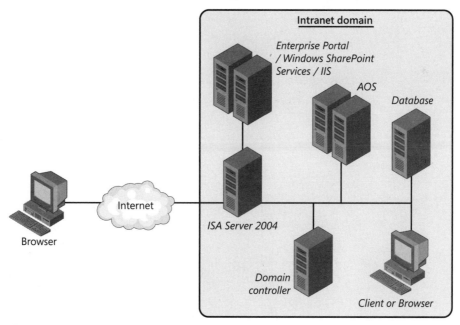

**Figure 10-4**  An EP topology.

# The Web Framework

The EP Web framework is the design-time and run-time Web infrastructure of MorphX. This includes the kernel, X++ classes, designer and debugging tools, data binding, security trimming, metadata store, and the mechanism for linking all of these components together. In combination with the EP Web Parts and Windows SharePoint Services, they constitute the Web user interface to Dynamics AX.

Weblets are the basic unit of the Dynamics AX Web elements that generate HTML. Web forms, Web reports, and Web menus are some of the specialized Weblets in Dynamics AX included for rapid Web development. Web forms allow you to quickly build a Web user interface by using pre-built Dynamics AX Web controls; these controls are then tied to the Dynamics AX data source and the event model to define the business logic. Reports and Web reports have a finer-grained designer surface (with grid-snapping, pixel-positioning, and so on) for defining the layout and binding to a data source, and they include built-in tools for generating summary reports and graphs. Web menus allow you to build and render the navigation hierarchy or site map. Dynamics AX comes with many other specialized, ready-to-use Weblets that can be used in the EP, such as the Category Browser Weblet, Favorite Record Weblet, and Questionnaire Weblet.

Developers can use these pre-built Weblets or build their own by using MorphX. Data retrieval, business logic, and presentation as defined in Web forms, reports, Web reports, or custom-built Weblets. The navigation and menu hierarchy are defined in Web menu items and Web menus. Web menu items are secured in the AOT by applying the security key.

Figure 10-5 shows all the Web nodes in the AOT.

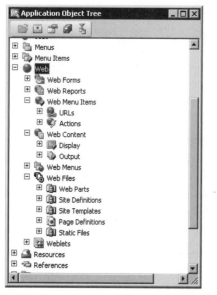

**Figure 10-5**   The Web nodes in the AOT.

# Web Forms

Web forms derive from Weblets and are generally the Web elements used for creating, editing, viewing, and listing business data from Dynamics AX in the EP. Essentially, you can consider a Web form to be a Web element that returns a stream of HTML about transactional data that can be rendered and displayed in a Web browser. One or more application tables can be set as the data source for Web forms. Dynamics AX includes several default Web form controls that can be used in Web forms. Programmed entirely in HTML, the Web form controls are like very thin wrappers of the standard HTML controls. Dynamics AX includes the following Web form controls: *WebButton*, *WebCheckBox*, *WebComboBox*, *WebDate*, *WebEdit*, *WebGrid*, *WebGroup*, *WebGuid*, *WebImage*, *WebInt64*, *WebInteger*, *Weblet*, *WebRadioButton*, *WebReal*, *WebStaticText*, *WebTab*, *WebTabPage*, and *WebUserDefined*.

The layout for all the controls, except *WebUserDefined*, is pre-built. This enables developers to perform rapid application development simply by binding the controls to the data source. If the development requires more granular control in regard to how the layout generates HTML, the *WebUserDefined* Web control can be useful, because its layout method can be overridden.

You can place Web form controls into groups by using a WebGroups control, and you can arrange them on the page by using standard HTML. This means that you position every element relative to other page elements, and that you cannot define absolute positions for the controls.

Web form controls also offer support for data lookup to provide a way for the user to fill in fields from a pre-populated list. The Web lookup uses the relations that are added to table fields or extended data types to list the possible values for the field. The *LookupButton* property on a Web control specifies whether a Lookup button must be displayed next to the control. The default setting is *Auto*, which displays the Lookup button. The *LookupMethod* property specifies how the lookup should be handled for the control. The default setting displays the lookup form or list in a separate browser window.

## Web Form Runtime

At run time, the EP Web framework instantiates an object of the *WebFormHTML* class. The *WebFormHTML* object reads the Web form's design and calls the appropriate *layoutControls* method passing the control's ID. This method then calls the control type–specific methods, such as *layoutText*, *layoutDate*, or *layoutButton*. These methods render the Web form controls by using the appropriate HTML controls. The *controlName* method on the *WebFormHTML* class returns a name that uniquely identifies the control, whether it is data-bound or not. This identifier is used by the *SetControls* method, which is called when the Web form is posted. The *SetControls* method does the opposite of the *layoutControls* method—it reads the values of the Web form controls and puts them back into the form's data sources by calling the *getParm* method on *WebSession* class, passing the unique control names provided by the layout methods. Figure 10-6 shows a simplified Web form HTML generation sequence diagram.

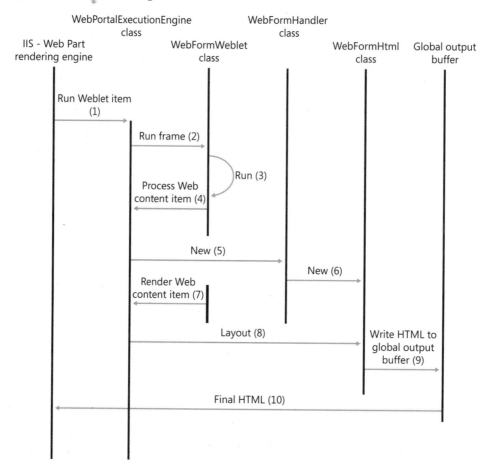

**Figure 10-6**   Web form HTML generation (simplified).

## Web Form Events

The EP is stateless. On every round trip to the server, pages are instantiated, processed, rendered, and disposed of. If a page needs to keep its state between server round trips, when a server-side event is processed, the ASP.NET page framework uses a hidden input control, referred to as ViewState, to store the state of the page and all the controls in that page in encoded format to persist between Web requests. A server round trip to the same page for processing a server-side event is commonly referred to as a postback. A postback occurs when a page is submitted in the browser or when the Web control on the page raises a server-side event that necessitates a postback. The EP Web framework persists the value of the Web controls in the ASP.NET ViewState during page postback. No custom coding is required to persist the Web control values between postbacks. However, information other than the values stored in ViewState must be handled separately.

The EP Web framework provides several events that allow you use X++ code to persist the values of variables and temporary tables into ViewState during postbacks in Web forms. The first such event is called the *loadViewState* event. You can use this event to load the in-memory variables from ViewState. The *loadViewState* event occurs before the *init* and *run* events are executed. After the *run* event lays out the controls and updates them with postback data, the framework updates the ViewState with postback data.

The second event to occur that is related to ViewState is the *loaded* event. By this time, the changes to the data source and Web controls have been applied, the controls on the Web page have been updated with postback data, and the ViewState of the page has been updated with postback data. This is the right place to use the in-memory variables retrieved from ViewState and subsequently update the Web controls, if necessary.

The third event related to ViewState is called *saveViewState*. This event can be used to save the in-memory variable into ViewState. The *SaveViewState* event occurs after the *layout* event.

Figure 10-7 shows the sequence of Web form events.

## Web Form Example

Imagine that you have been asked to create a Web page in your company's EP so that salespeople can create a sales order from anywhere on the Web. To accomplish this task, you create a Web form called *EPSalesTableCreateTunnel* and add data sources and Web controls. Because this Web form is designed like a wizard to make creation of sales orders more intuitive, the sales basket ID must be preserved between the pages of the wizard. To do this, a *salesBasketId* variable is declared in the class declaration. The value of *salesBasketId* is persisted into ViewState in the *saveViewState* event. Between page posts, the variable is loaded from ViewState in the *loadViewState* event. The following code illustrates this task.

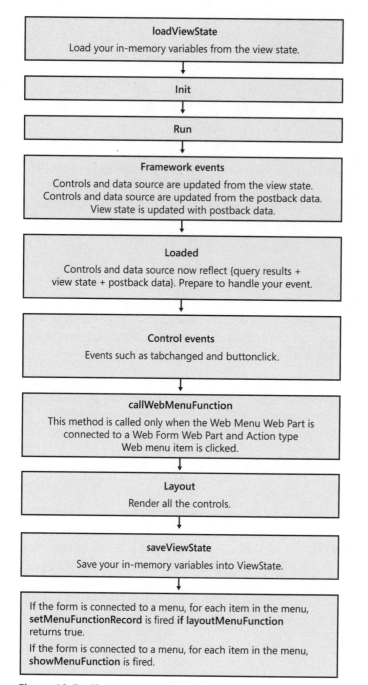

**Figure 10-7** The sequence of Web form events.

```
public class FormWebRun extends ObjectRun
{
SalesBasketId   salesBasketId;
#define.SalesBasketId('EPSalesTableCreateTunnel_SalesBasketId')
}
private void loadViewState()
{
 super();
 if ( this.viewStateContains(#SalesBasketId))
       salesBasketId = this.viewStateItem(#SalesBasketId);
}
private void init()
{
 if ( element.args().dataset() == tablenum(SalesBasket))
       salesBasket = element.args().record();
       salesBasketId = salesBasket.SalesBasketId;
}
private void loaded()
{
  super();
  if ( !salesBasketId)
       {
    salesBasket_da.create();
       salesBasketId = salesBasket.SalesBasketId;
       }
}
private void saveViewState()
{
  super();
  if ( salesBasketId)
       this.viewStateItem(#SalesBasketId,salesBasketId);
}
```

Figure 10-8 shows the *EPSalesTableCreateTunnel* Web form in the AOT, the property pane of the Web Form Web Part pointing to this Web content, and the run-time view.

# Reports and Web Reports

Reports and Web reports present and summarize business data in a ready-to-use format that helps the user analyze the business and make decisions. Reports are generally static and read-only, but advanced reports can be delivered as interactive Web pages with drilldown capabilities. Reports can also be presented as graphs with rich visualizations.

## Web Report Runtime

At run time, the *Run* method on the Web report Weblet instantiates and executes the Web report. It creates an instance of the *WebReportRunEx* class. This class extends the system class *ReportRun*, which generates a report with multiple output options, such as printing to a printer, previewing on screen, or sending to your own custom-built output device.

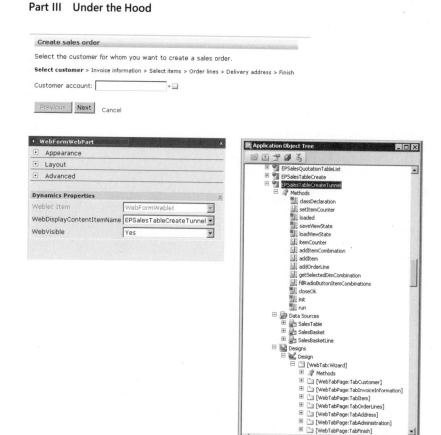

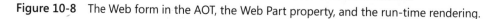

**Figure 10-8**    The Web form in the AOT, the Web Part property, and the run-time rendering.

To render the report on the EP, the kernel uses the *WebReportHTML* class to handle the run-time execution. *WebReportHTML* extends the *WebReportBase* class, which extends the system class *ReportOutputUser*. Generation of the HTML for the Web report takes place in the *WebReportHTML* class. Like Web forms, the *WebReportHTML* class uses HTML tables to arrange the sections and controls, thereby taking advantage of the browser's rendering engine. Although the kernel processes the report, it delegates the processing of the report to the *WebReportHTML* class, rather than printing or previewing it, thereby providing full control of the format and display of the report to the developer. When the Web report runs, the kernel calls the proper methods on the *WebReportHTML* object in exactly the same order as when the report is processed in the kernel and sent to the screen or the printer. For this purpose, the *ReportOutputUser* system class has several layout methods that can be overridden, thus giving the X++ class that extends it total display control of the report.

The first method called when a Web report is executed is the *startReport* method. The kernel passes the *PrintJobSettings* class for the report to the method, allowing you to specify any default settings for the Web report based on the information found in *PrintJobSettings*. After the kernel is finished processing the Web report, it calls the *endReport* method on the *WebReportHTML* object. The actual processing of the Web report takes place between these two calls. Based on the Web report design, all the other methods on the object will be called when the control flow from the kernel is passed on.

The methods in *WebReportHTML* are divided into two groups: methods that handle report sections and methods that handle formatting of the report control types (or fields). Typically, each section in the report has two methods (or events): a start method and an end method. Examples include *startPageHeaderSection*, *endPageHeaderSection*, *startBodySection*, *endBodySection*, *startProgrammableSection*, and *endProgrammableSection*.

Both start and end methods receive a parameter: an object of the system class for the particular section. The kernel, for example, passes an object of type *OutputBodySection* to the *startBodySection* method, which allows you to read body properties such as *ArrangeMethod* and *NoOfColumns* for the section and format the output of the method accordingly.

As a general rule, sections are arranged by using HTML tables, such as <TABLE> in the start method and </TABLE> in the end method, because they act as containers for report fields (as they do in standard reports). The organization of Web report content into HTML tables, rows, and cells gives Web reports several advantages over the strategy used when formatting standard reports. However, because the controls do not have absolute coordinates and sizes, this approach also has some limitations. The most obvious limitation is that you cannot control exactly where the controls are positioned on the Web page.

Figure 10-9 shows a simplified Web report HTML generation sequence diagram.

In reports, the *WebMenuItemType* and *WebMenuItemName* properties of the control assign a Web menu item to a control so that, when activated, the control calls the Web menu item to provide drillthrough capabilities. The *CSSClass* and *LabelCSSClass* properties let you assign a cascading style sheet class to the control and its label, respectively.

## Web Report Example

For example, consider a scenario in which you need to create a report in table format and set the style of the table rendered based on the properties set on the report. In such a case, you could use the *startPageHeaderSection* and *endPageHeaderSection* methods of the *WebReportHTML* class to insert the beginning and ending HTML table tags, along with the correct style elements. Later, the body section will be processed based on the report design.

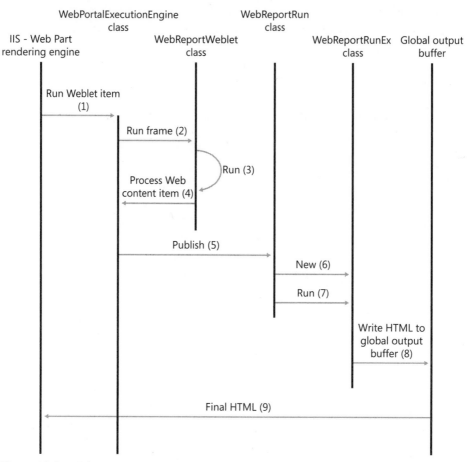

**Figure 10-9** Web report HTML generation (simplified).

```
public void startPageHeaderSection(OutputPageHeaderSection section)
{

    this.beginContainer();

        this.write('<table class="' + _cssClassReportHeader + '" border="0"
cellspacing="0" cellpadding="0">\n');

    if (!_isReportTemplate)
        this.beginRow();

}
public void endPageHeaderSection(OutputPageHeaderSection section)
{
    if (!_isReportTemplate)
        this.endRow();
```

```
        this.write('</Table>\n');
        this.endContainer();

        _isReportTemplate = false;

}
```

Figure 10-10 shows the EPSalesByRegion report in the AOT, the property pane of the Web Report Web Part pointing to this Web content, and the run-time view.

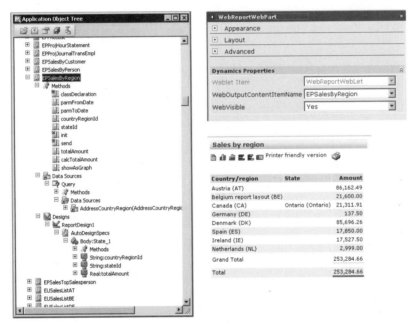

**Figure 10-10**   The report in the AOT, the Web Part property, and the run-time rendering.

# Weblets

Weblets are the basic unit of the Dynamics AX Web elements that generate HTML. If the needs of the Web page cannot be met by the standard design templates for Web forms and reports, Weblets can give you complete programmatic control of the presentation.

## Weblet Runtime

For the Weblet to be instantiated and called from the Web framework, it must have a certain set of properties and methods that control its behavior at design time and run time.

Properties control the layout and behavior of Weblets. The *WebLet* class offers an interface to manage the properties. The *addProp* method adds a property to the Weblet. The *addProp* method takes the name of the property and the default value for the property. The *Name* parameter must be the name of an extended data type. The *getProp* method retrieves the value of a property and takes the name of the property as a parameter and returns its value.

The following are two important methods of Weblets:

- **createProperties**   Creates the properties for the Weblet.

- **run**   Produces the HTML code for the Weblet and sends it to the browser. This method is called by the framework at run time, which is when the Web Part containing the Weblet is processed and sent to the browser.

## Weblet Example

The following is a code sample for a very simple example of the *WebDateTimeWebLet* class. The Weblet has two properties: one to show or hide the time, and one to show or hide the date.

```
class WebDateTimeWebLet extends WebLet
{
}
void createProperties()
{
    super();
    this.addProp(extendedTypeStr(ShowTime),TRUE);
    this.addProp(extendedTypeStr(ShowDate),TRUE);
}
str designView()
{
    str ret;

    ret += '<A>';
    if (this.getProp(extendedTypeStr(ShowDate)))
        ret += date2StrUsr(today());
    if (this.getProp(extendedTypeStr(ShowTime)))
    {
        if (ret)
            ret += ' ';

        ret += time2str(timeNow(),0,0);
    }
    ret += '</A>';
    return ret;
}

  void run()
{

    webSession().writeTxt(this.designView());
}
```

Figure 10-11 shows the *WebDateTimeWebLet* class in the AOT, the property pane of the Generic Web Part pointing to this Weblet, and the run-time view.

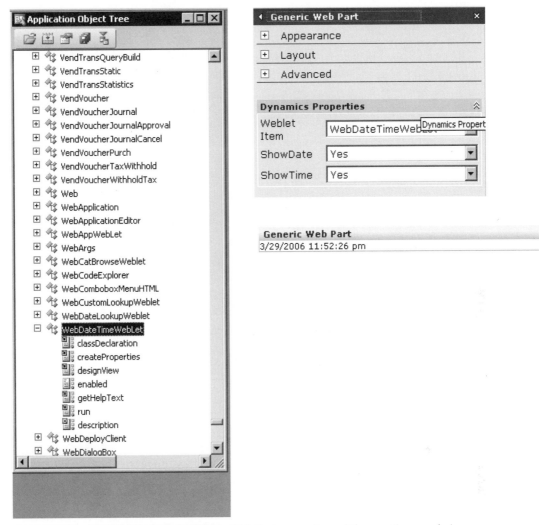

**Figure 10-11**    The Weblet in the AOT, the Web Part property, and the run-time rendering.

## Securing Web Elements

To securely expose Web forms and reports through Web Parts in Windows SharePoint Services, you must create a Web content node pointing to the Web form or report in the AOT. You can assign security keys, along with other configuration keys, to the Web content node. You can assign parameters if the Web forms or reports make use of parameters to exhibit different behavior on different pages. In custom-built Weblets, you can assign a security key at the Weblet level in the AOT. Figure 10-12 shows the *SecurityKey* property of a Web content node.

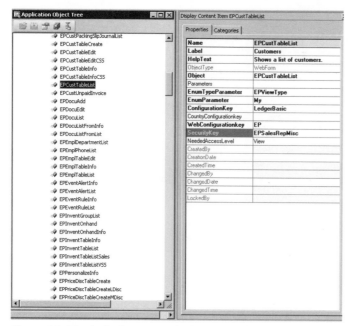

**Figure 10-12** Assigning a security key to Web content.

The primary level of security is at the Weblet level. For Web forms and reports, a second level of security is at the Web content level. These two levels of security are specific to Web elements. In addition, both Web and non-Web applications in Dynamics AX can be secured at the data access level by table, field, or record-level security settings. Figure 10-13 shows the security applied in EP Web Parts.

Using security keys is the primary way to set permission levels for groups in Dynamics AX. After you configure security keys to define the features that the application should include, the keys are used to grant permissions to the individual groups. Permissions are granted to groups to regulate how they are allowed to work with each object in a database. You can apply more granular control by creating your own groups, assigning appropriate permissions to those groups, and then adding users to those groups.

At logon, the security keys determine user access. Access depends on the user groups that the user belongs to and the company or domain of which the user is a member. Access to the individual security key can depend on its parent, so the calculation must be done hierarchically. Access to Web menu items, Web content, and Weblets can be set up in the User Group Permissions dialog box (accessible from Administration\Setup\ Security\User Group Permissions). You can use the Viewing list to apply a different view to the tree structure. Figure 10-14 shows the User Group Permissions dialog box.

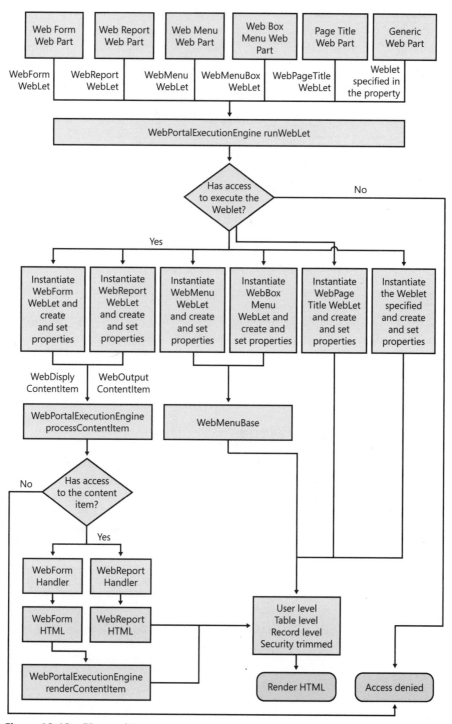

**Figure 10-13**   EP security.

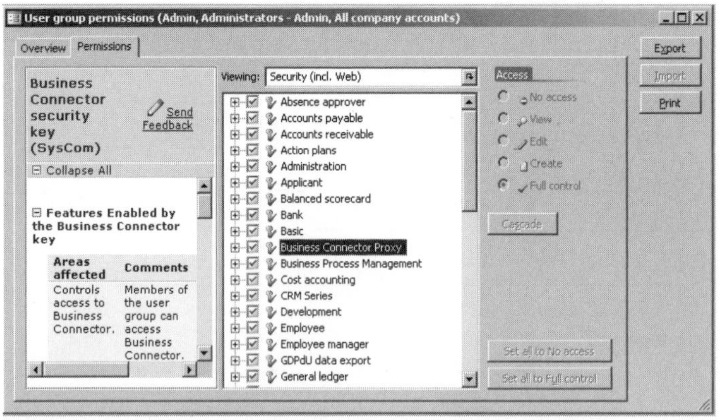

**Figure 10-14**    The User Group Permissions dialog box.

If a user does not have access to a Web menu item, that item will not appear on the Web menu. If the Web menu item is linked from other Web forms or reports for which the user has access, the item linked with the Web menu item appears as text, rather than as a link.

If the user does not have access to Web content or a Weblet on a Web page, the content or Weblet will not be rendered on the page. The Web Part properties also limit the items displayed in the drop-down list based on the user permissions for the underlying objects. Moreover, the types of operations that are allowed on these objects depend on the access level set for the objects on the groups to which the user belongs.

## Web Menu Items and Web Menus

Web menu items are the basic navigational tool in the Web framework. They can point to either a URL or a class. Web menu items can be secured by security keys. You can use menu items in Web menus as navigational elements on a Web page or in controls such as buttons on Web forms to provide links. You can hide or show the links based on user permissions. You can use Web menu items as the glue and navigation mechanism throughout the Web site to help you create sites that are dynamic and versatile.

The Web framework uses the *WebLink* class to generate hyperlinks. This class has all the properties and methods needed by the framework to pass information back and forth between the browser and the server. More importantly, it has a method that returns the URL for the link. *WebLink* also has several methods for passing record information.

A Web menu defines the hierarchical navigational scheme and comprises Web menu items, submenu headings, and references to other Web menus. Web menus can be included on the Web page through the Web Menu Web Part. Different orientation and layout options exist to allow flexible use of Web menus on Web pages. Figure 10-15 shows the AOT nodes for Web menus and Web menu items.

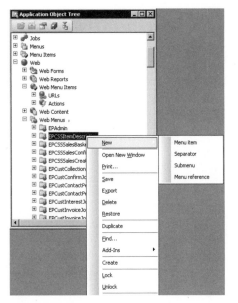

**Figure 10-15**   A Web menu and a Web menu item.

# Web Parts and Web Part Pages

Web Parts are pluggable and reusable Windows SharePoint Services components that generate HTML and provide the foundation for modular presentation of data. This data is easily integrated to assemble a Web page and support customization and personalization. The EP comes with a standard set of Web Parts that expose the business data from Dynamics AX. The Web Parts map to the Web elements in the Web framework. They include the following:

- **Web Form Web Part**   For rendering Web content of type display (Web forms)

- **Web Report Web Part**   For rendering Web content of type output (reports and Web reports)

- **Web Menu Web Part**   For rendering Web menus

- **Box Menu Web Part**   For rendering a Web menu as a list of tasks, mainly on the content portion of Web pages

- **Page Title Web Part**   For displaying the title of a Web page with the Dynamics AX label system

- **Generic Web Part**   For rendering any Weblet

Figure 10-16 shows the design surface of the EP Web Part Page with all of the EP Web Parts.

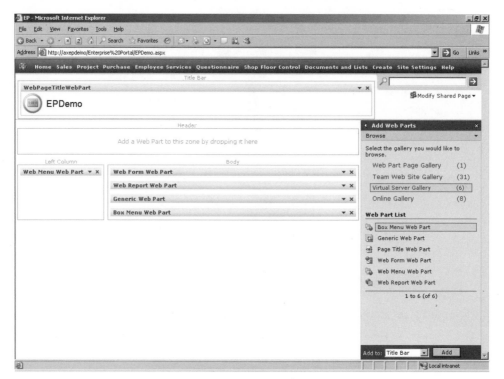

**Figure 10-16**   The EP Web Parts list on a Web Part Page.

In design mode, when the property pane is invoked for these Web Parts, the EP Web framework creates a Dynamics Web Property Manager (DWPM) object to get the property sheet information from Dynamics AX. The *editProperties* method of the corresponding *Weblet* class is called to get the properties and related items. The DWPM uses these properties, their types, and the values and dynamically adds server-side HTML controls to the property sheet. The user sees seamlessly defined properties for the Weblet through the Web Part in Windows SharePoint Services.

DWPM subscribes to the server-side control events for the controls it adds and receives notification through postback events about property value changes. DWPM then notifies the Weblet of the property change through the *propChanged* callback. After the properties are set on the Web Part, the DWPM calls the *createTextFromWeblet* method on the *WebLet* class to get the configuration string and persist it as a property of the Web Part. At run time, the Web framework gets the configuration string and instantiates the appropriate Weblets, generates HTML, and renders the assembled page.

When the Web Part Page is processed, Web Parts might need to exchange information and alter their content or functionality. Web Parts accomplish this by using standard connectable interfaces. A connectable interface is a set of methods used by the Web Part infrastructure to enable the transfer of information between Web Parts that do not have prior knowledge of each other.

Web Menu and Web Form Web Parts use this Web Part connection mechanism to pass the information required to identify a record in a Dynamics AX database, known as *record context*, to the pages invoked by menu items. The Web Form Web Part implements the *ICellProvider* interface, and the Web Menu Web Part implements the *ICellConsumer* interface. In the EP, the Web Part connection is an optional technique that is used when the menu needs to get the context from the Web form to pass to the invoked menu item, or when the Web form needs to control the elements displayed on the Web menu. Web Part connections are based on the notion of providers and consumers. The Web Form Web Part is the provider of record context, and the Web Menu Web Part is the consumer of this information when the Web Part connection is enabled. The Web Part connection can be enabled or displayed in Windows SharePoint Services design mode when the page contains one or more Web Menu Web Parts or Web Form Web Parts. Figure 10-17 shows the design view of a Web Part Page with connected Web Parts.

At run time, if the Web form is connected to the Web menu, the *showMenuFunction* method on the Web form is called for every Web menu item in the Web menu before rendering the menu link. The Web form controls whether the Web menu item is displayed for the given context.

For example, when the *EPSalesTableList* Web form is displayed, and the intention is to hide or show the *EPSalesTableCreate* link on the connected Web menu based on the *SalesType* listed, the *showMenuFunction* method on the *SalesTableList* Web form implements the following logic.

```
boolean showMenuFunction(MenuFunction mf)
{
    boolean ret;

    switch (mf.name())
    {
        case weburlitemstr(EPSalesTableCreate)   : ret = salesTable.SalesType == Sales
Type::Sales; break;

        default : ret = true; break;
    }

    return ret;
}
```

Moreover, for every Web menu item on the Web menu, the *setMenuFunctionRecord* method on the Web form is called and provides the Web form with the control to set the record context to the Web menu item for it to use. The *setMenuFunctionRecord* is called only when the *layoutMenuFunction* method on the Web form returns true.

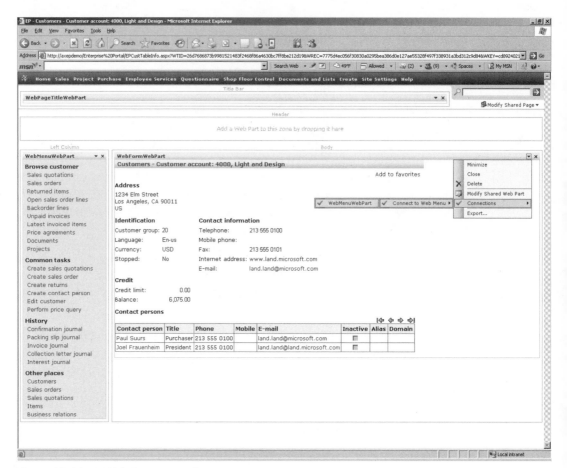

**Figure 10-17**   A Web Part connection page.

For example, when the *SalesTableList* Web form is connected to a Web menu, and it must set the record context to all the Web menu items in that Web menu except for the one named *EPCustInvoiceJournalListCSS*, the *setMenuFunctionRecord* method on the *Sales TableList* form implements the logic shown in the following sample code. This causes the record context of all the links in the Web menu (except *EPCustInvoiceJournalListCSS*) to be appended as a query string.

```
Public Common setMenuFunctionRecord(WebMenuFunction _menuFunction, Common _cursor)
{
    Common ret;

    ret = super(_menuFunction, _cursor);

    if (_menuFunction.name() == weburlitemstr(EPCustInvoiceJournalListCSS))
    {
        ret = null;
    }
```

```
    return ret;
}
```

The *callWebMenuFunction* method on the Web form is called once for the Web menu item when that Web menu item link is clicked. For example, if a *SalesQuotationList* Web Part page can be called from two different places, such as from a Customer page and a Business Relation page, and the Create SalesQuotation link on the SalesQuotationList page must pass the customer information or the business relation information, depending on where it was called from, the Web Part connection can be useful.

In such a scenario, the sales quotation table list Web form would implement a *callMenuFunction* method with logic that would only be invoked when the Web Form Web Part was connected to the Web Menu Web Part, as shown in the following code sample.

```
public boolean callMenuFunction(WebMenuFunction _menuFunction, Object _webLink)
{
    if (_menuFunction.name() == weburlitemstr(EPSalesQuotationTableCreate))
    {
        if (element.args().record())
        {
            switch(element.args().record().TableId)
            {
                case tablenum(CustTable) :
                _webLink.tableid(tablenum(CustTable));
                _webLink.record(element.args().record());
                _webLink.menufunction(new
WebUrlMenuFunction(weburlitemstr(EPSalesQuotationTableCreate)));
                break;

                case tablenum(smmBusRelTable) :
                _webLink.tableid(tablenum(smmBusRelTable));
                _webLink.record(element.args().record());
                _webLink.menufunction(new
WebUrlMenuFunction(weburlitemstr(EPSalesQuotationTableCreate)));
                break;

            }
        }
        else
        {
            _webLink.menufunction(new
WebUrlMenuFunction(weburlitemstr(EPSalesQuotationTableCreateTunnel)));
        }

        return false;
    }

    return true;
}
```

Figure 10-18 shows the Web Part life cycle in ASP.NET and the sequence of events relating to Web Part connection.

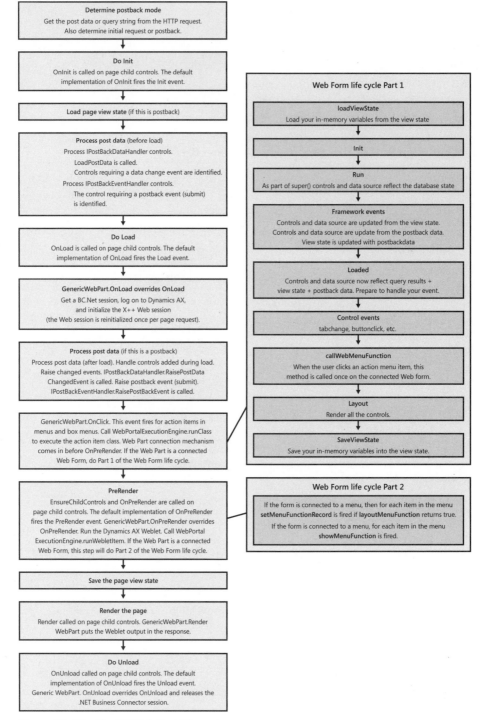

**Figure 10-18**   The EP Web Part life cycle.

# Web Files

SharePoint sites can be customized by using site definitions or custom templates built on existing site definitions. The site definitions encompass multiple files located on the file system on each Web server. These files define the structure and schema for the site. You can create new site definitions by copying the existing site definition files and modifying them to meet the needs of the sites that are created based on these site definitions. You create custom templates by using the user interface to customize existing sites and storing them as templates.

The EP site definition files are stored in the AOT under Web\Web Files\Site Definitions. The custom templates are stored under Web\Web Files\Site Templates. The Enterprise Portal Deployment Wizard, accessible from Administration\SetUp\Internet\Enterprise Portal \Manage Deployments, deploys these files from the AOT to the Web server file system and Windows SharePoint Services.

The EP includes one default site definition for each supported language. Each site definition has two configurations: one for authenticated users and another for public Internet users. The EP does not include any site templates. However, the AOT provides a mechanism for partners and customers to add custom templates and let the Enterprise Portal Deployment Wizard deploy these files.

The EP site definition contains the page templates embedded with the Web Menu Web Part to display the global menu and the Page Title Web Part to display the page title using Dynamics AX labels. So, when a page is created in the EP, these two Web Parts are already available on the Web page, creating consistency across all Web Part Pages in the EP and supporting rapid application development. Figure 10-19 shows some of the key files that constitute the site definition and their locations on the Web server.

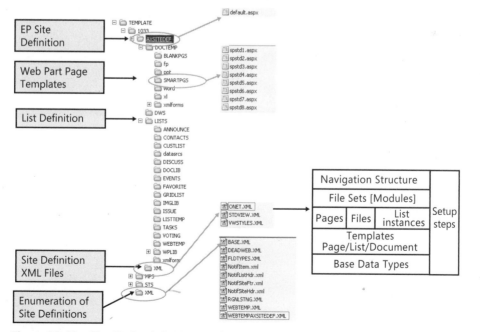

**Figure 10-19**   The EP site definition on the Web server.

The EP Web Parts are packed into one Web Part package and kept in the AOT under Web\ Web Files\Web Parts. If necessary, partners and customers can add their own Web Part package under this node, and the EP will deploy these files to the Global Assembly Cache on the Web server and add a safe control entry in the Web.config file.

The Web Part Pages display one or more Web Parts. Web Parts provide an easy way to build powerful Web pages that display a variety of information, ranging from a Dynamics AX data view of a list in the current site to external data presented in custom-built Web Parts. You create Web Part Pages in Windows SharePoint Services by using Microsoft Internet Explorer. You simply drag Web Parts onto Web Part Pages and set their properties by using pre-populated lists. You can edit Web Part Pages by using either Microsoft Office FrontPage or Internet Explorer. You can use Internet Explorer to edit a page and change its Web Parts, the order of the Web Parts, and Web Part properties. You can use Office FrontPage for logo or graphic insertion, document library or list customization, theme and style application, and so on. Pages edited with FrontPage, however, cannot be imported into the AOT.

All the Web Parts on a Web page share the same Dynamics AX Web session. You can import Web Part Pages created in the EP site in Windows SharePoint Services into the AOT as page definitions by using the Import Page tool from the Web menu items of type URL. The page definitions are stored in the AOT under Web\Web Files\Page Definitions.

The page definitions imported into the AOT automatically create pages when a site is created with the EP site definition. The *PublicPage* property of the page definition node determines whether the page should be created on the public site. All the pages are created for the authenticated site. The page definition *Title* property, if used, must be set to a label so that the page displays the localized title when used with different language settings.

Style sheets and other necessary files, such as lookup files and images for the EP, are kept under Web\Web Files\Static Files. The style sheets are referred to by the Web Parts. Each Web Part applies the current theme and uses it to refer to the corresponding EP style sheets.

For example, if the folder name of the currently applied theme in the EP site is called After-noon, the Web Part refers to the EPAfternoon.css file from the Enterprise Portal folder. This folder is found on the Web server under <*drive*>:\Program Files\Common Files\Microsoft Shared\web server extensions\60\TEMPLATE\LAYOUTS.

If the Web Part does not find a corresponding file, the default EP style sheet is applied. Dynamics AX includes a few default style sheets for EP mapping to some of the most commonly used Windows SharePoint Services themes. However, partners and customers can extend these and create style sheets that map to any Windows SharePoint Services theme. Windows SharePoint Services also allows you to create new themes.

## The Import Page and Deploy Page Tools

The Import Page tool and the Deploy Page tool provide a seamless integration between the AOT and the Windows SharePoint Services Enterprise Portal site. The Import Page tool allows pages created in Windows SharePoint Services to be pulled into the AOT from the Web menu items of type URL. The new page definitions are in XML format and stored under Web\Web Files\Page Definitions.

Importing pages into the AOT as page definitions allows the pages to be automatically created when a Windows SharePoint Services site is created with the EP site definition. This allows the pages to use the Dynamics AX labels for the page titles so that the same page definitions can be used for sites in different languages.

You can also deploy the page definitions at the individual page level. This allows you to import pages created in Windows SharePoint Services (set as the AOT site in Administration \Setup\Internet\Enterprise Portal\Web Sites in the Dynamics AX client) into the AOT as page definitions by using the standard Dynamics AX Import and Export utilities (accessible under Administration\Periodic\Data Export/Import). Then you can deploy the newly created or updated page definitions to the current SharePoint site as Web Part Pages without having to delete and re-create the site, thereby avoiding problems with data migration from the old site to the new site.

The Import Page and Deploy Page tools use the AOT site setting specified in the Web Sites dialog box as the source or target SharePoint site. Figure 10-20 shows the AOT with the Import Page and Deploy Page menus.

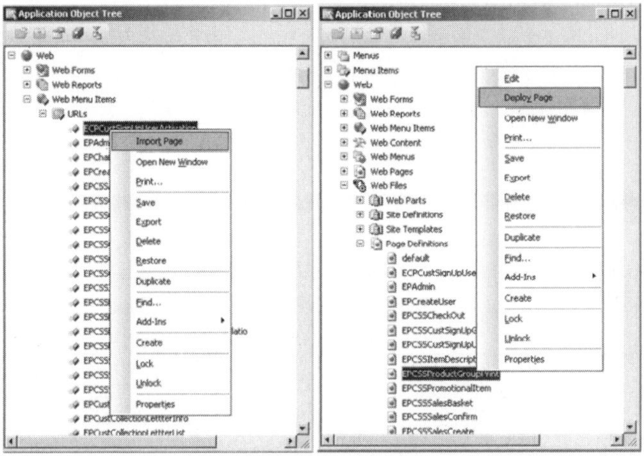

**Figure 10-20**   The Import Page and Deploy Page tools.

## Record Context and Encryption

Record context is the interface for passing information through the query string to a Web Part Page to retrieve a record from Dynamics AX. The EP uses record context to locate a record in the Dynamic AX database and display it in a Web form for viewing and editing.

Some of the parameters of the query string to the EP Web Part Page as record context are as follows:

- WTID = Table ID
- WREC = Rec ID
- WFID = Field ID
- WKEY= Unique Record KEY (the field identifier and the value of the field for the record to be retrieved)

These parameters are passed either in a query string or in post data on Web pages. If they were passed in clear text, an unauthorized user could view data or perform actions by guessing and manipulating their values. To help secure the EP, Dynamics AX encrypts these parameters by default on the front-end Web server itself. This makes it impossible to guess or manipulate the parameters. For debugging and Web development purposes, the administrator may turn the encryption off in the Enterprise Portal Parameters dialog box, which is located in Administration \Setup\Internet\Enterprise Portal\Parameters. If the record-level security and other data-level security are already active and no security threat exists, turning off the encryption could result in better performance. However, keeping encryption turned on is highly recommended.

Whether encryption is on or off, the functionality of the Web elements in the EP must remain the same. A URL generated for one user cannot be used by any other user. And, if the encryption expiration interval is set, a user cannot use the URL generated for him or her after the specified number of days has elapsed. The encryption key is stored in the database and protected by the Application Object Server (AOS) and Business Connector Proxy accounts.

## Web Page Development Flow

To put the information in this section into practice, consider the following steps of a developer whose task is to create a Web page that displays data from a table in Dynamics AX.

| Step | Details |
| --- | --- |
| Step 1: Create a Web form in the AOT under Web\Web Forms. | Create a Web form in MorphX, set the data source, business logic, and user interface controls, and store the Web form in the AOT. |
| Step 2: Create Web content under Web\Web Content. | Create Web content in the AOT, point it to the Web form created, and set the security and configuration keys and parameters. Store the Web content in the AOT. |

| Step | Details |
| --- | --- |
| Step 3: Create a Web page in Windows Share-Point Services. | Create a Web page in Windows SharePoint Services, using the Web Form Web Part and other Web Parts, such as Web Menu Web Part, as needed. Point the Web Part properties to the respective items in the AOT, and store the Web page in the SharePoint site. |
| Step 4: Create a Web menu item in the AOT under Web\Web Menu Items. | Create a Web menu item in the AOT, set the URL property to the page created in the SharePoint site, and store the Web menu item in the AOT. |
| Step 5: Import the page definition from Web\Web Menu Items, and set the page title in Web\Web Files\Page Definitions. | Import the page definition on the Web menu item saved in the AOT. This creates a node under Page Definitions in Web\Web Files in the AOT. Set the PageTitle and ImageResource properties of the newly created page definition node, and store it in the AOT. |
| Step 6: Add the Web menu item to the Web menu under Web\Web Menus. | Add the Web menu item to the Web menu in the AOT so that it appears on Web pages that have the Web Menu Web Part and points to the Web menu. |

The following steps describe how to display data from the CustTable table in the EP.

| Task | Steps |
| --- | --- |
| Task 1: Create a Web form. | 1.  Start the Dynamics AX client. |
| | 2.  Press CTRL+D to open the AOT, or click the **AOT** button on the toolbar. Open a second instance of the AOT and position it next to the first. |
| | 3.  In the left AOT window, expand the **Data Dictionary** node. |
| | 4.  Expand the **Tables** node. |
| | 5.  Locate the *CustTable* table. This is the main table that stores customer master file information. |
| | 6.  In the right AOT window, expand the **Web** node. |
| | 7.  Right-click the **Web Forms** node, and then click **New Web Form**. |
| | 8.  Expand the new Web form. Then drag the *CustTable* table identified in Step 5 from the left AOT window onto the data sources of the new Web form in the right AOT window. |
| | 9.  Expand the **Designs** node of the new Web form. |
| | 10. Right-click **Design**, point to **New Control**, and then click **WebGrid**. |
| | 11. Right-click the new **WebGrid** control, and then click **Properties**. |
| | 12. Set the *DataSource* to *CustTable*. |
| | 13. Right-click **WebGrid**, point to **Add New Control**, and then click **WebEdit**. |
| | 14. Right-click the new **WebEdit** control, and then click **Properties**. |
| | 15. Set the *DataSource* to *CustTable* and the *DataField* to *Name*. |
| | 16. Click **Save All** on the AOT toolbar of the right AOT window. |

| Task | Steps |
|------|-------|
| Task 2: Create Web content. | 1. In the left AOT window, expand **Web**, expand **Web Content**, and locate **Display**. |
|  | 2. In the right AOT window, expand **Web**, expand **Web Forms**, and locate the new Web form created in Task 1. |
|  | 3. Drag the Web form from the right AOT window to the Web **Content\Display** node in the left AOT window. |
|  | 4. Click **Save All** on the AOT toolbar of the left AOT window. |
| Task 3: Create a Web page. | 1. In Internet Explorer, navigate to the home page of the EP by entering the URL. |
|  | 2. Click **Create** on the global menu. |
|  | 3. Scroll to the bottom of the page and click **Web Part Page**. |
|  | 4. Type a name for the page, select the **Header, Left Column**, and **Body** layout templates, and then select the Document Library as the Enterprise Portal. |
|  | 5. Click Create. |
|  | 6. Drag **WebFormWebPart** from **Web Part List** on the right side to the Body section. |
|  | 7. Click the down arrow on the **WebFormWebPart**, and then click **Modify Shared Web Part**. |
|  | 8. For **WebDisplayContentItemName**, select the Web content created in Task 2. |
|  | 9. Click **OK**. |
| Task 4: Create a Web menu item. | 1. Start the Dynamics AX client. |
|  | 2. Press CTRL+D to open the AOT, or click the **AOT** button on the toolbar. |
|  | 3. In the AOT, expand the **Web** node, expand **Web Menu Items**, and locate **URLs**. |
|  | 4. Right-click **URLs**, and then click **Create New URL**. |
|  | 5. Right-click the new URL item, and then click **Properties**. |
|  | 6. Click the URL property, and then click **Lookup** to open the **Browse for Folder** dialog box. |
|  | 7. Navigate to the **Enterprise Portal** folder and expand it. |
|  | 8. Select the Web page created in Task 3, and then click **OK**. |
|  | 9. Click **Save All** on the AOT toolbar of the right AOT window. |
| Task 5: Import the page definition and set the page title. | 1. Right-click the new URL item and then click **Import Page**. |
|  | 2. In the AOT, expand the **Web** node, expand **Web Files**, expand **Page Definitions**, and locate the new node created as a result of importing the page in the preceding step. |
|  | 3. If the page needs a title, right-click the **Page Definition** node and set the PageTitle property to a label. If no title is needed, clear the PageTitle and ImageResource properties of the **Page Definition** node. |

| Task | Steps |
|------|-------|
| Task 6: Add the Web menu item to the Web menu. | 1. Start the Dynamics AX client. |
| | 2. Press CTRL+D to open the AOT, or click the **AOT** button on the toolbar. |
| | 3. In the AOT, expand the **Web** node, and then expand **Web Menus**. |
| | 4. Locate the Web menu to which the new Web menu item will be added. For example, locate the **EPHomeForEmployee** Web menu, and then expand the **Browse** node. |
| | 5. Right-click the **Browse** node, point to **New**, and then click **Menu item**. A new menu item is created in this node. |
| | 6. Right-click and set the *MenuItemType* property to *Url*, and then set the *MenuItemName* property to the Web menu item created in Task 4. |
| | 7. Click **Save All** on the AOT toolbar of the right AOT window. |

The newly created page will be available from the EP site, including a new link to the page on the EP home page.

# Content Management

Organizations today generate abundant information that is stored in various locations and in many different formats. However, if this information is largely inaccessible to people working for the organization, they cannot leverage the value of the information in their daily tasks. A great deal of knowledge and insight is often contained in overlooked or inaccessible content.

Web portals can be viewed as a mechanism by which disparate information can be aggregated and to which access can be systematically provided to anyone who needs the information. The EP combines the rich content management and collaboration functionality of Windows SharePoint Services with the ability to access business data in one location. In addition to a central document store, Windows SharePoint Services provides a completely customizable and extendable rich metadata store and a list infrastructure to support any ad hoc semi-structured data needs, such as announcements, links, discussion boards, issue tracking, surveys, calendaring (including presence information), and personalization.

The EP also exposes the document handling functionality of Dynamics AX. You can attach notes and files to records by using the Dynamics AX document handling functionality. When you create notes, you flag them as internal or external, which allows you to control which documents the notes will appear on. For example, you could set internal notes on a sales order to print on a packing list but not on an invoice. Any file that can be launched from the user environment can be attached to a record within Dynamics AX from the client, as well as from the EP.

# Common Search

Search is an intrinsic and essential feature of any Web portal, providing quick and easy access to the information that people need. Business information exists in many forms. Along with structured data stored in databases of business systems, volumes of unstructured information are stored in documents and collaboration content. When too much information is stored in many places and in many forms, users often spend enormous amounts of time using traditional methods to look for the right information and lose focus on their primary task.

The EP provides users with the ability to search both business data and SharePoint site content to locate data quickly. The Dynamics AX Data Crawler indexes business data stored in the Dynamics AX database, and Windows SharePoint Services indexes SharePoint lists and documents. Common search in the EP combines both of these result sets as one search result. The search results from all sources are presented in a combined and consistent way and display the details of items when opened. A seamless user experience ensures that the search behavior is integrated into the EP in the way that users interact with the portal.

Windows SharePoint Services uses Microsoft SQL Server full-text search for documents and lists. The search capability is not available with installations of the Desktop Engine version of SQL Server (WMSDE/MSDE); it is available only with SQL Server databases. After SQL Server is configured to support full-text indexing, you can enable or disable Windows SharePoint Services search by using the SharePoint Central Administration page.

Dynamics AX uses the Data Crawler to index business data. The Data Crawler is configured and executed from the Dynamics AX client by clicking Basic\Setup\Data Crawler. The tables and fields that are indexed by the Data Crawler are configurable. If either the Data Crawler or the Windows SharePoint Services search engine is not enabled and configured, Dynamics AX data cannot be searched in the EP.

Common search uses the *SearchLinkRefType* and *SearchLinkRefName* properties of the underlying table to generate the link on the search results page for Data Crawler search queries. For example, the *CustTable* table has the *SearchLinkRefType* property set to *URL* and the *SearchLinkRefName* property set to *EPCustTableList*. When the Data Crawler indexes the *CustTable* table and a search query matches the record stored in the table, the search results page displays the matching customer records with links to the *EPCustTableList* Web page.

By enforcing table-level security, record-level security, access type (internal or external), and menu-level security, Dynamics AX displays only the search results for records to which the user has access. If the user is not a valid Dynamics AX user, the Dynamics AX section of the search results page is not displayed.

Figure 10-21 shows the components of common search.

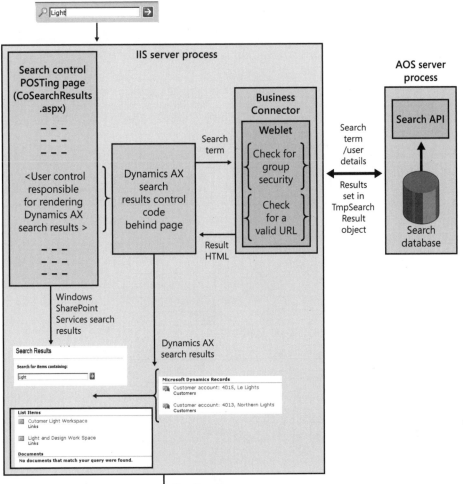

**Figure 10-21**   The EP common search components.

If a user conducts a search from within a SharePoint list or document library, the results are restricted to that list or document library, and the search experience is the same as for any Windows SharePoint Services site. If a user conducts a search from a Web Part Page, the common search combines the search results from both Windows SharePoint Services and the Dynamics AX Data Crawler. The diagram in Figure 10-22 illustrates the common search flow.

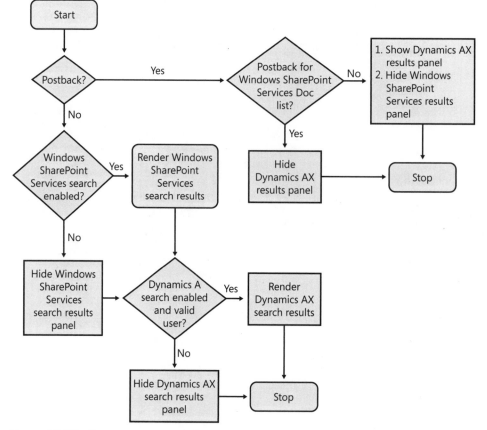

**Figure 10-22**    The common search flow.

# Security

In the EP, Dynamics AX security is layered on top of, and depends on, the security of underlying products and technologies, such as Windows SharePoint Services and IIS. For externally facing sites, communication security and firewall configurations are also important for helping to secure the EP.

The EP has two configurations in its site definition. The first configuration in the site definition, referred to as Microsoft Dynamics Public, allows Internet customers or prospective customers to view product catalogs, request customer accounts, and so on. The second configuration, referred to as the Microsoft Dynamics Enterprise Portal, is the complete portal for self-service scenarios involving intranet or extranet users for authenticated employees, vendors, and customers.

The Microsoft Dynamics Public configuration has anonymous authentication enabled in both IIS and Windows SharePoint Services so that anyone on the Web can access it. To connect to Dynamics AX, it uses a built-in Dynamics AX user account called Guest. The Guest account is part of the EP Guest user group, which has limited access to Dynamics AX components necessary for the public site to function. The Microsoft Dynamics Enterprise Portal configuration has Integrated Windows authentication or basic authentication over Secure Sockets Layer (SSL) enabled in IIS and Windows SharePoint Services.

This secured site restricts access to users with Active Directory directory accounts who are configured as Dynamics AX users with Web site access enabled for that particular site by the Dynamics AX administrator. You use the User Relations dialog box (accessed from Administration\Setup) to configure users with an employee, vendor, or business relation, or a customer account and contact. Then you can grant them access to the EP sites through Site groups for that Windows SharePoint Services EP site.

Both types of EP site use the Business Connector proxy account to establish connections to the AOS. The Windows SharePoint Services application pool must be configured with a Microsoft Windows domain user account, and this account must be specified as the Dynamics AX Business Connector proxy account for both sites to function. After the connection is established, the EP uses either LogonAsGuest or LogonAs, depending on the type of EP site for the current user, to activate the Dynamics AX security mechanism. Dynamics AX provides various means and methods to limit user access, such as placing restrictions on individual tables and fields, limiting the availability of application features through configuration keys, and controlling user-level security with security keys.

EP security is role based. This means that you can easily group tasks associated with a business function into a role, such as Sales or Consultant, and assign users to this role to give them the necessary permissions on the Dynamics AX objects to perform those tasks in the EP. To give users access to more functionality, you can assign them to more than one role.

The Enterprise Portal Configuration Wizard imports the predefined user group rights from the Resources node in the AOT. This set of roles can easily be extended by importing the user group permissions into the AOT under the Resources node. You assign a user to a role by simply adding the user to the corresponding user groups.

In addition to the Dynamics AX elements, the EP includes SharePoint lists and document libraries, which are secured with SharePoint site groups. The Dynamics AX user groups play no role in controlling access to the SharePoint lists and documents. However, for consistency and simplicity of the EP roles concept, a standard set of SharePoint site groups provides access to a specific set of document libraries and lists when the site is created. You can add new roles by modifying the XML file in the AOT under the Web Files node. Based on their SharePoint site group membership, Dynamics AX users are granted various levels of permission on these Windows SharePoint Services objects.

Figure 10-23 shows the sequence of interactions between the EP components.

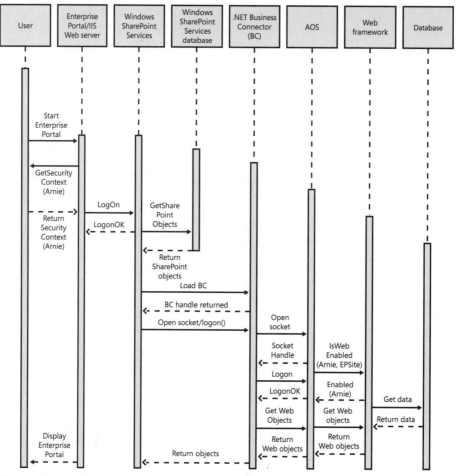

**Figure 10-23** The EP sequence.

# Chapter Summary

This chapter introduced Web development in the Enterprise Portal and provided a detailed look into design and run-time aspects of the Web framework. Through examples, it also demonstrated how to customize and extend the EP to meet your business needs. This chapter covered content management and search functionality in the EP, and it also described how Windows SharePoint Services is used as the Web platform for the Dynamics AX EP. This chapter also covered the security aspects of the EP in detail.

# Chapter 11
# Configuration and Security

The objectives of this chapter are to:

- Introduce the IntelliMorph layout technology.

- Explain how the license and configuration systems affect application functionality throughout the system.

- Describe the security framework and discuss data access security.

## Introduction

Microsoft Dynamics AX 4.0 is targeted toward businesses whose size, location, language, and line of business vary widely. Security system configuration, personalization, and presentation layout become significant features when you are implementing and using the system.

This chapter describes how the Dynamics AX 4.0 application runtime implements configuration and security and how these concepts determine the interface that the user sees. IntelliMorph is the unique technology for designing and developing the application forms, reports, menus, and menu items. The IntelliMorph technology encompasses essential framework elements that influence the final output within licensing, configuration, and security. The licensing and configuration frameworks give you the option to license application modules, thus providing access to various application areas. You may also enable and disable functionality independently of the licensing.

This chapter discusses security in the context of the application runtime, and it also offers details about important security aspects to consider when developing the application. The last section in this chapter covers the concept of data access security, which makes it possible to differentiate business data access across user profiles. This feature enables query construction to extend the table permission options available in Microsoft SQL Server. The feature that differentiates business data access is called the record level security framework.

# IntelliMorph

Although Dynamics AX is an international product with support for multiple countries, languages, company sizes, and industries within the same deployment, it is also an extremely productive development platform that ensures a uniform yet very configurable and automatically arranged layout of application functionality. The unique presentation technology is based on model element properties, configuration and security settings, and personalization, which together lay out the presentation controls on forms, reports, menus, menu items, and corresponding Web elements for each individual user. The technology is called IntelliMorph, and it works with both the rich client and the Web client types in Dynamics AX.

A primary requirement of the IntelliMorph technology design was preparation for international distribution, but with a different approach than other enterprise resource planning (ERP) products; IntelliMorph had to be ready for multiple countries in multiple languages within the same deployment, and it had to offer the same user experience, regardless of the user interface language. This necessitated the design of a metadata-driven and property-driven user interface in which forms, reports, menus, and menu items would react to both global and local configuration and security settings. A positive side-effect of this design is that users can personalize the interface in multiple ways. The personalization has been extended even further in Dynamics AX 4.0, in which an individual user can reference all rich client forms as individual favorites to which they can attach any query.

IntelliMorph automatically arranges functionality based on license codes, configuration and security keys, and personalization—without programmable changes. Figure 11-1 illustrates the filtering structure for the layout of elements such as form, report, menu, and Web.

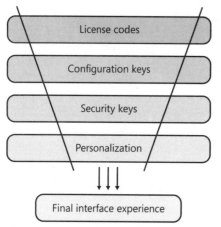

**Figure 11-1**    IntelliMorph presentation structure.

The layout includes the license code that opens the parent configuration key, which holds either the security key references or the configuration key children to the security keys.

Security keys determine access to the menu items that reference available functionality for user groups and individual users. An individual user profile can be connected to multiple user groups, and the complete collection of permissions comprises the maximum security level. The final factor in the interface experience is personalization, which allows the user to modify the user interface by hiding, showing, and configuring the presentation controls.

The elements and their interactions and dependencies are described in greater detail in the following sections, which include a discussion on personalization.

> **Note**   Presentation of the user interface is not limited to support for the IntelliMorph technology; it also provides a rich set of design options for developing Microsoft Windows forms with many different control types, such as ActiveX or ListView controls. Dynamics AX reports also come with their own designer that allows you to visually design a report while using both the X++ syntax and the properties window for arranging and formatting.

# Best Practices

Having an understanding of how the IntelliMorph technology works can help you develop the run-time presentation for application extensions. If you follow the best practice design rules and patterns, you can optimize your use of the IntelliMorph technology and ensure a uniform application run-time interface. The best practice principles focus on using the default property settings for the presentation controls that determine how to present elements and functionality. They also cover the general use of labels, field groups, extended data types, auto groups, security and configuration keys, and menu items. The standard Dynamics AX application is developed using all the best practice rules and patterns, which provide a uniform way of interacting with the application and the underlying business logic. Chapter 4, "The MorphX Development Tools," provides a description of the Best Practices tool. You can find details on the rules and patterns in the Microsoft Dynamics AX SDK.

## Principles for Forms

Designing application forms can be a very time-consuming task if you always design from scratch, especially if your application must run in a multiple-language deployment. This is why the best practice is to create forms and reports by dragging and dropping as often as possible and setting very few properties manually. Occasionally, the system's default property values might not suit the current situation, which is why almost any property can be customized.

When you design the layout of a form for which a table or view is used as the underlying data source, the same field groups and field structures in the original Tables and Views nodes in the Application Object Tree (AOT) will be available in the form node, providing that you moved the table or view by dragging it from one of these nodes to the form's Data Sources node. This gives you the flexibility to move field groups or individual fields from the pool of field groups and fields in the form's Data Sources node to the form's Design node. The data sources should be configured to use the Dynamics AX AutoJoin system that ensures that data is synchronized when two forms are linked. When you work with the layout and property settings, you must keep the Auto or Default settings. This optimizes the use of the auto-arrange technology and limits the need to move pixels to unify and align the form presentation with the rest of the application.

When designing forms, follow the recommendations in the following list where possible to optimize use of the auto-arrange technology. Most patterns are property settings on the form design.

- Use default settings where possible, especially for the attributes *Left*, *Top*, *Width*, *Height*, *Frame*, *WindowResize*, *WindowType*, and *HideToolbar*.

- Use the *DataGroup* attribute when using tables or views as data sources.

- When using the *DataGroup* attribute, change the *AutoDataGroup* property to *Yes*. This adjusts the overall behavior based on the data source behavior.

- Use labels instead of hard-coded strings.

- Add Help text (status bar Help) as labels instead of hard-coded strings.

- Use the *TitleDatasource* property to provide a better and more visible data experience for the user.

- Set the *AutoDeclaration* property to *Yes* if the control features must be accessible from X++ code.

- Use the AutoJoin system where possible.

If your customers require a very unique user experience, there are no design restrictions that prevent you from completely remodeling the user interface. The only disadvantage is that training, flexibility, and upgrade become somewhat more complex.

## Principles for Reports

IntelliMorph is even more important for reports than it is for forms. The best practices for reports primarily involve retaining the default settings for properties. When you design a report, knowledge about the environment in which the report will execute is often unavailable. This type of information includes the following:

- The size of the paper in the user's printer

- The length or content of the labels according to the user's installation profile and language

- Which fields are disabled by security and configuration key settings

- The length of the fields (extended data types) in the user's installation

- The sort order of the data sent to the report

- Whether the user wants to print using the *subtotals* setting or just the *totals* setting
- The default settings for font and font size
- The number of records in the tables from which the report gets its data

You can create two kinds of report designs: Auto (AutodesignSpecs) or Generated (design). You can use Auto for all normal reports and Generated for reports with special functional requirements that cannot be implemented with Auto designs. You can also use the Generated design for reports for which the design is determined externally, such as:

- Reports that are forms with externally determined layouts and where the information is expected to display in very specific positions.
- Reports that are forms for which the design is likely to be adjusted to the customer needs at deployment time. Invoices are one example. Most controls should have their positions fixed (not set to Auto) to simplify moving them by using the Report Designer.

You should follow these design patterns when possible:

- Use default property settings where possible, especially for Orientation, Width, Label, Width of label, and formatting information because fixed settings cause the report controls to disregard the IntelliMorph auto-arrange technology available from the property window.
- Use the Auto design report type when possible.

## Working with IntelliMorph

IntelliMorph provides numerous options for personalizing Dynamics AX forms. These options allow you to move controls, set properties on controls, and add extra fields to forms. Forms are customized at application run time, and settings are saved on a per-user basis. The personalization options can be invoked from multiple places, depending on the type of personalization. The personalization options use the same framework whether a column is hidden via the Command entry on the menu bar, moved within the form runtime by using the mouse, or renamed by using the advanced personalization form.

The advanced personalization form, shown in Figure 11-2, provides the user with customization options.

By using this tool, the user can change the tab page order, move elements around, remove fields, add additional fields from existing form data sources, rename the field, prevent the field content from being edited, change the default field length, and even choose among multiple versions of the form presentation. The personalizations can be shared if, for example, a department wants a common presentation that is different from the standard company presentation and does not want to modify the global form layout.

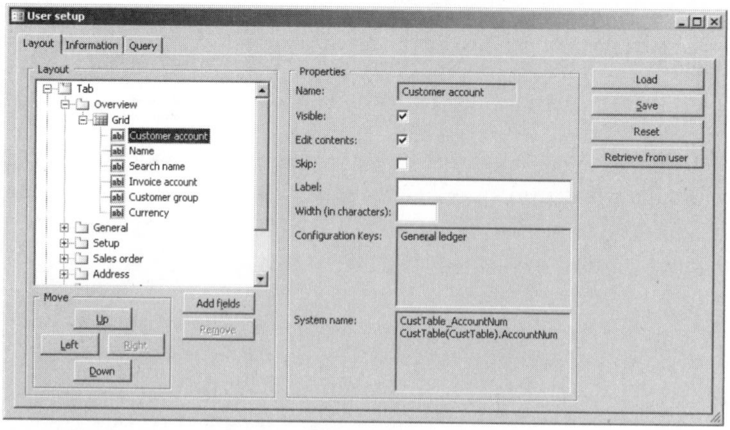

**Figure 11-2**   The advanced personalization form.

To make user personalization work, you must define different levels of personalization by using the form design properties *AllowUserSetup* and *AllowAdd*. There are four levels of personalization as presented in Table 11-1.

**Table 11-1   Personalization Levels**

| Personalization Level | Description | AllowUserSetup | AllowAdd |
|---|---|---|---|
| 1. Limit user personalization of forms | Only the size and position of the form can be changed. You cannot change the properties on the individual controls. Because the position and size of the form are saved (the size is saved if the *SaveSize* property is set to *Yes*), there will be an entry for this form in the *SysLastValue* table, even though no personalization is allowed. | No | No |
| 2. Enable customization of controls | You can change the behavior of individual controls, but you cannot move them or add new controls. You can define personal values for the following properties: *Enabled, Visible, Skip, Width,* and *Label text.* | Restricted | No |
| 3. Enable customization of layout | You can adjust properties on controls and move controls between containers. You can move controls from within the Setup form by dragging or by using the navigation buttons. You can move grid columns within the grid by dragging them directly onto the form. Because this feature gives the user the option to create a tab page that encompasses all the information normally entered for a given record or grid, most forms should support this level of personalization. | Yes | Restricted |

**Table 11-1   Personalization Levels**

| Personalization Level | Description | *AllowUserSetup* | *AllowAdd* |
|---|---|---|---|
| 4. Enable customization of layout and content | You can customize the layout and add new fields from the Setup form. To support this level of personalization, you must move all code to the data source fields. The added controls do not have any code. The properties are the default values for this type of control and data. You can add data fields only. You cannot add unbound controls or controls bound to display methods. | *Yes* | *Yes* |

These personalization levels also depend on how X++ code on the form is used. The kernel can automatically restrict the user setup level if the methods that take the position of the control into account are overridden.

# Licensing and Configuration

Dynamics AX allows licensing of application modules, multiple user types, languages, server technology, the Web framework, database logging, record-level security, development tools, run-time execution, and integration frameworks. The system elements and application modules are locked by license codes that must be unlocked by license keys.

Unlocking a license code is the initial step in configuration of the Dynamics AX system because the license codes reference the configuration key that links to the physical functionality. You unlock the license code by using the License Information form, shown in Figure 11-3, which is accessed from Administration\Setup\System\License Information.

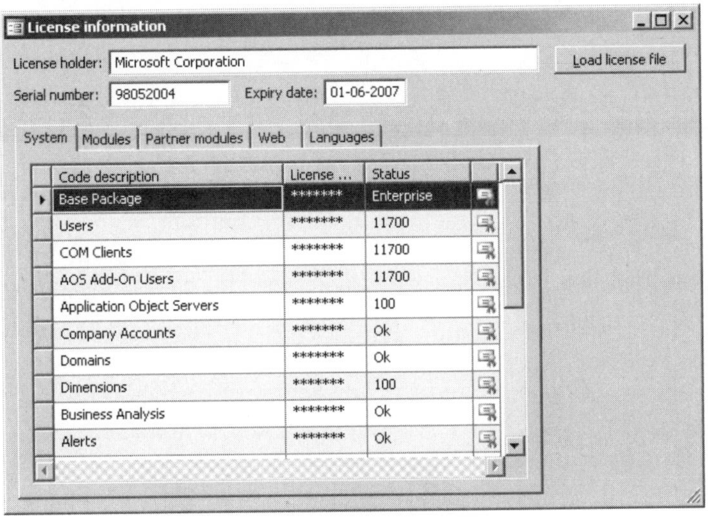

**Figure 11-3**   The License Information form.

You enter the license codes manually or import them by clicking the Load License File button. All the license codes and license files available for import are supplied by Microsoft through the Microsoft Partner Program.

The license codes are validated individually based on the license holder name, serial number, expiration date, and the license key being entered or imported. The validation process either accepts the license key and updates the status field with *counts*, *names*, or *OK* or returns a negative result in the Infolog form.

> **Note**   Standard customer licenses do not contain an expiration date. Licenses for other uses, such as evaluation, independent software vendor projects, education, and training, do include an expiration date. When a license reaches its expiration date, the system changes execution mode and becomes a restricted demo product for a limited amount of time.

The license code elements themselves are created in the AOT and divided into five tab pages, as shown in Figure 11-3, based on the type of functionality that they relate to. The grouping is determined by a license code property, and sorting inside the groups is handled by the *Sys-LicenseCodeSort* table and its *createSortIdx* method. The Partner Modules tab allows you to include licensed partner modules. Partners can sign an agreement with Microsoft that gives other partners and customers the opportunity to purchase and request partner-developed functionality. You may contact your local Microsoft subsidiary for more details about the program.

## The Configuration Hierarchy

The license codes reside at the top of the configuration hierarchy. This is the entry point for working with the configuration system that surrounds all the application modules and system elements available within Dynamics AX. The configuration system is based on approximately 200 multiple configuration keys that are used to enable and disable functionality in the application for the entire deployment. Each license key controls access to a specific set of functions; when a key is disabled, its functionality is automatically removed from the database and the user interface. This means that the application runtime renders presentation controls only for menu items that are associated with the active configuration key or where no configuration key is available.

The relationship between license codes and configuration keys is very comprehensive. An individual license key is not only the enabler for a variety of configuration keys, but it also removes the visibility of configuration keys and their functions throughout the entire system if the license key is *not* valid. Removing configuration keys with invalid license keys reduces the configuration complexity. For example, if a license key is not entered or not valid in the license information form (accessed from Administration/Setup/System), the Configuration form hides it and displays only the valid license keys and the configuration and security keys that depend on them. This reduces the number of security keys to be configured when creating user groups. (User groups, which are essential to the security subsystem, are described later in this chapter.) Figure 11-4 shows the system-wide configuration hierarchy followed by most functionalities within an implementation, with the exception of those that do not comply with best practices for developing Dynamics AX application modules.

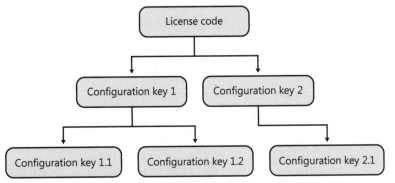

**Figure 11-4**   The configuration hierarchy.

The configuration hierarchy might seem complex. However, easy-to-use administrator check-lists and forms, such as the License formation, Configuration, and Permission forms, reduce the initial complexity.

## Configuration Keys

The application modules and the underlying business logic that license codes and configuration keys enable are available when Dynamics AX is deployed. This means that everything from forms, reports, and menus to data elements and the Data Dictionary, as well as the entire development environment, is already present, existing in a temporary state where the elements do not affect the enabled functionality.

Using the configuration hierarchy shown in Figure 11-4, you can enable parent configuration keys with valid license keys to appear in the global configuration form by navigating to Administration\Setup\System\Configuration. The parent configuration keys controlled by the license codes appear with a red padlock overlay and cannot be disabled; any configuration key children displayed below the parent can be changed. Parent configuration keys with no children are not available from the configuration form.

> **Note**   Parent configuration keys can exist without an attached license key. These will be available for the administrator to enable or disable at all times from within the Configuration form.

The Dynamics AX configuration philosophy is to enable functionality when needed, rather than remove superfluous functionality like other ERP systems do. The consequence of this philosophy is that the system starts minimized by default. This means that all child configuration keys are disabled. An example of the Configuration form and the minimized approach is shown in Figure 11-5.

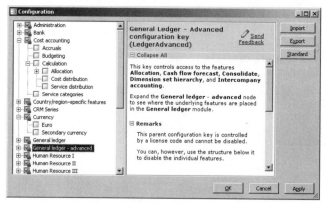

**Figure 11-5** The Configuration form.

As a more detailed example, consider a company buying the Trade module license code. The company wants most of the functionality in the module, but it does not do business with other countries. The company therefore chooses to disable the Foreign Trade configuration key.

By using the configuration key flow chart shown in Figure 11-6, an administrator can determine whether a configuration key is enabled and what it would take to eventually enable it, which depends on the parent of the configuration key.

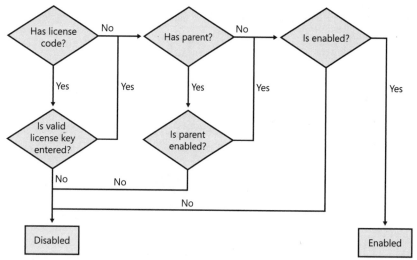

**Figure 11-6** Configuration key flowchart.

# Using Configuration Keys

An important part of the application development process is mapping extensions to the configuration-based and role-based security frameworks that integrate the extensions into the complete solution. Correctly using the configuration keys throughout the system can make enterprise-wide deployment very powerful, flexible, and economical when divisions, regions, or sites all use the same deployment platform and customize local deployment by using configuration keys, rather than developing specific customizations in each installation. Individualized development, though, cannot be entirely avoided because of the nature of businesses and their development needs.

Configuration keys affect the Data Dictionary, presentation, and navigation infrastructure directly, meaning that a configuration key property can be referenced on all relevant elements. Table 11-2 lists the elements that can be directly affected by configuration keys.

**Table 11-2   Configuration Key References**

| Grouping | Element types |
| --- | --- |
| Data Dictionary | Tables including Fields and Indexes |
| | Maps |
| | Views |
| | Extended data types |
| | Base enumerations |
| | License codes |
| | Configuration keys |
| | Security keys |
| | Perspectives |
| Windows Presentation and Navigation | Menus |
| | Display—Menu items |
| | Output—Menu items |
| | Action—Menu items |
| Web Presentation and Navigation | URL—Web menu items |
| | Action—Web menu items |
| | Display—Web content |
| | Output – Web content |
| | Web menus |
| | Weblets |
| Documentation References | System documentation |
| | Application developer documentation |
| | Application documentation |
| | HTML Help files |

Enabling the configuration keys also means invoking hierarchical structures of role-based security options, providing system administrators with an extremely flexible and dynamic framework for setting up user security. The role-based security hierarchy supports use without configuration keys when it is necessary for specific kinds of implementations. Figure 11-7 illustrates a frequently used security hierarchy in which the configuration key is the gatekeeper for interaction with the functionality underneath.

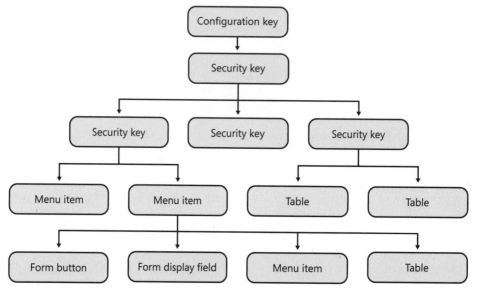

**Figure 11-7**   Security keys as permission gates.

The hierarchy is based on security keys that, working together with user groups, act as permission gates that allow users to see, invoke, and work with the user interface, business logic, and rules represented by menu items, submenu items, tables, buttons, and fields.

This introduction to the role-based security hierarchy provides a high-level overview of the concept. The particular hierarchy shown in Figure 11-8 demonstrates how the *LedgerBasic* configuration key opens for a subset of the Vendor functionality that is managed by a sub-hierarchy of security keys. The sub-hierarchy is the link to functionality such as the Purchase Order form and the Vendor form that are referenced via Display menu items. These Display menu items explicitly reference specific tables to decrease the complexity of security configuration.

This illustration does not depict all possible elements and combinations within the security hierarchy, which would include such things as reports, classes, Web elements, or how country-specific functionality is invoked for an individual user.

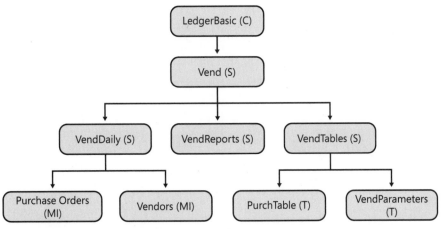

**Figure 11-8**   A security hierarchy example.

# The Security Framework

The security framework within Dynamics AX uses the Microsoft Windows Integrated Security platform and Active Directory directory service to authenticate user or system interactions before they are authorized by the Dynamics AX role-based security. Using Windows authentication allows automatic logon to the Dynamics AX application without collecting user name and password information.

A Windows-authenticated user can be associated with only one Dynamics AX user but can be shared between multiple Windows users. The application role for the individual Dynamics AX user is determined by the user groups with which the role is associated, and it defines the user interface actions that a user is authorized to perform and the data that the user is authorized to view and modify. You can create an application role by adding all the necessary functionality to one user group, or you can create a collection of user groups that defines the entire application role. User groups can be shared by multiple Dynamics AX users, as shown in Figure 11-9.

**Note**   Windows authentication is the only authentication scheme available in Dynamics AX 4.0. The option to work with the SQL Server authentication, available in earlier versions, no longer exists.

## Organizing Security

The role-based Dynamics AX security framework is comprised of users, company accounts, domains, user groups, table and field permissions, and record-level security. Organization of application security in Dynamics AX is associated with security keys and their relationships with menu items, form controls, tables, and fields, which together operate as the connection layer between the application logic and the application role configuration. The security keys reduce the complexity of setting up the overall security of individual user groups per domain because the references to configuration keys can remove unused functionality. Parent security keys can enable or disable entire application modules. Subcategories of application modules are structured by using the method that matches the main menu structure.

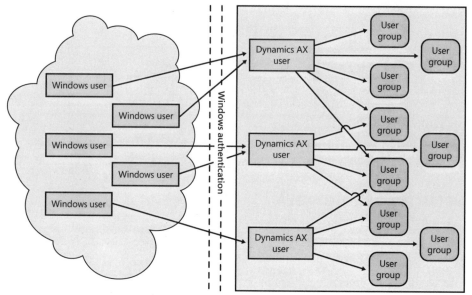

**Figure 11-9**   Authentication overview.

The flow chart in Figure 11-10 illustrates how authorization is validated for the individual user group and how configuration keys and parent security keys affect the final security access.

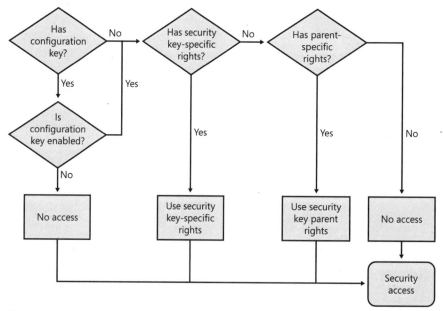

**Figure 11-10**   Validation of authorization.

> **Note**  Configuration keys and parent security keys are element properties that are added to the individual security key. When adding the properties, only one of the two properties can be used at a time because a configuration key indicates that the security key is the parent and the parent property indicates that the security key is a subcategory.

When you create security keys, the parent security keys function as the application module keepers for the underlying child security key categories: Daily, Setup, Journals, Inquiries, Reports, Periodic, Miscellaneous, and Tables. These categories define the user interface for the substructure of the application module within the Dynamics AX main menu. This makes it easy to relate the main menu items with the security elements when configuring user group permissions.

> **Tip**  To simplify the navigation experience, all application modules use category naming.

The security keys control the initial permission levels to functionality within the application, but they depend on the menu items and the table permissions framework for detailed security configuration. The permissions are assigned to user groups within their corresponding domains using the following five permission levels:

- **No access**  Members of the user group cannot access the item or any sub-items that the item controls.

- **View access**  Members of the user group are allowed to view the item, but they cannot use it.

- **Edit access**  Members of the user group are allowed to view and use the item.

- **Create access**  Members of the user group are allowed to view and use the item, and they can also add new items.

- **Full control**  Members of the user group have full access to the item, and no commands are disabled. Members can also provide additional rights in special cases if full access is given to the administration items.

> **Note**  The security framework presents only the user interface elements that the users have access to, and it handles the appropriate access level for individual users. Security is applied on the user interface, which is the user's entry to the application through menus, menu items, reports, and forms.

Permission levels are assigned and accessible from the user group permission form, which facilitates the entire permission assignment process beyond simple node creation.

# Applying Security

The process for applying the security framework to the Dynamics AX application includes the following seven steps, which must be performed after the licensing and generic configuration is completed:

1. Create users.

2. Create user groups.

3. Create company accounts.

4. Create domains.

5. Set permissions for user groups and domain combinations.

6. Set table and field access.

7. Set record-level security.

## Domains

Configuring the security of the Dynamics AX application involves the use of domains. A domain is a collection of one or more company accounts that allow you to define user groups with the same permissions in a company with several subsidiary businesses, while allowing the same user groups to have other permissions within other companies. Domains make it easier to maintain user group security when several companies use the same security profile.

> **Note**   A single company account can belong to more than one domain.

Domains allow great flexibility in the configuration of user group permissions. They can generate a strict security policy, in which each user group in each domain is a distinct entity with absolutely no access between groups or domains, or one user group can have company account access to similar group data, forms, and modules across multiple domains. The latter option simplifies the access configuration of corporate services such as controllers, multi-site planners, human resource functions, and other functions that centralize or share assignments and tasks. Figure 11-11 illustrates how domains and user groups can work together in multiple ways within the same security framework.

The domain security key *SysOpenDomain* controls access to information about users, user groups, company accounts, and domains. Using the domain security key in user groups provides access to records in all domains.

> **Note**   Dynamics AX includes only one domain by default: Admin. The Admin domain always includes all companies. It cannot be removed, and no companies can be deleted. Use the Admin domain for any user groups that need access to all companies. When the license key domain is not purchased, domains are still visible and functioning, but access is limited to the Admin domain only.

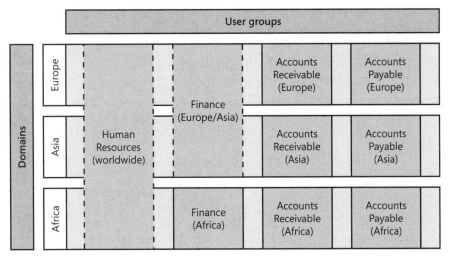

**Figure 11-11**   An example of the relationship between domains and user groups.

## User Group Permissions

Permissions and user rights are granted to groups, which allows the system administrator to define a set of users that share common security privileges. When you add a user to a group, you give the user all the permissions and user rights assigned to that group. By default, user groups cannot access any menus, reports, forms, tables, or fields in Dynamics AX. User groups can be shared between all Dynamics AX user types: Windows users, Web users, or anonymous users, such as Business Connector users.

> **Note**   A user who is a member of more than one group inherits the highest permissions level of the two groups. A user cannot access the application without being added to at least one user group.

When configuring group permissions, the system administrator works with a hierarchical security tree that represents all the available security keys and includes application module access, individual permission levels, and Help text that explains the security element. The User Group Permissions form allows for configuration of high-level permissions and very detailed permission levels for individual user groups. Figure 11-12 shows the configuration interface that system administrators work with to assign permissions.

You can use the User Group Permissions form to display the security elements by selecting one of the following Viewing filters, which are available at the top of the form:

- **Security**   Windows-relevant security elements, sorted alphabetically
- **Security (Incl. Web)**   All security elements, including Web-specific elements (such as activity centers, deployment options, and cross functions), sorted alphabetically
- **Country/Region-Specific**   Legacy functions relevant for the individual countries and regions, sorted alphabetically

■ **Main Menu**    Functions structured according to the main menu within the Dynamics AX application runtime

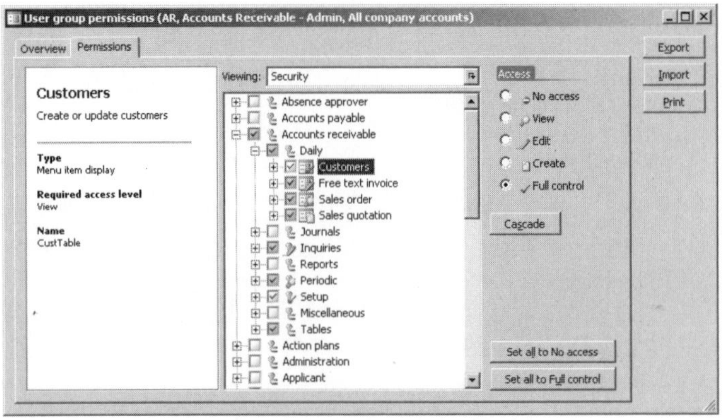

**Figure 11-12**    The User Group Permissions form.

These elements are the main overview elements, but additional filters will be available if the menu node does not have a parent, such as Task Panes or Tools. This means that customized menus can be presented automatically in the filter, if the preceding criteria are met.

If you set the permission level to Full Control on the parent node key, security key children, menu items, and tables will inherit the same permissions. However, if you set any other permission level, permissions will not be inherited below the parent menu item. If a permission level is required for the entire sub-tree, the Cascade button grants the current permission level when clicked.

> **Important**    If you change permissions for a user group, especially if you demote permissions, you should follow the best practice of instructing all group members to restart their Dynamics AX client, so the permission changes will take effect.

## Record-Level Security

Within any enterprise, some users are restricted from working with certain sensitive data for reasons regarding confidentiality, legal obligations, or company policy. In Dynamics AX, authorization for access to sensitive data is managed via the table-based record level security (RLS) framework that builds on the restrictions enforced by user group permissions. With user group permissions, you restrict access to menus, forms, and reports for group members. The RLS framework allows you to add additional restrictions to the information displayed in reports and on forms. These restrictions are automatically applied by the Dynamics AX application runtime when the application requests data from the database table included in the RLS framework. The restrictions are included by extending the WHERE clause within the SQL statement with the defined RLS query details.

Common uses of record-level security include the following situations:

- Allowing members of a sales user group to see only the accounts they manage
- Prohibiting financial data from appearing on forms or reports for a specific user group
- Prohibiting account details or account IDs from appearing on forms or reports for a specific user group
- Restricting form and report data according to location, country, or region

When you enable record-level security, you select user groups and the appropriate database table by using the Record Level Security wizard, and then you execute a query that specifies the fields and criteria to be applied. The query criteria are specified using the generic Query form and are added to the individual database table that was chosen with the wizard. Note that record-level security is configured per company, so the wizard and criteria definitions must be executed for each company.

> **Important**    If an application role that uses multiple user groups has record-level security applied on a certain table within a company account, maximum access is given to the role. For example, if one user group has no record-level security for the *Customer* table and another user group allows users to see only a subset of the customers, the user will have access to all customers.

The following is the process for enabling record-level security for a user group for a particular database table:

1. Start the Record Level Security wizard.
2. Select a user group.
3. Select tables.
4. Complete the wizard.
5. Mark an available table, and then click *Query*.
6. Add the query criteria.

By default, the tables in the wizard are presented based on the *TableGroup* property with the value set to Main, and they are grouped according to the parent security key matching the main menu structures. Setting the value to Main results in a subset of the tables. However, you can expand the selection by clicking *Show All Tables*.

The RLS framework is automatically invoked by the kernel when criteria has been applied to database tables, but it could require additional work in certain situations, such as the following:

- Using display and edit methods
- Using a *FormListControl*, *FormTreeControl*, or *TableListControl* control to show data
- Using a temporary table as a data source

Whenever a display or edit method is used to return a value from another row, you must evaluate the business impact of displaying this data. If your evaluation shows signs of unwanted information disclosure, you should perform an explicit authorization in X++ code to check permissions before calling these methods. The following code shows an explicit authorization.

```
if (hasSecurityKeyAccess(securitykeyNum(mySecurityKey), AccessType::View))
{
myMethod();
}
if (hasMenuItemAccess(menuItemDisplayStr(myMenuItem), MenuItemType::Display)))
{
myMethod();
}
DictTable dictTable = new DictTable(tablenum(myTable));
if (dictTable.rights >= AccessType::Insert))
{
myMethod();
}
if (isConfigurationkeyEnabled(configurationkeyNum(myConfigurationKey))
{
myMethod();
}
```

 **Note**    For more security-related information on using display and edit methods, refer to the Microsoft Dynamics AX SDK.

Populating a *FormListControl*, *FormTreeControl*, or *TableListControl* control with data from a query can lead to unwanted information disclosure. In such cases, you must manually activate the record-level security, as shown here.

```
public void run
{
CustTable custTable;
super();
// Ensure that record-level security is used.
custTable.recordLevelSecurity(true);
while select custTable
{
listView.add(custTable.name);
}
}
```

When the form cache is filled with data from a temporary table, you must ensure that the data conforms to the record-level security. This includes tables declared as temporary in the code, as illustrated in the following code example, and tables in the AOT whose *Temporary* property is set to Yes.

```
public void run
{
CustTable custTable, tmpDatasource;
;
// Ensure that record-level security is used.
custTable.recordLevelSecurity(true);
while select custTable
{
tmpDataSource.data(custTable);
tmpDataSource.insert();
}
formDataSource.setTmp();
formDataSource.checkRecord(false);
formDataSource.setTmpData(tmpDatasource);
super();
}
```

Record-level security is not required in the following situations:

■ When the value is calculated

■ When the value is based only on fields in the current record

# Security Coding

The development of Dynamics AX 4.0 included many new Trustworthy Computing initiatives for more secure, private, and reliable computing experiences. The following sections focus on these security initiatives and how they affect security coding. Specifically, this section covers table permissions, code access security, impersonation in batch execution, and the best practice rules for ensuring deployment-wide compliance.

## Table Permissions

The table permissions framework provides security for tables that reside in the database and are available through the AOT. Annotating specific create, read, update, and delete operations on tables, combined with assigning user group permissions on tables, enables the Application Object Server (AOS) to authorize individual user permissions on tables.

For each table described in the AOT, a new property is introduced, called *AOSAuthorization*. The property describes the operations that may be performed on a table when combined with user permissions set on the User Group Permissions form. The illustration in Figure 11-13 shows the table property *AOSAuthorization* and its available values.

The *AOSAuthorization* property is an enumeration with the possible values described in Table 11-3.

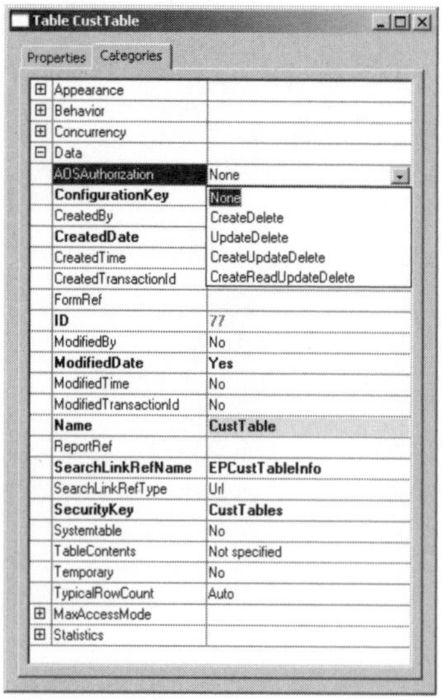

**Figure 11-13** The table property form.

**Table 11-3** *AOSAuthorization* Values

| Value | Description |
| --- | --- |
| *None* | No AOS authorization validation is performed (default value). |
| *CreateDelete* | Create and delete authorization validation is performed on the AOS. |
| *UpdateDelete* | Update and delete authorization validation is performed on the AOS. |
| *CreateUpdateDelete* | Create, update, and delete authorization validation is performed on the AOS. |
| *CreateReadUpdateDelete* | All operations are validated on the AOS. |

To secure the database tables even further, you must have a set of Data Manipulation Language (DML) validation routines at the AOS server location when inserting, reading, updating, or deleting records from the database tables. The following four system-defined methods are included in the Override Method group to support the routine validation, located in the AOT under Data Dictionary\Table\Methods:

- *AOSValdiateDelete*
- *AOSValidateInsert*
- *AOSValidateRead*
- *AOSValidateUpdate*

Table 11-4 describes the behavior of the AOS when authorizing an authenticated user on a table, including the user group permissions setting and the *AOSAuthorization* property value.

**Table 11-4**  *AOSAuthorization* **Property Values**

| | | Property value | | | | |
|---|---|---|---|---|---|---|
| | | **None** | **Create** | **Read** | **Update** | **Delete** |
| **User** | **No Access** | Success | Failure | Failure | Failure | Failure |
| **group** | **View** | Success | Failure | Success | Failure | Failure |
| **access** | **Edit** | Success | Failure | Success | Success | Failure |
| **value** | **Create** | Success | Success | Success | Success | Failure |
| | **Full Control** | Success | Success | Success | Success | Success |

## Code Access Security

The Code Access Security (CAS) framework provides methods that can make APIs more secure against invocation attempts by non-trusted code (code that does not originate in the AOT). If you extend the *CodeAccessPermission* class, a derived class can determine whether code accessing the API is trusted by checking for the appropriate permission.

If the API executes on the server tier, the impact of malicious code that could exploit the API is more severe in a shared environment, and the utilization should be secured. To secure a class that executes on the server tier, follow these steps:

1. Derive a class that cannot be extended from the *CodeAccessPermission* class.

2. Create a method that returns the class parameters.

3. Create a constructor for all of the class parameters that store permission data.

4. Override the *CodeAccessPermission::isSubsetOf* method to compare the derived permission class with *CodeAccessPermission* to determine the existence of the required permissions for invoking the API that you want to secure.

5. Override the *CodeAccessPermission::copy* method to return a copy of an instance of the class created in the first step. This helps prevent the class object from being modified and passed to the API that is being secured.

6. Call the *CodeAccessPermission::demand* method before executing the API functionality that you are securing. The method checks the call stack to determine whether the permission required to invoke the API has been granted to the calling code.

Additional information about code access security and securing APIs is available in the Microsoft Dynamics AX SDK.

## Batch Jobs

Dynamics AX 4.0 introduces a new and more secure type of batch job that uses impersonation. Rather than executing the batch job type as the user who is running the batch process, you can now use the new *runAs* function to execute it as the Dynamics AX user who initially submitted the job. When this type of batch processing is used, the user who initiates the batch processing cannot interact with the batch job or view its output. Dynamics AX 4.0 includes support for batch processing that does not use the *runAs* function. Batch-enabled classes in Dynamics AX that do not use the *runAs* function can easily be changed to do so, if appropriate.

> **Note** When you move batch jobs to use the *runAs* function, you must ensure that there are no additional Dynamics AX application run-time interactions.

To identify possible run-time interactions, use any of the following methods:

- Perform a manual code review.

- Identify transition exceptions in the Infolog by converting the X++ class to a server-bound batch job (see the following syntax example), submitting the X++ class for batch processing, and checking the Infolog for transition exceptions.

- Identify client-server interactions using the client/server trace by submitting the unmodified X++ class for batch processing and checking the client/server trace for client/server interactions.

If you discover any run-time interactions, you should eliminate them by refactoring the application logic involved. When the class is ready to use the *runAs* function, you must override a method shown to return true, as shown here.

```
public boolean runsImpersonated()
{
    return true;
}
```

> **Note** Classes in batch journals are executed according to whether they are legacy or use *runAs*. In other words, a batch journal can contain a mixture of batch run modes.

## Best Practice Rules

Applying the principles of Microsoft's Trustworthy Computing effort involved adding about 50 new rules to the Best Practice tool to help you validate your application logic and ensure that it complies with the new security initiatives. The new rules are grouped under General Checks\Trustworthy Computing in the Best Practice Parameters dialog box, as shown in Figure 11-14. The Best Practice Parameters dialog box is accessible from Tools\Options.

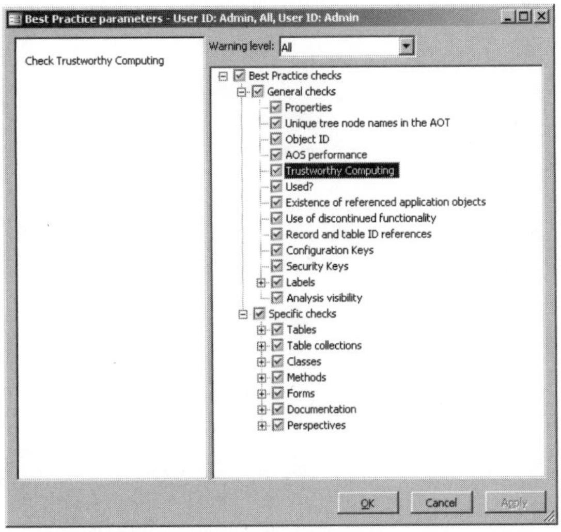

**Figure 11-14**   The Best Practice Parameters dialog box with Trustworthy Computing rules.

# Chapter Summary

This chapter described how IntelliMorph, licensing, configuration, security, and record-level security affect the Dynamics AX application run-time experience. These features help you implement Dynamics AX applications that must operate in multi-site, multi-user, or multilanguage environments.

Chapter 12

# The Database Layer

The objectives of this chapter are to:

- Describe the transaction semantics of the X++ language and explain how database transactions are supported by the Microsoft Dynamics AX 4.0 application runtime.

- Introduce record and company identification.

- Provide an overview of the Unicode support available in Dynamics AX 4.0.

- Introduce the database access layer in the application runtime.

- Discuss the database-triggering methods that are available on record buffer instances.

- Explain the concept of temporary tables and describe when and how they are used.

## Introduction

The Dynamics AX 4.0 application runtime provides a set of strong features that can help you quickly design international features. These runtime features store data in a database without requiring you to consider user locales or the databases that Dynamics AX supports.

This chapter describes how the application runtime supports the concept of atomicity, consistency, isolation, durability (ACID) transactions in a multiple-user environment and explains the intricacies of the two supported concurrency models: optimistic concurrency and pessimistic concurrency. When committing the transactions, identification is important at both the individual record level and the company level. This chapter also describes how identifiers work across application areas. Dynamics AX provides full support for the concurrent handling of multiple languages, which is accomplished through full Unicode support by the application runtime.

Two sections in this chapter focus on how the Dynamics AX implements a database abstraction layer. Queries executed using specialized X++ methods provide operations support that is independent of the supported databases. Combined with the ability to write X++ code tied to specific database triggers, this makes it easy to write code that is reused all over the application, whether specific data is accessed through a rich client or a Web client or through X++.

The last section of the chapter discusses the concept of temporary tables. Temporary tables make it possible to have local database data that is isolated from other users, but that can be accessed as if it were stored directly in the database with other shared data. The concept of temporary tables is also important for understanding when you are designing an application that allows the licensing of multiple modules; when designing the modules, you need not consider whether they are enabled or disabled.

# Transaction Semantics

The X++ language includes the statements *ttsbegin*, *ttscommit*, and *ttsabort* for marking the beginning and ending of database transactions. It is important to understand how the execution of X++ code outside and inside a transaction scope affects the data that is retrieved from the database because of the difference in isolation levels, and also how the transaction scope affects exception handling. This section describes *tts*-prefixed statements, isolations levels, and exception handling, as well as the two concurrency models that Dynamics AX supports.

This section includes examples of how these X++ statements affect interaction with Microsoft SQL Server 2000. The X++ statements executed in the application are written in lowercase letters (*select*, for example), and SQL statements parsed to and executed in the database are written in uppercase letters (SELECT, for example). This chapter also includes the use of specific SQL hints and functions. These are not described completely, so you are advised to consult the SQL Server Reference documentation for a detailed description.

An instance of a Dynamics AX table type is both a record object and a cursor object. The remainder of this chapter refers to this combined object as a *record buffer*.

## Transaction Statements

A transaction in X++ starts with *ttsbegin* and ends with either *ttscommit* or *ttsabort*. The use of these statements does not necessarily result in the following equivalent statements being sent to SQL Server 2000: BEGIN TRANSACTION, COMMIT TRANSACTION, and ROLLBACK TRANSACTION. Instead, when a transaction is initiated with a *ttsbegin* statement, implicit transactions are turned on. The transaction will not start until an SQL Data Manipulation Language (DML) statement is executed, so it will start when SELECT, UPDATE, INSERT, or DELETE is executed. When *ttscommit* or *ttsabort* is executed, the equivalent statements

COMMIT TRANSACTION and ROLLBACK TRANSACTION execute only if a transaction has been initiated. This is illustrated in the following X++ code, in which the comments show the SQL statements that will be sent and executed by the database. The remaining code samples in this chapter contain the same notation, with the SQL statement shown as comments.

```
boolean b = true;
;
ttsbegin; // Transaction is not initiated here.
update_recordset custTable // First DML statement within transaction
    setting creditMax = 0; // SET IMPLICIT_TRANSACTIONS ON
if ( b == true )
    ttscommit; // COMMIT TRANSACTION
else
    ttsabort; // ROLLBACK TRANSACTION
```

You can, however, have nested levels of transaction blocks to accommodate encapsulation and allow for reuse of business logic. This involves the notion of transaction level, also known as ttslevel, and nested transaction scopes involving inner and outer transaction scopes.

> **Note**   Consider a class developed to update a single customer record within a transaction. This class would contain a *ttsbegin/ttscommit* block, which states the transaction scope for the update of the single instance of the customer. This class can be consumed by another class, which selects multiple customer records and updates them individually by calling the first class. If the entire update of all the customers were executed as a single transaction, the consuming class would also contain a *ttsbegin/ttscommit* block, stating the outer transaction scope.

When X++ code is executed outside a transaction scope, the transaction level is 0. However, when a *ttsbegin* statement is executed, the transaction level is increased by one, and when a *ttscommit* statement is executed, the transaction level is decreased by one. Not until the first DML statement is executed after the transaction level has changed from 0 to a higher level will the SET IMPLICIT_TRANSACTIONS ON statement be sent to the database. And only when the transaction level is decreased from 1 to 0 and a transaction has begun will the COMMIT TRANSACTION statement be sent. Assuming that a transaction has begun, the execution of *ttsabort* causes a ROLLBACK TRANSACTION statement to be sent to the database and the transaction level to be reset to 0.

The following example illustrates the use of nested transactions and TRANSACTION statements sent to the database, as well as the changes in the transaction level.

```
static void UpdateCustomers(Args _args)
{
    CustTable custTable;
    ;
    ttsbegin; // Transaction level changes from 0 to 1.
```

```
        while select forupdate custTable
            where custTable.CustGroup == '40' // SET IMPLICIT_TRANSACTIONS ON
        {
            ttsbegin;    // Transaction level changes from 1 to 2.

            custTable.CreditMax = 1000;
            custTable.update();

            ttscommit;   // Transaction level changes from 2 to 1.
        }

        ttscommit;// COMMIT TRANSACTION - Transaction level changes from 1 to 0.
    }
```

**Note**  The current transaction level can always be queried by calling *appl.ttslevel()*. The returned value is the current transaction level.

It is important that the number of *ttsbegin* statements balance the number of *ttscommit* statements. If the Dynamics AX application runtime discovers that the *ttsbegin* and *ttscommit* statements are not balanced, an error dialog box (shown in Figure 12-1) is presented to the user, or an error with the following text is written to the Infolog: "Error executing code: Call to TTSCOMMIT without first calling TTSBEGIN."

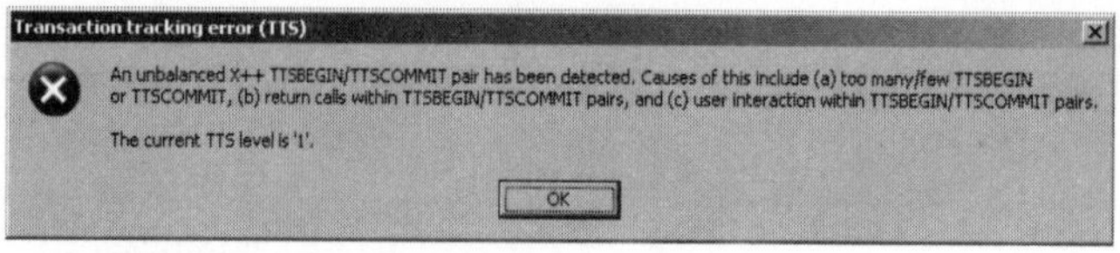

**Figure 12-1**  An unbalanced transaction level error.

**Note**  It might be necessary, in the event of an unbalanced TTS error, to log out of the Dynamics AX client to reset the transaction level. This would also roll back the started transaction in the database.

## Isolation Levels

When Dynamics AX is installed running on a SQL Server 2000 database, two different isolation levels are used. The first isolation level is READ UNCOMMITTED, which is used when the Dynamics AX application runtime executes outside a transaction scope. The second is the READ COMMITTED isolation level, which is used when a transaction scope is entered. The default isolation level for every database process opened by the application runtime is READ UNCOMMITTED; when the first *ttsbegin* statement executes, the isolation level in the process changes to READ COMMITTED, and when a *ttsabort* statement or the final *ttscommit* statement executes, the isolation level in the process switches back to READ UNCOMMITTED.

The change of isolation levels is accomplished by executing the following statements in SQL Server 2000: SET TRANSACTION ISOLATION LEVEL READ UNCOMMITTED, SET TRANSACTION ISOLATION LEVEL READ COMMITTED.

Note that changes in isolation levels always occur when the first *ttsbegin* statement, the first *ttsabort* statement, and the final *ttscommit* statement execute. The following code is identical to the previous example, except that the comments now track the changing isolation levels.

```
static void UpdateCustomers(Args _args)
{
    CustTable custTable;
    ;
    ttsbegin; // SET TRANSACTION ISOLATION LEVEL READ COMMITTED

    while select forupdate custTable
        where custTable.CustGroup == '40'
    {
        ttsbegin;

        custTable.CreditMax = 1000;
        custTable.update();

        ttscommit;
    }

    ttscommit; // SET TRANSACTION ISOLATION LEVEL READ UNCOMMITTED
}
```

The main reason for using the READ UNCOMMITTED isolation level outside a transaction scope is to prevent readers from getting blocked behind writers. If the Dynamics AX application runtime used only the READ COMMITTED isolation level inside and outside transactions, any selection of records from a table that is currently being updated by another process and not yet committed would be blocked because the other process would have an exclusive lock on the record. Note that this is the default behavior when using SQL Server 2000. To understand how Dynamics AX uses other databases, refer to Appendix C, "Source Code Changes Required for Upgrade."

However, using the READ UNCOMMITTED isolation level implies that uncommitted changes made by other processes are not isolated from the process that executes an uncommitted read from the database. You should avoid manipulating the database with information that is read uncommitted because the read information could potentially be rolled back or be in an inconsistent state. If you want to manipulate the database, the information used should be a committed version; it is important to re-read data inside the transaction scope or use other means to ensure that inconsistent or rolled back data is not used. This subject is discussed in greater detail in the section titled "Concurrency Models," later in this chapter.

> **Note**   Transactions are generally defined as having four properties, known as ACID (atomicity, consistency, isolation, durability) properties:
>
> **Atomicity:** Every operation in the transaction is either committed or rolled back.
>
> **Consistency:** When committed, the transaction should leave the database in a consistent state.
>
> **Isolation:** Uncommitted changes are not visible to other transactions.
>
> **Durability:** After a transaction is committed, the changes are permanent, even in the event of system failure.

Any scenario in Dynamics AX may use more than one database process when executing. The Dynamics AX application runtime may use both a process with a *READ UNCOMMITTED* isolation level and another process with a *READ COMMITTED* isolation level within the same scenario. This generally occurs when a *READ UNCOMMITTED* process is used where an open cursor still exists and the application runtime needs to start a transaction. In such a situation, the application runtime uses an additional *READ COMMITTED* process for the execution of statements within the transaction block.

This is illustrated in the following example, in which it is assumed that all records in *custTable* are not fetched immediately when executing the select statement because of the number of records in the table. This means that the cursor for selecting the *custTable* records is not closed when the *ttsbegin* statement executes. The application runtime, therefore, uses an additional process to update the *vendTable* record.

```
static void UpdateVendors(Args _args)
{
    CustTable custTable;
    VendTable vendTable;
    ;

    while select custTable // SELECT executed by process running
                           // READ UNCOMMITTED isolation level
    {
        ttsbegin;           // New process used running
                            // READ COMMITTED isolation level
        if (custTable.VendAccount)
        {
            vendTable = VendTable::find(custTable.vendAccount, true);

            vendTable.custAccount = custTable.accountNum;
            vendTable.update();
        }
        ttscommit;
    } // The READ UNCOMMITTED process is again used when fetching
      // additional records from the database.
}
```

## Enforcing Uncommitted Reads in Transactions

As stated at the beginning of this section, readers can get blocked behind writers when using the *READ COMMITTED* isolation level in SQL Server 2000. You can, however, select uncommitted data within a transaction scope even though the isolation level is set to *READ COMMITTED*. You accomplish this by executing *selectLocked(false)* on a record buffer before selecting any rows with it. This adds the NOLOCK hint to the SELECT statement, which is parsed to the database; consequently, uncommitted records are read, and the reader is not blocked.

The previous code example can be changed so that all changes to the *vendTable* records are committed on a set basis instead of row by row, while still reading uncommitted *custTable* records, as shown here.

```
static void UpdateVendors(Args _args)
{
    CustTable custTable;
    VendTable vendTable;
    ;
    ttsbegin;  // READ COMMITTED isolation level

    custTable.selectLocked(false); // enforcing uncommitted read
    while select custTable // SELECT … FROM CUSTTABLE WITH(NOLOCK) …
    {
        if (custTable.VendAccount)
        {
            vendTable = VendTable::find(custTable.vendAccount, true);

            vendTable.custAccount = custTable.accountNum;
            vendTable.update();
        }
    }
    ttscommit;
}
```

As explained earlier, enforcing uncommitted reads should be done with great care and consideration.

**Note**   The use of *selectLocked(false)* has no impact when used outside a transaction scope. It will not enforce a committed read within a *READ UNCOMMITTED* isolation level.

## Implicit Transactions

As explained earlier, implicit transactions are turned on when the first DML statement executes within a transaction. Similarly, implicit transactions are turned off when the first DML statement executes after the database process is used again outside the transaction scope. This is done by issuing the SET IMPLICIT_TRANSACTIONS OFF statement in the database. This causes any insert, update, or delete statement sent to the database in this mode to be automatically committed. Although possible, it is generally not advisable or a best practice to execute these statements outside a transaction scope because these statements are committed instantly to the database. This prevents you from rolling back the database later in the event of an error.

## Transaction IDs

Each transaction in Dynamics AX may be given a unique transaction ID by the Application Object Server (AOS). However, the AOS supplies such an ID only if one of the following circumstances is true:

- A record is inserted into a table in which the *CreatedTransactionId* property is set to Yes.
- A record is updated on a table in which the *ModifiedTransactionId* property is set to Yes.
- The X++ code explicitly requests a transaction by calling *appl.curTransactionsId(true)*.

Allocation and type of the transaction ID are explained in the "Record Identifiers" section, later in this chapter.

## The AOS Process Pool

The AOS does not open a new process in the database every time a process is needed. An open process that is no longer needed is placed in a pool of processes from which the AOS selects when it needs an additional process. The processes in the pool use a *READ UNCOMMITTED* isolation level and have implicit transactions turned off after they are used, unless they will be used to start a transaction. If the intention is to start a transaction, the isolation level is immediately changed and reverted before it is released to the pool.

# Concurrency Models

The Dynamics AX application runtime has built-in support in metadata and in the X++ language for the two concurrency models used when updating data in the database: optimistic concurrency and pessimistic concurrency.

The optimistic concurrency model is new with Dynamics AX 4.0. The previous version supported only pessimistic concurrency. The optimistic model is also referred to as *optimistic concurrency control* (OCC), which is the term used in properties and in the application runtime.

The differences between the two models are the methods they use to avoid "last writer wins" scenarios and, consequently, the timing of locks requested in the database.

**Note**   In a "last writer wins" scenario, two or more processes select and update the same record with different data, each believing that it is the only process updating that record. All processes commit their data, assuming that their version has been stored in the database. In reality, only the data from the last writing process is stored in the database. The data from the other processes is stored only for a moment, but there is no indication that their data was overwritten and lost.

**Caution**   Dynamics AX allows you to develop "last writer wins" X++ code intentionally and unintentionally. This can happen if you do not select records for update before actually updating them, and simply skip the transaction check by calling *skipTTSCheck(true)* on the record buffer.

The two models are managed very generically by the Dynamics AX runtime, and it is not necessary for you to decide whether to use pessimistic or optimistic concurrency when writing transactional X++ code. You can switch from using pessimistic concurrency to optimistic concurrency by merely changing a property on a table.

The following example illustrates what happens from a locking perspective when executing the X++ code by using pessimistic concurrency and running SQL Server 2000. The *select* statement contains the *forupdate* keyword that instructs the application runtime to execute a SELECT statement in the database with an UPDLOCK hint added. This instructs the database to acquire an update lock on all the selected records, to be held until the end of the transaction, thereby ensuring that no other process can modify the rows. But it does not prevent other readers from reading the rows, assuming that they do not require an update lock. Later, when the *update* method is called, an UPDATE statement is executed in the database, knowing that no other process has been able to modify the record since it was selected. At the same time, the update lock is transformed into an exclusive lock, which is held until the transaction is committed to the database. The exclusive lock blocks readers requiring an update lock and other writers. On SQL Server 2000, it even blocks readers merely requesting to read a committed version of the record. The X++ code is shown here.

```
static void UpdateCreditRating(Args _args)
{
    CustTable custTable;
    ;
    ttsbegin;
    while select forupdate custTable // SELECT … WITH (UPDLOCK)
                                     // Acquire an update lock.
    {
        if (custTable.CreditMax < custTable.balanceMST())
        {
            if (custTable.CreditMax < 1000)
                custTable.CreditRating = 'Good customer';
            else
                custTable.CreditRating = 'Solid customer';
```

```
                custTable.update();        // UPDATE ... WHERE ACCOUNTNUM = <Id>
                                           // Acquire an exclusive lock.
        }
    }
    ttscommit;
}
```

The following X++ code illustrates the same scenario shown in the preceding code, but it uses optimistic concurrency and SQL Server 2000. The *select* statement contains the *forupdate* keyword, which instructs the application runtime to execute a *SELECT* statement in the database with a NOLOCK hint added. This instructs the database to enforce an uncommitted read—thus overriding the *READ COMMITTED* isolation level—and not acquire any locks. Because no locks are held by the process, other processes can potentially modify the same rows. When the *update* method is called, an UPDATE statement is executed in the database, at which time a predicate is added to determine whether the *RecVersion* field still contains the value that it contained when the record was originally selected.

**Note**   The *RecVersion* field was introduced as part of the optimistic concurrency implementation in Dynamics AX. The field is a 32-bit integer with a default value of 1, which is changed to a random value when the record is updated.

If the *RecVersion* check fails when executing the UPDATE statement, another process has modified the same record. If the check does not fail, an exclusive lock is acquired for the record and the record is updated. In the event of a failure, the Dynamics AX application runtime throws an update conflict exception. Code for optimistic concurrency is shown here.

```
static void UpdateCreditRating(Args _args)
{
    CustTable custTable;
    ;
    ttsbegin;
    while select forupdate custTable // SELECT ... WITH (NOLOCK)
                                     // Enforce uncommitted read.
    {
        if (custTable.CreditMax < custTable.balanceMST())
        {
            if (custTable.CreditMax < 1000)
                custTable.CreditRating = 'Good customer';
            else
                custTable.CreditRating = 'Solid customer';

            custTable.update();        // UPDATE ... WHERE ACCOUNTNUM = <Id>
                                       // AND RECVERSION = <RecVersion>
                                       // Acquire an exclusive lock.
        }
    }
    ttscommit;
}
```

The two models differ in concurrency and throughput. The concurrency difference lies in the number of locks held at the time of commit. Whether the preceding scenario is executed using the optimistic or pessimistic model does not affect the number of exclusive locks held by the process because the number of *custTable* records to update is the same. When you use the pessimistic model, the update locks are held for the remainder of the *custTable* records that were not updated. When you use the optimistic model, no locks are held on rows that are not updated. The optimistic model allows other processes to update these rows, and the pessimistic model prevents other processes from updating these rows, which results in lower concurrency. However, the optimistic model involves a risk: The update could fail because other processes can update the same rows.

Regarding throughput, the optimistic model is better than the pessimistic model. Fewer database resources are used because fewer locks are acquired. However, in case of an update failure, the optimistic model must retry, which leads to inferior throughput.

To illustrate the difference in the models, assume that the preceding X++ code example selected 100 *custTable* rows. However, only 35 of these rows were updated, and the updated rows were distributed evenly among the 100 selected rows. Using the pessimistic concurrency model, a graphical representation would appear as shown in Figure 12-2.

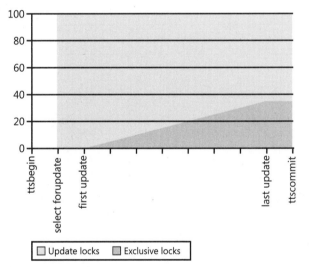

**Figure 12-2**   Update and exclusive locks using the pessimistic concurrency model.

If, however, the optimistic concurrency model were used, the picture would look slightly different, as shown in Figure 12-3. There would still be the same number of exclusive locks, but there would be no update locks. Also notice that no locks would be held from the time of the selection of the rows until the first record was updated.

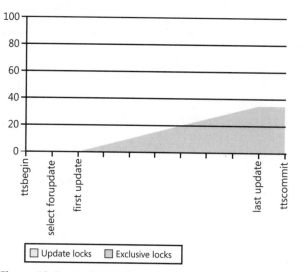

Figure 12-3   Update lock and exclusive locks using the optimistic concurrency model.

When choosing between the two models, you must consider the potential risk or likelihood of an update conflict. If the risk is minimal, the optimistic concurrency model will most likely fit the scenario; if the risk is not minimal, the pessimistic concurrency model might be your best choice. But the estimated cost of handling an update conflict and retrying can also influence your decision.

> **Note**   Although all of the preceding examples mention updates only, the same *RecVersion* check is made when deleting records, and it is therefore also applicable in those scenarios.

## Concurrent Scenarios

When two processes attempt to update the same record at the same time, locking, blocking, or potential failure could occur, depending on the concurrency model. The following scenario illustrates the behavior differences when two processes using SQL Server 2000 attempt to update two fields on the same records using pessimistic and optimistic concurrency.

Figure 12-4 illustrates pessimistic concurrency, in which Process 1 selects the *CustTable* record with a *forupdate* keyword and holds an update lock on the records. When Process 2 attempts to read the same record, also with a *forupdate* keyword, it is blocked behind the lock acquired by Process 1. Process 1 continues to set the new customer group and updates the record, and it converts the update lock into an exclusive lock. But Process 1 must commit before the locks can be released and Process 2 can continue by acquiring the update lock and reading the record. Process 2 can then set the new credit maximum, update the record, and commit the transaction.

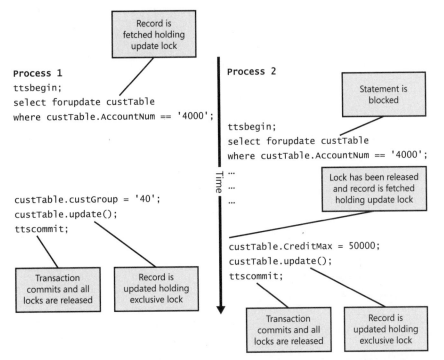

The figure contains the following text labels:

Record is fetched holding update lock

**Process 1**
```
ttsbegin;
select forupdate custTable
where custTable.AccountNum == '4000';
```

**Process 2**

Statement is blocked

```
ttsbegin;
select forupdate custTable
where custTable.AccountNum == '4000';
```

...
...
...

Lock has been released and record is fetched holding update lock

```
custTable.custGroup = '40';
custTable.update();
ttscommit;
```

Time

```
custTable.CreditMax = 50000;
custTable.update();
ttscommit;
```

Transaction commits and all locks are released

Record is updated holding exclusive lock

Transaction commits and all locks are released

Record is updated holding exclusive lock

**Figure 12-4**   Simultaneous update of the same record using pessimistic concurrency.

Figure 12-5 illustrates one possible outcome of the same two processes executing, using optimistic concurrency. Process 1 selects the same *CustTable* record with the *forupdate* keyword, but no locks are acquired or held for the remainder of the transaction. Process 2 can therefore select the same record in the same way, and both processes will hold a record with a *RecVersion* value of 789. Process 1 again sets the customer group field to a new value, updates the record, and acquires an exclusive lock. At the same time, the selected *RecVersion* is compared to the value in the database to ensure that no other processes have updated the same record, and then the *RecVersion* field is assigned a new value of 543. Process 2 takes over and assigns a new credit maximum value and executes an update. As the database first attempts to acquire an exclusive lock on the record, Process 2 gets blocked behind the lock of Process 1 on the same record until Process 1 commits and releases its locks. Process 2 can then acquire the lock, but because the selected *RecVersion* of 789 is not equal to the value of 543 in the database, the update fails and an update conflict is thrown.

If, however, Process 1 updates its changes before Process 2 selects the record, the two processes would complete successfully. This is shown in Figure 12-6, in which Process 2 reads the updated version where the *RecVersion* value is 543. Although Process 2 is blocked behind Process 1 when it tries to update the record, the *RecVersion* check does not fail when Process 1 commits and releases its locks because Process 2 has read the uncommitted version from Process 1.

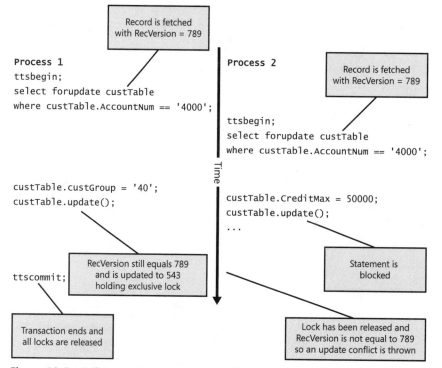

**Figure 12-5** Failing simultaneous update of the same record using optimistic concurrency.

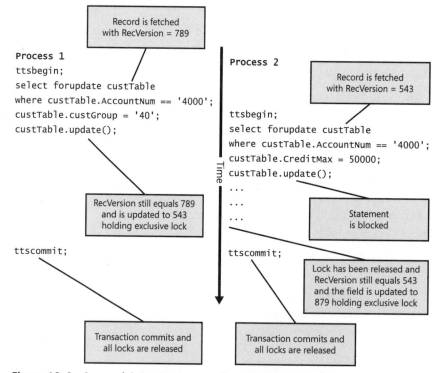

**Figure 12-6** Successful simultaneous update of the same record using optimistic concurrency.

The examples shown in Figures 12-5 and 12-6 illustrate how the application runtime behaves when the same record is updated by two processes. The following section describes how the runtime behaves when the same record is updated more than once within the same process.

## Disconnected Updates of the Same Record

Consider a scenario in which two separate pieces of application logic in the same process have copied the same record into two separate buffers, both with the intent of updating different fields on each of the buffers. Both records would have been selected with the *forupdate* keyword added to the *select* statement. In a pessimistic concurrency scenario, both select statements would request an update lock, but because the select statements are both executed with the same database process, they would not lock or block each other. In an optimistic concurrency scenario, both select statement would retrieve the same value for the *RecVersion* field but would not, of course, acquire any locks.

When the two pieces of application logic consequently changed and updated each of their records, the Dynamics AX application runtime would not encounter a problem when using pessimistic concurrency because each update statement would merely update its changed fields by using the primary key to locate the record in the database. However, when the application logic uses optimistic concurrency, the first update statement would determine whether the selected *RecVersion* value was equal to the value in the database and also update the *RecVersion* to a new value. But when the second update statement executed, it ought to fail because the selected *RecVersion* value would no longer match the value in the database. Fortunately, the Dynamics AX application runtime manages this situation. When the update statement is executed, the application runtime locates all other buffers holding the same record that have been retrieved with the *forupdate* keyword and changes the *RecVersion* value on these buffers to the value in the database. The second update, therefore, does not fail.

The following X++ code illustrates the behavior of the Dynamics AX application runtime when the same record is copied into three different buffers. Two of the select statements also include the *forupdate* keyword and copy the record into the *custTableSelectedForUpdate* and *custTableUpdated* buffers. When the *creditMax* field on the *custTableUpdated* buffer changes and is later updated in the database, the *RecVersion* field in the *custTableUpdated* buffer changes to the new value in the database—but now the *RecVersion* field in the *custTableSelected-ForUpdate* buffer also changes to the same value. The *RecVersion* field in the *custTableSelected* buffer does not change, however, because the record was retrieved without the *forupdate* keyword. The X++ code is shown here.

```
static void RecVersionChange(Args _args)
{
    CustTable custTableSelected;
    CustTable custTableSelectedForUpdate;
    CustTable custTableUpdated;
    ;
    ttsbegin;
```

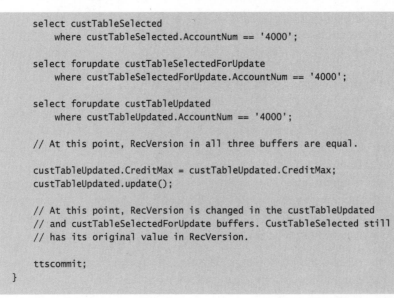

```
    select custTableSelected
        where custTableSelected.AccountNum == '4000';

    select forupdate custTableSelectedForUpdate
        where custTableSelectedForUpdate.AccountNum == '4000';

    select forupdate custTableUpdated
        where custTableUpdated.AccountNum == '4000';

    // At this point, RecVersion in all three buffers are equal.

    custTableUpdated.CreditMax = custTableUpdated.CreditMax;
    custTableUpdated.update();

    // At this point, RecVersion is changed in the custTableUpdated
    // and custTableSelectedForUpdate buffers. CustTableSelected still
    // has its original value in RecVersion.

    ttscommit;
}
```

**Caution**    When multiple processes want to simultaneously update the same record, the application runtime prevents the "last writer wins" scenario by either acquiring update locks when using pessimistic concurrency or performing the *RecVersion* check when using optimistic concurrency. However, nothing in the database or the application runtime prevents the "last writer wins" scenario if disconnected application logic within the same scenario and database process changes the same field by using two different buffers.

## Using Relative Updates to Prevent Update Conflicts

Dynamics AX has always included built-in support for relative updates. But it was not until the introduction of optimistic concurrency that this support became truly useful. Relative updates can be applied only to fields of type integer and real. You apply them by changing the *FieldUpdate* property from the default value of Absolute to Relative, as shown in Figure 12-7.

The difference between an absolute update and a relative update is that an absolute update submits *FIELD* = <*new value*> in the *UPDATE* statement sent to the database, and a relative update submits *FIELD* = *FIELD* + <*delta value*>. The delta value is the difference between the originally selected value and the newly applied value. So if the *SalesQty* field on the *SalesLine* table were changed from 2 to 5, the update statement would contain either *SALESQTY* = 5 or *SALESQTY* = *SALESQTY* + 3, depending on whether the *FieldUpdate* property on the *SalesQty* field was set to *Absolute* or *Relative*.

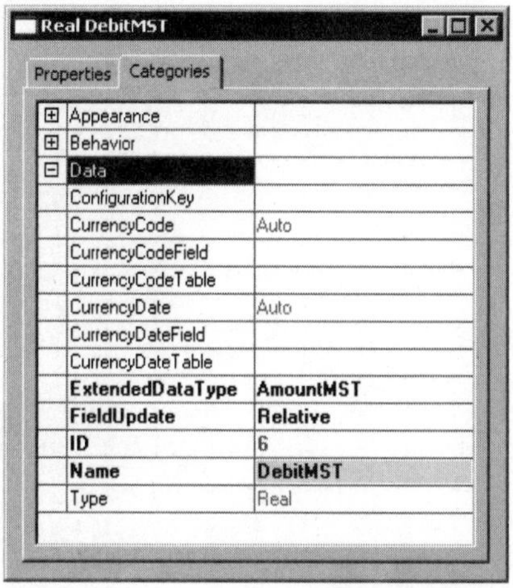

Figure 12-7   The *FieldUpdate* table field property.

When you use relative updates, it is neither what the previous value in the database was nor what it will become that is important to the updating of the application logic. The only important thing is that the difference is added to the value in the database. If all fields being updated in an update statement use relative updates and the record was selected using optimistic concurrency, the *RecVersion* check is not added to the update statement. This is because the previous value is not important, and therefore it is not important whether any other process changed the value between the select and the update.

Using relative updates on tables combined with pessimistic concurrency has no benefit because an update lock will be acquired when the application logic selects the record, so no other processes can update the same record between the select and the update.

**Warning**   Relative updates should not be used for fields on which decisions are being made by the application logic if the select is made using optimistic concurrency. You cannot guarantee that any decision will be made based on the actual value of the field. For example, a Boolean field should not be set to true or false based on whether a relative updated field is equal to zero because another process could update the relative field at the same time. The Boolean field would be set based on the value in memory, which might not be the value that is eventually written to the database.

## Choosing a Concurrency Model During Development

When developing applications in Dynamics AX, you can control the use of a concurrency model on two levels; the first is at a table level by setting a property on the table definition in the Application Object Tree (AOT), and the second is by enforcing a specific model in X++ code.

Figure 12-8 shows the table-level setting, in which the *OccEnabled* property can be set to either Yes (the default value) or No.

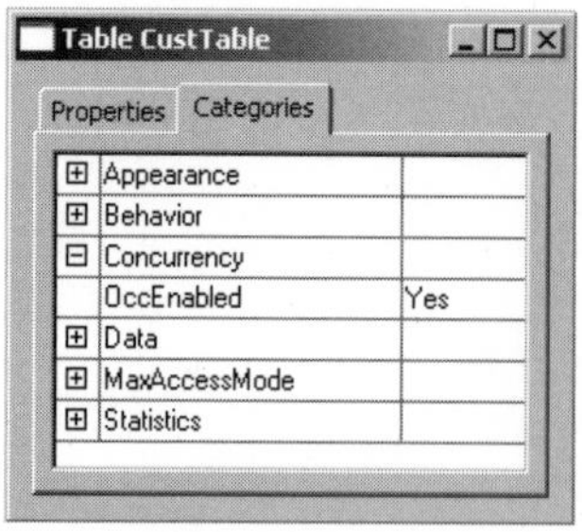

Figure 12-8   An optimistic concurrency control table property.

When the runtime has to execute a statement such as *select forupdate custTable where custTable.AccountNum == '4000'*, the application runtime consults the *OccEnabled* property on the table and translates the statement into an SQL statement with either a NOLOCK hint or an UPDLOCK hint added to the SELECT statement.

The concurrency model setting on the tables in Dynamics AX is based on an assessment of whether the risk of update conflict is minimal for the majority of the daily business scenarios in the application in which the specific table is updated or deleted. The scenarios can be found by using the cross-reference system in Dynamics AX or by searching for places in the X++ code where the table is either updated or deleted. If a table is never updated or deleted in the X++ code, the execution of the code will not be influenced by whether the table is OCC-enabled because the table will be manipulated only from a rich client form or a Web client form. Because the form application runtime does not use the table-level setting when updating records, the *OccEnabled* property is set to Yes by default on these tables.

**Note**   Only about 25 tables of the approximately 2,100 tables in the SYS layer do not use optimistic concurrency.

If a minority of the business scenarios require the use of a different concurrency model, they should be handled individually by applying statement-level concurrency code.

**Note**   No select statements needed to be rewritten for the development of Dynamics AX 4.0 because of the new interpretation of the *forupdate* keyword. The code base for the existing update scenarios was completely reusable. It was necessary to use the new keywords only for the scenarios that needed a behavior different from the table setting.

The statement-level concurrency control can be applied by exchanging the *forupdate* keyword with either *optimisticlock* or *pessimisticlock*. This enforces the use of either optimistic or pessimistic concurrency in a scenario in which the keyword is used and will overrule the table-level setting. In case of enforced pessimistic concurrency, the select statement would be written as follows: *select pessimisticlock custTable where custTable.AccountNum == '4000'*.

> **Note**   You can also control the concurrency model with the use of a variable by calling the *concurrencyModel(ConcurrencyModel concurrencyModel)* method on a cursor and parsing the concurrency model as the parameter. The *ConcurrencyModel* type is an enumeration type. A similar method is available on the *QueryBuildDataSource* class, and you can even specify the concurrency model in metadata when defining a query element in the AOT.

You should enforce pessimistic concurrency when serialization is necessary; serialization is implemented by requiring an update lock on a record in the database. The lock prevents two processes from entering the same scenario because entering requires an update lock. Only the process holding the update lock can enter the scenario, and the other process is blocked until the lock is released. The serializing select statement should therefore include the *pessimistic-lock* keyword.

> **Best Practices**   Enforcing pessimistic concurrency by using the *pessimisticlock* keyword is a best practice for developing serialization logic, although you can implement the same pessimistic concurrency behavior by using the *forupdate* keyword on a table where pessimistic concurrency is chosen at the table level. The X++ code explicitly states that an update lock is required; more importantly, the scenario will not fail if the table property is changed. The *OccEnabled* property can be changed through customization in higher layers.

You should enforce optimistic concurrency in situations in which it is apparent that the optimistic model would improve concurrency and throughput compared to the pessimistic model, especially when use of the pessimistic model would cause major blocking because of update locks that are never converted into exclusive locks. For example, optimistic concurrency is enforced in the Dynamics AX consistency check classes, where you can assume that only a few records are in an inconsistent state and therefore need to be corrected and updated.

> **Best Practices**   You should explicitly state the use of optimistic concurrency in the X++ code if the scenario always qualifies for the use of this model.

## Setting a Concurrency Model Globally

You can disable the table-level concurrency settings at run time. This has a global impact on the business logic. You have access to a Concurrency Model Configuration form from the Administration menu, in which you can override the table-level setting and enforce either optimistic or pessimistic concurrency for all tables. The property on the tables will not change, but when the Dynamics AX application runtime interprets the *forupdate* keyword, it uses the global setting, rather than the table-level setting. The global setting honors the interpretation of the *optistimiclock* or *pessimisticlock* keywords, so optimistic and pessimistic concurrency are still enforced in scenarios in which these keywords are used.

> **Warning**   You should disable the table-level settings with great care only after considerable testing in a non-production environment, and only if you completely understand and accept all the consequences of the change.

## Optimistic Concurrency and Exception Handling

Although exception handling is described in Chapter 5,"The X++ Programming Language," it deserves special attention in a discussion of optimistic concurrency because an *UpdateConflict* exception is thrown when the application runtime discovers an update conflict. The *Update-Conflict* exception is the only exception that can be caught both inside and outside a transaction scope. All other exceptions in the X++ programming language can be caught only outside a transaction scope. When the update conflict exception is caught inside a transaction scope, the database is not rolled back, as it is when caught outside a transaction scope.

Update conflict exceptions can be caught inside a transaction scope so that you can catch the exception, execute compensating logic, and then retry the update. The compensating logic must insert, update, or delete records in the database to get to a state in which you can retry the application logic.

You might find it very difficult, however, to write compensation logic that reverts all changes within a given scenario and makes it possible to retry the application logic from a consistent state. This is especially true because it is possible to customize the update methods to manipulate records in other tables. These changed records are then not compensated for by the compensation logic, which might be located in a completely different element. Because of these difficulties, the standard Dynamics AX application does not attempt to compensate for changes to database records and retry within a transaction scope. The implemented X++ code to catch the update conflict exception and retry outside transaction scopes uses the X++ code pattern shown in the following example. The validation on the returned value from *appl.ttsL evel()* determines whether the exception is caught inside or outside the transaction. If the exception is caught inside a transaction scope, the exception is simply thrown again. If the exception is caught outside a transaction scope, the transaction is retried unless the scenario has already been retried a certain number of times, in which case the application logic stops trying and throws an *UpdateConflictNotRecovered* exception. In Dynamics AX, the maximum number, which is set in the *OCCRetryCount* macro element in the AOT, is 5.

```
#OCCRetryCount
catch (Exception::UpdateConflict)
{
    if (appl.ttsLevel() == 0)
    {
        if (xSession::currentRetryCount() >= #RetryNum)
        {
            // Don't retry anymore.
            throw Exception::UpdateConflictNotRecovered;
```

```
        }
        else
        {
            // Transaction is rolled back, so retry.
            // Possible additional code here
            retry;
        }
    }
    else
    {
        // Rethrow exception because execution is within transaction.
        throw Exception::UpdateConflict;
    }
}
```

## Concurrency Models in Forms

The execution of the rich client and Web client form application runtime always uses optimistic concurrency when updating and deleting records in forms. This means that the form application runtime does not use the *OccEnabled* property on the tables.

In a Dynamics AX installation that uses SQL Server 2000, records are always read into the form by using an uncommitted isolation level, and when records are updated or deleted, the *RecVersion* check is performed. This prevents an extra round trip to the database to reselect the record and requires an update lock. This was not the case in earlier versions of Dynamics AX, in which optimistic concurrency was not implemented.

## Repeatable Read

If a scenario does not need to modify any data and merely needs to be assured that the same data can be read numerous times within a transaction scope without changes to data, the scenario can use the new repeatable read option supported in Dynamics AX. You ensure repeatable read by issuing the following select statement, which includes the *repeatableread* keyword:

```
select repeatableread custTable where custTable.CustGroup == '40';
```

When Dynamics AX running with SQL Server 2000 executes the preceding statement, it adds a REPEATABLEREAD hint to the SQL SELECT statement, which is parsed to the database. This ensures that a shared lock is held until the end of the transaction on all records selected by the statement. Because this prevents any other process from modifying the same records, it guarantees that the same record can be reselected and that the field values will remain the same.

> **Note** The *repeatableread* option only prevents the records from being updated or deleted. It does not prevent insertion of new records that match the criteria applied when the shared locks were acquired. The same SELECT statement may therefore return more rows the second time it is executed.

# Record Identifiers

When a transaction scope is committed and a record set is inserted in the database table, the inserted record gets a unique record identifier assigned by the Dynamics AX application runtime. The record identifiers are also referred to as record IDs, and *RecID* is the column name. The record IDs are 64-bit integers that are used throughout the application to ensure data integrity. MorphX automatically creates *RecID* fields in all Dynamics AX application tables and system tables. They cannot be removed from the tables like normal fields because they are defined by the MorphX environment.

> **Note** The Transaction ID framework uses the same numbering scheme for unique identification transactions across the application and within the company accounts. It is also modified to use a 64-bit integer as the transaction identifier. This is the same approach used in earlier versions of the application.

The record ID allocation method uses a sequential numbering scheme to allocate record identifiers to all rows inserted in the Dynamics AX database. Sequential numbering is not strictly required (numbers can be used out of sequence, manually modified, or skipped), but duplicates are not allowed.

## Allocation

Record identifiers are allocated by the AOS as needed when a record is about to be inserted in the database. Each AOS allocates blocks of 250 record identifiers, which are allocated per table. So each AOS holds an in-memory pool of up to 249 record identifiers per table. When the entire pool for a table is used, the AOS allocates 250 new record identifiers for that table.

There is no guarantee that records inserted in the same table will have sequential record identifiers if they are inserted by different instances of the AOS. There is also no guarantee that the sequence of record identifiers will not be fragmented. Used record identifiers are not reclaimed when transactions are aborted. Unused record identifiers are lost when an AOS is stopped. Because of the 64-bit integer scheme, the available number of record identifiers is inexhaustible, and the fragmentation has no practical impact.

The *SystemSequences* database table holds the next available record identifier block for each table. Note that the allocation of record identifiers is not per company (as it was in earlier versions of Dynamics AX), but per table.

Inserted records always have a record identifier, but they can also have a company account identifier (*DataAreaID*) for grouping all data that belongs to a legal business entity. If data in a table must be saved per company (meaning that the developer has set the *SaveDataPer-Company* table property to Yes), the Dynamics AX application runtime will always apply the *DataAreaID* column as part of every index and every database access command.

In Dynamics AX 4.0, you may have multiple instances of a record ID within the same company, as long as they do not occur within the same table. The co-existence of identical record IDs is possible because the generator that creates the individual identifier exists on a per-table basis, and the uniqueness of the record includes the table ID in the reference. All companies share the same record ID allocator per table, which ensures that there is only one instance of each record identifier across all companies within a particular table.

Figure 12-9 shows the differences in generation and allocation between Dynamics AX 4.0 and its predecessors.

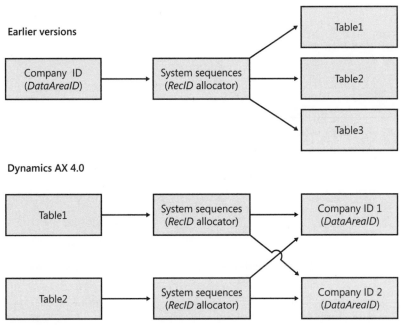

**Figure 12-9**   Record identifier allocation comparison.

In Dynamics AX 4.0, the record ID type changed from 32-bit to 64-bit integer to prevent particularly high-volume customers from running out of available record IDs. Another reason for the change was to balance the requirements for maximum performance, minimum impact on customer and partner extensions, database upgrade time, and code upgrade time. The 64-bit integer enhancement allows for a total of 18,446,744,073,709,551,615 (0xFFFF FFFF FFFF FFFF) record identifiers and provides more flexibility in allocating certain ranges for specific purposes.

In Dynamics AX 4.0, the record ID range, equivalent to the entire 32-bit range used in earlier versions, is reserved to support existing customers when they upgrade. This approach is the safest and most efficient model and can be implemented without modifying any record identifiers, including foreign key references to record identifiers. Only the content of the sequence number allocation table is modified during upgrade. The range from 0x0000 0001 0000 0000 through 0x7FFF FFFF FFFF FFFF is used for new records in Dynamics 4.0 to prevent possible conflict with data from previous versions.

Figure 12-10 illustrates the new allocation range for record IDs using the 64-bit integer, and it also shows where the *SystemSequences* database table operates. The complete identifier range is essentially divided into three groups (upgrade, new, and future), thus extending the existing record ID range of use from $2^{32}$ to $2^{63}$-1 numbers.

OxFFFF FFFF FFFF FFFF

OxFFFF FFFF 8000 0000
OxFFFF FFFF 7FFF FFFF

0x8000 0000 0000 0000
0x7FFF FFFF FFFF FFFF

0x0000 0001 0000 0000
0x0000 0000 FFFF FFFF

0x0000 0000 8000 0000
0x0000 0000 7FFF FFFF

☐ Upgrade range only
◼ Reserved – do not use
☐ All new record IDs

**Figure 12-10**   Record identifier allocation ranges.

# Administration

The numbering scheme is administrated automatically by the Dynamics AX application runtime and can be divided into administration of the individual record ID and the record ID block. The record IDs are managed in memory at the AOS cache level, whereas the block allocation uses the *SystemSequences* database to get information about the next record ID block value (*NextVAL*), native Dynamics AX table IDs (*TabID*), and the corresponding *DataAreaID*. By default, the administration tool set provides very limited manipulation possibilities for the database administrator, who can set the next block value but cannot manipulate the next individually assigned record ID. However, the *SystemSequence* system class can be used to manually alter the automatic record ID assignment behavior, but only for local block assignment.

 **Caution**    To avoid destruction of data integrity and to maintain the inter-table referencing, use the *SystemSequence* class with the utmost caution.

The entities in the *SystemSequences* table are not created when synchronizing the table definition from the MorphX Data Dictionary, nor does the record ID block of 250 numbers get allocated when starting the AOS. The entity is created the first time that a record is inserted into the table.

# Upgrade

The enhanced record identification is based on a 64-bit integer and requires existing 3.0 installations to upgrade. The upgrade process for the record ID requires changes to the 3.0 application that must be made before starting the application and data upgrade. The record ID data pre-upgrade is handled by the Dynamics AX DB Upgrade Preparation tool. However, some prerequisites must be met before you can use the tool. Additionally, the existing application logic must be upgraded to support the 64-bit integer.

With the Dynamics AX DB Upgrade Preparation tool, partners and customers use a stand-alone Microsoft Windows application tool that prepares the 3.0 database for the automatic data upgrade handled by Dynamics AX 4.0. The database preparation is required because the Dynamics AX 4.0 database has been subject to fundamental and significant changes, including:

- Unicode enabling.
- Record identification extension (*RecID*).
- OCC implementation.

The Dynamics AX DB Upgrade Preparation tool reads the 3.0 database and re-populates the new database with Unicode data types (*nchar*, *nvarchar*, and *ntext*) in place of the Multibyte Character Set (MBCS) data types. In addition, the record identification references and the transaction identification reference fields are converted from 32 bit to 64 bit (data type *int64* instead of *int*). For relevant tables, optimistic concurrency control is enabled.

Focusing on the record identification, the Dynamics AX DB Upgrade Preparation tool comes with some preliminary MorphX elements to query the AOT for possible elements that need further investigation before initiation of the pre-upgrade process. The elements exist as an export file called PrivateProject_UpgradeColumnList.xpo, which is available on the product CD in the DatabaseUpgrade folder. Unfortunately, the Dynamics AX DB Upgrade Preparation tool cannot locate existing record identifier references that are packed inside containers and stored in the database. Such record identifier references must be moved to a dedicated field before the upgrade. When investigating Microsoft Axapta 3.0 modifications for packed containers containing record identifiers, look for:

- Classes that extends the *SysPackable* class.
- Fields that contains a record identification packed inside the *pack()* method of that class.
- The packed data containers that are subsequently saved to a database table.

If the 3.0 code has such modifications, you must do the following before running the Dynamics AX DB Upgrade Preparation tool to ensure that data import and export can correctly handle record identifications:

1. Create a dedicated field in the relevant table to store the record identification reference.
2. Unpack existing packed data and move it to the dedicated field.

Other tool prerequisites include the following:

- The Axapta 3.0 SPx system must be installed and running.
- A new and empty Dynamics AX 4.0 database must be created by using the installation program.

When all prerequisites are met, the Dynamics AX DB Upgrade tool can be run, but only once. The tool requires read access to the source database and write access to the target database.

The introduction of the 64-bit integer as record identifiers also requires the application logic to be upgraded because the internal references do not comply with the Dynamics AX 4.0 best practices. For changes to the application logic and metadata, see Appendix C, "Source Code Changes Required for Upgrade."

# Company Identifiers

The business and system information in Dynamics AX is associated with company accounts and their interaction with the database tables. Several company accounts can share the same database infrastructure and use the same application logic. However, they must each have their own set of data that cannot be directly accessed from other company accounts. Tables in an application may also contain information that can be reused by several company accounts. This design involves the following elements:

- **Companies**   A company account can be based on one or more virtual company accounts. When you add data to a table that is not in a virtual company account, the data is stored directly in the company account.
- **Virtual companies**   A virtual company account is a collection of data from several company accounts that is common to all the companies and uses a list of one or more table collections to define the tables that it contains. The data in the tables included in the table collections is stored in the virtual company account. The end user cannot work

directly in a virtual company account, but the contents of the shared tables can be changed through the company account.

■ **Table collections**   A table collection is a specification of a list of table names. Table collections define a graph of tables that have no foreign-key relationships with tables outside the table collection. Table collections are defined by developers. Each table and view in the system can occur only once in any one table collection, but tables and views can be added to more than one table collection. A table collection stores no table data; only companies and virtual companies store data.

The Dynamics AX application runtime uses these components to provide a powerful framework for integrating and optimizing the available and required business data across the enterprise, allowing chosen processes and structures to be centralized. This also improves data integrity because identical information is administrated only once and does not have to be saved in multiple companies. Another significant benefit is that users do not perceive the virtual company as a separate company account because it is completely transparent to users who are using the current company account.

Figure 12-11 illustrates how the three virtual company accounts interact with company accounts and how a virtual company account can have multiple *table collections associated with the individual virtual company account.* Company AAA and Company BBB share the maintenance of currencies, whereas Company CCC and Company DDD share the chart of accounts. All companies share the maintenance of zip codes and countries. The last virtual company account also shows how company accounts can use multiple virtual company accounts.

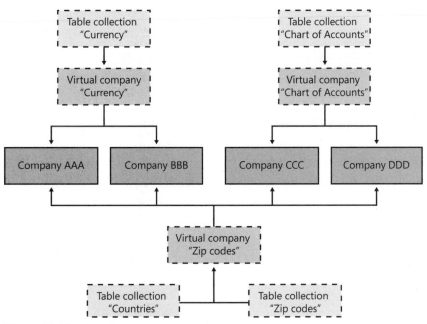

**Figure 12-11**   Company account overview.

Company accounts translate the organizational structures of the enterprise into elements that can be configured using Dynamics AX applications. Building the company structures by using company accounts involves the following straightforward steps:

1.  Create company accounts.

2.  Create table collections.

3.  Create virtual company accounts and associate the company accounts.

When you create a table collection, the foreign keys must not be part of the table in a virtual company where the key is in the (non-virtual) company. When developing the table collection, you might have to adjust the data model to get the full benefit of the collection. Figure 12-12 shows the location of the table collection within the AOT and the tables included in the particular table collection.

**Figure 12-12**   Table collections in the AOT.

# Identification

Company accounts are identified by any three characters within the Unicode-supported character set in arbitrary combination, covering both real company accounts and virtual company accounts. This enables the Dynamics AX application to host thousands of companies within the same database using the same application logic. When choosing identification characters, be aware of characters that can affect the generated SQL statement (such as reserved words, !,",""", and so on) because the company identifier is an important part of the statement.

> **Note**   The company accounts feature is subject to licensing. You cannot create more than three company accounts or unlimited virtual company accounts until you acquire the Company Accounts license. This license removes the default three-company account limit.

The *DataArea* table, which is used by the application runtime when saving data, stores information about company accounts. The *SaveDataPerCompany* table property determines, on a table level, whether data should be saved per company or exist as general available data without company account affiliation. If the property is set to Yes, the *DataAreaID* column is applied automatically for storing the company account reference.

The data flow diagram in Figure 12-13 illustrates how records are evaluated before they are inserted into tables. The process for inserting records into non-company-specific tables is important to recognize because data will be related across companies, installation, database, AOT, tracing, or OLAP and is therefore accessible from all company accounts.

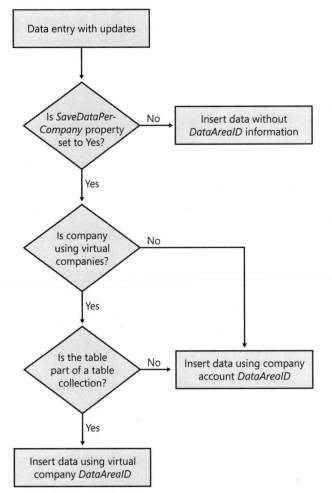

**Figure 12-13**   A data flow diagram for inserting data.

## Changing the Company Account

The company account context can be changed at run time by using multiple methods, but you can also change the context at startup time by using the configuration utility or by adding a company parameter directly in the application shortcut. Within the application runtime, users can launch the selection form to change the context by double-clicking the company name in the system's status bar or by clicking File\Open\Company on the menu bar.

Changing the company account from within the code is even more interesting when working across company accounts, such as with consolidations, sales between operations, or multi-site planning. MorphX supports changing of the company account by using the *changeCompany* function in X++, which also exists as a reserved keyword. The *changeCompany* statement alters the database settings to another (separate) company account. The syntax of the statement is:

changeCompany ( expression ) { `statement` }

In the preceding statement, *expression* is a string that defines the company to be used. The statement is executed on the new company. The following code example shows how to use this statement.

```
static void main()
{
    CustTable custTable;
    ;

    // Assume that we are running in company 'dat'.
    changeCompany('dmo') //Default company is now 'dmo'.
    {
        custTable = null;
        while select custTable
        {
            // custTable is now selected in company 'dmo'.
        }
    }
    // Default company is now set back to 'dat'.

    changeCompany('int') // Default company is now 'int'.
    {

    // Clear custTable to let the select work on the new default company.
        custTable = null;

        while select custTable
        {
            // custTable is now selected in company 'int'.
        }
    }
    // Default company is now 'dat' again.
}
```

The *changeCompany* function is heavily used by the classes tagged *InterCompany**, but it can also be found elsewhere.

## External Accessibility

You can access the company-specific data in Dynamics AX from external sources by using the COM Business Connector or the .NET Business Connector and the X++ application logic for extracting or modeling the required datasets, or by using the Application Integration Framework (AIF). You can also access the data by interacting directly with the database.

Working directly with the database is often the preferred approach for consultants not experienced with Dynamics AX because the database tools are well known, but this approach can be challenging if virtual company accounts are part of the company account dataset. The database does not include any information about references between company accounts and virtual company accounts.

You can use business views to expose a collection of data as self-contained database views that provide an accurate picture of a company's status translated into human-readable format. Using business views can also provide valuable details about natively calculated fields (based on either edit or display methods), enumeric field values, grouping of data, and company accounts, thereby increasing the data visibility for external parties. The Dynamics AX administrator defines and populates the business view to the database for further external processing. Creating business views does not necessarily require changes to the application logic or data dictionary because creation is handled from the application side and is data driven. Business views use existing tables and views from the AOT, but they create new database views within the same transactional database that the application runtime uses.

The process for creating business views is as follows:

1. Create database view prefixes.
2. Manage the virtual company accounts from within business views.
3. Define the company accounts collection.
4. Define groups of particular values, such as colors, numbers, text, and so on.
5. Define calculated fields by company accounts.
6. Manage the enumeric field values.
7. Create and define the business view.
8. Synchronize the created business view with the database.

# Unicode Support

In Dynamics AX 4.0, the application runtime completely supports Unicode and multiple-locale input and output without the risk of data loss. The previous version of Dynamics AX provided support for data storage in the database as Unicode data as well as handling of Asian characters in double-byte character sets, but the application runtime did not support multiple codepage characters or Unicode. In any given installation, only one character set was supported because data from one character set written to the database might not get correctly converted into another character set. This could lead to loss of data when incorrectly converted data was eventually written back to the database.

This problem is completely eliminated in Dynamics AX 4.0, but developers and end users should still be aware that Unicode support does not imply multiple locale sorting and comparison or other features such as multiple time zone functionality or multiple country-specific functionality.

> **Note**   Dynamics AX 4.0 supports storing Unicode data only, so the option Initialize database for Unicode in the Axapta 3.0 Configuration Utility is no longer available.

## Databases

The Dynamics AX application runtime supports only Unicode data types in the database, so all data persists in the N-prefixed versions of the data types in SQL Server and Oracle. These are the NVARCHAR and NTEXT data types in SQL Server and the NVARCHAR2 and NCLOB data types in Oracle. When you upgrade to Dynamics AX 4.0, the conversion from non-Unicode to Unicode is handled as part of the upgrade process.

> **Note**   Although the upgrade process handles the conversion of text stored in VARCHAR, TEXT, and the equivalent Oracle data types, text could still be stored in fields of type container, which persists in columns in the database of type IMAGE in SQL Server and BLOB in Oracle. These values are not converted during the upgrade process, but the Dynamics AX application runtime will convert non-Unicode data to Unicode data when the values are read from the database and extracted from the container field.

SQL Server 2000 and SQL Server 2005 store Unicode data using the UCS-2 encoding scheme, and Oracle Database 10g stores Unicode data using the UTF-16 encoding scheme. This means that every Unicode character generally uses 2 bytes, but in special cases 4 bytes, to store the single character. The required disk space to store the database is therefore higher for a Dynamics AX 4.0 installation than it is for installations of previous versions, given the same amount of tables and data. The required disk space is not doubled, however, because only string data is affected by the conversion to Unicode; the *int, real, date,* and *container* data types do not consume additional space in the database.

As the amount of space needed to store the data increased, so did the time required to read and write data because more bytes had to be read and written. This, of course, also affects the size of packages sent between the client tier and the server tier, and on to the database tier. Because the package size is the same in Axapta 3.0 and Dynamics AX 4.0, the number of packages is increased in Dynamics AX 4.0.

When you create the database to be used for the Dynamics AX installation, you can specify a collation. Collation determines the sorting order for data retrieved from the database and the comparison rules used when searching for the data.

> **Note**   Although specification of collations at lower levels than the database instance (such as at the column level) is supported by SQL Server 2000, SQL Server 2005, and Oracle Database 10*g*, it is not supported by the Dynamics AX application runtime.

Because the collation is specified at the database instance level, the Dynamics AX application runtime supports sorting using the collation setting only; it does not support sorting using a different locale. Dynamics AX supports input and output according to multiple locales, but not sorting and comparison according to multiple locales.

## The Application Runtime

The Dynamics AX application runtime supports Unicode through the use of UTF-16 encoding, which is also the primary encoding scheme used by Microsoft Windows 2000, Windows XP, and Microsoft Windows Server 2003. The use of UTF-16 encoding makes the Dynamics AX application surrogate-aware; it can handle more than 65,536 Unicode characters, which is the maximum number of Unicode characters supported by the UCS-2 encoding scheme. Dynamics AX generally uses only 2 bytes to store the Unicode character, but it uses 4 bytes when it needs to store supplementary Unicode characters. Supplementary characters are stored as surrogate pairs of 2 bytes each. An example of a supplementary character is the treble clef music symbol shown in Figure 12-14. The treble clef symbol has the Unicode code point 01D120 expressed as hexadecimal number.

**Figure 12-14**   An example of a supplementary character.

Although the application runtime uses UTF-16 encoding and the SQL Server back-end database uses UCS-2 encoding, you will not experience loss of data. This is because the SQL Server database is surrogate safe; it stores a Unicode character occupying 4 bytes of data as two unknown 2-byte Unicode characters. It retrieves the character in this manner as well, and returns it intact to the application runtime.

The maximum string length of a table field is, however, parsed directly as the string length to use when creating the NVARCHAR type column in the database. This means that a string field with a maximum length of 10 characters results in a new column in the SQL Server database with a maximum length of 10 double bytes. A maximum length of 10, therefore, does not necessarily mean that the field can contain 10 Unicode characters. For example, a string field can store a maximum of 5 treble clef symbols, with each occupying 4 bytes, totaling 20 bytes, which is equivalent to the maximum length of 10 double bytes declared for the column in the database. This does not cause problems, though, because the expected use of supplementary characters is minimal, especially in an application such as Dynamics AX 4.0. Supplementary characters are currently used, for example, for mathematical symbols, music symbols, and rare Han characters.

The Dynamics AX application runtime also supports the use of temporary tables that are stored either in memory or in files. The temporary tables use an indexed sequential access method (ISAM)–based architecture, which does not support the specific setting of collations, so data stored in temporary tables is sorted locale invariant and case insensitive. The indexes on the temporary tables have a similar behavior, so searching for data in the temporary table is also locale invariant and case insensitive.

The application runtime also performs string comparisons in a local-invariant and case-insensitive manner. However, some string functions, such as the *strlwr* and *strupr* functions, use the user's locale.

> **Important**   String comparison has changed slightly in Dynamics AX 4.0 compared to the previous version. Dynamics AX 4.0 still ignores case when comparing strings, but it does not ignore diacritics, meaning that the letter A is different from the letter Ä. The previous version ignored most, but not all, diacritics. For example, the letter A was equal to Ä, but not equal to Å.

## The MorphX Development Environment

The MorphX development environment also supports Unicode. You can write X++ code and define metadata that contains Unicode characters. However, you can define elements only in the dictionary, which conforms to the ASCII character set, and you can declare variables only in X++, which also conforms to the ASCII character set. The remaining metadata and language elements allow the use of all Unicode characters. This means that you can write comments in X++ using Unicode characters, as well as string constants in X++ and in metadata.

All strings and string functions in the X++ language support Unicode characters, so the *strlen* function returns the number of Unicode characters in a string, not the number of bytes or double bytes used to store the Unicode characters. Therefore, a string that contains only the treble clef symbol, as shown earlier, has a string length of 1, rather than 2, even though it uses two double bytes to store the single Unicode character.

> **Important**   Because SQL Server stores Unicode characters using UCS-2 encoding, it could return a different value when using the LEN function in Transact-SQL (T-SQL). A column that contained a single treble clef symbol stored by the Dynamics AX application would return a length of 2 when using the LEN function because the treble clef symbol is stored as two unknown Unicode characters in the database. The Dynamics AX application runtime does not use or expose the LEN function, so this behavior is not an issue for users of the Dynamics AX application; it arises only if the database is accessed directly from other programs or if you write direct SQL statements from within X++, thereby circumventing the database access layer.

## Files

File support in Dynamics AX 4.0 has been extended to support reading, creation, and writing of Unicode files. All text files written by the Dynamics AX application runtime are created as Unicode files, and all text files that are part of the Dynamics AX installation are Unicode files. The application runtime also, however, supports reading of non-Unicode files.

Two new file I/O classes have been introduced that allow you to implement X++ code that reads and writes Unicode text files: *TextIO* and *CommaTextIO*. These classes are equivalent to the *AsciiIO* and *CommaIO* ASCII character set classes. You should use these classes instead of the ASCII file I/O classes to avoid losing data when writing to files. However, you might encounter scenarios in which market, legal, or proprietary requirements demand the use of the ASCII file I/O classes.

## DLLs and COM Components

All areas of Dynamics AX 4.0 that use DLLs and COM components use the Unicode-enabled versions of the DLLs. The *createFile* method in the *WinApi* class has been replaced with the *CreateFileW* implementation, rather than the *CreateFileA* implementation of the *createFile* function, because *CreateFileW* supports Unicode and *CreateFileA* supports ANSI. When parsing parameters to the functions in X++ code, the parameters are defined as *ExtTypes::WString* when parsing in Unicode characters, whereas the *ExtTypes::String* expects non-Unicode characters to be parsed.

The code highlighted in bold in the following copy of the *createFile* method in Dynamics AX 4.0 has been changed to support Unicode.

```
#winapi
client static int createFile(str fileName, int flags = #OPEN_ALWAYS,
                                          int access = 0)
{
    DLL          _winApiDLL      = new DLL(#KernelDLL);
    DLLFunction _createFile      = new DLLFunction(_winApiDLL,'CreateFileW');

    _createFile.returns(ExtTypes::DWord);
```

Part III  Under the Hood

```
        _createFile.arg(ExtTypes::WString);
        _createFile.arg(ExtTypes::DWord);
        _createFile.arg(ExtTypes::DWord);
        _createFile.arg(ExtTypes::DWord);
        _createFile.arg(ExtTypes::DWord);
        _createFile.arg(ExtTypes::DWord);
        _createFile.arg(ExtTypes::DWord);

        return _createFile.call(fileName,access,0,0,
                           flags,#FILE_ATTRIBUTE_ARCHIVE,0);
    }
```

The *Binary* helper class used for COM interoperability and DLL function calls has also been changed. A *wString* function has been added to support Unicode characters to complement the existing *string* function.

# Database Access

The Dynamics AX application runtime supports the following three database platforms:

- SQL Server 2000
- SQL Server 2005
- Oracle Database 10g

However, as mentioned earlier, it is usually not necessary for you to focus on the underlying database because most of the differences in the databases are abstracted away by the application runtime. Unless an individual database offers very specific features, you can be almost certain that application logic developed using one database platform will execute without problems on the other platforms.

The Dynamics AX application runtime also supports the concurrent use of temporary tables where data is stored in files. You use these tables for temporary storage of records, and the application runtime uses them to mirror database records. Temporary tables are described near the end of this chapter.

Figure 12-15 shows how the execution of an update method on a record buffer in the application logic results in subsequent execution of application runtime logic. The database layer decides how to issue the correct statement through the appropriate API based on the installed database, the table itself, and how the table is mapped to the underlying database.

As shown in the diagram, database statements to the SQL Server 2000 and SQL Server 2005 database platforms are invoked through the Open Database Connectivity (ODBC) interface, and statements to Oracle Database 10g are invoked through the Oracle Call Interface (OCI).

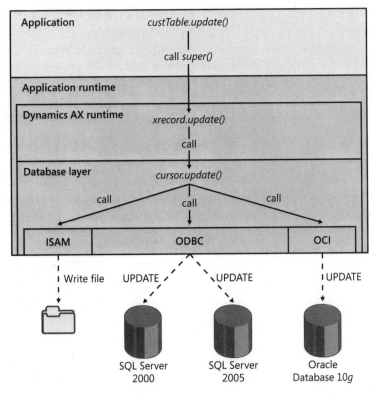

**Figure 12-15**   The database abstraction layer and platform support.

# Database Synchronization

When tables with fields and indexes are defined by using the AOT, they eventually become tables in a database. Through its database layer, the Dynamics AX application runtime synchronizes the tables defined in the application with the tables in the database. Synchronization is invoked when:

- A Dynamics AX application is installed or upgraded.
- Newly licensed modules and configurations are enabled.
- A table is created, changed, or deleted.
- An extended data type is changed.

The Dynamics AX application runtime uses one-way synchronization in which the table definitions in the Dynamics AX application are the master, and the database schemas in the database reflect the definitions inside Dynamics AX. If the database schemas do not match the table definitions in Dynamics AX, the schemas are modified to match the table definitions in Dynamics AX when the application is synchronized against the database.

Not all tables, fields, and indexes defined in Dynamics AX are reflected in the database. A table is synchronized to the database if it is not defined in metadata as a temporary table (its *temporary* property is set to Yes) and the associated configuration key is not disabled. The configuration key could be explicitly disabled, or it could be implicitly disabled if the associated license key is not enabled. A field is synchronized to the database if the content should be stored in the database (its *SaveContents* property is set to Yes) and the associated configuration key is not disabled. An index will be synchronized to the database if it is enabled (its *Enabled* property is set to Yes) and the associated configuration key is not disabled.

When you compare a table defined in Dynamics AX to the corresponding table in the database, the database table could contain fewer columns than defined fields in Dynamics AX and fewer indexes than defined in Dynamics AX. The indexes in the database could also contain fewer columns than defined because a defined field might not be enabled, preventing it from appearing in the database index.

> **Important**   There is no guarantee that the application runtime can synchronize the database if a configuration key is disabled while there is data in the database because re-creating the indexes could result in duplicate values in the index.

However, the Dynamics AX runtime applies several system fields to each table, which are synchronized to the database. The database table could therefore contain more columns than shown when you view the table definition in the AOT. Also, in certain circumstances, the Dynamics AX runtime includes an extra column in a database index to make it unique.

The Dynamics AX application runtime applies the columns shown in Table 12-1 to the tables in the database based on whether the following system fields are enabled on the table.

**Table 12-1   Dynamics AX System Fields**

| Dynamics AX system field | Database column | Table property |
|---|---|---|
| RecID | RECID | Always |
| recVersion | RECVERSION | Always |
| dataAreaId | DATAAREAID | SaveDataPerCompany = Yes |
| createdBy | CREATEDBY | CreatedBy = Yes |
| createdDate | CREATEDDATE | CreatedDate = Yes |
| createdTime | CREATEDTIME | CreatedTime = Yes |
| createdTransactionId | CREATEDTRANSACTIONID | CreatedTransactionId = Yes |
| modifiedBy | MODIFIEDBY | ModifiedBy = Yes |
| modifiedDate | MODIFIEDDATE | ModifiedDate = Yes |
| modifiedTime | MODIFIEDTIME | ModifiedTime = Yes |
| modifiedTransactionId | MODIFIEDTRANSACTIONID | ModifiedTransactionId = Yes |

The Dynamics AX application runtime requires a unique index on each table in the database to ensure that it can specifically identify each record in the database through the use of an index. The application runtime always ensures that at least one unique index exists on each table in the database; if no indexes are defined on the table or they are all disabled, the application runtime creates a *RecID* index as if the *CreateRecIdIndex* property had been set to Yes on the table. If indexes exist but none are unique, the application runtime estimates the average key length of each index, chooses the index with the lowest key length, and make this index unique by appending the RECID column.

If you want data in the tables to be saved per company (you set the *SaveDataPerCompany* property to Yes), the application runtime always applies the DATAAREAID column as the first column on every index.

> **Note**   Because a table definition inside the Dynamics AX application is the master definition, and the database schemas are always changed to reflect the Dynamics AX table definitions, it is difficult—if not impossible—to attach a Dynamics AX application to an existing legacy database.

## Table, Column, and Index Naming

The tables and columns in the database generally have the same name as defined in Dynamics AX. Indexes, however, are prefixed with I_<table id>. Any index on the SALESTABLE table in the database is therefore prefixed with I_366 because the ID for the SalesTable table in Dynamics AX is 366. The Dynamics AX application runtime allows a maximum of 30 characters for names in the database, so if names of tables, fields, or indexes exceed this number, they are truncated to 30 characters including the appended ID of the table, field, or index. For example, a table named LedgerPostingJournalVoucherSeries with an ID of 1014 becomes LEDGERPOSTINGJOURNALVOUCHE1014.

> **Tip**   If the *name* method is called on a *dictTable*, *dictField*, or *dictIndex* object with *DbBackend::Sql* as a parameter, as in *dictTable.name(DbBackend::Sql)*, the method will return the exact name in the database.

## Left and Right Justification

The Dynamics AX application runtime provides support for left and right justification of fields of type *string*. By default, *string* fields are left justified, and values are stored without modification in the database. However, if a *string* field is right justified, the value is prefixed with enough blanks when inserted into the database that all available space in the field is used. When values from a right-justified field are selected from the database, the application runtime removes the blanks. The application logic does not know whether a field is right or left justified because both left-justified and right-justified fields appear the same when used in the X++ application code.

When the application runtime formulates WHERE clauses in DML statements, it must determine whether fields are left justified or right justified because it adds extra blanks to a search value when searching for values equal to, lower than, higher than, and not equal to a field in the database. The application runtime adds extra blanks to the variable in a statement like the following when parsing the statement to the database. In the following statement, assume that the *accountNum* field is right justified.

```
select custTable where custTable.accountNum == '4000'
```

The statement parsed to the database looks like this.

```
SELECT ... FROM CUSTTABLE A WHERE A.ACCOUNTNUM = '            4000'
```

But if the search condition contains wildcard characters, as in the following X++ select statement, the application runtime must remove the blanks from the field being searched by applying LTRIM to the statement.

```
select custTable where custTable.accountNum like '4%';
```

This produces the expected result of selecting all *custTable* records where the *accountNum* field starts with '4', and the preceding X++ statement produces a statement like the following.

```
SELECT ... FROM CUSTTABLE A WHERE LTRIM(A.ACCOUNTNUM) LIKE '4%'
```

The introduction of the LTRIM function in the WHERE clause prevents both of the supported databases from searching in an index for the value in *accountNum*, which could have a severe effect on the performance of the statement.

> **Note**   None of the preceding SQL statements are a clear match to the statement parsed to either of the databases; they are intended to serve as examples only. The application runtime applies some additional functions when the LIKE operator is used.

The application runtime also applies LTRIM if a right-justified field is compared with a left-justified field. In the following select statement written in X++, assume that *accountNum* is right justified and *accountRelation* is left justified.

```
select priceDiscTable
notexists join custTable
where priceDiscTable.accountRelation == custTable.accountNum
```

The statement parsed to the database wraps the right-justified column in an LTRIM function, and looks like this.

```
SELECT … FROM PRICEDISCTABLE A
WHERE NOT EXISTS (SELECT 'x' FROM CUSTTABLE B
WHERE A.ACCOUNTRELATION=LTRIM(B.ACCOUNTNUM))
```

As mentioned earlier, this behavior could have a severe effect on performance, so you should decide whether this possible degradation of performance is acceptable before you change a field from left to right justification.

## Placeholders and Literals

The database layer in the Dynamics AX application runtime formulates SQL statements containing either placeholders or literals—that is, variables or constants. Whether the application runtime chooses to use placeholders instead of literals has nothing to do with using variables or constants when the statements are formulated in either X++ or the application runtime. The following X++ *select* statement that selects the minimum price for a given customer contains constants and a variable.

```
select minof(amount) from priceDiscTable
where priceDiscTable.Relation        == PriceType::PriceSales &&
      priceDiscTable.AccountCode      == TableGroupAll::Table  &&
      priceDiscTable.AccountRelation == custAccount
```

The statement is parsed to the SQL Server 2000 database when placeholders are used, as shown here.

```
SELECT MIN(A.AMOUNT) FROM PRICEDISCTABLE A
WHERE DATAAREAID=@P1 AND RELATION=@P2
AND ACCOUNTCODE=@P3 AND ACCOUNTRELATION=@P4
```

The statement is parsed as follows when literals are used. Assume that the statement is executed in the 'dat' company and that you are searching for the lowest price for customer '4000'.

```
SELECT MIN(A.AMOUNT) FROM PRICEDISCTABLE A
WHERE DATAAREAID=N'dat' AND RELATION=4
AND ACCOUNTCODE=0 AND ACCOUNTRELATION=N'4000'
```

As you can see, the use of constants or variables in the formulation of the statement in X++ has no effect on the use of placeholders or literals when the SQL statement is formulated. However, using *join* or specific keywords in the statement when formulating the statement in X++ does have an effect.

The default behavior of Dynamics AX is that placeholders are used, but if the Dynamics AX Server Configuration Utility option Use Literals In Complex Joins From X++ is selected, statements containing joins will use literals if the application runtime considers the statement to be a complex join. The application runtime determines that a join is complex if the statement contains two or more tables associated with the following table groups: Main, Worksheet-Header, WorksheetLine, Transaction, and Miscellaneous. Tables associated with the Group and Parameter table groups are not included when determining whether the join is complex.

**Note**    The SYS layer in Dynamics AX contains approximately 1,800 ordinary tables, and about 700 of these are associated with the Group and Parameter table groups.

Figure 12-16 shows an example of the *TableGroup* property in the list of metadata properties for a table.

| Table CustTable | |
|---|---|
| **Properties** **Categories** | |
| ⊞ Appearance | |
| ⊟ Behavior | |
|   AnalysisSelection | Auto |
|   **CacheLookup** | **NotInTTS** |
|   **ClusterIndex** | **AccountIdx** |
|   **CreateRecIdIndex** | **Yes** |
|   IsLookup | No |
|   **PrimaryIndex** | **AccountIdx** |
|   SaveDataPerCompany | Yes |
|   **TableGroup** | **Main** |
| ⊞ Concurrency | |
| ⊞ Data | |
| ⊞ MaxAccessMode | |
| ⊞ Statistics | |

**Figure 12-16**    The *TableGroup* property defined for *CustTable*.

**Note**    The Dynamics AX Server Configuration Utility option Use Literals In Complex Joins From X++ is selected by default when you install Axapta 3.0 and cleared when you install or upgrade to Dynamics AX 4.0.

The difference between using placeholders and literals lies mainly in the ability of the database to reuse execution plans and the accuracy of the calculated execution plan. When literals are used in a statement, the query optimizer in the database knows the exact values being searched for and can therefore use its statistics more accurately; when placeholders are used, the optimizer does not know the values. But because the execution plan is based on the exact values when literals are used, it cannot be reused when the same statement is parsed again with different search values. Placeholders, however, do allow reuse of the execution plan. Whether placeholders or literals result in the best performance depends on three factors:

■ How often the same statement is executed with different values

- How much better the query optimizer is at calculating the optimal execution plan when the exact values are known

- The total time required to execute the actual statement

Usually, however, both approaches result in similar execution plans; placeholders are generally preferred because execution plans can be reused, which results in better performance overall.

You can explicitly state that a join statement should always use placeholders when the SQL statement is formulated by the application runtime, regardless of the table group settings on the tables in the statement and the Server Configuration Utility options. You do this by adding the *forceplaceholders* keyword to the statement in X++, as shown in the following select statement (which would use literals if the previously mentioned Server Configuration Utility option were selected).

```
select forceplaceholders priceDiscTable
notexists join custTable
where priceDiscTable.accountRelation == custTable.accountNum
```

The alternate keyword *forceliterals* is also available in X++. This keyword explicitly causes literals to be used when the application runtime formulates the SQL statements.

**Tip**   The Query framework also allows you to explicitly state whether placeholders or literals should be used for a given query by calling *query.literals(1)* to enforce literals, *query.literals(2)* to enforce placeholders, and *query.literals(0)* to let the application runtime decide which to use. Unfortunately, no enumeration is available from the Dynamics AX application runtime to use in place of these integer constants, but the macros *#QueryLiteralsDefault*, *#QueryForceLiterals*, and *#QueryForcePlaceholders* are available from the Query macro library.

## The Dynamics AX Type System vs. the Database Type System

Because Dynamics AX application table definitions are the master for the table definitions in the database, the Dynamics AX application runtime also explicitly controls the mapping between the Dynamics AX data types and types in the supported databases. Table 12-2 describes the mapping between the Dynamics AX type system and the database type systems.

**Table 12-2   Dynamics AX and Database Type Systems**

| Dynamics AX | SQL Server 2000 | SQL Server 2005 | Oracle Database 10*g* |
|---|---|---|---|
| int | INT | INT | NUMBER(10,0) |
| real | NUMERIC(28,12) | NUMERIC(28,12) | NUMBER(32,16) |
| string (fixed length) | NVARCHAR(length) | NVARCHAR(length) | NVARCHAR2(length) |

**Table 12-2   Dynamics AX and Database Type Systems**

| Dynamics AX | SQL Server 2000 | SQL Server 2005 | Oracle Database 10g |
|---|---|---|---|
| string (memo) | NTEXT | NTEXT | NCLOB |
| date | DATETIME | DATETIME | DATE |
| time | INT | INT | NUMBER(10,0) |
| enum | INT | INT | NUMBER(10,0) |
| container | IMAGE | IMAGE | BLOB |
| guid | UNIQUEIDENTIFIER | UNIQUEIDENTIFIER | RAW(16) |
| int64 | BIGINT | BIGINT | NUMBER(20,0) |

Database types that are not shown in this table are not supported by the Dynamics AX application runtime.

# The Database Log and Alerts

Dynamics AX includes two features that base their functionality on the fact that data has been manipulated in tables: the Database Log and Alerts. Both features use information exposed by the Dynamics AX application runtime when specific data is manipulated and when the application runtime uses configuration data entered into a Dynamics AX framework table from the application. The configuration that identifies which statements to trace and log is stored in the *Databaselog* table provided by the application runtime. When a statement is executed that should be traced and logged, the application is notified by executing a callback method on the *Application* class.

Figure 12-17 illustrates a scenario in which Dynamics AX is configured to log updates to *custTable* records. When the *custTable.update* method is called, it invokes the base version of the *update* method on the *xrecord* object by calling *super()*. The base version method determines whether database logging has been configured for the given table and the update statement by querying the *Databaselog* table. If logging is enabled, a call is made to the *log-Update* method on the *Application* object, and the X++ application logic inserts a record into the *SysDataBaseLog* table.

The scenario is the same for inserts, deletes, and renaming of the primary key, as well as for raising of events that triggers alerts.

You can use the application runtime table *Databaselog* to configure all the logging and eventing because it contains a *logType* field of type *DatabaseLogType*, which is an enumeration that contains the following four values for the Database Log feature: Insert, Delete, Update, and RenameKey. It also contains the following four values for the Alert feature: EventInsert, EventDelete,

EventUpdate, and EventRenameKey. When the application runtime queries the *Databaselog* table, it therefore queries for the configuration of a specific type of logging on a given table.

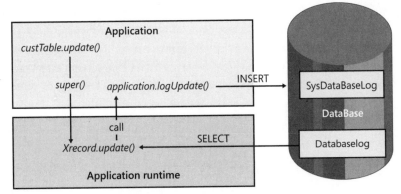

**Figure 12-17**   Logging database updates.

Table 12-3 shows the correlation between the Database Log and Alert configuration. It shows what triggers the log or event, which method on *Application* the callback is made to, and to which table the log or event is logged.

**Table 12-3   Database Log and Alert Implementation Details**

| Logged event | Triggering method on *Xrecord* class | Callback method on *Application* class | Where logged |
|---|---|---|---|
| Database insert | *insert* method | *logInsert* method | *SysDataBaseLog* |
| Database update | *update* method | *logUpdate* method | *SysDataBaseLog* |
| Database delete | *delete* method | *logDelete* method | *SysDataBaseLog* |
| Database rename primary key | *renamePrimaryKey* method | *logRenameKey* method | *SysDataBaseLog* |
| Insert event | *insert* method | *eventInsert* method | *EventCUD* |
| Update event | *update* method | *eventUpdate* method | *EventCUD* |
| Delete event | *delete* method | *eventDelete* method | *EventCUD* |
| Rename primary key event | *renamePrimaryKey* method | *eventRenameKey* method | *EventCUD* |

**Note**   The application runtime does not query the *Databaselog* table in the database every time a trigger method is executed because the AOS caches all records in memory when first needed. When records are changed in the *Databaselog* table, the cached version must therefore be flushed. You do this by calling *SysFlushDatabaseLogSetup::main()* from X++, which not only flushes the cached memory on the current AOS, but also informs other AOSs that they should flush their caches as well. The other AOSs read the flush information from the database at pre-defined intervals, so they are flushed with a minor delay.

# Database-Triggering Methods

A record buffer contains a variety of instance methods, and when called directly or indirectly, it results in statements or affects the number of statements sent to the database. Some of the methods can be called explicitly, and some are called implicitly by the Dynamics AX application runtime. Some of the methods are final, and others can be overridden. All the base versions of these methods are implemented on the *xRecord* system class. This section offers an overview of these methods and describes how the Dynamics AX application runtime interprets the execution of these methods and other built-in constructs in the X++ language. It also explains how this interpretation results in different SQL statements being parsed to the database for execution.

## The *insert, update,* and *delete* Methods

The three main methods used on the record buffer to manipulate data in the database are the *insert, update,* and *delete* methods. Each method when called results in an INSERT statement, an UPDATE statement, or a DELETE statement being parsed from the AOS to the database where each statement manipulates a single row.

> **Note**   If a *RecID* index exists on the table when the Dynamics AX application runtime formulates an UPDATE or a DELETE statement, RECID is used as a predicate in the WHERE clause to find the record. Otherwise, the shortest unique index will be used as the predicate.

All three methods can be overridden on each table individually, and they all follow the same pattern as the *insert* method, shown in the following code. The *super* call to the base class method makes the application runtime formulate the SQL DML statement and parse it to the database. Consequently, with an overridden method implemented by a developer, an application can execute additional X++ code before or after the statement is parsed to the database.

```
public void insert()
{
    // Additional code before insertion record
    super(); // The SQL statement is formulated when executing super();
    // Additional code after insertion of record
}
```

Although none of the three methods explicitly contains the *server* or *client* method modifier, all three methods are always executed on the tier where the data source is located. This means that the methods are executed on the server tier, but the methods on a temporary table may be executed on either the client tier or the server tier. Applying the *server* or *client* method modifier to these methods does not change this behavior.

There are also three equivalent methods for inserting, updating, and deleting: *doInsert*, *doUpdate*, and *doDelete*. Each method executes the same run-time logic as the base class version of the *insert*, *update*, and *delete* methods; using these methods circumvents any X++ logic in the overridden versions of *insert*, *update*, and *delete*, so use them with caution. The *doInsert*, *doUpdate*, and *doDelete* methods cannot be overridden.

> **Caution**   If you override the *insert*, *update*, and *delete* methods, you should honor the application runtime logic in the base class methods. If the logic in the methods is moved to a class hierarchy, make sure that the X++ code there executes the equivalent *doInsert*, *doUpdate*, and *doDelete* methods on the record buffer. If this is not possible because of an error, an exception should be thrown.

In addition to the *insert* and *update* methods, the record buffer also contains a *write* method that can be overridden. Execution of this methods leads to execution of either the *update* method or the *insert* method, depending on whether the record has already been inserted.

> **Caution**   Any X++ application logic written in an overridden version of the *write* method will be executed only if the method is explicitly called from other X++ code, or when records are inserted or updated from rich client forms or Web client forms. If you have written X++ code using this method, you should be aware of this limitation and consider migrating the code to the *insert* or *update* method.

As with the *insert*, *update*, and *delete* methods, the *write* method is forced by the application runtime to execute on the tier where the data source is located, no matter what is stated in the definition of the method.

## Selecting Rows

The record buffer also contains the overridable method *postLoad*. It is not necessary to execute *postLoad* from X++ because the application runtime executes it when records are retrieved from the database by the AOS. When you override the method, the *super* call copies the retrieved buffer to the original record buffer that is accessible through the *orig* method. Before an overridden *postLoad* method calls the base class method, the state of the original buffer is undefined.

> **Caution**   Any application logic written in the *postLoad* method should be light-weight code because it executes every time a record of this type is retrieved from the database. You should always consider whether the X++ code could be written elsewhere, such as in a display method.

The application runtime also forces the *postLoad* method to execute on the tier where the data source is located. Assuming that the table is not temporary and multiple records are retrieved by a client, the *postLoad* method executes on all the retrieved records sent from the database to the AOS before they are sent individually by the AOS to the client.

# Validating Rows

The record buffer contains two sets of validation methods that can be overridden. These are the previously existing methods (*validateField*, *validateWrite*, and *validateDelete*) and the new set of methods introduced in Dynamics AX 4.0: *aosValidateRead*, *aosValidateInsert*, *aosValidateUpdate*, and *aosValidateDelete*.

The difference between the two sets of methods is that the *validateField*, *validateWrite*, and *validateDelete* methods are invoked only from rich client and web client forms or if called directly from X++ code; *aosValidateInsert*, *aosValidateUpdate*, and *aosValidateDelete* are invoked implicitly from the *insert*, *update*, and *delete* base version methods, respectively, and the *aosValidateRead* method is invoked when the application retrieves records from the database.

The *aosValidate* methods prevent reading, writing, or deleting, so they should return a Boolean value of false if the user is not allowed to perform the operation that the method is validating. If the method returns false, an error is written to the Infolog and an *Exception::Error* is thrown by the Dynamics AX application runtime. The form application runtime also writes an error to the Infolog if any of the validate methods return false. When a validate method is called from X++ code, the calling method determines how to handle a validate method that returns false.

# Changing the Default Behavior

The record buffer contains a dozen methods used to change the default behavior of DML statements issued in X++ code. All the methods except one can be called with a Boolean parameter to change the default behavior, and they can all be called without a parameter to query the current status. None of the methods can be overridden.

The following methods on the record buffer influence how the application runtime interprets *select* statements that use the record buffer.

### The *SelectForUpdate* Method

Calling *selectForUpdate(true)* on a record buffer replaces the use of the *forupdate* keyword in a select statement. The following piece of X++ code

```
custTable.selectForUpdate(true);
select custTable where custTable.AccountNum == '4000';
```

is equal in behavior to this code.

```
select forupdate custTable where custTable.AccountNum == '4000';
```

Depending on the concurrency model settings on the table, a NOLOCK or UPDLOCK hint is added to the SELECT statement parsed to SQL Server 2000.

**Tip**   If you use the Query framework instead of select statements to retrieve records, it is also possible to retrieve these records as if a *forupdate* keyword had been used by calling *update(true)* on the *QueryBuildDataSource* object.

### The *concurrencyModel* Method

Calling *concurrencyModel(ConcurrencyModel::OptimisticLock)* on a record buffer replaces the use of the *optimisticlock* keyword, and calling *concurrencyModel(ConcurrencyModel::Pessimistic-Lock)* replaces the use of the *pessimisticlock* keyword. The following piece of X++ code

```
custTable.concurrencyModel(ConcurrencyModel::OptimisticLock);
select custTable where custTable.AccountNum == '4000';
```

is equal in behavior to this code.

```
select optimisticlock custTable where custTable.AccountNum == '4000';
```

This method overrules any concurrency model setting on the table and causes the addition of a NOLOCK or UPDLOCK hint to the SELECT statement parsed to SQL Server 2000. The type of hint depends on whether the *OptimisticLock* or the *PessimisticLock* enumeration value was parsed as a parameter when the application logic called the *concurrencyModel* method.

**Tip**   If you use the Query framework instead of select statements to retrieve records, it is possible to retrieve these records by using a specific concurrency model by calling *concurrency-Model(ConcurrencyModel::OptimisticLock)* or *concurrencyModel(ConcurrencyModel::Pessimistic-Lock)* on the *QueryBuildDataSource* object.

### The *selectWithRepeatableRead* Method

Calling *selectWithRepeatableRead(true)* on a record buffer replaces the use of the *repeatableread* keyword in a select statement. The following piece of X++ code

```
custTable.selectWithRepeatableRead(true);
select custTable where custTable.AccountNum == '4000';
```

is equal in behavior to this code.

```
select repeatableread custTable where custTable.AccountNum == '4000';
```

Using this keyword results in the addition of a REPEATABLEREAD hint to the SELECT statement parsed to SQL Server 2000.

> **Tip**   If you use the Query framework instead of select statements to retrieve records, it is possible to retrieve these records with a REPEATABLEREAD hint as well, by calling *selectWith-RepeatableRead(true)* on the *QueryBuildDataSource* object.

### The *readPast* Method

Calling *readPast(true)* on a record buffer results in the addition of a READPAST hint to the SELECT statement parsed to SQL Server 2000, which causes the database to skip rows on which an exclusive lock is held. The record is simply not read. This method has no equivalent keyword that can be used in a select statement.

> **Note**   Enforcing *readPast* in an installation using SQL Server 2005 on a select statement with no additional hints has no effect. SQL Server 2005 does not skip records on which an exclusive lock is held; it only returns the previous committed version.

### The *selectLocked* Method

Calling *selectLocked(true)* on a record buffer results in the addition of a NOLOCK hint to the SELECT statement parsed to SQL Server 2000, which causes the select statement to allow the reading of uncommitted records. Calling this method outside a transaction scope has no effect because the default isolation level in SQL Server 2000 is READ UNCOMMITTED, and the method has no equivalent keyword that can be used in a select statement.

### The *skipTTSCheck* Method

The record buffer also contains a method that affects the behavior of updates and deletes. Calling *skipTTSCheck(true)* on a record buffer makes it possible to later call *update* or *delete* on the record buffer without first selecting the record for update. The following code, in which a *custTable* record is selected without a *forupdate* keyword and is later updated with *skipTTSCheck* set to true, will therefore not fail.

```
static void skipTTSCheck(Args _args)
{
    CustTable custTable;

    ttsbegin;

    select custTable where custTable.AccountNum == '4000';
    custTable.CreditMax = 1000;
```

```
        custTable.skipTTSCheck(true);
        custTable.update();

        ttscommit;

    }
```

The execution of the *update* method will not throw an error in this example because the Dynamics AX application runtime will not verify that the buffer was selected with *forupdate* or an equivalent keyword. In a pessimistic concurrency scenario, no update lock would be acquired before the update, and in an optimistic concurrency scenario, the *RecVersion* check would not be made. This could lead to "last writer wins" scenarios, as described earlier in this chapter.

If the *skipTTSCheck* method had not been called in the preceding scenario, the application runtime would have thrown an error and presented the following in the Infolog: "The operation cannot be completed, since the record was not selected for update. Remember TTS-BEGIN/TTSCOMMIT as well as the FORUPDATE clause."

## Set-Based DML Statements

As explained in the preceding sections, *insert*, *update*, and *delete* methods are available on the buffer to manipulate data in the database. The buffer also offers the less frequently used *write*, *doInsert*, *doUpdate*, and *doDelete* methods for use when writing application logic in X++ code. All these methods are recordset methods; when they are executed, at least one statement is sent to the database, representing the INSERT, UPDATE, or DELETE statement being executed in the database. Each execution of these statements therefore results in a call from the AOS to the database server in addition to previous calls to select and retrieve the records.

The X++ language contains set-based insert, update, and delete operators, as well as set-based classes, that can reduce the number of round trips made from the AOS to the database tier. The Dynamics AX application runtime may downgrade these set-based operations to row-based statements because of metadata setup, overriding of methods, or the configuration of the Dynamics AX application. The record buffer, however, offers methods to change this behavior and prevent downgrading. I discuss the set-based statements and the remaining methods on the record buffer in Chapter 17, "Performance."

# Temporary Tables

By default, any table defined in the AOT is mapped in a one-to-one relationship to a table in the underlying relational database. Any table may, however, be mapped to an ISAM file–based table that is available only during the runtime scope of the AOS or a client. This mapping can take place as follows:

- At design time by setting metadata properties

- At configuration time by enabling licensed modules or configurations

- At application run time by writing explicit X++ code

The ISAM file contains data and all the indexes defined on the table that maps to the temporary table that the file represents. Because working on smaller datasets is generally faster than working on larger datasets, the Dynamics AX application runtime monitors the space needed for the dataset. If the number exceeds 128 kilobytes (KB), the dataset is written to the ISAM file; everything is kept in memory if the consumed space is less than 128 KB. Switching from memory to file has a significant effect on performance. A file with the syntax *$tmp<8 digits>.$$$* is created when data is switched from memory to file. You can monitor the threshold limit by noting when this file is created.

> **Note** A small test run by the product development team using the Dynamics AX demo data showed that 220 *CustTable* records could be stored in the temporary table before data was written to the file. However, this number will vary depending on the amount of data in each record.

Although the temporary tables do not map to a relational database, all the DML statements in the X++ language are valid for tables operating as temporary tables. Some of the statements are executed by the application runtime in a downgraded fashion because the ISAM file functionality does not offer the same amount of functionality as a relational database. Therefore, set-based operators always execute as record-by-record operations.

## Using Temporary Tables

Any table that acts as a temporary table is, indeed, temporary. When you declare a record buffer of a temporary table type, the table will not contain any records, so you must insert records to work with the temporary table. The temporary table and all the records will be lost when no more declared record buffers point to the temporary dataset.

Memory and file space are not allocated to the temporary table before the first record is inserted, and the table resides on the tier where the first record was inserted. For example, if the first insert occurs on the server tier, the memory is allocated on this tier, and eventually a file will also be created on the server tier. The tier on which the record buffer is declared or subsequent inserts, updates, or deletes are executed is insignificant.

> **Important** A careless temporary table design could lead to a substantial number of round trips between the client and the server and result in degraded performance.

A declared temporary record buffer contains a pointer to the dataset. If two temporary record buffers are used, they point to different datasets by default, even though the table type is the same. To illustrate this, the X++ code in the following example uses the *TmpLedgerTable* temporary table defined in Dynamics AX 4.0. The table contains three fields: *AccountName*, *AccountNum*, and *CompanyId*. The *AccountNum* and *CompanyId* fields are both part of a unique index, *AccountNumIdx*. This is illustrated in Figure 12-18.

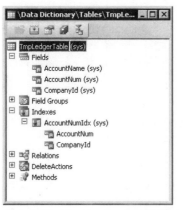

**Figure 12-18**   The *TmpLedgerTable* temporary table.

The following X++ code shows two record buffers of the same type and how the same record can be inserted in both of the record buffers. Because the record buffers point to two different datasets, a "duplicate value in index" failure will not result, as it would if both record buffers had pointed to the same temporary dataset or if the record buffers had been mapped to a database table.

```
static void TmpLedgerTable(Args _args)
{
    TmpLedgerTable tmpLedgerTable1;
    TmpLedgerTable tmpLedgerTable2;
    ;
    tmpLedgerTable1.CompanyId = 'dat';
    tmpledgerTable1.AccountNum = '1000';
    tmpLedgerTable1.AccountName = 'Name';
    tmpLedgerTable1.insert(); // Insert into tmpLedgerTable1's dataset.

    tmpLedgerTable2.CompanyId = 'dat';
    tmpledgerTable2.AccountNum = '1000';
    tmpLedgerTable2.AccountName = 'Name';
    tmpLedgerTable2.insert(); // Insert into tmpLedgerTable2's dataset.
}
```

To share the same dataset, you must call the *setTmpData* method on the record buffer, as illustrated in the following similar X++ code in which the *setTmpData* method is called on the second record buffer and parsed in the first record buffer as a parameter.

```
static void TmpLedgerTable(Args _args)
{
    TmpLedgerTable tmpLedgerTable1;
```

```
    TmpLedgerTable tmpLedgerTable2;
    ;
    tmpLedgerTable2.setTmpData(tmpLedgerTable1);

    tmpLedgerTable1.CompanyId = 'dat';
    tmpLedgerTable1.AccountNum = '1000';
    tmpLedgerTable1.AccountName = 'Name';
    tmpLedgerTable1.insert(); // Insert into shared dataset.

    tmpLedgerTable2.CompanyId = 'dat';
    tmpLedgerTable2.AccountNum = '1000';
    tmpLedgerTable2.AccountName = 'Name';
    tmpLedgerTable2.insert(); // Insert will fail with dublicate value.
}
```

The preceding X++ code will fail on the second insert with a "duplicate value in index" error because both record buffers point to the same dataset. You would notice similar behavior if, instead of calling *setTmpData,* you simply assigned the second record buffer to the first record buffer, as illustrated here.

```
    tmpLedgerTable2 = tmpLedgerTable1;
```

However, the variables would point to the same object, which means that they use the same dataset.

When you want to use the *data* method to copy data from one temporary record buffer to another, where both buffers point to the same dataset, you should write the copy like this.

```
    tmpLedgerTable2.data(tmpLedgerTable1);
```

> **Warning**   The connection from the two record buffers to the same dataset would be lost if the code were written as *tmpLedgerTable2 = tmpLedgerTable1.data()*. The temporary record buffer would be assigned to a new record buffer in which only the data part is filled in, but with a connection to a new dataset.

As mentioned earlier, when no record buffer points to the dataset, the records in the temporary table are lost, the allocated memory is freed, and the file is deleted. This is illustrated in the following X++ code example, in which the same record is inserted twice using the same record buffer. However, because the record buffer is set to null between the two inserts, the first dataset is lost, so the second insert will not result in a duplicate value in the index because the new record is inserted into a new dataset.

```
static void TmpLedgerTable(Args _args)
{
    TmpLedgerTable tmpLedgerTable;
    ;
    tmpLedgerTable.CompanyId = 'dat';
    tmpledgerTable.AccountNum = '1000';
    tmpLedgerTable.AccountName = 'Name';
    tmpLedgerTable.insert(); // Insert into first dataset.

    tmpLedgerTable = null; // Allocated memory is freed
                           // and file is deleted.
    tmpLedgerTable.CompanyId = 'dat';
    tmpledgerTable.AccountNum = '1000';
    tmpLedgerTable.AccountName = 'Name';
    tmpLedgerTable.insert(); // Insert into new dataset.
}
```

These temporary table examples do not include use of *ttsbegin* and *ttscommit* statements. This is because you must call the *ttsbegin*, *ttscommit*, and *ttsabort* methods on the temporary record buffer to work with transaction scopes on temporary tables. The *ttsbegin*, *ttscommit*, and *ttsabort* statements only affect manipulation of data related to ordinary tables that are mapped to relational database tables. This is illustrated in the following X++ code where the value of the *accountNum* field is printed to the Infolog even though the *ttsabort* statement was executed.

```
static void TmpLedgerTableAbort(Args _args)
{
    TmpLedgerTable tmpLedgerTable;

    ttsbegin;
    tmpLedgerTable.CompanyId = 'dat';
    tmpledgerTable.AccountNum = '1000';
    tmpLedgerTable.AccountName = 'Name';
    tmpLedgerTable.insert(); // Insert into table.
    ttsabort;

    while select tmpLedgerTable
    {
        info(tmpLedgerTable.AccountNum);
    }
}
```

To successfully abort the inserts of the table in the preceding scenario, you must instead call the *ttsbegin* and *ttsabort* methods on the temporary record buffer, as shown here.

```
static void TmpLedgerTableAbort(Args _args)
{
    TmpLedgerTable tmpLedgerTable;
```

```
        tmpLedgerTable.ttsbegin();
        tmpLedgerTable.CompanyId = 'dat';
        tmpledgerTable.AccountNum = '1000';
        tmpLedgerTable.AccountName = 'Name';
        tmpLedgerTable.insert(); // Insert into table.
        tmpLedgerTable.ttsabort();

        while select tmpLedgerTable
        {
            info(tmpLedgerTable.AccountNum);
        }
    }
```

When you work with multiple temporary record buffers, you must call the *ttsbegin*, *ttscommit*, and *ttsabort* methods on each record buffer because there is no correlation between the individual temporary datasets.

**Important**   When exceptions are thrown and caught outside the transaction scope, where the *ttsabort* statement has already been called by the Dynamics AX application runtime, temporary data is not rolled back.

When you work with temporary datasets, make sure that you are aware of how the datasets are used inside and outside transaction scopes.

**Important**   It is generally not a problem that the *ttsbegin*, *ttscommit*, and *ttsabort* statements have no impact on temporary data if the temporary record buffer is not declared until after the first *ttsbegin* statement is executed. This only means that the record buffer will be out of scope and the dataset destroyed if an exception is thrown and caught outside the transaction scope.

The database-triggering methods on temporary tables behave in almost the same manner as with ordinary tables, with a few exceptions. When the *insert*, *update*, and *delete* methods are called on the temporary record buffer, they do not call any of the database-logging or event-raising methods on the application class if database logging or alerts have been set up for the table.

**Note**   In general, you cannot set up logging or eventing on defined temporary tables. However, because ordinary tables may be changed to temporary tables, logging or eventing could already be set up. Changing the behavior of an ordinary table is described later in this chapter.

Delete actions are also not executed on temporary tables. Although you can set up delete actions, the Dynamics AX application runtime does not try to execute them.

**Tip**   You can query a record buffer for acting on a temporary dataset by calling the *isTmp* record buffer method, which returns true or false depending on whether the table is temporary.

Dynamics AX allows you to trace SQL statements, either from within the rich client or from the Dynamics AX Configuration Utility or the Dynamics AX Server Configuration Utility. However, SQL statements can be traced only if they are sent to the relational database. Manipulation of data in temporary tables cannot be traced by using these tools.

## Design-Time Setting

As explained earlier, you can make a table temporary during various phases of a Dynamics AX implementation. To define a table as temporary, you change the *Temporary* property on the table from the default value of No to Yes. This prevents a matching table from being created in the underlying relational database when the table is synchronized against the database. Instead, memory or a file is allocated for the table when needed. Figure 12-19 shows the *Temporary* property on a table where the value is set to Yes, thereby marking the table as temporary at design time.

| Table TmpABC | |
|---|---|
| **Properties** Categories | |
| ⊞ Appearance | |
| ⊞ Behavior | |
| ⊞ Concurrency | |
| ⊟ Data | |
| AOSAuthorization | None |
| **ConfigurationKey** | **LogisticsAdvanced** |
| CreatedBy | No |
| CreatedDate | No |
| CreatedTime | No |
| CreatedTransactionId | No |
| FormRef | |
| **ID** | 443 |
| ModifiedBy | No |
| ModifiedDate | No |
| ModifiedTime | No |
| ModifiedTransactionId | No |
| **Name** | **TmpABC** |
| ReportRef | |
| SearchLinkRefName | |
| SearchLinkRefType | Url |
| SecurityKey | |
| Systemtable | No |
| TableContents | Not specified |
| **Temporary** | **Yes** |
| TypicalRowCount | Auto |
| ⊞ MaxAccessMode | |
| ⊞ Statistics | |

**Figure 12-19**   Marking a table as temporary at design time.

 **Best Practices**   Tables that are defined as temporary at design time should have a table name prefixed or postfixed with *Tmp*. This improves readability of the X++ code when temporary tables are explicitly used.

## Configuration-Time Setting

When you define a table by using the AOT, you can attach a configuration key to a table by setting the *ConfigurationKey* property on the table. The property belongs to the Data section of the table properties, as illustrated in Figure 12-19.

When the Dynamics AX application runtime synchronizes the tables to the database, it synchronizes tables for licensed modules and enabled configurations only. Whether a table belongs to a licensed module or an enabled configuration depends on the settings in the *ConfigurationKey* property. If the configuration key is enabled, the table is synchronized to the database; if the configuration key is not enabled, the table is disabled and behaves like a temporary table. Therefore, a runtime error does not occur when the application runtime interprets X++ code that accesses tables that are not enabled.

**Note**    Whether a configuration key is enabled is not important to a table that is already set as temporary. The table remains temporary, even though its configuration key is disabled, and you can expect the same behavior regardless of the configuration key setting.

## Application Runtime Setting

You may also use X++ code to turn an ordinary table into a temporary table and use it as such. You do this by calling the *setTmp* method on the record buffer. From then on, the record buffer will be treated as though the *Temporary* property on the table were set to Yes.

**Note**    You cannot define a record buffer of a temporary table type and turn it into an ordinary table. One reason for this, among many, is that there is no underlying table in the relational database.

The following X++ code illustrates use of the *setTmp* method, in which two record buffers of the same type are defined; one is made temporary, and all records from the database are inserted into the temporary version of the table. The temporary record buffer will therefore point to a dataset containing a complete copy of all the records from the database belonging to the current company.

```
static void TmpCustTable(Args _args)
{
    CustTable custTable;
    CustTable custTableTmp;
    ;
    custTableTmp.setTmp();
    ttsbegin;
    while select custTable
    {
        custTableTmp.data(custTable);
        custTableTmp.doInsert();
    }
    ttscommit;
}
```

Notice that the preceding X++ code uses the *doInsert* method to insert records into the temporary record buffer. It does this to prevent execution of the overridden *insert* method. This method inserts and updates records in other tables that are not switched automatically to temporary mode just because the *custTable* record buffer is temporary.

> **Caution**   You should use great care when changing an ordinary record buffer to a temporary record buffer because application logic in overridden methods that manipulates data in ordinary tables could be inadvertently executed. This could happen if the temporary record buffer is used in a form and the form application runtime makes the call to the database-triggering methods.

## Chapter Summary

This chapter described how the Dynamics AX application runtime supports database access, record and company identification, transactions, and multiple languages. This support allows you to implement applications within Dynamics AX that operate in a multi-user and multi-language environment and can run on multiple databases and in different configurations.

# Chapter 13
# Advanced MorphX Forms

The objectives of this chapter are to:

- Demonstrate features of MorphX forms that go beyond the features of typical data entry forms.

- Describe how forms are instantiated.

- Describe how to modify multiple forms without modifying their definitions.

## Introduction

Experienced business developers can very quickly create a suitable user interface with MorphX forms. Sometimes, though, you might want more than just a form with a grid and some tab pages. This chapter shows you, by example, how to leverage some of the more advanced features of MorphX forms. But remember, when deviating from standard development tasks, your progress will be slower and more complicated.

The example in this chapter builds an extension to several hundred forms in the system, without modifying any of them. The change is entirely programmatic. The goal of the change is to better integrate the Document Handling feature with forms. With Document Handling, a user can attach a note to any record in Microsoft Dynamics AX 4.0. The note follows the record throughout the system. You typically use this feature to keep track of correspondence with customers, vendors, and other external entities. You can also attach files to notes, which is useful for keeping track of design documents, such as blueprints and specifications.

By default, you can access the Document Handling feature only by clicking a toolbar icon. The example in this chapter embeds the Document Handling functionality directly in all affected forms. This gives the user easy access to attached documents and enables creation of new documents with a single mouse click.

The example in this chapter is implemented in five chronological steps. The first step is to gain control when a form is instantiated. The next step is to modify the form by adding controls before the form is displayed. The added controls are then populated with data. At this point in the example, the form looks good, but it lacks user interaction, so the next step is to react accordingly to user interface events. Finally, the example provides mechanics that allow a form to opt out of the extension of functionality.

# Capturing Form Instantiation

You must first establish that you do not want to modify all the forms in the system manually. You would never complete the task, and such an approach would cause problems during future upgrades. This section offers a more intelligent solution.

All forms in Dynamics AX are created through the *ClassFactory* class. The Dynamics AX runtime calls the *formRunClassOnClient* method to create instances of forms. The *args* parameter, shown in the following code, contains the name of the form element to create.

```
client static FormRun formRunClassOnClient(Args args)
{
    SysSetupFormRun sysSetupFormRun;
;
    sysSetupFormRun = new SysSetupFormRun(args);
    return sysSetupFormRun;
}
```

You can substitute certain forms by changing the form name in the *args* parameter before the instance is created. But to achieve your goal, you must change the appearance of forms, not substitute them. Notice that a specialization of the *FormRun* class is created. The system defines the *FormRun* class, and you cannot change its implementation. However, the specialization—called *SysSetupFormRun*—is an application-defined class, meaning that you can modify it to accommodate your needs.

When a form is opened, *init* is the first method called. The *init* method creates instances of all the form controls from the metadata definition in the Application Object Tree (AOT). Before *init* is called, you have only a *FormRun* instance and a *Form* instance, which represents the form element definitions. The *FormRun* instance is actually a *SysSetupFormRun* instance (see Figure 13-2, later in this chapter, for this relationship). After *init* is executed, you also have instances of all the form controls necessary to display the form. These include pixel positions, widths, heights, and so on.

The example for this chapter constructs a class named *MyDocuPane*. Here is the definition.

```
class MyDocuPane
{
    SysSetupFormRun formRun;
    Form form;

    public void new(FormRun _formRun)
    {;
        formRun = _formRun;
        form = formRun.form();
    }
    public void beforeInit()
    {
    }
    public void afterInit()
    {
    }
    public void update(common _common)
    {
    }
}
```

Notice how you extract the *Form* instance from *FormRun* in the *new* method. Also notice the three empty methods, which are invoked from the *SysSetupFormRun* class. The following code example shows how to apply the two *init* methods in the *SysSetupFormRun* class. The changes to the *SysSetupFormRun* class appear in bold.

```
public class SysSetupFormRun extends FormRun
{
    ...
    MyDocuPane docuPane;
    public void init()
    {;
        docuPane = new MyDocuPane(this);

        docuPane.beforeInit();
        //Call init on the base class (FormRun).
        super();

        docuPane.afterInit();
        SysSecurityFormSetup::loadSecurity(this);
    }
}
```

Adding a member variable to a class in a hierarchy always requires a recompile of the class and all classes that extend it. You can do this by running the Compile Forward tool found on the Add-ins submenu. In addition, you must restart the Dynamics AX client because form instances already exist in memory.

After a restart, the class is called each time a form is opened, regardless of the form. The class is even called when the progress bar is displayed because the progress bar is also a form. Because the goal of this example is to add Document Handling capabilities to forms, limiting the forms you target makes sense. First, Document Handling must be active. Second, target forms can be defined as forms with one data source that belong to the main table group. The following code adds a method determining whether a form is a target to the *MyDocuPane* class.

```
private boolean isTargetForm()
{
    FormBuildDataSource formBuildDataSource;
    DictTable dictTable;

    //Only target forms when document handling is active.
    if (infolog.docuHandlingActive())
    {
        if (form.dataSourceCount() == 1)
        {
            //Get the first (and only) data source.
            formBuildDataSource = form.dataSource(1);
            dictTable = new DictTable(formBuildDataSource.table());
            if (dictTable &&
                dictTable.tableGroup() == TableGroup::Main)
            {
                return true;
            }
        }
    }
    return false;
}
```

Notice how the *FormBuildDataSource* instance finds the table used as a data source on the form and how reflection determines which group the table belongs to. Because the result of this method is constant for each form, you call it only once and save the return value in a member variable, as shown here.

```
class MyDocuPane
{
    ...
    boolean isTargetForm;
    public void new(FormRun _formRun)
    {
        ...
        isTargetForm = this.isTargetForm();
    }
    ...
}
```

# Adding Design Controls at Run Time

The next step is to modify all forms that meet the target criteria. Everything you can do in the AOT is also possible programmatically. You can modify the form programmatically before it is initialized by using the form design-time API.

From a programming perspective, the easiest way to determine which steps are required to add controls at run time is to perform the steps in the AOT and mentally note all steps performed. The goal in the example is to add an HTML ActiveX control to the form, dock it to the left side of the form, set a fixed pixel width, and set a dynamic height, so the control resizes with the form. Doing this in the AOT is quite simple, and you can do it on any of the target forms, such as *CustTable*.

Programmatically, you can accomplish the same by following the steps shown here.

```
public void beforeInit()
{
    FormBuildDesign design = form.design();
    FormbuildActiveXControl buildActiveX;
    #Help

    if (isTargetForm)
    {
        buildActiveX = design.addControl(FormControlType::ActiveX, 'myActiveX');
        buildActiveX.className(#WebBrowserClassName);
        buildActiveX.leftMode(FormLeft::LeftEdge);
        buildActiveX.heightMode(FormHeight::ColumnHeight);
        buildActiveX.width(150);
    }
}
```

The *className* specified in the preceding code is the *progId* for the Microsoft WebBrowser ActiveX control, which is part of Microsoft Internet Explorer. The *progId* is defined in the *Help* macro. To learn more about ActiveX components in general, refer to MSDN. The control's *leftMode* property is set to FormLeft::LeftEdge, which docks the control on the left side of the form; similarly, the *heightMode* property is set to FormHeight::ColumnHeight, which anchors the control to the top and bottom of the form, and the *width* property is set to 150 pixels. Now each target form has an ActiveX control capable of showing HTML text on the left side. You can open any target from the main menu to validate it.

**Tip**   You can find documentation of all kernel APIs under the System Documentation node in the AOT.

# Populating the Control

The controls are now laid out as planned. However, an HTML control without any content is not very useful. This section shows how to find the run-time instance of the ActiveX control, which is where you must send the HTML text. As already mentioned, the run-time controls are instantiated in the form's *init* method. The following code finds the run-time instance of the ActiveX control from the form design.

```
class MyDocuPane
{
    FormActiveXControl activeX;
    ...
    public void afterInit()
    {
        if (isTargetForm)
        {
            activeX = formRun.design().controlName('myActiveX');
        }
    }
}
```

As the preceding code shows, you gain access to the run-time controls by calling the *design* method on the *formRun* object, and you query the controls by their names. Notice the duality between the *beforeInit* and *afterInit* methods. There are two sets of APIs: a design-time version and a run-time version. The type names for the design-time version contain the word *Build*.

> **Tip**   The *FormNotify* method on the *Info* class is automatically invoked by the runtime when certain form events, caused by user actions, occur. The following are supported events: form opened, form closed, got focus, lost focus, record changed, and document handling icon clicked. You can add event logic in this method as required.

To be notified each time the record in the form changes, go to the *SysSetupFormRun* class and modify the *docCursor* method. The *docCursor* method is called from the *formNotify* method on the *Info* class so that Document Handling can receive the selected record. The following example changes the *docCursor* method on the *SysSetupFormRun* class by calling the *update* method, so notification occurs when it is time to update the contents of the ActiveX control.

```
Common docCursor()
{    Common common;
    if (infolog.docuHandlingActive())
    {        common = super();
        docuPane.update(common);
        return common;
    }
    return null;
}
```

Now it is time to implement the *update* method. *Common* is the base type for all table types. It can contain a record from any table. The *update* method takes the currently selected record as a *common* parameter, generates HTML text, and writes it to the ActiveX control, using a helper method on the *SysHelp* class, as shown here.

```
class MyDocuPane
{
    FormActiveXControl activeX;
    ...

    public void update(common _common)
    {
        str html;
    ;
        if (isTargetForm)
        {
            html = this.generateHTML(_common);
            SysHelp::showHTML(activeX, html);
        }
    }
}
```

To see the contents of the *generateHTML* method, review the complete example listing at the end of this chapter. For the purpose of this chapter, the HTML generation is kept as simple as possible. If you want, you can fine-tune the styles to get exactly the output that you want.

Now all the target forms have an HTML ActiveX control on the left side that contains a list of all the Document Handling notes for the currently selected record. The HTML content has a hyperlink to create a new note and a hyperlink for each existing node. The steps in the next section provide the ability to react when these hyperlinks are clicked.

# Reacting to User Interface Events

Reacting to user interface events is usually simple—you just override the event method, or, for ActiveX, choose the ActiveX event from the ActiveX Explorer. However, the form definition in the AOT does not contain the ActiveX control because it was added at run time, so you need another way to receive event notification.

The run-time form system can be told where to look for and invoke the event methods. This subsystem is enabled by calling the *controlMethodOverload* method on the *formRun* class with a *true* parameter. Then the form looks for methods on the *formRun* object. The method's name must adhere to a strict naming convention: <ControlName>_<MethodName>. An example of a method name using this naming convention is *myButton_clicked*. When an event is fired, and the method is not found on the *formRun* object, it defaults to the event method on the control. The method must also have the same return type and parameters as the event method.

In this example, you cannot add the method to the *formRun* type because this requires that you also change the definition of all target forms in the AOT. Instead, you can tell the form on which object to look for the event methods by passing the object to the *controlMethodOverload-Object* method. The following code enables this subsystem.

```
public void beforeInit()
{
    ...
    if (isTargetForm)
    {
        formRun.controlMethodOverload(true);
        formRun.controlMethodOverloadObject(this);
        ...
    }
}
```

So far, this does not change anything because the class contains no event methods. The following code adds an event method for the ActiveX event *onevent_BeforeNavigate2*, which is fired when a user clicks a hyperlink.

```
void myActiveX_onEvent_BeforeNavigate2(
    COM _pDisp,
    COMVariant /* variant */ _URL,
    COMVariant /* variant */ _Flags,
    COMVariant /* variant */ _TargetFrameName,
    COMVariant /* variant */ _PostData,
    COMVariant /* variant */ _Headers,
    COMVariant /* boolean */ _Cancel)
{
    ...
}
```

For the entire implementation, see the listing at the end of this chapter.

# Form Opt Out

At this point in the example implementation, all the forms that constitute the target forms will be affected. In some scenarios, however, you might want to exclude a specific form from the targets. For example, you would want to exclude a form that already uses the *controlMethod-Overload* subsystem, because only one class can be registered to receive the control method events. The form is captured too early in the form initialization process to determine whether *controlMethodOverload* will be used by the form itself. If the form itself uses *controlMethodOverload*, it will inadvertently unregister your class, breaking your event-handling logic.

To give a form a chance to support opting out of a service or feature , you can determine whether the form implements a certain method, and if it does, call it to see if it needs to opt out.

**Note**   Forms in Dynamics AX cannot implement interfaces in the object-oriented sense. Interfaces provide compile-time safe mechanisms for inter-object communication, which is a stronger alternative than the late-binding mechanism used in this example. However, interfaces are not supported for forms.

The method profile to look for can be chosen arbitrarily. In this example, the following code defines the method profile to look for.

```
public boolean useMyDocuPane()
{
}
```

Any form that needs to opt out can add this method as a new method and let it return false. The following code calls this method in the *isTargetForm* method.

```
private boolean isTargetForm()
{
    ...
    object formRunObj;

    if (infolog.docuHandlingActive())
    {
        if (formHasMethod(formRun, IdentifierStr(useMyDocuPane)))
        {
            formRunObj = formRun;
            if (!formRunObj.useMyDocuPane())
                return false;
        }
    ...
    }
}
```

Notice how reflection is indirectly used to verify that the form implements the *useMyDocuPane* method. If it does, it is invoked. Because the *FormRun* type does not have this method, you will receive a compiler error if you try to call it directly on the *formRun* object. Because you have already determined that the method exists, you can assign the *formRun* object to the general *object* type. The compiler accepts any method called on the *object* type, and the runtime will perform late binding to the method.

Now each form can opt out to prevent the Document Handling pane from being embedded in the form.

# The Final Result

The result of the code examples shown in the preceding sections can be seen in Figure 13-1. The figure shows how the code modifies the customer form without actually modifying the form definition itself.

Figure 13-2 shows a Unified Modeling Language (UML) object model diagram of the classes used and modified in this chapter.

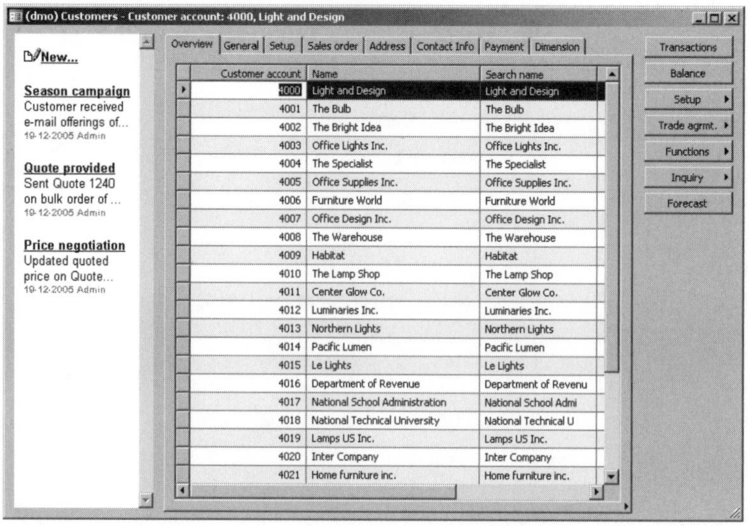

**Figure 13-1**    The customer form with *MyDocuPane* enabled.

Listings 13-1 and 13-2 show all the source code used to achieve the desired result. Listing 13-1 shows the implementation for capturing form instantiation. *SysSetupFormRun* is an existing class. The changes made to the class appear in bold.

**Listing 13-1**    The changes to the *SysSetupFormRun* class.

```
public class SysSetupFormRun extends FormRun
{
    ...
    MyDocuPane docuPane;
    public void init()
    {;
        docuPane = new MyDocuPane(this);

        docuPane.beforeInit();
        super();
        docuPane.afterInit();
        SysSecurityFormSetup::loadSecurity(this);
    }

    Common docCursor()
    {       Common common;
        if (infolog.docuHandlingActive())
        {
            common = super();
            docuPane.update(common);
            return common;
        }
        return null;
    }
}
```

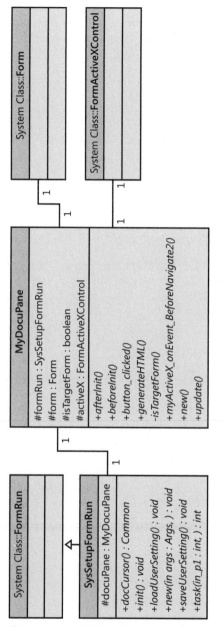

**Figure 13-2**   A UML object model of the final implementation.

Listing 13-2 shows the full implementation of the Document Handling pane constructed in this chapter.

**Listing 13-2**    The complete source code for the *MyDocuPane* class.

```
class MyDocuPane
{
    SysSetupFormRun formRun;
    Form form;
    boolean isTargetForm;
    FormActiveXControl activeX;
    #Define.myProtocol(@'myDocu:\\')

    public void new(FormRun _formRun)
    {;
        if (_formRun)
        {
            formRun = _formRun;
            form = formRun.form();
            isTargetForm = this.isTargetForm();
        }
    }

    private boolean isTargetForm()
    {
        FormBuildDataSource formBuildDataSource;
        DictTable dictTable;
        object formRunObj;

        //Only target forms when document handling is active.
        if (infolog.docuHandlingActive())
        {
            if (formHasMethod(formRun, IdentifierStr(useMyDocuPane)))
            {
                formRunObj = formRun;
                if (!formRunObj.useMyDocuPane())
                    return false;
            }

            //Get the first (and only) data source.
            if (form.dataSourceCount() == 1)
            {
                formBuildDataSource = form.dataSource(1);
                dictTable = new DictTable(formBuildDataSource.table());
                if (dictTable &&
                    dictTable.tableGroup() == TableGroup::Main)
                {
                    return true;
                }
            }
        }
        return false;
    }

    public void beforeInit()
    {
        FormBuildDesign design = form.design();
        FormbuildActiveXControl buildActiveX;
        #Help
```

```
        if (isTargetForm)
        {
            buildActiveX = design.addControl(FormControlType::ActiveX, 'myActiveX');
            buildActiveX.className(#WebBrowserClassName);
            buildActiveX.leftMode(FormLeft::LeftEdge);
            buildActiveX.heightMode(FormHeight::ColumnHeight);
            buildActiveX.width(150);
        }
    }

    public void afterInit()
    {
        if (isTargetForm)
        {
            activeX = formRun.design().controlName('MyActiveX');
        }
    }
    public void update(common _common)
    {
        str html;
    ;
        if (isTargetForm)
        {
            html = this.generateHTML(_common);
            SysHelp::showHTML(activeX, html);
        }
    }
    str generateHTML(Common _common)
    {
        DocuRef docuRef;
        str html = '<html><body><Font size="2" face="Arial">';

        html += @'<a href="'+#myProtocol+'new"><img border=0 src="'+
            SysResource::getImagePath(ResourceStr(WebForm_NewRecord))+
            '"><B>New...</B></a><p>';

        while select docuRef
            where docuRef.RefCompanyId == _common.dataAreaId
               && docuRef.RefTableId == _common.TableId
               && docuRef.RefRecId == _common.RecId
        {
            html += '<B><a href="'+strfmt(#myProtocol+'%1',
                record2Dynakey(docuRef))+'">';
            html += docuRef.Name+'</a></B><br>';
            html += docuRef.Notes+'<br>';
            html += '<font color="gray" size="1">';
            html += strfmt("%1 %2", docuRef.createdDate,
                docuRef.createdBy)+'</font><p>';
        }

        html += '</font><body><html>';
        return html;
    }
    void myActiveX_onEvent_BeforeNavigate2(
        COM _pDisp,
```

```
        COMVariant /* variant */ _URL,
        COMVariant /* variant */ _Flags,
        COMVariant /* variant */ _TargetFrameName,
        COMVariant /* variant */ _PostData,
        COMVariant /* variant */ _Headers,
        COMVariant /* boolean */ _Cancel)
    {
        Args args;
        FormRun callFormRun;
        str action;
        FormObjectSet dataSource;

        if (strStartsWith(_url.variant().bStr(), #myProtocol))
        {
            action = substr(_url.variant().bStr(),
                        strLen(#myProtocol)+1, maxInt());
            //We take care of navigation from here...
            _cancel.boolean(true);

            args = new Args(formStr(DocuView));
            callFormRun = ClassFactory::formRunClassOnClient(args);
            callFormRun.init();
            callFormRun.run();
            dataSource = callFormRun.dataSource(1);

            switch (action)
            {
                case 'new':
                    datasource.create();
                    break;

                default:
                    datasource.findRecord(
                        dynaKey2Record(action, tableNum(DocuRef)));
                    break;
            }

            callFormRun.wait();
        }
    }
}
```

# Chapter Summary

This chapter described how to implement a Document Handling pane that is automatically added to certain forms. This included discussions on how to:

- Capture form instantiation.
- Use reflection on the form to find its methods.
- Add controls at run time.

- Capture events to the automatically added controls.

- Call a method on forms and validate its existence.

The techniques used in the chapter, especially those that describe how to add controls at run time, can be applied in many scenarios.

The implementation approach used in this chapter is also used in the Dynamics AX application, in which the same approach is leveraged through the SysListPanel framework. The framework shows two list panels with buttons that allow you to move items between them. An example of this is the *Users* form, on which you assign users to user groups.

# Chapter 14
# Reflection

The objectives of this chapter are to:

- Introduce the concept of reflection.

- Demonstrate the capabilities and limitations of the available reflection system functions and APIs.

## Introduction

Reflection is a programmatic discoverability mechanism of the application model. In other words, reflection gives you APIs for reading and traversing the element definitions. By using the reflection APIs in the MorphX development environment, you can query metadata as though it were a table, an object model, or a tree structure.

You can do interesting things with the reflection information. The Reverse Engineering tool is an excellent example of the power of reflection. Based on element definitions in MorphX, the tool generates Unified Modeling Language (UML) models that can be browsed in Microsoft Office Visio. Chapter 13, "Advanced MorphX Forms," shows how reflection is used at run time to determine whether a form meets certain criteria.

Reflection also allows you to invoke methods on objects. This will be of little value to business application developers who construct class hierarchies properly. For framework developers, it is much more valuable. Suppose, for example, you want to programmatically write any record to an XML file that includes all of the fields and display methods. Reflection allows you to determine the fields and their value and also invoke the display methods to capture their return values.

X++ features a set of system functions that can be used for reflection, as well as three reflection APIs. The reflection system functions are:

- **Intrinsic functions**   A set of functions that allows you to refer to an element's name or ID in a compile time–safe manner

- ■ **The *TypeOf* system function**    A function that returns the primitive type for a variable
- ■ **The *ClassIdGet* system function**    A function that returns the ID of the class for an instance of an object

The reflection APIs are:

- ■ **Table data**    A set of tables that contains all element definitions. The tables give you direct access to the contents of the .aod files. You can query for the existence of elements and certain properties, such as created by, created time, and created date. You cannot retrieve information about the contents or structure of each element.

- ■ **Dictionary**    A set of classes that provides a type-safe mechanism for reading metadata from an object model. *Dictionary* classes provide basic and more abstract information about elements in a type-safe manner. With few exceptions, this API is read-only.

- ■ **Treenodes**    A class hierarchy that provides the Application Object Tree (AOT) with an API that can be used to create, read, update, and delete any piece of metadata or source code. This API can tell you everything about anything in the AOT. You navigate the treenodes in the AOT through the API and query for metadata in a non-type-safe manner. This API also allows you to programmatically create, update, and delete elements and sub-elements in the AOT. This topic is, however, beyond the scope of this chapter.

# Reflection System Functions

The X++ language features a set of system functions that can be used to reflect on elements. They are described in the following sections.

## Intrinsic Functions

You should use intrinsic functions whenever you need to reference an element from within X++ code. Intrinsic functions provide a way to make a type-safe reference. The compiler will recognize the reference and verify that the element being referenced exists. If the element does not exist, the code will not compile. Because elements have their own life cycles, a reference does not remain valid forever; an element may be renamed or deleted. Using intrinsic functions ensures that you will be notified at compile time of any broken references. A compiler error early in the development cycle is always better than a run-time error later.

All references made by using intrinsic functions are captured by the Cross-Reference tool. This means that you can determine where any element is referenced, regardless of whether the reference is in metadata or code. Note that this works only for the elements included in the Cross-Reference tool. The Cross-Reference tool is described in Chapter 4, "The MorphX Development Tools."

Consider these two implementations:

```
print "MyClass";          //Prints MyClass
print classNum(MyClass);  //Prints MyClass
```

They result in exactly the same thing: the string "MyClass" is printed. As a reference, the first implementation is weak. It will eventually break, which will result in time spent debugging. The second implementation is strong and unlikely to break. If you were to rename or delete *MyClass*, you could use the Cross-Reference tool to do an impact analysis of your changes and correct any broken references.

You can reference all elements in the AOT by their names by using the intrinsic function *<ElementKind>Str*. Some elements also have an ID by which they can be referenced with the intrinsic function *<ElementKind>Num*. Intrinsic functions are not limited to parent objects; they also exist for class methods, table fields, indexes, and methods. More than 50 intrinsic functions are available. Here are a few examples of intrinsic functions.

```
print fieldNum(MyTable, MyField);    //Prints 50001
print fieldStr(MyTable, MyField);    //Prints MyField
print methodStr(MyClass, MyMethod);  //Prints MyMethod
print formStr(MyForm);               //Prints MyForm
```

An element's ID is assigned when the element is created. The ID is an application model layer–dependant sequential ID. In the preceding example, 50001 is the ID assigned to the first element created in the USR layer. The ID scheme is explained in Chapter 1, "Architectural Overview."

Two other intrinsic functions are worth noting: *identifierStr* and *literalStr*. *IdentifierStr* allows you to refer to elements when a more feature-rich intrinsic function is not available. *IdentifierStr* provides no compile-time checking and no cross-reference information. Using the *IdentifierStr* function is much better than using a literal, however, because the intention of referring to an element is captured. If a literal is used, the intention is lost—the reference could be to user interface text, a file name, or something completely different. The Best Practices tool detects use of *identifierStr* and issues a best practice warning.

The Microsoft Dynamics AX runtime automatically converts any reference to a label identifier to the label text for the label identifier. In most cases, this is the desired behavior; however, you can avoid the conversion by using *LiteralStr*. *LiteralStr* allows you to refer to a label identifier without converting the label ID to the label text, as shown here.

```
print <;$QD>@SYS1<;$QD>;             //Prints time transactions
print literalStr(<;$QD>@SYS1<;$QD>); //Prints @SYS1
```

In the first line of the example, the label identifier (@SYS1) is automatically converted to the label text (Time transactions). In the second line, the reference to the label identifier is not converted.

## The *TypeOf* System Function

The *TypeOf* system function takes a variable instance as a parameter and returns the primitive type of the parameter. Here is an example.

```
int i = 123;
str s = "Hello world";
MyClass c;
Guid g = newGuid();

print typeOf(i);   //Prints Integer
print typeOf(s);   //Prints String
print typeOf(c);   //Prints Class
print typeOf(g);   //Prints Guid
pause;
```

The return value is an instance of the *Types* system enumeration. It contains an enumeration for each primitive type in X++.

## The *ClassIdGet* System Function

The *ClassIdGet* system function takes an object as a parameter and returns the class ID for the class element of which the object is an instance. If the parameter passed is Null, the function returns the class ID for the declared type. Here is an example.

```
MyBaseClass c;
print classIdGet(c);  //Prints 50001

c = new MyDerivedClass();
print classIdGet(c);  //Prints 50002
pause;
```

This function is particularly useful when determining the type of an object instance. Suppose you need to determine whether a class instance is a particular class. The following example shows how *ClassIdGet* can be used to determine the class ID of the *_anyClass* variable instance. If the *_anyClass* variable really is an instance of *MyClass*, it is safe to assign it to the variable *myClass*.

```
void myMethod(object _anyClass)
{
    MyClass myClass;
```

```
    if (classIdGet(_anyClass) == classNum(MyClass))
    {
        myClass = _anyClass;
        ...
    }
}
```

Notice the use of the intrinsic function, which evaluates at compile time, and the use of *classIdGet*, which evaluates at run time.

Because it does not take inheritance into account, this sort of implementation is likely to break the object model. In most cases, any instance of a derived *MyClass* class should be treated as an actual *MyClass* instance. The logic to handle inheritance was rather cumbersome to implement correctly in the previous version of Dynamics AX, but two new static methods on *SysDictClass* in version 4.0 make it trivial. The new methods are *is* and *as*, which you will recognize if you are familiar with C#. The *is* method returns true if the object passed in is of a certain type, and the *as* method can be used to cast an instance to a particular type. The *as* method returns null if the cast is invalid.

These two methods also take interface implementations into account. So with the *as* method, you can cast your object to an interface. Here is a revision of the preceding example using the *as* method.

```
void myMethod(object _anyClass)
{
    MyClass myClass = SysDictClass::as(_anyClass, classNum(MyClass));
    if (myClass)
    {
        ...
    }
}
```

Here is an example of an interface cast.

```
void myMethod2(object _anyClass)
{
    SysPackable packableClass =
        SysDictClass::as(_anyClass, classNum(SysPackable));
    if (packableClass)
    {
        packableClass.pack();
    }
}
```

> **Note** This book promotes customization through inheritance using the Liskov substitution principle. In object-oriented programming, the Liskov substitution principle is a particular definition of subtype that was introduced by Barbara Liskov and Jeannette Wing in a 1993 paper entitled "Family Values: A Behavioral Notion of Subtyping." When you follow the Liskov substitution principle, you substitute one implementation of a class with another implementation by using inheritance. The class being substituted must have its constructor encapsulated, so the developer has to modify the construction of the original class in only one place. This is why you will find static *construct* methods on most classes in Dynamics AX. The substituted class must inherit from and behave as the original class. The primary benefit is minimization of the layering shadow, which makes code upgrade much easier. *Dict* classes and *SysDict* classes, good examples of class substitution, are discussed later in this chapter.

# Reflection APIs

The X++ system library includes three APIs that can be used to reflect on elements. They are described in the following sections.

## The Table Data API

Suppose that you want to find all classes whose names begin with *Invent* and that have been modified within the last month. The following example shows one way to do it.

```
static void findInventoryClasses(Args _args)
{
    UtilElements utilElements;

    while select name from utilElements
        where utilElements.RecordType == UtilElementType::Class
            && utilElements.Name like 'Invent*'
            && utilElements.ModifiedDate == today()-30
    {
        info(strfmt("%1", utilElements.Name));
    }
}
```

The *UtilElements* table provides access to all elements. The *RecordType* field holds the element kind. Other fields in the *UtilElements* table that can be reflected on are *Name*, *CreatedBy*, *CreatedTime*, *CreatedDate*, *ModifiedBy*, *ModifiedTime*, and *ModifiedDate*.

Because of the nature of the table data API, the *UtilElements* table can also be used as a data source in a form or report. A form showing the table data is available from Tools\ Development Tools\Application Objects\Application Objects. In the form, you can use the standard query capabilities to filter and search the data.

As you learned in Chapter 2, "The MorphX Development Environment," some elements have sub-elements associated with them. For example, a table has fields and methods. This parent/child association is captured in the *ParentId* field of the sub-element. The following job finds all static method elements on the *CustTable* table element by selecting only table static method elements whose *parentId* equals the *CustTable*'s table ID.

```
static void findStaticMethodsOnCustTable(Args _args)
{
    UtilElements utilElements;

    while select name from utilElements
        where utilElements.recordType == UtilElementType::TableStaticMethod
            && utilElements.parentId == tableNum(CustTable)
    {
        info(strfmt("%1", utilElements.name));
    }
}
```

Notice the use of field lists in the *select* statements in the examples in this section. Each record in the table also has a *binary large object (BLOB)* field that contains all the metadata, source code, and bytecode. This *BLOB* field cannot be interpreted from X++ code, so you do not need to fetch it. When you specify a file list to the *select* statement with fields from the primary index, fetching the actual record is avoided, and the *select* statement will return the result much faster. The primary index contains these fields: *RecordType*, *ParentId*, *Name*, and *UtilLevel*.

The *UtilLevel* field contains the layer of the element. The following job finds all parent elements in the USR layer.

```
static void findParentElementsInUSRLayer(Args _args)
{
    UtilElements utilElements;

    while select recordType, name from utilElements
        where utilElements.parentId == 0
            && utilElements.utilLevel == UtilEntryLevel::usr
    {
        info(strfmt("%1 %2", utilElements.recordType, utilElements.name));
    }
}
```

As you learned in Chapter 1, elements can have IDs. The *UtilElements* table cannot provide ID information. To get ID information, you must use the *UtilIdElements* table. The two tables are both views on the elements in the .aod files; the only difference is the inclusion of the *ID* field in the *UtilIdElements* table. The following is a revision of the previous job that also reports IDs.

```
static void findParentElementsInUSRLayer(Args _args)
{
    UtilIdElements utilIdElements;

    while select RecordType, Id, Name from utilIdElements
        where utilIdElements.ParentId == 0
            && utilIdElements.UtilLevel == UtilEntryLevel::usr
    {
        info(strfmt("%1 %2 %3",
            utilIdElements.RecordType,
            utilIdElements.Name,
            utilIdElements.Id));
    }
}
```

Although this section has discussed two tables that contain the .aod files, all of the application data files have a table reflection API similar to the ones discussed so far. Table 14-1 provides an overview.

**Table 14-1   Reflection Tables**

| Table names | Description |
|---|---|
| *UtilElements UtilIdElements* | Tables containing the .aod files, which contain elements. |
| *UtilElementsOld UtilIdElements-Old* | Tables containing the .aod files in the Old application folder. This information is useful during code upgrades. |
| *UtilApplHelp* | Tables containing the .ahd files, which contain end-user online Help information. |
| *UtilApplCodeDoc* | Tables containing the .add files, which contain developer documentation information for elements. |
| *UtilCodeDoc* | Tables containing the .khd files, which contain developer documentation information for Dynamics AX system APIs. |

All the tables listed in Table 14-1 have an associated helper class. These classes contain a set of static methods that are generally helpful. All of the classes have the same name as the table, prefixed with an *x*.

Suppose that you want to report the AOT path for *MyForm* from the table *utilIdElements*. You could use the *xUtilIdElements* function to return this information, as in the following code.

```
static void findAOTPathForMyForm(Args _args)
{
    UtilIdElements utilIdElements = xUtilIdElements::find(
        UtilElementType::Form, FormStr(MyForm));

    if (utilIdElements)
        info(xUtilIdElements::getNodePath(utilIdElements));
}
```

> **Note**   When you use the table data API in an environment with version control enabled, the values of some of the fields will be reset during the build process. In the build process, .xpo files are imported into empty layers in Dynamics AX. The values of the *CreatedBy*, *CreatedTime*, *CreatedDate*, *ModifiedBy*, *ModifiedTime*, and *ModifiedDate* fields are set during this import process and therefore do not survive from build to build.

## The Dictionary API

The dictionary API is a type-safe reflection API that can reflect on many elements. The following code sample is a revision of the preceding example that finds inventory classes by using the dictionary API. You cannot use this API to get information about when an element was modified. Instead, this example reflects a bit more on the class information and only lists abstract classes.

```
static void findAbstractInventoryClasses(Args _args)
{
    Dictionary dictionary = new Dictionary();
    int i;
    DictClass dictClass;

    for(i=1; i<=dictionary.classCnt(); i++)
    {
        dictClass = new DictClass(dictionary.classCnt2Id(i));

        if (dictClass.isAbstract() &&
            strStartsWith(dictClass.name(), 'Invent'))
        {
            info(strfmt("%1", dictClass.name()));
        }
    }
}
```

The *Dictionary* class provides information about which elements exist. With this information, you can instantiate a *DictClass* object that provides specific information about the class, such as whether the class is abstract, final, or an interface, which class it extends, whether it implements any interfaces, and its methods. Notice that the *DictClass* class can also reflect on interfaces. Also notice how the class counter is converted into a class ID; this is required because the IDs are not listed consecutively.

When you run this job, you will notice that it is much slower than the implementation that uses the table data API—at least the first time you run it! The job performs better after the information is cached.

Figure 14-1 shows the object model for the dictionary API. As you can see, some elements cannot be reflected upon by using this API.

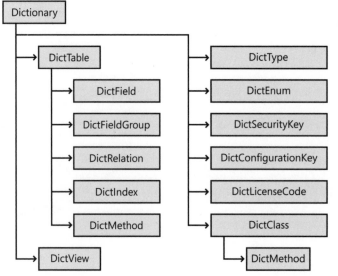

**Figure 14-1**    The object model for the dictionary reflection API.

Starting at the *Dictionary* class level is unnecessary when using this API. The following example revises the *FindStaticMethodsOnCustTable* from the preceding code by using the dictionary API. It also reports the method parameters of the methods.

```
static void findStaticMethodsOnCustTable(Args _args)
{
    DictTable dictTable = new DictTable(tableNum(CustTable));
    DictMethod dictMethod;
    int i;
    int j;
    str parameters;

    for (i=1; i<=dictTable.staticMethodCnt(); i++)
    {
        dictMethod = new DictMethod(
            UtilElementType::TableStaticMethod,
            dictTable.id(),
            dictTable.staticMethod(i));

        parameters = '';
        for (j=1; j<=dictMethod.parameterCnt(); j++)
        {
            parameters += strfmt("%1 %2",
                extendedTypeId2name(dictMethod.parameterId(j)),
                dictMethod.parameterName(j));

            if (j<dictMethod.parameterCnt())
                parameters += ', ';
        }
        info(strfmt("%1(%2)", dictMethod.name(), parameters));
    }
}
```

As mentioned earlier, reflection can also be used to invoke methods on objects. This example invokes the static *Find* method on the table *CustTable*.

```
static void invokeFindOnCustTable(Args _args)
{
    DictTable dictTable = new DictTable(tableNum(CustTable));
    CustTable customer;
;
    customer = dictTable.callStatic(
        tableStaticMethodStr(CustTable, Find), '4000');

    print customer.Name;    //Prints Light and Design
    pause;
}
```

Notice the use of the intrinsic function *tableStaticMethodStr* to make a reference to the *Find* method.

You can also use this API to instantiate class and table objects. Suppose that you want to select all records in a table with a given table ID. The following example shows how.

```
void findRecords(TableId _tableId)
{
    DictTable dictTable = new DictTable(_tableId);
    Common common = dictTable.makeRecord();
    FieldId primaryKeyField = DictTable.primaryKeyField();

    while select common
    {
        info(strfmt("%1", common.(primaryKeyField)));
    }
}
```

First, notice the call to the *makeRecord* method that instantiates a table cursor object that points to the correct table. You can use the *select* statement to select records from the table. If you wanted to, you could also insert records by using the table cursor. Notice the syntax used to get a field value out of the cursor object; this syntax allows any field to be accessed by its field ID. This example simply prints the content of the primary key field. The *makeObject* method on the class *DictClass* can be used to create an object instance of a class.

All the classes in the dictionary API discussed so far are defined as system APIs. On top of each of these is an application-defined class that provides even more reflection capabilities. These classes are named *SysDict<ElementKind>*, and each class extends its counterpart in the system API. For example, *SysDictClass* extends *DictClass*.

Consider the following example. Table fields have a property that specifies whether the field is mandatory. The *DictField* class returns the value of the mandatory property as a bit set in the return value of its *flag* method. Testing of a bit set is somewhat cumbersome, and if the implementation of the flag changes, the consuming applications will break. The *SysDictField* class encapsulates the bit-testing logic in a *mandatory* method. Here is how the method is used.

```
static void mandatoryFieldsOnCustTable(Args _args)
{
    DictTable dictTable = new DictTable(tableNum(CustTable));
    SysDictField sysDictField;
    int i;

    for (i=1; i<=dictTable.fieldCnt(); i++)
    {
        sysDictField = new SysDictField(
            dictTable.id(), dictTable.fieldCnt2Id(i));

        if (sysDictField.mandatory())
            info(sysDictField.name());
    }
}
```

You might also want to browse the *SysDict* classes for static methods. Many of these provide additional reflection information and better interfaces.

Notice how all the examples instantiate the dictionary classes by using their *new* constructor. An alternative way exists that some developers find helpful, but it should be avoided. Recall the hierarchy of the objects shown in Figure 14-1. A parent object can return an instance of a child object, as shown here.

```
DictTable dictTable = new DictTable(tableId);
DictField firstField, nextField;
firstField = dictTable.fieldObject(dictTable.fieldNext(0));
nextField = dictTable.fieldObject(dictTable.fieldNext(dictField.id()));
```

The primary reason to avoid this construct is that you cannot substitute *Dict* classes with *SysDict* classes. If you ever need reflection methods available only on the *SysDict* classes, you must refactor the code. Writing the code so that it is easy to substitute the class will make refactoring easier and lower the risk of introducing bugs in the refactoring process. Another reason to avoid this construct is the lack of API consistency. The examples used in this section that instantiate dictionary classes all follow the same structure, which is consistent for all the classes in the dictionary API.

## The Treenodes API

The two reflection APIs discussed so far both had limitations. The table data API can reflect only on the existence of elements and a small subset of element metadata. The dictionary API can reflect in a type-safe manner but only on the element types that are exposed through this API.

The treenodes API can reflect on everything, but as always, power comes at a cost. The treenodes API is harder to use than the other reflection APIs discussed. It can cause memory and performance problems, and it is not type-safe.

The following example revises the example from the section "The Table Data API" to find inventory classes by using the treenodes API.

```
static void findInventoryClasses(Args _args)
{
    TreeNode classesNode = TreeNode::findNode(@'\Classes');
    TreeNodeIterator iterator = ClassesNode.AOTiterator();
    TreeNode classNode = iterator.next();
    ClassName className;

    while (classNode)
    {
        className = classNode.treeNodeName();
        if (strStartsWith(className, 'Invent'))
            info(strfmt("%1", className));

        classNode = iterator.next();
    }
}
```

First, notice how you find a node in the AOT based on the path as a literal. The *AOT* macro contains definitions for the primary AOT paths. For readability reasons, the examples in this chapter do not use the macro. Notice the use of a *TreeNodeIterator* class to loop over the classes.

If you stay at the class level in the AOT, you will not encounter problems, but be careful if you go any deeper. Tree nodes in MorphX contain data that is not managed by the Dynamics AX runtime, and the memory of the nodes is not automatically deallocated. For each parent node that is expanded, the *TreenodeRelease* method should be called to free the memory. For an example of this, see the *doTreeNode* method on the *SysBpCheck* class.

The following small job prints the source code for the *doTreeNode* method by calling the *AOTgetSource* method on the *treenode* object for the *doTreeNode* method.

```
static void printSourceCode(Args _args)
{
    TreeNode treeNode =
        TreeNode::findNode(@'\Classes\SysBpCheck\doTreenode');
    ;
    info(treeNode.AOTgetSource());
}
```

The treenodes API provides access to the source code of nodes in the AOT. You can use the class *ScannerClass* to turn the string that contains the source code into a sequence of compilable tokens.

The following code revises the preceding example to find mandatory fields on the table *CustTable*.

```
static void mandatoryFieldsOnCustTable(Args _args)
{
    TreeNode fieldsNode = TreeNode::findNode(
        @'\Data Dictionary\Tables\CustTable\Fields');

    TreeNode field = fieldsNode.AOTfirstChild();

    while (field)
    {
        if (field.AOTgetProperty('Mandatory') == 'Yes')
            info(field.treeNodeName());

        field = field.AOTnextSibling();
    }
}
```

Notice the alternate way of looping over sub-nodes. Both this and the iterator approach work equally well. The only way to determine that a field is mandatory with this API is to know that your node models a field and that field nodes have a property named *Mandatory*, which is set to Yes (not to True) for mandatory fields.

Use the *Properties* macro when referring to property names. It contains text definitions for all property names. By using this macro, you avoid using literal names, as in reference to *Mandatory* in the preceding example.

Unlike the dictionary API, which cannot reflect all elements, everything can be reflected with the treenodes API. This fact is exploited in the *SysDictMenu* class, which provides a type-safe way to reflect on menus and menu items by wrapping information provided by the treenodes API in a type-safe API. The following job prints the structure of the *MainMenu* menu, which typically is shown in the Navigation Pane.

```
static void printMainMenu(Args _args)
{
    void reportLevel(SysDictMenu _sysDictMenu)
    {
        SysMenuEnumerator enumerator;

        if (_sysDictMenu.isMenuReference() ||
            _sysDictMenu.isMenu())
        {
            setPrefix(_sysDictMenu.label());
```

```
            enumerator = _sysDictMenu.getEnumerator();
            while (enumerator.moveNext())
                reportLevel(enumerator.current());
        }
        else
            info(_sysDictMenu.label());
    }

    reportLevel(SysDictMenu::newMainMenu());
}
```

Notice how the *setPrefix* function is used to capture the hierarchy and how the *reportLevel* function is called recursively.

The treenodes API also allows you to reflect on forms and reports, as well as their structure, properties, and methods. The Compare tool in MorphX uses this API to compare any node with any other node. The *SysTreeNode* class contains a *TreeNode* class and implements a cascade of interfaces, which makes *TreeNode* classes consumable for the Compare tool and the Version Control tool. The *SysTreeNode* class also contains a powerful set of static methods.

The *TreeNode* class is actually the base class of a larger hierarchy. You can cast instances to specialized *TreeNode* classes that provide more specific functionality. The hierarchy is not fully consistent for all nodes. You can browse the hierarchy in the AOT by clicking System Documentation, clicking Classes, right-clicking TreeNode, pointing to Add-Ins, and then clicking Application Hierarchy.

The *xUtil* classes shown in the table data API examples contain methods for transitioning between the class paradigm of *TreeNode* classes and the table paradigm of *UtilElements* tables. Here is an example.

```
TreeNode node1 = TreeNode::findNode(@'\Data Dictionary\Tables\CustTable');
UtilElements utilElements = xUtilElements::findTreeNode(custTableNode);
TreeNode node2 = xUtilElements::getNodeInTree(utilElements);
```

Although this section has only discussed the reflection functionality of the treenode API, you can use the API just as you would use the AOT designer. You can create new elements and modify properties and source code. The Wizard Wizard uses the treenode API to generate the project, form, and class implementing the wizard functionality. You can also compile and get layered nodes and nodes from the Old Application folder (located in Documents And Settings\All Users\Application Data\Microsoft\Dynamics AX 4.0\Ax Application\Appl\ Standard\Old). The capabilities that go beyond reflection are very powerful, but proceed with great care. Obtaining information in a non-type-safe manner requires caution, but writing in a non-type-safe manner can lead to cataclysmic situations.

# Chapter Summary

This chapter introduced the concept of reflection and showed examples of the three reflection APIs. The examples are designed so that you can compare the APIs and pick the one that matches your needs. You are encouraged to try using the reflection APIs, especially the dictionary API. This chapter also explained why you should always use intrinsic functions, rather than hard-coded text, when referring to elements.

For more examples on the use of reflection APIs, review the *SysBPCheck* classes. These classes essentially validate anything worth validating in metadata and source code for any node in the AOT, and they make heavy use of all three of the reflection APIs.

# Chapter 15
# System Classes

The objectives of this chapter are to:

- Introduce the global session classes: *appl*, *infolog*, *classFactory*, and *versionControl*.

- Explain the startup sequence of Microsoft Dynamics AX 4.0.

- Show how to extend the X++ function library by using the *Global* class.

- Introduce the collection classes in Dynamics AX 4.0 and show examples of how they can be used.

- Discuss how to use collections optimally and effectively.

## Introduction

Dynamics AX 4.0 provides a rich set of classes on which to build your application. Some of these classes are defined by the system and are sometimes referred to as *kernel classes*. Others are defined in X++ in the Application Object Tree (AOT) and are typically prefixed with *Sys*.

This chapter is a collection of important classes not covered elsewhere in this book. The chapter describes only the most commonly used system classes. The product documentation included with Dynamics AX 4.0 includes additional class documentation.

## The Global Session Classes

The Dynamic AX runtime features a wide range of classes that can be instantiated when needed. Also, five objects are globally available for the duration of the client session: *appl* (an instance of *Application*), *infolog* (an instance of *Info*), *classFactory* (two instances of *Class-Factory*), and *versionControl* (an instance of *VersionControl*). Only four objects are listed because two objects share the name *classFactory*. (This is explained later in the chapter.) By using the debugger, you can access these objects on the Globals tab in the Variables window.

All of the global session classes are defined in the AOT, so you can modify existing methods and add new methods. Because they are special classes, they appear after all other classes in the Classes category.

The primary purpose of these classes is to provide type-safe run-time support for event generation. These classes provide a set of methods that are invoked by the runtime and can be overridden by the application. This provides a type-safe event implementation. If a method is not overridden, the system-defined implementation is invoked. By overriding methods, the application can take action based on parameters passed to the methods. For example, the *formNotify* method on the *infolog* object is invoked by the runtime when certain form events occur.

The classes also serve a secondary purpose. They provide a set of useful API-like methods that can return various static information about the client and the server, such as their location on the network, their version numbers, and so on.

# The Startup Sequence

The global session classes are instantiated as soon as the runtime is initialized. Figure 15-1 shows the startup sequence.

The first call from the runtime into X++ is when the *appl* object is created as an instance of the *Application* class. An interesting thing happens next—the *Application* constructor calls the *syncApplTables* method. You might know that during installation of Dynamics AX, the Installation Checklist includes a synchronization step that prepares the database for storing data. You might wonder, then, how the database stores information entered before the synchronization step, such as license codes and the progress in the checklist. All kernel-defined tables are synchronized every time Dynamics AX starts. The same applies to the application tables defined in the *syncApplTables* method. For performance reasons, synchronization occurs only when the table definitions have changed.

After instantiation of *appl* come the instantiation of *infolog* on the client tier, *classFactory* on the server, *classFactory* on the client, and finally, *versionControl* on the client tier. At this point, all the global session classes are instantiated. You should not place logic in the constructors of these classes. If the logic fails for some reason, you might not be able to start the Application Object Server (AOS) because it follows the same startup sequence as the client. If you cannot start the AOS, you cannot start any clients, you cannot debug, and you cannot fix the problem. You would have to find a system backup in your archives.

If you need to execute logic during startup, you should implement it in one of the *startupPost* methods. If you want the logic to run on the server tier, you must implement it in the *Application* .*startupPost* method; if you want it to run on the client tier, implement it in the *Info.startupPost* method. These two methods are reserved for your business logic needs. They are intentionally kept empty in the SYS layer and will not be modified in future versions of Dynamics AX. The *startupPost* methods are provided to allow you to avoid changing to the two *startup* methods.

The *startup* methods are for system initialization, and they are modified with each version. If you overlayer one of the *startup* methods, Dynamics AX will probably not start after an upgrade because your changes prevent new initialization logic from executing.

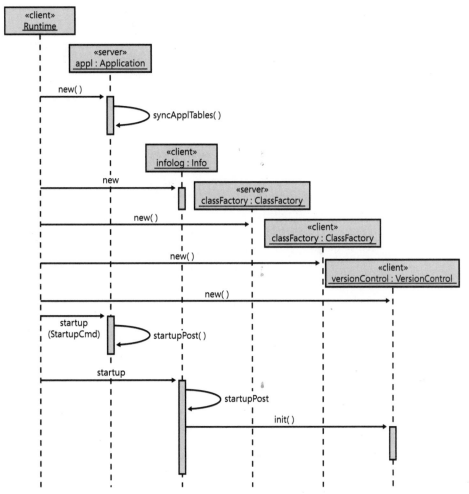

**Figure 15-1**   The startup sequence.

If you require business logic to be executed on a startup command passed to the client in the format ax32.exe –startupcmd=<*myCommand*>, you can use the SysStartupCmd framework. The SysStartupCmd framework is called from both *Application.startup* and *Info.startup*.

## The *Application* Class

The most important feature of the *Application* class is that it runs on the server. Each client session has its own instance of this class on the server. The *Application* class cannot be used for client-to-client communication. You always have an instance of the class available in the global object *appl*; you should never create your own instance.

Here is an example of the *appl* object used in X++.

```
appl.setDefaultCompany('DAT');
```

The *setDefaultCompany* method changes the current company accounts.

Methods on this class are called when database synchronization starts, when records are inserted, updated, or deleted, and when transaction scope begins, is aborted, or is committed.

## The *Info* Class

The *Info* class runs on the client tier. You always have an instance of the class available named *infolog*; you should never create your own instance of this class.

Methods on this class are called when a form is opened and closed, when the data source in a form changes record, and when the client enters idle mode. The *Info* class also provides visualization of messages sent to the Infolog message logging subsystem. When an exception is thrown or the *error*, *warning*, *info*, or *checkFailed* methods are called, a message is posted to the Infolog message queue. When the client enters idle mode, it processes all the messages and displays them in the Infolog form. You can find methods such as *copy*, *cut*, *clear*, *add*, *import*, and *export* on the *Info* class. These methods allow you to modify the queue before it is processed. The following example illustrates the queue.

```
container data;
print infolog.line(); //Prints 0

info("Post this information message to the Infolog queue");
warning("Post this warning message to the Infolog queue");
error("Post this error message to the Infolog queue");

print infolog.line();      //Prints 3
data = infolog.cut(2, 3); //From = 2, To = 3
print infolog.line();      //Prints 1
...
infolog.view(data);
```

## The *ClassFactory* Class

As the name of this class indicates, *ClassFactory* is a factory. At run time, two instances of the *ClassFactory* class exist, and they share name *classFactory*. However confusing the implementation details might sound, this is a powerful concept. When you call a method on *classFactory* from code running on the client, you are calling the *classFactory* object on the client tier; when you call a method on *classFactory* from code running on the server, you are calling the *classFactory* object on the server tier. Therefore, you will never make a call across tiers, which impedes performance, when calling a method on *classFactory*. If the *appl* and *infolog* objects are thought of as cousins that reside on the two tiers, the two *classFactory* objects are twins.

Because they are two instances of the same class, the *classFactory* objects do not share member variables. If you set a value on the client instance, you cannot retrieve it on the server instance. Remember this when debugging the *ClassFactory* class.

The *classFactory* objects are called when the runtime must instantiate forms, reports, and certain system dialogs, such as the Label Editor, Query form, and Compiler Output form. If you need to instantiate a new form or report, you should use the factory. The following code shows how to correctly instantiate a form.

```
Args args = new Args(formStr(<FormName>));
FormRun formRun = classFactory.formRunClass(args);
```

By instantiating all forms through the same factory, you can substitute forms and, at run time, change forms. This is discussed in detail in Chapter 13, "Advanced MorphX Forms."

## The *VersionControl* Class

The *VersionControl* class is used for MorphX version control of elements and is covered in depth in Chapter 4, "The MorphX Development Tools."

## The *SysGlobalCache* Class

As you consider possible uses for these global session class instances, the first thing you might think of is storage of global variables. This is exactly what these classes should be used for, and you do not even have to modify them. The *appl*, *infolog*, and *classFactory* objects each hold an instance of the *SysGlobalCache* class. This means that you have a cache on the client, the server, and your current tier.

If your design calls for the use of global variables, you should reconsider your design. Global variables accessed and modified from multiple places can make your source code fail in unpredictable ways, typically far from the real problem. This makes debugging hard. Steve McConnell, in his book *Code Complete, Second Edition*, expressed it well:

> While the road to programming hell is paved with global variables, class data presents
> far fewer risks.

As the *SysGlobalCache* name implies, it should be used for caching of information, preferably static information. If the cache is not updated, it will remain there for the duration of the client session.

Here is an example of the correct use of the *SysGlobalCache* class.

```
public static client server List myStaticList()
{
    SysGlobalCache cache = classFactory.globalCache();

    List list = cache.get(classStr(MyClass), funcName(), null);

    if (!list)
    {
        // Populate list.
        list = new List(...);
        ...
        cache.set(classStr(MyClass), funcName(), list);
    }
    return list;
}
```

First, notice the use of the global cache on *classFactory*. The *classFactory* object is used because the static method can run on both the client and server tiers. The first time it is called on each tier, you populate the list and cache it.

Also notice the parameters to the *get* method. The first two parameters are the key to the cached values inside the global cache. You use an intrinsic function to indicate which class owns this cached information. You use the system function *funcName* as the second parameter. This function returns the type name of the class and the name of the current method. In the preceding example, this is *MyClass.myStaticList*.

The example could also have used the intrinsic function *staticMethodStr(MyClass, myStaticList)*. However, the use of *funcName* makes the implementation more robust because it ensures encapsulation. If the code is copied into another method, it will not access the same cache because *funcName* will evaluate to something different. If the intrinsic function approach were used, it would access the same cache, and you would have taken the first step toward "programming hell."

The third parameter to the *get* method is the value returned if the cache is empty. This is required on the API because the cache can hold instances of any type, even primitive types, table types, and container types.

# The *Global* Class

The *Global* class contains about 250 default static methods. Each of these methods can be considered an extension to the built-in functions in the X++ language. Normally, when referring to a static method on a class in X++, you must use the following syntax.

```
ClassName::methodName(...);
```

However, the compiler treats the methods on the *Global* class in a special way. It allows you to omit the reference to the class name. These two lines have the same meaning.

```
Global::info(...);
info(...);
```

The *info* method on the *Global* class is typically used to send an informational message to the *Infolog* form.

This compiler feature can make X++ code more readable. If you find yourself referring to the same method from many places or repeatedly implementing the same trivial functionality, you should consider adding new methods to the *Global* class.

In Dynamics AX 4.0, the *strStartsWith* method is added to the *Global* class, as shown here.

```
static boolean strStartsWith(str _string, str _potentialStart)
{
    if (substr(_string, 1, strlen(_potentialStart)) == _potentialStart)
        return true;
    return false;
}
```

This method qualifies for the *Global* class because it is generally useful, and because it hides the trivial implementation details of determining whether the start of a string matches another string. If the implementation changes (because a faster algorithm is found, for example), only the single method that encapsulates the implementation details must be changed, rather than all instances across the program. This encapsulation also makes the X++ code simpler, allowing you to focus on the problem domain instead of on low-level string implementation details.

To decide whether a method belongs on the *Global* class or is better suited to another class, you must consider the context provided by the class name when it is used. When it is placed on *Global*, the context is effectively lost because the class name is omitted. Other classes also have a collection of static methods, such as the *SysDictClass* and *WinApi* classes. Consider the context provided by specifying the class name in these two cases.

```
WinApi::getTickCount();
SysDictClass::as(...);
```

In the first example, the reference to *WinApi* tells the developer consuming the method that it will call into a wrapped Microsoft Windows API. In the second example, the *SysDictClass* tells the developer that the functionality is related to reflection of classes. This information will be lost if the *getTickCount* and *as* methods are placed on *Global*.

You should also consider the discoverability of your methods. When you place a method on *Global*, the user will not benefit from IntelliSense functionality unless he or she explicitly writes the name of the *Global* class; in this case, the readability will suffer if the method name is left in the written source code. If you place your method on a class, where it logically belongs, the user needs to know only of the existence of that particular class. The user can then browse to it when necessary. Most experienced X++ developers are aware of the *WinApi* class. Very few, if any, know all 200 methods on the class, nor do they need to.

If you are still learning the X++ language, you might want to browse the *Global* class for useful methods that can make your work easier. The built-in functions available in X++ complement the methods on the *Global* class by providing general-purpose functions easily consumable from X++. You can find all the X++ functions listed in the AOT under System Documentation\Functions.

The *Global* class is also a special class and is therefore listed at the end of the Classes category in the AOT, along with the global session classes discussed in the preceding section.

# The Collection Classes

The class library in Dynamics AX contains a useful set of collection classes. A collection class can contain instances of any valid X++ type, including objects. The collection classes, *Set*, *List*, *Map*, *Array*, and *Struct*, are sometimes referred to as foundation classes or, in earlier versions of the product, Axapta Foundation Classes (AFC).

All collection classes are kept in memory, so pay attention to their size when you insert instances in them. If you need to handle huge amounts of data, you should consider alternatives such as temporary tables or partly on-disk X++ arrays.

The elements inserted in the collections can be retrieved by traversing the collection class or by performing a lookup in it. To decide which collection class to use, you must consider your data and how you want to retrieve it. The following sections explain each collection class.

## The *Set* Class

A *Set* object is a collection that may hold any number of distinct values of any given X++ type. All values in the *Set* must have the same type. An added value that is already stored in the *Set* is ignored and does not increase the number of elements in the *Set*. The elements are stored in a way that facilitates looking up the elements. The following example illustrates this by creating a *Set* object with integers and adding 100, 200, and 200 (again) to the set.

```
Set set = new Set(Types::Integer);
;
set.add(100);
set.add(200);
set.add(100);
```

```
print set.toString(); //{100, 200}
print set.elements(); //2
print set.in(100);    //true
print set.in(150);    //false
pause;
```

A set is particularly useful in situations in which you want to sort elements as the elements in the set are sorted when inserted, or when you want to track objects. Here is an example from the *AxInternalBase* class.

```
protected boolean isMethodExecuted(str _methodName, ...)
{
    if (setMethodsCalled.in(_methodName))
        return true;

    setMethodsCalled.add(_methodName);
    ...
    return false;
}
```

The *setMethodsCalled* object keeps track of which methods have been executed.

As Figure 15-2 shows, you can perform logical operations on a *Set*. You can create a union of two sets, find the difference between two sets, or find the intersection between two sets.

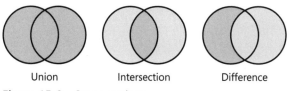

Union          Intersection          Difference

**Figure 15-2**   *Set* operations.

The logical operations are illustrated programmatically here.

```
Set set1 = new Set(Types::String);
Set set2 = new Set(Types::String);
;
set1.add('a');
set1.add('b');
set1.add('c');

set2.add('c');
set2.add('d');
set2.add('e');

print Set::union(set1, set2).toString();        // {a, b, c, d, e}
print Set::intersection(set1, set2).toString(); // {c}
print Set::difference(set1, set2).toString();   // {a, b}
print Set::difference(set2, set1).toString();   // {d, e}
pause;
```

## The *List* Class

*List* objects are structures that may contain any number of elements that are accessed sequentially. A *List* may contain values of any X++ type. All the values in the *List* must be of the type defined when creating the *List*. Elements may be added at either end of the *List*. A *List* is similar to a *Set*, except a *List* can contain the same element several times, and elements in a *List* are kept in the order in which they were inserted. Here is an example that shows insertion of integers into a list of integers. Note that the last integer values are inserted at beginning of the list.

```
List list = new List(Types::Integer);
;
list.addEnd(100);
list.addEnd(200);
list.addEnd(100);
list.addStart(300);

print list.toString();  // 300, 100, 200, 100
print list.elements();  // 4
pause;
```

## The *Map* Class

*Map* objects associate one key value with another value. Figure 15-3 illustrates this.

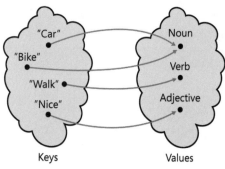

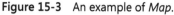

**Figure 15-3**   An example of *Map*.

You can use any type as the key and value, including class and record types. The key and the value do not have to be of the same type. Lookups in a *Map* are efficient, which makes *Map* objects useful for caching of information.

Multiple keys may map to the same value, but one key can map to only one value at a time. Adding a key and value pair to a place where the key is already associated with a value changes the association so that the key maps to the new value.

The following example shows how to populate a *Map* with the keys and values shown in Figure 15-3 and subsequently perform a lookup.

```
Map map = new Map(Types::String, Types::Enum);
Word wordType;
;
map.insert("Car", Word::Noun);
map.insert("Bike", Word::Noun);
map.insert("Walk", Word::Verb);
map.insert("Nice", Word::Adjective);

print map.elements(); //4;

wordType = map.lookup("Car");
print strfmt("Car is a %1", wordType); //Car is a Noun
pause;
```

A *Map* throws an exception if *lookup* is called for a non-existing key. You can call *exists* to verify that a key exists before calling *lookup*. This is particularly useful inside transactions, where you cannot catch the exception gracefully. Here is an example.

```
if (map.exists("Car"))
    wordType = map.lookup("Car");
```

## The *Array* Class

An *Array* object may hold instances of any one given type, including objects and records (unlike the arrays built into the X++ language). The values are stored sequentially. An *Array* can expand as needed, so you do not have to specify its size at the time of instantiation. As with arrays in X++, the indexing of *Array* objects is one-based (that is, counting of elements begins with one, not zero).

```
Array array = new Array(types::class);

array.value(1, new Point(1, 1));
array.value(2, new Point(10, 10));
array.value(4, new Point(20, 20));

print array.lastIndex();            //4
print array.value(2).toString();    //(10, 10)
pause;
```

The *Point* class is declared in a later example, in the section on serialization.

# The *Struct* Class

*Struct* objects may hold a variety of values of any X++ type. A *Struct* collects information about a specific entity. For example, you can store information such as inventory item identifier, name, and price and treat this compound information as one instance.

*Struct* objects allow you to store information in much the same way that you do with classes and tables. You can think of a *Struct* as a lightweight class. A *Struct* object exists only in the scope of the code in which it is instantiated. It does not provide polymorphism like most classes, or persistence like tables. The main benefits of using a *Struct* are that you can dynamically add new elements and you are not required to create a new type definition in the AOT.

As shown in the following example, accessing elements in a *Struct* is not strongly typed because you reference *Struct* objects by using a literal string. You should use a *Struct* only when absolutely necessary. The *Struct* was introduced as a collection class to communicate with the property sheet API, described in Chapter 3, "The MorphX Designers."

Here is an example of how to use a *Struct*.

```
Struct item = new Struct("int Id; str Name");
;
item.value("Id", 1000);
item.value("Name", "Bike");

print item.toString();    //id=1000; Name="Bike"

item.add("Price", 299);
print item.toString();    //id=1000; Name="Bike"; Price=299
print item.fields();      //3
print item.fieldName(1);  //Id
print item.fieldType(1);  //int
print item.value("Id");   //1000
pause;
```

Performance is an interesting topic related to the use of classes, tables, and the *Struct* class. Suppose you needed a composite type to store values. For this discussion, the composite type is a point composed of two real values: *x* and *y*. You could model this in three ways:

- By using a *Struct* with two fields, *x* and *y*.

- By defining a new class, in which the constructor takes *x* and *y* as parameters, and using two access methods to retrieve the values.

- By defining a table with two fields, *x* and *y*. You do not have to insert records into the physical (or temporary) table; you use the record only to store the point in memory.

You could benchmark these three implementations by creating 5,000 instances of points, adding these to a *Set*, traversing the *Set*, and accessing all the point values. Figure 15-4 shows the remarkable result.

**Figure 15-4**   Performance of *Struct* objects, classes, and tables as composite types.

The first two implementations are comparable, but the third is five to seven times faster. The difference in performance is a result of the overhead in instantiation of objects and the number of method calls. A method call in X++ has a small overhead, which, in scenarios involving the database, is negligible. However, in this case, instantiation and method calls are the slowest operations performed.

The performance difference between the *Struct* and class implementations is simply a result of the difference in the number of method calls. In the *Struct* implementation, you must instantiate the *Struct* and call the *value* method for both *x* and *y*. For the class implementation, you can instantiate and set the values through the constructor in one method call. For the table implementation, you can set the field values directly without a single method call, and also without instantiating an object. The following code was used to measure the performance.

```
//Struct implementation
for (i=1; i<=5000; i++)
{
    pointStruct = new struct("real x; real y");
    pointStruct.value("x", i);
    pointStruct.value("y", i);

    set.add(pointStruct);
}

//Class implementation
for (i=1; i<=5000; i++)
{
    pointClass = new Point(i, i);

    set.add(pointClass);
}

//Table implementation
for (i=1; i<=5000; i++)
{
    pointTable.x = i;
    pointTable.y = i;

    set.add(pointTable);
}
```

When accessing the values, the struct and class implementations perform poorly because a method call is required; the table implementation is much faster.

> **Note**   When you insert a table type into a collection class, a memory copy operation is performed. Although table types in X++ are reference types, they behave as value types when inserted in collection classes.

If your implementation calls for fast in-memory storage and retrieval of composite types, you should favor using a table implementation. The tree view provided by the Permissions tab in Administration\User Permissions is built with the table approach. This implementation generates a deep and complex tree structure in a matter of seconds. Earlier versions of Dynamics AX applied the class approach, and in those versions it took significantly longer to build a much simpler tree. For more information about improving performance, see Chapter 17, "Performance."

## Traversal

You can traverse your collections by using either an enumerator or an iterator. When the collection classes were first introduced in Dynamics AX, the iterator was the only option. But because of a few obscure drawbacks that appear as hard-to-find errors, enumerators were added, and iterators were kept for backward compatibility. To highlight the subtle differences, the following code shows how to traverse a collection with both approaches.

```
List list = new List(Types::Integer);
ListIterator iterator;
ListEnumerator enumerator;
;
//Populate list.
...

//Traverse using an iterator.
iterator = new ListIterator(list);
while (iterator.more())
{
    print iterator.value();
    iterator.next();
}

//Traverse using an enumerator.
enumerator = list.getEnumerator();
while (enumerator.moveNext())
{
    print enumerator.current();
}
```

The first difference is the way in which the iterator and enumerator instances are created. For the iterator, you call *new*, and for the enumerator, you get an instance from the collection class by calling the *getEnumerator* method. In most cases, both approaches will work equally well. However, when the collection class resides on the opposite tier from the tier on which it is traversed, the situation is quite different. For example, if the collection resides on the client tier and is traversed on the server tier, the iterator approach fails because the iterator does not support cross-tier referencing. The enumerator does not support cross-tier referencing either, but it doesn't have to because it is instantiated on the same tier as the collection class. Traversing on the server tier using the client tier enumerator is quite network intensive, but the result is logically correct. Because some code is marked as *Called From,* meaning that it can run on either tier, depending on where it is called from, you could have broken logic if you use iterators, even if you test one execution path. In many cases, hard-to-track bugs such as this surface only when an operation is executed in batch mode.

> **Note**   In earlier versions of Dynamics AX, this problem was even more pronounced because development and testing sometimes took place in two-tier environments, and this issue surfaces only in three-tier environments.

The second difference between iterators and enumerators is the way in which the traversing pointer moves forward. In the iterator approach, you must explicitly call both *more* and *next;* in the enumerator approach, the *moveNext* method handles these needs. Most developers have inadvertently implemented an endless loop at least once, simply because they forgot to move a pointer. This is not a significant problem, but it does cause an annoying interruption during the development phase.

If you always use the enumerator, you will not encounter either of the preceding issues. The only situation in which you cannot avoid using the iterator is when you must remove elements from a *List* collection. The following code shows how this is accomplished.

```
List list = new List(Types::Integer);
ListIterator iterator;
;
list.addEnd(100);
list.addEnd(200);
list.addEnd(300);

iterator = new ListIterator(list);
while (iterator.more())
{
    if (iterator.value() == 200)
        iterator.delete();
    iterator.next();
}
print list.toString(); //{100, 300}
pause;
```

# Serialization

Serialization is the operation of converting an object to a bit stream of data that is easily persisted or transported over the network. Deserialization is the opposite operation, in which an object is created from a bit stream. Serializing an object into a stream and later deserializing the stream into a new object must create an object whose member variables are identical to the original object.

> **Note**   The Application frameworks RunBase and SysLastValue rely heavily on serialization. Classes in these frameworks implement the *SysPackable* interface, which requires implementation of *pack* and *unpack* methods.

All collection classes support serialization. The bit stream generated is in the form of a container, which is a value type. This is particularly useful when you are collecting information on one tier and want to transfer it to the opposite tier.

The following code shows a typical example, in which several records are placed in a map on the server tier and are consumed on the client tier. The benefit of using this approach (rather than simply returning a reference to the map object on the server tier) is the reduced number of client/server calls. The following implementation contains only one client/server call, calling the *generateMap OnServer* method. If the reference approach were used, each call to the enumerator would also be a client/server call, typically resulting in at least two client/server calls per element in the map. Here is the implementation using serialization.

```
client class MyClass
{
    private static server container generateMapOnServer()
    {
        Map map = new Map(typeId2Type(typeId(RecId)), Types::Record);
        // Populate map.
        ...
        // Serialize the map.
        return map.pack();
    }
    public void consumeMap()
    {
        // Deserialize the map.
        Map map = Map::create(MyClass::generateMapOnServer());
        mapEnumerator enumerator = map.getEnumerator();

        //Traverse map.
        while (enumerator.moveNext())
        {
            ...
        }
    }
}
```

In the preceding example, the *Map* object contains types, which are easy to serialize. The collection class is capable of serializing primitive X++ types and records. If a collection contains classes, the classes must provide an implementation of a *pack* method and a *create* method for the collection to be serializable. Here is an implementation of a serializable *Point* class.

```
class Point
{
    real x;
    real y;

    public void new(real _x, real _y)
    {;
        x = _x;
        y = _y;
    }

    public container pack()
    {
        return [x, y];
    }

    public static Point create(container _data)
    {
        real x;
        real y;
        [x, y] = _data;
        return new Point(x, y);
    }

    public str toString()
    {
        return strfmt('(%1, %2)', x, y);
    }
}
```

The following example is just one way of modeling a line by using a *Set* of *Point* classes. Notice how a new line instance is created by serializing and deserializing the line object.

```
Set line = new Set(Types::Class);
Set newLine;
;
line.add(new Point(0, 0));
line.add(new Point(2, 5));

print line.toString();      // {(0, 0), (2, 5)}

//Create a new instance.
newLine = Set::create(line.pack());
print newLine.toString();  // {(0, 0), (2, 5)}
pause;
```

# Bringing It All Together

You have seen how collection classes allow you to collect instances of objects and values. The collection classes provide conceptually simple structures. The classes *Set*, *List*, *Map*, *Array*, and *Struct* are easy to understand and just as easy to use. If you do a cross-reference to find all the places in the existing code where they are used, their usefulness is evident.

Sometimes, however, these collection classes are too simple to meet certain requirements. Suppose you needed to model a shape. In this case, having a *List* of points would be useful. Points can be modeled as a *Struct* because the collection classes can contain objects, and an instance of a collection class is an object. You can combine collections classes to create, for example, a list of maps, a set of lists, or a set of lists of maps.

The *SysGlobalCache* class, described earlier in this chapter, is a good example of combining collection classes. It uses a map of maps of a given type. An example of a global cache instance is illustrated in Figure 15-5.

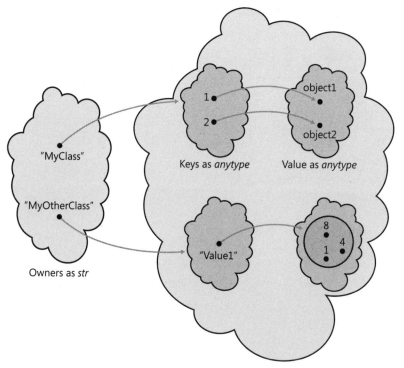

**Figure 15-5**    An example of internal structure in *SysGlobalCache*.

The values in the first *Map* are always strings (type *str*); this string is referred to as the *owner* of the entry in the cache. Each of these values maps to another instance of *Map* in which the types of the key and value are determined by the consumer of the cache. This way, the cache can be used to store instances of several types.

The values in the *SysGlobalCache* example shown in Figure 15-5 could be inserted by this code.

```
globalCache.set(classStr(MyClass), 1, object1);
globalCache.set(classStr(MyClass), 2, object2);
globalCache.set(classStr(MyOtherClass), "Value1", myIntegerSet);
```

Now examine how this is implemented inside the *SysGlobalCache* class, shown in the next code sample. The class has only one member variable, *maps*, which is instantiated in the *new* method as a mapping of strings to classes. The first time a value of type *value* is inserted in the cache, using the *set* method, a new instance of *Map*, named *map*, is created. The *owner* string is mapped to this *map* object in the *maps* member variable. The *map* object maps values of the *key* type to values of the *value* type. The types are determined by using the *typeOf* function. The *key* and *value* pair is then inserted in *map*. The *get* method is implemented to retrieve values from the cache. To retrieve the values, the following two lookups must be performed:

- A lookup in the owner-to-map *Map* to get the key-to-value *Map*.

- A lookup in the key-to-value *Map* using the *key* to find the *value*.

If either lookup fails, the default return value specified as a parameter is returned.

```
class SysGlobalCache
{
    Map maps;

    private void new()
    {
        maps = new Map(Types::String, Types::Class);
    }

    public boolean set(str owner, anytype key, anytype value)
    {
        Map map;
        if (maps.exists(owner))
        {
            map = maps.lookup(owner);
        }
        else
        {
            map = new Map(typeOf(key), typeOf(value));
            maps.insert(owner, map);
        }
        return map.insert(key, value);
    }

    public anytype get(str owner, anytype key, anyType returnValue = '')
    {
        Map map;
        if (maps.exists(owner))
```

```
        {
            map = maps.lookup(owner);
            if (map.exists(key))
                return map.lookup(key);
        }
        return returnValue;
    }
    ...
}
```

# Other Collection Classes

A few other collection classes are worth mentioning. They do not share the same structure as the collection classes explained so far, but you can use them for collecting instances.

## The *Stack* Class

A stack is a structure in which you can add and remove instances from the top. This kind of structure, resembling a stack of plates, is sometimes described as a last in, first out (LIFO) structure. You add an instance to the top by calling *push*, and you remove the top instance by calling *pop*. The *Stack* class in Dynamics AX can hold only instances of containers. Because containers can contain any value type, you can still create a stack of integers, strings, dates, and so on.

Here is an example of how to use *Stack*.

```
Stack stack = new Stack();
;
stack.push([123]);
stack.push(["My string"]);

print conpeek(stack.pop(), 1);  //My string
print conpeek(stack.pop(), 1);  //123
pause;
```

## The *StackBase* Class

Because the *Stack* class is limited to holding container instances, an improved stack was implemented called *StackBase*. The *StackBase* class provides the same functionality as the *Stack* class, except that it can hold instances of any given type.

Here is an example of how to use *StackBase*.

```
StackBase stack = new StackBase(Types::Class);
;
stack.push(new Point(10, 10));
stack.push(new Struct("int age;"));
```

```
print stack.pop().toString();   //(age:0);
print stack.pop().toString();   //(10, 10)
pause;
```

### The *RecordSortedList* Class

If you have a list of records that you must either sort or pass as a parameter, you can use the *RecordSortedList* class. This collection class can hold only record types. When you insert a record in the list, it is sorted according to one or more fields that you specify. Because sorting takes place in memory, you can specify any fields, rather than just those for which a table index already exists. The combined sorting fields must constitute a unique key. If you need to sort by a non-unique field, you can add the *RecId* field, which is guaranteed to be unique, as a sorting field.

Here is an example in which customers are sorted by city by using *RecordSortedList*.

```
RecordSortedList list = new RecordSortedList(tableNum(CustTable));
CustTable customer;
boolean more;
;
//Sort by City, RecId.
list.sortOrder(fieldNum(CustTable, City), fieldNum(CustTable, RecId));

//Insert customers in the list.
while select customer
{
    list.ins(customer);
}

//Traverse the list.
more = list.first(customer);
while (more)
{
    info(strfmt("%1, %2", customer.Name, customer.City));
    more = list.next(customer);
}
```

# Chapter Summary

This chapter covered three important concepts. First, it introduced the global session classes. You learned when these classes are instantiated and how to reference their global instances. You also learned about the objectives and uses of global session classes. This chapter also discussed extending the X++ language by adding your own methods to the *Global* class. Finally, this chapter introduced collection classes and provided examples of their use. You learned how to traverse the collections by using enumerators, and you also saw how to create more complex collections by combining collection classes.

# Chapter 16
# Unit Testing

The objectives of this chapter are to:

- Introduce the practice of unit testing.

- Describe how to write unit tests.

- Provide insight into the design of the Unit Test framework and explain how to extend it.

## Introduction

A complete Unit Test framework is a new feature in Microsoft Dynamics AX 4.0. A unit test is a piece of code that exercises another piece of code and ascertains that it behaves correctly. The developer who implements the unit to be tested typically writes the unit test. Thought leaders in this area recommend writing unit tests as early as possible, even before writing a single line of the unit's code. This principle is called test-driven development.

Writing unit tests early forces you to consider how your code will be consumed; this in turn makes your APIs easier to use and understand, and it results in constructs that are more likely to be robust and long-lasting. With this technique, you must have at least one unit test for each requirement; a failing unit test indicates an unfulfilled requirement. Development efforts should be targeted at making the failing unit test succeed—no more, no less.

To reap the full benefits of unit testing, you should execute test cases regularly, preferably each time code is changed. The Unit Test framework in Dynamics AX supports you regardless of your approach to writing unit tests. For example, the unit test capabilities are fully embedded in MorphX, and you can easily toggle between writing test cases and writing business logic.

When implementing unit tests, you write a test class, also referred to as a *test case*. Each test case has several test methods that exercise the object being tested in a particular way. As you build your library of test cases, you will find that you need to organize them into groups. Test cases can be grouped into test suites. The simplest way to do this is to use test projects, which are simply special kinds of Application Object Tree (AOT) projects.

# Test Cases

To implement a unit test case, you must create a new class that extends the *SysTestCase* class, which is a part of the Unit Test framework. You should give the class the same name as the class it is testing, suffixed with *Test*. This is illustrated in the following example, where a unit test for the *Stack* class is declared.

```
class StackTest extends SysTestCase
{
}
```

If you were to run the unit test at this point, you would find that zero tests were run and zero tests failed.

This default naming convention tells the Unit Test framework which test class to collect code coverage data for. If the default test class name does not suit your needs, you can override the *testsElementName* method. You can also override the *testsElementType* method to set the kind of element for which the framework will collect code coverage data.

To create a useful test, you must add one or more test methods to the class. All test method names must start with *test*. The test methods must return void and take no parameters. In the following code, a test method is added to the *StackTest* class.

```
void testPushPop()
{
    //Create an instance of the class to test.
    Stack stack = new Stack();
    ;
    //Push 123 to the top of the stack.
    stack.push([123]);
    //Pop the value from the stack and assert that it is 123.
    this.assertEquals([123], stack.pop());
}
```

Within each test method, you should exercise the object you test and confirm that it behaves correctly. Running the unit test at this point tells you that one test was run and zero tests failed.

Your testing needs should be met by the assertion methods available on *SysTestCase* (which extends *SysTestAssert*), as shown in Table 16-1.

**Table 16-1   Assertion Methods on the *SysTestCase* Class**

| Method | Parameters | Action |
|---|---|---|
| *assertEquals* | *(anyType, anyType)* | Asserts that two values are equal. When the argument is of type *object*, the *equal* method is called to compare them. |
| *assertFalse* | *(boolean)* | Asserts that the value is false. |
| *assertNotEqual* | *(anyType, anyType)* | Asserts that two values are different. |
| *assertNotNull* | *(object)* | Asserts that the value is not null. |
| *assertNotSame* | *(object, object)* | Asserts that the objects referenced are not the same. |
| *assertNull* | *(object)* | Asserts that the value is null. |
| *assertRealEquals* | *(real, real [, real delta])* | Asserts that real values differ with no more than the delta. |
| *assertSame* | *(object, object)* | Asserts that the objects referenced are the same. |
| *assertTrue* | *(boolean)* | Asserts that the value is true. |

If an assertion fails, the test method fails. You can configure the framework to stop at first failure or continue with the next test method in the Unit Test Parameters dialog box at Tools\Development Tools\Unit Test\Parameters. The following code adds a new failing test method.

```
//Test the qty method, which returns the quantity of values on the stack.
void testQty()
{
    //Create an instance of the class to test.
    Stack stack = new Stack();
    ;
    //Push 123 to the top of the stack.
    stack.push([123]);
    //Pop the value from the stack and assert that it is 0.
    this.assertEquals(0, stack.qty());
}
```

Running the unit test at this point shows that two tests were executed and one failed. The failing test appears in the Infolog, as shown in Figure 16-1. Clicking Edit opens the X++ editor on the assert call that failed.

You can also do your own validation logic and call *fail* if none of the assertion methods suit your needs. Here is an example in which a performance criterion of three seconds for 1000 push/pop operations is tested.

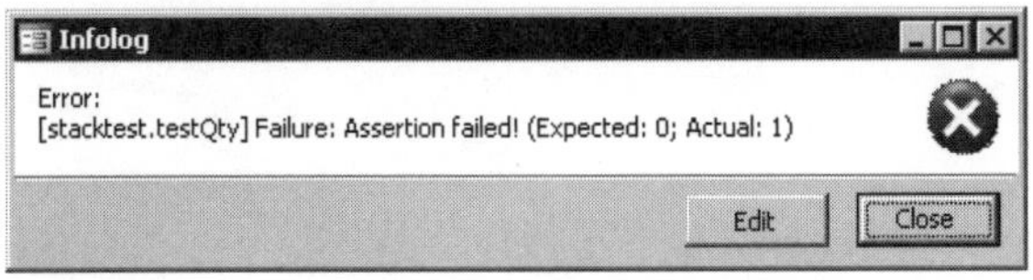

**Figure 16-1**   A failing unit test in the Infolog.

```
void testPerformance()
{
    Stack stack = new Stack();
    //Get the number of milliseconds since the PC was started.
    int startTick = WinApi::getTickCount();
    int i;
    ;
    for(i=1; i<=1000; i++)
    {
        stack.push([i]);
        stack.pop();
    }
    //Must complete in 3000 milliseconds.
    if (WinApi::getTickCount() - startTick > 3000)
    {
        this.fail("Performance criteria not met!");
    }
}
```

You might have noticed code redundancy in the three test methods shown so far. In many cases, initialization code is required before the test method can run. Instead of duplicating this code in all test methods, you can refactor it into the *setUp* method. If teardown logic is required, you can place it in the *tearDown* method. When the framework runs a test method, it instantiates a new test case class, which is followed by calls to *setUp* and test methods, and finally a call to the *tearDown* method. This prevents in-memory data from one test method from affecting another test method. Test suites, which are covered in the next section, provide ways to isolate data persisted in the database between test case and methods. The following code uses the *setUp* method to refactor the sample code.

```
class StackTest extends SysTestCase
{
    Stack stack;

    public void setUp()
    {;
        super();
        //Create an instance of the class to test.
        stack = new Stack();
    }
    void testPushPop()
    {;
        stack.push([123]);
        this.assertEquals([123], stack.pop());
    }
    ...
}
```

The Unit Test framework also supports testing of exceptions. If a method is expected to throw an exception, you can instruct the framework to gracefully handle this. If you expect an exception and none is thrown, the framework reports the test case as failed. You inform the framework that an exception is expected by calling *parmExceptionExpected([boolean, str])*. You can specify an exception text that must exactly match the text thrown with the exception, or the test case will fail. You should not write more asserts after the method call expected to throw an exception because execution should never get that far. The following code adds a test method that expects an exception message to be thrown.

```
void testFailingPop()
{;
    //Assert that an exception is expected.
    this.parmExceptionExpected(true, "Stack is empty!");

    //Call the method expected to throw an exception.
    stack.pop();
}
```

The sample test case now has four test methods. By following these steps, you can run the test case from MorphX:

1. Right-click the method, point to Add-ins, and then click Run tests.

2. Type the name in the Test toolbar, and then click Run.

3. Start the Dynamics AX client with the command line
   **-StartupCmd=RunTestProject_<*Name of test case class*>**

If you wanted to run the test case programmatically, you could use a test runner class. To do this, you would typically place the following logic in your test class's *main* method, which is invoked when you press F5 in the X++ editor.

```
static void main(args _args)
{
    SysTestRunner runner = new SysTestRunner(classStr(StackTest));
    SysTestListenerXML listener =
        new SysTestListenerXML(@"c:\tmp\StackTest.xml");
    ;
    runner.getResult().addListener(listener);
    runner.run();
}
```

Notice that you also register a listener. If you did not register a listener, you would not know the result of the test. Listeners are described later in this chapter.

# Test Suites

Test suites serve two purposes:

- **Collection of test cases and test suites**   A test suite can contain any number of test cases and other test suites. This allows test cases to be grouped in a hierarchy.

- **Test case isolation**   Each test case could have different needs for isolation, depending on what data it will change. In fact, each method within the test case could have a need for isolation.

Dynamics AX includes the following four test suites that provide different levels of isolation:

- *SysTestSuite*   This is the default test suite. It provides no isolation. You can override the *setUp* and *tearDown* methods, if necessary. Note that these methods are not the same as the *setUp* and *tearDown* methods on the test case.

- *SysTestSuiteCompanyIsolateClass*   This test suite constructs an empty company account for the entire test class and runs each test method in the company account. After all test methods have been executed, the company account is deleted.

- *SysTestSuiteCompanyIsolateMethod*   This test suite constructs an empty company account for each test method and runs the test method in the company account. After the test methods have been executed, the company account is deleted. This is the highest isolation level provided. It does, however, have a noticeable effect on performance.

- *SysTestSuiteTTS*   This test suite wraps each test method in a transaction. After the test method has been completed, the transaction is aborted. This provides a fast alternative to the company isolation suites, but it has a couple of limitations:

  - Exceptions cannot be handled gracefully. Exceptions thrown inside a transaction abort the transaction automatically and cannot be caught inside the transaction.

  - Test cases that require data to be committed cannot use this test suite.

For each test case, you can override the *createSuite* method to select the appropriate suite for your test case. The following code shows how to use the company isolation test suite in the *StackTest* class.

```
public SysTestSuite createSuite()
{;
    return new SysTestSuiteCompanyIsolateClass(this);
}
```

Using test projects to group test cases into suites is recommended. You can, however, create your own class extending from *SysTestSuite* and programmatically add test cases and other test suites to it. You can run each test suite in one of the following ways:

- Type the name in the Test toolbar, and then click Run.

- Start the Dynamics AX client with the command line
  **-StartupCmd=RunTestProject_<*Name of test suite class*>**

- Implement a static *main* method similar to the one shown in the test case example.

The following code shows the entire *StackTest* test case. Notice the refactoring and the changes in *testQty* to make the test case succeed.

```
class StackTest extends SysTestCase
{
    Stack stack;

    public SysTestSuite createSuite()
    {;
        return new SysTestSuiteCompanyIsolateClass(this);
    }
    public void setUp()
    {;
        super();
        stack = new Stack();
    }
    void testPushPop()
    {;
        stack.push([123]);
        this.assertEquals([123], stack.pop());
    }
    void testQty()
    {;
        stack.push([100]);
        this.assertEquals(1, stack.qty());
        stack.push([200]);
        this.assertEquals(2, stack.qty());
        stack.clear();
        this.assertEquals(0, stack.qty());
    }
    void testPerformance()
    {
        int startTick = WinApi::getTickCount();
        int i;
        ;
        for(i=1; i<=1000; i++)
        {
            stack.push([i]);
            stack.pop();
        }
        //Must complete in 3 seconds
        if (WinApi::getTickCount() - startTick > 3000)
```

```
        {
            this.fail("Performance goals not met!");
        }
    }
    void testFailingPop()
    {;
        this.parmExceptionExpected(true, "Stack is empty!");
        stack.pop();
    }
    static void main(args _args)
    {
        // This method illustrates how to run a test case programmatically.
        SysTestRunner runner = new SysTestRunner(classStr(StackTest));
        SysTestListenerXML listener =
            new SysTestListenerXML(@"c:\tmp\StackTest.xml");
        ;
        runner.getResult().addListener(listener);
        runner.run();
    }
}
```

# Test Projects

The easiest way to group test cases is to use a test project. You can create a test project with the project designer in MorphX. The test project can contain groups of test case classes and references to other test projects. You create a new test project by selecting the project type Test Project when creating either a shared or private project. A test project can also contain references to other test projects, which allows the project to scale across many development teams. You create a reference by right-clicking the project root node and selecting New Reference To Test Project.

Figure 16-2 shows a test project that includes a group of common tests containing the test case example and references to two other test projects.

**Figure 16-2**   A test project that contains references and a test case.

Each test project has its own settings that are persisted with the project definition. This allows you to specify test project settings that follow the project, even through import and export, redeployment, and so on.

You can run a test project in several ways:

- Right-click it, and then click Run.

- Type the name in the Test toolbar, and then click Run.

- Start the Dynamics AX client with the command line
  **-StartupCmd=RunTestProject_<*Name of test project*>**

- Use the version control functionality during check-in. Check-in stops if the test fails.
  You specify the project to run during check-in in Tools\Development Tools\Version
  Control\Setup\System Settings.

## The Test Toolbar

When you are working with unit testing, you should open the Test toolbar. You access the Test
toolbar, shown in Figure 16-3, from Tools\Development Tools\Unit Test\Show Toolbar.

| Test: | StackTest | ▼ | Run | Reset | 4 run, 0 failed | ✓ | Details | ☒ |

**Figure 16-3**   The Test toolbar.

You can type the name of the test case, test suite, or test project that you want to run,
click Run to execute it, and then, to get information about the result, click Details to
open the Test Jobs window. The Test Jobs window shows you the following information
collected during the test execution:

- The status of each test case

- Environmental information

- Timing (when the test started and stopped, the duration of the test, and so on)

- Code coverage, when enabled

- Information sent to the Infolog during the test case execution

> **Note**   The information displayed in the Test Jobs window is collected by the database
> listener. It is automatically registered when you run a test by using the toolbar.

## Code Coverage

The Unit Test framework can collect code coverage information during execution, including a
percentage value that indicates how thoroughly you have tested your unit. It also allows you to
focus your implementation of the test cases on the parts not covered by other test cases. The Test
Jobs window also offers a line-by-line view of the code lines visited. You can enable code coverage
in the Unit Test Parameters dialog box at Tools\Development Tools\Unit Test\Parameters.
However, because much more data is collected, enabling code coverage when executing unit tests

affects performance during execution dramatically. Figure 16-4 shows an example of the code coverage recorded by the *testFailingPop* method from the preceding test case example.

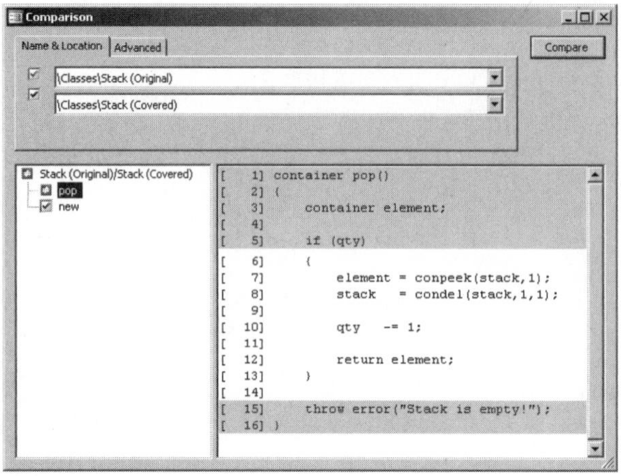

**Figure 16-4**   Visualization of code coverage.

The lines highlighted in grey are the lines visited during execution (lines 1–5 and 15–16). The lines not highlighted have not been visited (lines 6–14).

# Test Listeners

The value of running a test case is dramatically increased if good reporting options exist. When running a test case or a suite of tests, you can enable one or more listeners. Each listener produces its unique output. Dynamics AX includes many listeners, allowing output to text files, XML files, the database, the Infolog, the Message window, the Print window, and the Progress bar. You can enable test listeners in the Unit Test Parameters dialog box.

Here is the XML generated by the XML listener when you run the *StackTest* unit test.

```xml
<?xml version="1.0" encoding="utf-8" standalone="yes"?>
<!-- Created by SysTestListenerXML -->
<test-results date="11-12-2005" time="10:51:34" success="false">
  <test-suite name="stacktest" time="52" success="true" coverage="61.54">
    <results>
      <test-case name="stacktest.testConstruct" time="0" success="true" coverage="9.62" />
      <test-case name="stacktest.testFailingPop" time="31" success="true"
coverage="23.08" />
      <test-case name="stacktest.testPushPop" time="0" success="true" coverage="50.00" />
      <test-case name="stacktest.testQty" time="21" success="true" coverage="30.77" />
    </results>
  </test-suite>
</test-results>
```

> **Note**   Listeners that generate a file write the file to the application log directory. The only way to change the file name and location is to manually register a listener, which was shown in the complete listing of a test suite earlier in the chapter.

If you must create a new listener to output to a type of media not supported by default, you can do so by following these steps:

1.  Create your own listener class implementing the *SysTestListener* interface. Alternatively, you can inherit from one of the existing test listeners. The methods on your class are invoked when events such as the start and end of test suites and test cases occur and when test cases fail. A *SysTestListenerData* object is passed to each method. The object contains information about the test case or suite, coverage data, and much more. By extracting the information, you can generate output to suit your needs.

2.  Modify the base enumeration *SysTestListeners*. You must add an entry that has the same name as your listener class and a label of your choice. This causes the listener to appear in the test parameters form.

## Object Model

This chapter has so far described the classes in the Unit Test framework and how they interact. Figure 16-5 shows this information as a Unified Modeling Language (UML) object model.

Note that the *SysTestCase* class implements quite a few interfaces. In fact, the Unit Test framework can use any class that implements the *SysTestable* interface as a test case. The other interfaces can be implemented for more control. It is, however, far easier to create test case classes that extend the *SysTestCase* base class. (For simplicity, Figure 16-5 does not show the *SysTestSuite* derived classes or the *SysTestListener* derived classes.)

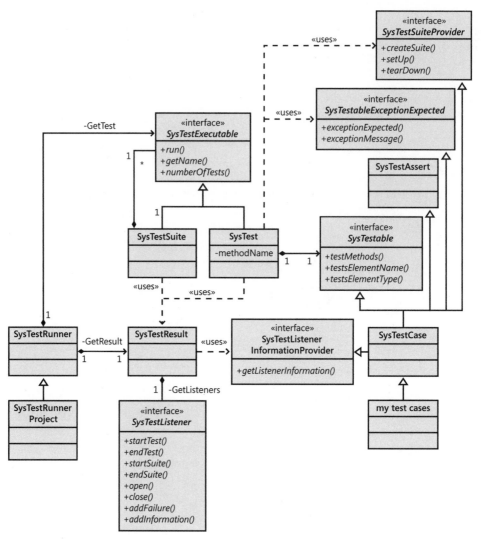

**Figure 16-5**   A UML diagram of the Unit Test framework.

# Chapter Summary

This chapter introduced the unit testing capabilities of Dynamics AX and provided an example of how to write a unit test. If you are managing an implementation project for Dynamics AX, you should advocate testing and support your team members in any way required. At first glance, it might seem like more work, but the investment will be well worth the effort. If you are a team member on a project that does not do unit testing, you should convince your manager of the benefits. Plenty of recent literature describes this in great detail. If you have a hard time convincing your manager of the benefits of writing unshippable code, you have several options. One dubious option is to secretly write your own test cases for your own features. As the benefits become obvious to your managers and peers, you may win them over. Another option is to find an employer that takes software construction more seriously.

# Chapter 17
# Performance

The objectives of this chapter are to:

- Describe how to control the execution of logic in a three-tier environment and what to consider when designing and implementing X++ code.

- Explain how to optimize database performance and minimize database interaction by using set-based operators and caching, limiting locking, and optimizing *select* statements.

- Introduce the tools available in the Microsoft Dynamics AX 4.0 development environment for monitoring client/server calls, database calls, and code execution.

## Introduction

Performance is often an afterthought. Many development teams rarely pay attention to performance until later in the development process or, more critically, after a customer reports severe performance problems in the production environment. After a feature is implemented, making more than minor performance improvements is often too difficult. But if you know how to use the performance optimization features in Dynamics AX, you can create designs that allow for optimal performance within the boundaries of the Dynamics AX development and run-time environments.

In this chapter, I describe what to consider when developing features to be executed in a three-tier environment in which X++ code can be executed on either the client tier or the server tier. I also introduce the performance-enhancing features available within the development environment, such as set-based operators for database interaction, caching, which can be set up in metadata or directly in code, and the optimistic concurrency control for limiting database locking. I conclude the chapter by describing some of the performance-monitoring tools available within the Dynamics AX development environment that provide a reliable foundation for monitoring client/server calls, database activity, and X++ code execution.

# Client/Server Performance

As described in Chapter 1, "Architectural Overview," Dynamics AX is a three-tier client/server application; the Dynamics AX application runtime supports the execution of application runtime logic on either the client tier or the server tier.

> **Note**    The Dynamics AX application runtime does not support development of application logic to be executed on the database tier.

By default, all X++ code is defined as "called from," meaning that the method is executed on the tier from which the call is made. Class instance methods, however, execute on the tier where the object is instantiated.

It is preferable to execute database-intensive application logic as close to the database as possible, which is on the server tier, and to execute user-interaction application logic as close to the end user as possible, which is on the client tier. This minimizes round trips from the client to the server. Round trips involve sending packages between the two tiers, which usually occurs across a network with a certain bandwidth and latency, affecting performance. At the same time, communication between the client and server is synchronous, meaning that the client waits until the server has finished executing the call from the client to the server, and vice versa.

> **Note**    It is debatable whether CPU-intensive application logic that does not involve user and database interaction should be allowed to execute on the client tier or should always be pushed to the server tier. The client tier normally serves only one user and his or her applications, and the server serves processes from multiple users. However, the power of the server is greater than that of the client, so at development time it is difficult to determine which tier has the most resources to execute the logic at run time. Minimizing the client/server traffic has been a development goal in the last several versions of Dynamics AX, but moving execution of CPU-intensive application logic to a specific tier has not been a goal.

## Controlling the Execution of Logic

To control where application logic is executed, the Dynamics AX application runtime supports setting metadata or writing specific method modifiers by using X++. The *client* and *server* method modifiers can be applied to instance and static table methods and static class methods. When you apply the *client* modifier, the method is always executed on the client tier, and when you apply the *server* modifier, the method is always executed on the server tier. If the caller is on a tier other than the tier specified on the calling method, the application logic continues to execute on the tier specified in the calling method. The calling tier then waits until the calling method exits or the called tier invokes a method, which forces it back.

The specific execution of class instance methods is controlled by the *RunOn* property on the class. The property can be set to *Called from*, *Server*, or *Client*. If the property is set to *Called from*, an object of that type is instantiated on the instantiating tier, and all instance methods are also executed on that tier. If the property is set specifically to *Server* or *Client*, the object is instantiated on the specified tier, and all instance methods are also executed on this tier. You can change the *RunOn* property on a derived class only if the *RunOn* property on the base class is set to *Called from*. A derived class inherits the property value of the parent class if the property is set to *Client* or *Server*.

By default, table instance and static methods are executed as "called from" if neither the *server* nor the *client* modifier is specified. You can, however, specify both *client* and *server* as modifiers in the same method, but doing so does not influence where the method is executed; it signals that the developer of the method has evaluated the method and decided that it should be executed as "*called from*" and should not be client bound or server bound.

> **Note**   By default, insert, update, and delete methods on the tables are always server bound, even though it is not stated in the definition of the method. The methods cannot be forced to the client because any *client* modifier is simply ignored by the Dynamics AX application runtime.

If neither the *client* nor the *server* modifier is specified in static class methods, the methods are executed on the tier specified by the *RunOn* property on the class. Specifying both *client* and *server* in these methods does, however, force the methods to be executed as "*called from*" and thereby disregard the property value on the class.

> **Note**   You can specify the *client* and *server* modifiers on class instance methods and in form and report methods, but these are ignored by the application runtime.

When a class is executed from a menu item, it is possible to specify on the menu item whether the class should be executed on the server, the client, or the calling tier. This is because the menu item elements also contain a *RunOn* property, which can be set to the same values and the equivalent class property. However, the menu item property cannot overrule the class setting.

## Optimizing Client/Server Calls

When you develop classes and table methods, you should consider whether the class should be allowed to be instantiated on both the client and server tiers, or only on one tier. This decision depends on the application logic implemented in the methods. When you develop classes, you should also think about the application programming interface (API), especially when you develop server-bound classes to be used by application logic executed on the client tier.

Consider the following X++ example, in which the server-bound *ServerClass* class is instantiated. Two variables are parsed to the object, and then a result is returned. This X++ code results in at least five round trips between the client and the server: one when instantiating the server-bound class, two when parsing the variables, one when requesting the result, and a final call when the *ServerClass* object handle loses scope. The object will subsequently be destroyed on the server tier.

```
static void CallingServerClass(Args _args)
{
    ServerClass serverClass;
    int         result;
    ;
    serverClass = new ServerClass();      // Call to server
    serverClass.parmVariable1(20);        // Call to server
    serverClass.parmVariable2(30);        // Call to server
    result = serverClass.result();        // Call to server

                                          // Destroy object - Call to server
}
```

You can reduce the number of calls by bundling the calls to the *parm* methods with the call to the *result* method, as shown in the following X++ code.

```
static void CallingServerClass(Args _args)
{
    ServerClass serverClass;
    int         result;
    ;
    serverClass = new ServerClass();      // Call to server
    result = serverClass.result(20, 30);  // Call to server

                                          // Destroy object - Call to server
}
```

This reduces the number of server calls by two and reduces the total calls to three. The optimal solution is not to instantiate the server-bound object on the client tier, but merely to call a server-bound static method on the class, as shown in the following X++ code.

```
static void CallingServerClass(Args _args)
{
    int         result;
    ;
    result = ServerClass::calcResult(20,30); // Single call to server
}
```

The same optimization can be considered for server-bound table methods. If multiple server-bound methods are called sequentially from the client tier, the individual calls can be bundled into a single server-bound method, which then makes the individual calls to the other methods.

## Parsing Parameters by Reference and Value

When the client tier has an object handle to a server object, the server sometimes queries the client tier by calling the client to determine whether the tier still contains handles to the object. Otherwise, the server tier will destroy the object. If the server tier also has handles to client objects, the client performs the same query. This, of course, happens as shown in the preceding examples when a server-bound object is instantiated on the client tier. However, it also happens if an object is instantiated on the client tier and is then parsed as a parameter to a server-bound method. In this case, object handles to the same object exist on both tiers, which results in extra client/server calls to determine whether these objects can be destroyed.

Instead of parsing the object by reference from one tier to the other, you may consider parsing it by value. This means that values are parsed to the other tier, which is then used to instantiate a new object of the same type. Then two different and disconnected objects exist on either tier, making it unnecessary for the tier to keep track of object handles across the tier.

> **Note**   Parsing by value is automatically supported by the RunBase framework. The RunBase framework packs variables in a container, parses the container to the opposite tier, and then unpacks the container and instantiates a new object from the variables in the container.

## Reports and Forms

Dynamics AX reports can be executed on either the client or the server. Exactly where to execute the report is defined by the menu item that opens the report. If reports are executed on the server but displayed on the client, the individual pages are generated on the server and sent to the client. If a report is executed on the client, the client renders and generates the report pages.

Rich forms are always executed on the client, which results in client/server traffic when fetching and manipulating records. In addition, display methods can degrade form performance because the displayed methods are executed by the form application runtime whenever it refreshes the forms control displaying the value. A server-bound display method could cause a substantial number of client/server calls, especially if the display method is shown in a grid in which the returned value from multiple display methods is shown at the same time. You can, however, cache the value from the display methods by calling the *cacheAddMethod* method on the *FormDataSource* object. The form application runtime then caches the returned values and refreshes them only when the record is modified or re-read.

# Transaction Performance

The previous section focused on limiting traffic between the client and server tiers, but these tiers are just two of the three tiers involved when a Dynamics AX application is executed. The last tier is the database tier, and it is also important to optimize the exchange of packages between the server tier and the database tier. This section focuses on optimizing the transactional part of the execution of application logic. The Dynamics AX application runtime helps you minimize calls made from the server tier to the database tier by supporting set-based operators and caching of data. However, you should also focus on reducing the amount of data sent from the database tier to the server tier. Not only will the data be fetched faster from the database, but fewer packages will be sent back and less memory will be consumed. All these efforts will promote faster execution of application logic, which will result in smaller transaction scopes, less locking and blocking, and improved concurrency and throughput.

## Set-Based Data Manipulation Operators

As briefly mentioned in Chapter 12, "The Database Layer," in the discussion of database-triggering methods, the X++ language contains specific operators and classes to enable set-based manipulation in the database. The set-based constructs have an advantage over record-set constructs—they make fewer round trips to the database. The following X++ code example, showing the selection of several *custTable* records and where each is updated with a new value in the *creditMax* field, illustrates that a round trip is required for the execution of the *select* statement and for each execution of the *update*.

```
static void UpdateCustomers(Args _args)
{
    CustTable custTable;
    ;
    ttsbegin;

    while select forupdate custTable
        where custTable.CustGroup == '40' // Round trip to database
    {
        custTable.CreditMax = 1000;
        custTable.update(); // Round trip to database
    }

    ttscommit;
}
```

In a scenario in which 100 *custTable* records qualify for the *update* because the *custGroup* fields is equal to '40', the number of round trips would be 1 *select* + 100 *updates* = 101 round trips. The number of round trips for the *select* statement might be slightly higher, depending on the number of *custTable* records that can be retrieved simultaneously from the database and sent to the Application Object Server (AOS).

Theoretically, the preceding scenario could be rewritten to result in only one round trip to the database by changing the X++ code as indicated in the following example. The example shows how to use the *update_recordset* operator, resulting in a single SQL UPDATE statement being parsed to the database.

```
static void UpdateCustomers(Args _args)
{
    CustTable custTable;
    ;
    ttsbegin;

    update_recordset custTable setting creditMax = 1000
        where custTable.CustGroup == '40'; // Single round trip to database

    ttscommit;
}
```

For several reasons, however, the specific use of a *custTable* record buffer would not result in only one round trip. This is described in the following sections on each of the set-based constructs supported by the Dynamics AX application runtime. These sections also describe features available that would allow you to modify the preceding scenario to ensure a single round trip to the database, even with the use of a *custTable* record buffer.

> **Important**   None of the following set-based operations improves performance when used on temporary tables. The Dynamics AX application runtime always downgrades set-based operations on temporary tables to record-based operations. This is true regardless of how the table became a temporary table (whether specified in metadata in the table properties, disabled because of the configuration of the Dynamics AX application, or explicitly stated in the X++ code using the table). Also, the downgrade by the application runtime always invokes the *doInsert*, *doUpdate*, and *doDelete* methods on the record buffer, so no application logic in the overridden methods is executed.

## The *insert_recordset* Operator

The *insert_recordset* operator enables the insertion of multiple records into a table in one round trip to the database. The following X++ code illustrates the use of the operator as the code copies sizes from one item to another item. The item to which the sizes are copied is selected from *inventTable*.

```
static void CopySizes(Args _args)
{
    InventSize  inventSizeTo;
    InventSize  inventSizeFrom;
    InventTable inventTable;
    ;
```

```
        ttsbegin;
        insert_recordset inventSizeTo (ItemId, InventSizeId, Description, Name)
            select itemId from inventTable
                where inventTable.ItemId == 'PB-Metal Shade'
            join inventSizeId, description, name from inventSizeFrom
                where inventSizeFrom.ItemId == 'PB-Plastic Shade';
        ttscommit;
    }
```

The round trip to the database involves the execution of three statements in the database:

- The *select* part of the *insert_recordset* statement is executed where the selected rows are inserted into a temporarily created new table in the database. The syntax of the *select* statement when executed in Microsoft SQL Server 2000 is similar to *SELECT <field list> INTO <temporary table> FROM <source tables> WHERE <predicates>*.

- The records from the temporary table are inserted directly into the target table using syntax such as *INSERT INTO <target table> (<field list>) SELECT <field list> FROM <temporary table>*.

- The temporary table is dropped with the execution of *DROP TABLE <temporary table>*.

This approach has a tremendous performance advantage over inserting the records one by one, as shown in the following X++ code, which addresses the same scenario as the previous X++ code.

```
    static void CopySizes(Args _args)
    {
        InventSize   inventSizeTo;
        InventSize   inventSizeFrom;
        InventTable inventTable;
        ;
        ttsbegin;
        while select itemId from inventTable
                where inventTable.ItemId == 'PB-Metal Shade'
            join inventSizeId, description, name from inventSizeFrom
                where inventSizeFrom.ItemId == 'PB-Plastic Shade'
        {
            inventSizeTo.ItemId        = inventTable.ItemId;
            inventSizeTo.InventSizeId  = inventSizeFrom.InventSizeId;
            inventSizeTo.Description    = inventSizeFrom.Description;
            inventSizeTo.Name           = inventSizeFrom.Name;
            inventSizeTo.insert();
        }
        ttscommit;
    }
```

If 10 sizes were copied, this scenario would result in one round trip caused by the *select* statement and an additional 10 round trips caused by the inserts, totaling 11 round trips.

The *insert_recordset* operation could be downgraded, however, from a set-based operation to a record-based operation. This occurs if any of the following is true:

- The table is entire-table cached.

- The *insert* method or the *aosValidateInsert* method is overridden on the target table.

- Alerts have been set to be triggered by inserts into the target table.

- The Database Log has been configured to log inserts into the target table.

The Dynamics AX application runtime automatically handles the downgrade and internally executes a scenario similar to the *while select* scenario shown in the preceding example.

> **Important**   When the Dynamics AX application runtime checks for overridden methods, it only determines whether the methods are implemented. It does not determine whether the overridden methods contain only the default X++ code. A method is therefore considered to be overridden by the application runtime, even though it contains the following X++ code:
>
> ```
> public void insert()
> {
>     super();
> }
> ```
>
> Any set-based insert is then downgraded. It is therefore important that you delete such a method to avoid the downgrade with its performance ramifications.

You can, however, avoid any downgrade caused by the previously mentioned functionality, unless the table is entire-table cached. The record buffer contains methods that turn off the checks that the application runtime performs when determining whether the *insert_recordset* operation should be downgraded. Calling *skipDataMethods(true)* prevents the check that determines whether the *insert* method is overridden, and calling *skipAosValidation(true)* prevents the check on the *aosValidateInsert* method. Calling *skipDatabaseLog(true)* prevents the check that determines whether the Database Log is configured to log inserts into the table, and calling *skipEvents(true)* prevents the check that determines whether any alerts have been set to be triggered by the *insert* event on the table. The following X++ code, which includes the call to *skipDataMethods(true)*, therefore ensures that the *insert_recordset* operation is not downgraded because the *insert* method is overridden on the *InventSize* table.

```
static void CopySizes(Args _args)
{
    InventSize  inventSizeTo;
    InventSize  inventSizeFrom;
    InventTable inventTable;
    ;
    ttsbegin;
    inventSizeTo.skipDataMethods(true) // Skip override check on insert.
    insert_recordset inventSizeTo (ItemId, InventSizeId, Description, Name)
        select itemId from inventTable
```

```
            where inventTable.ItemId == 'PB-Metal Shade'
        join inventSizeId, description, name from inventSizeFrom
            where inventSizeFrom.ItemId == 'PB-Plastic Shade';
    ttscommit;
}
```

Skip methods must be used with extreme caution to avoid implementing X++ code in the *insert* method that will not get executed, events not being raised, logs not being created, and so on. If you override the *insert* method, you should use the cross-reference system to determine whether any X++ code calls *skipDataMethods(true)*, or the X++ code could fail to execute the *insert* method. Moreover, when you implement calls to *skipDataMethods(true)*, make sure that not executing the X++ code in the overridden *insert* method will not lead to data inconsistency.

Note that the skip methods can be used only to influence whether the *insert_recordset* operation is downgraded. If a call to *skipDataMethods(true)* is implemented to prevent downgrading because the *insert* method is overridden, the overridden version of the *insert* method will eventually be executed if the operation is still downgraded. The operation would be downgraded, if, for example, the Database Log had been configured to log inserts into the table. In the previous example, the overridden *insert* method on the InventSize table would be executed if the Database Log were configured to log inserts into the InventSize table because the *insert_recordset* operation would then revert to a *while select* scenario in which the overridden *insert* method would get called.

## The *update_recordset* Operator

The behavior of the *update_recordset* operator is very similar to that of the *insert_recordset* operator. This is illustrated by the following piece of X++ code, in which all sizes for an item are updated with a new description.

```
static void UpdateSizes(Args _args)
{
    InventSize  inventSize;
    ;
    ttsbegin;
    update_recordset inventSize
        setting Description = 'This size is for item PB-Metal Shade'
        where inventSize.itemId == 'PB-Metal Shade';
    ttscommit;
}
```

The execution of the *update_recordset* operation results in one statement being parsed to the database, which in SQL Server 2000 uses a syntax similar to *UPDATE <table> <SET> <field and expression list> WHERE <predicates>*. As with the *insert_recordset* operator, this operator also provides a tremendous improvement in performance over the record-based version, in which each record is updated individually. This is shown in the following X++ code, which serves the same purpose as the preceding example. The code selects all the records qualified for update, sets the new description value, and updates the record.

```
static void UpdateSizes(Args _args)
{
    InventSize  inventSize;
    ;
    ttsbegin;
    while select forupdate inventSize
        where inventSize.itemId == 'PB-Metal Shade'
    {
        inventSize.Description = 'This size is for item PB-Metal Shade';
        inventSize.update();
    }
    ttscommit;
}
```

If 10 records qualified, one *select* statement and 10 *update* statements would be parsed to the database, rather than the single *update* statement that would be parsed by using the *update_recordset* operator.

The *update_recordset* operation could also be downgraded if specific methods have been overridden or because of the configuration of the Dynamics AX application. This occurs if any of the following is true:

- The table is entire-table cached.

- The *update* method, the *aosValidateUpdate* method, or the *aosValidateRead* method is overridden on the target table.

- Alerts have been set up to be triggered by *update* queries into the target table.

- The Database Log has been configured to log *update* queries into the target table.

The Dynamics AX application runtime automatically handles the downgrade and internally executes a scenario similar to the *while select* scenario shown in the preceding example.

You can avoid any downgrade caused by the previously mentioned functionality, unless the table is entire-table cached. The record buffer contains methods that turn off the checks that the application runtime performs when determining whether the *update_recordset* operation should be downgraded. Calling *skipDataMethods(true)* prevents the check that determines whether the *update* method is overridden, and calling *skipAosValidation(true)* prevents the checks on the *aosValidateUpdate* and *aosValidateRead* methods. Calling *skipDatabaseLog(true)* prevents the check that determines whether the Database Log is configured to log updates to records in the table, and calling *skipEvents(true)* prevents the check to determine whether any alerts have been set to be triggered by the *update* event on the table.

As I explained earlier, the skip methods should be used with great caution, and you should take the same precautions before using the skip methods in combination with the *update_recordset* operation. Again, using the skip methods only influences whether the *update_recordset* operation is downgraded to a *while select* scenario. If the operation is downgraded, the database logging, alerting, and execution of overridden methods will occur, even though the respective skip methods have been called.

> **Tip**   If an *update_recordset* operation is downgraded to a *while select* scenario, the *select* statement uses the concurrency model specified at the table level. You can apply the *optimistic-lock* and *pessimisticlock* keywords to the *update_recordset* statements and enforce a specific concurrency model to be used in case of downgrade.

### The *delete_from* Operator

The *delete_from* operator is similar to the *insert_recordset* and *update_recordset* operators in that it parses a single statement to the database to delete multiple rows. The following X++ code shows deletion of all sizes for an item.

```
static void DeleteSizes(Args _args)
{
    InventSize  inventSize;
    ;
    ttsbegin;
    delete_from inventSize
        where inventSize.itemId == 'PB-Metal Shade';
    ttscommit;
}
```

This code parses a statement to SQL Server 2000 in a similar syntax to *DELETE <table> WHERE <predicates>* and executes the same scenario as the following X++ code that uses record-by-record deletes.

```
static void DeleteSizes(Args _args)
{
    InventSize  inventSize;
    ;
    ttsbegin;
    while select forupdate inventSize
        where inventSize.itemId == 'PB-Metal Shade'
    {
        inventSize.delete();
    }
    ttscommit;
}
```

Again, the use of *delete_from* is preferred with respect to performance because a single statement is parsed to the database, rather than the multiple statements that the record-by-record version parses.

Like the downgrading *insert_recordset* and *update_recordset* operations, the *delete_from* operation could also be downgraded, and for similar reasons. Downgrade occurs if any of the following is true:

- The table is entire-table cached.

- The *delete* method, the *aosValidateDelete* method, or the *aosValidateRead* method is overridden on the target table.

- Alerts have been set up to be triggered by deletes into the target table.

- The Database Log has been configured to log deletes into the target table.

Downgrade also occurs if delete actions are defined on the table. The Dynamics AX application runtime automatically handles the downgrade and internally executes a scenario similar to the *while select* scenario shown in the preceding example.

You can avoid downgrade caused by the previously mentioned functionality, unless the table is entire-table cached. The record buffer contains methods that turn off the checks that the application runtime performs when determining whether to downgrade the *delete_from* operation. Calling *skipDataMethods(true)* prevents the check that determines whether the delete method is overridden, and calling *skipAosValidation(true)* prevents the checks on the *aosValidateDelete* and *aosValidateRead* methods. Calling *skipDatabaseLog(true)* prevents the check that determines whether the Database Log is configured to log deletion of records in the table, and calling *skipEvents(true)* prevents the check that determines whether any alerts have been set to be triggered by the *delete* event on the table. Calling *skipDeleteActions(true)* prevents the check that determines whether any delete actions are defined in metadata on the table.

The preceding descriptions about the use of the skip methods, the no-skipping behavior in the event of downgrade, and the concurrency model for the *update_recordset* operator are equally valid for the use of the *delete_from* operator.

**Note**  The record buffer also contains a *skipDeleteMethod* method. Calling the methods as *skipDeleteMethod(true)* has the same effect as calling *skipDataMethods(true)*. It actually invokes the same Dynamics AX application runtime logic, so you can use the *skipDeleteMethod* in combination with *insert_recordset* and *update_recordset*, although it might not improve the readability of the X++ code.

## The *RecordInsertList* and *RecordSortedList* Classes

In addition to the set-based operators, Dynamics AX also allows you to use the *RecordInsertList* and *RecordSortedList* classes when inserting multiple records into a table. When the records are ready to be inserted, the Dynamics AX application runtime packs multiple records into a single package and sends it to the database. The database executes individual inserts for each record in the package. This is illustrated in the following example, in which a *RecordInsertList* object is instantiated and each record to be inserted into the database is added to the *RecordInsertList* object. When all records are inserted into the object, the *insertDatabase* method is called to ensure that all records are inserted into the database.

```
static void CopySizes(Args _args)
{
    InventSize          inventSizeTo;
    InventSize          inventSizeFrom;
    InventTable         inventTable;
    RecordInsertList    recordInsertList;
    ;
    ttsbegin;
    recordInsertList = new RecordInsertList(tableNum(InventSize));

    while select itemId from inventTable
            where inventTable.ItemId == 'PB-Metal Shade'
        join inventSizeId, description, name from inventSizeFrom
            where inventSizeFrom.ItemId == 'PB-Plastic Shade'
    {
        inventSizeTo.ItemId         = inventTable.ItemId;
        inventSizeTo.InventSizeId   = inventSizeFrom.InventSizeId;
        inventSizeTo.Description     = inventSizeFrom.Description;
        inventSizeTo.Name           = inventSizeFrom.Name;
        recordInsertList.add(inventSizeTo); // Insert records
                                            // if package is full.

    }
    recordInsertList.insertDatabase();      // Insert remaining records
                                            // into database.

    ttscommit;
}
```

If the Dynamics AX application runtime discovers that enough records have been added to the *RecordInsertList* object to constitute a package, the records are packed, parsed to the database, and inserted individually on the database tier. This check is made when the *add* method is called. When the *insertDatabase* method is called from the application logic, the remaining records are therefore inserted with the same mechanism.

Using these classes has an advantage over the *while select* scenario: Fewer round trips are made from the AOS to the database because multiple records are sent simultaneously. However, the number of INSERT statements in the database remains the same.

> **Note**   Because the timing of insertion into the database depends on the size of the record
> buffer and the package, you should not expect a record to be selectable from the database
> until the *insertDatabase* method has been called.

The preceding scenario can be rewritten to use the *RecordSortedList* class instead of the
*RecordInsertList* class, as shown in the following X++ code.

```
static void CopySizes(Args _args)
{
    InventSize          inventSizeTo;
    InventSize          inventSizeFrom;
    InventTable         inventTable;
    RecordSortedList    recordSortedList;
    ;
    ttsbegin;
    recordSortedList = new RecordSortedList(tableNum(InventSize));
    recordSortedList.sortOrder(fieldNum(InventSize, ItemId),
                            fieldNum(InventSize, InventSizeId));

    while select itemId from inventTable
            where inventTable.ItemId == 'PB-Metal Shade'
        join inventSizeId, description, name from inventSizeFrom
            where inventSizeFrom.ItemId == 'PB-Plastic Shade'
    {
        inventSizeTo.ItemId        = inventTable.ItemId;
        inventSizeTo.InventSizeId  = inventSizeFrom.InventSizeId;
        inventSizeTo.Description    = inventSizeFrom.Description;
        inventSizeTo.Name          = inventSizeFrom.Name;
        recordSortedList.ins(inventSizeTo); //No records will be inserted.
    }
    recordSortedList.insertDatabase();//All records are inserted in database.
    ttscommit;
}
```

When the application logic uses a *RecordSortedList* object, the records are not parsed and
inserted in the database until the *insertDatabase* method is called. The number of round trips
and INSERT statements executed is the same as for the *RecordInsertList* object.

Both *RecordInsertList* objects and a *RecordSortedList* objects can be downgraded in application
logic to record-by-record inserts, in which each record is sent in a separate round trip to the
database and the INSERT statement is subsequently executed. This occurs if the *insert*
method or the *aosValidateInsert* method is overridden, or if the table contains fields of type
container or memo. Downgrade does not occur if the Database Log is configured to log
inserts or alerts that have been set to be triggered by the *insert* event on the table. The database
logging and eventing occurs on a record-by-record basis after the records have been sent and
inserted into the database.

When instantiating the *RecordInsertList* object, you can specify that the *insert* and *aosValidate-Insert* methods be skipped. You can also specify that the database logging and eventing be skipped if the operation is not downgraded.

## Restartable Jobs and Optimistic Concurrency

In multiple scenarios in the Dynamics AX application, the execution of some application logic involves manipulating multiple rows from the same table. Some scenarios require that all rows be manipulated within a single transaction scope; if something fails and the transaction is aborted, all modifications are rolled back, and the job can be restarted manually or automatically. Other scenarios commit the changes on a record-by-record basis; in case of failure, only the changes to the current record are rolled back, and all previously manipulated records are already committed. When a job is restarted in this scenario, it starts where it left off by skipping all the records already changed.

An example of the first scenario is shown in the following code, in which all *update* queries to the *custTable* records are wrapped into a single transaction scope.

```
static void UpdateCreditMax(Args _args)
{
    CustTable    custTable;
    ;
    ttsbegin;
    while select forupdate custTable where custTable.creditMax == 0
    {
        if (custTable.balanceMST() < 10000)
        {
            custTable.creditMax = 50000;
            custTable.update();
        }
    }
    ttscommit;
}
```

An example of the second scenario, executing the same logic, is shown in the following code, in which the transaction scope is handled on a record basis. Note that you must reselect each individual *custTable* record inside the transaction for the Dynamics AX application runtime to allow the update of the record.

```
static void UpdateCreditMax(Args _args)
{
    CustTable    custTable;
    CustTable    updateableCustTable;
    ;
    while select custTable where custTable.creditMax == 0
    {
        if (custTable.balanceMST() < 10000)
```

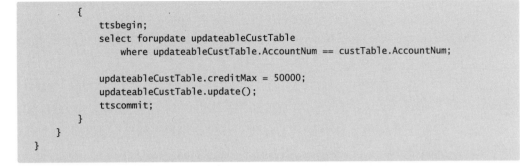

```
        {
            ttsbegin;
            select forupdate updateableCustTable
                where updateableCustTable.AccountNum == custTable.AccountNum;

            updateableCustTable.creditMax = 50000;
            updateableCustTable.update();
            ttscommit;
        }
    }
}
```

In a scenario in which 100 *custTable* records qualify for the update, the first example would involve one *select* and 100 *update* statements being parsed to the database, and the second example would involve one large *select* query and 100 single ones, plus the 100 *update* statements. So the first scenario would execute faster than the second, but the first scenario would also hold the locks on the updated *custTable* records for a longer period of time because it would not commit for each record. The second example demonstrates superior concurrency over the first example because locks are held for a short period of time.

The implementation of the optimistic concurrency model in Dynamics AX 4.0 resulted in the ability to take advantage of the benefits offered by both of the preceding examples. In Dynamics AX 4.0, you can select records outside a transaction scope and update records inside a transaction scope, but only if the records are selected optimistically. This is shown in the following example, in which the *optimisticlock* keyword is applied to the *select* statement while maintaining a per-record transaction scope. Because the records are selected with the *optimisticlock* keyword, it is not necessary to reselect each record individually within the transaction scope. For a detailed description of the optimistic concurrency model, see Chapter 12.

```
static void UpdateCreditMax(Args _args)
{
    CustTable    custTable;
    ;
    while select optimisticlock custTable where custTable.creditMax == 0
    {
        if (custTable.balanceMST() < 10000)
        {
            ttsbegin;
            custTable.creditMax = 50000;
            custTable.update();
            ttscommit;
        }
    }
}
```

This approach provides the same number of statements parsed to the database as in the first example, with the improved concurrency from the second example because commits execute on a record basis. This example will still not perform as fast as the first because it has the extra burden of the per-record transaction management. You could optimize the example even further by committing on a scale somewhere between all records and the single record, without decreasing the concurrency considerably. However, the appropriate choice of commit frequency always depends on the circumstances of the job.

> **Best Practices**    You can use the *forupdate* keyword when selecting records outside the transaction if the table has been enabled for optimistic concurrency at the table level. However, the best practice is to explicitly use the *optimisticlock* keyword because the scenario will not fail if the table-level setting is changed. Using the *optimisticlock* keyword also improves the readability of the X++ code because the explicit intention of the developer is stated in the code.

# Caching

The Dynamics AX application runtime supports the enabling of single-record and set-based caching of records. Set-based caching can be set in metadata by switching a property on a table definition or writing explicit X++ code, which instantiates a cache. Regardless of how caching is set up, you do not need to know which caching method is used because the application runtime handles the cache transparently. But to optimize the use of the cache, you must understand how each caching mechanism works.

The Microsoft Dynamics AX SDK contains a good description of the individual caching possibilities and how they are set up. This section focuses on how the caches are implemented in the Dynamics AX application runtime and what you should expect when using the individual caching mechanisms.

## Record Caches

You can set up three types of record caching on a table by setting the *CacheLookup* property on the table definition. The following are the three record-caching values:

- *Found*
- *FoundAndEmpty*
- *NotInTTS*

One additional value (besides *None*) is *EntireTable*, which is a set-based caching option that is described later in this section.

The three record-caching possibilities are fundamentally the same. The difference lies in what is cached and when cached values are flushed. For example, the *Found* and *FoundAndEmpty* caches are preserved across transaction boundaries, but a table that uses the *NotInTTS* cache does not use the cache when first accessed inside a transaction scope—it uses it in consecutive *select* statements, unless a *forupdate* keyword is applied to the *select* statement. The following X++ code example describes when the cache will be used inside and outside a transaction scope, when a table uses the *NotInTTS* caching mechanism, and where the *AccountNum* field is the primary key. The comments in the X++ code describe when the cache will be used and when it will not. In the example, it appears that the first two *select* statements after the *ttsbegin* command will not use the cache. The first will not use the cache because it is the first statement inside the transaction scope, and the second will not use the cache because the *forupdate* keyword is applied to the statement. The use of the *forupdate* keyword forces the application runtime to look up the record in the database because the previously cached record was not selected with the *forupdate* keyword applied.

```
static void NotInTTSCache(Args _args)
{
    CustTable custTable;
    ;
    select custTable                            // Look up in cache. If record
        where custTable.AccountNum == '4000';   // does not exist, look up
                                                // in database.

    ttsbegin;                                   // Start transaction.

    select custTable                            // Cache is invalid. Look up in
        where custTable.AccountNum == '4000';   // database and place in cache.

    select forupdate custTable                  // Look up in database because
        where custTable.AccountNum == '4000';   // forupdate keyword is applied.

    select custTable                            // Cache will be used.
        where custTable.AccountNum == '4000';   // No lookup in database.

    select forupdate custTable                  // Cache will be used because
        where custTable.AccountNum == '4000';   // forupdate keyword was used
                                                // previously.

    ttscommit;                                  // End transaction.

    select custTable                            // Cache will be used.
        where custTable.AccountNum == '4000';
}
```

If the table had been set up with *Found* or *FoundAndEmpty* caching in the preceding example, the cache would have been used when executing the first *select* statement inside the transaction, but not when the first *select forupdate* statement was executed.

> **Note**   By default, all Dynamics AX system tables are set up using a *Found* cache. This cannot be changed.

For all three caching mechanisms, the cache is used only if the *select* statement contains equal-to (==) predicates in the *where* clause that exactly match all the fields in the primary index of the table. The *PrimaryIndex* property on the table must therefore be set to the unique index used when accessing the cache from application logic.

The following X++ code examples show when the Dynamics AX application runtime will try to use the cache and when it will not. The cache will be used in the first *select* statement only; the remaining three statements do not match the fields in the primary index, so they will all perform lookups in the database.

```
static void UtilizeCache(Args _args)
{
    CustTable custTable;
    ;
    select custTable                          // Will use cache because only
        where custTable.AccountNum == '4000'; // the primary key is used as
                                              // predicate.

    select custTable;                         // Cannot use cache because no
                                              // "where" clause exists.

    select custTable                          // Cannot use cache because
        where custTable.AccountNum > '4000';  // equal to (==) is not used.

    select custTable                          // Will not use cache because
        where custTable.AccountNum == '4000'  // where-clause contains more
        &&     custTable.CustGroup == '40';   // predicates than the primary
                                              // key.
}
```

**Note**   The *RecId* index, which is always unique on a table, can be set as the *PrimaryIndex* in the table's properties. You can therefore set up caching using the *RecId* field.

The Dynamics AX application runtime ensures that all fields on a record are selected before they are cached. The application runtime therefore always changes a field list to include all fields on the table before submitting the SELECT statement to the database when it cannot find the record in the cache. The following X++ code illustrates this behavior.

```
static void expandingFieldList(Args _args)
{
    CustTable custTable;
    ;
    select creditRating  // The field list will be expanded to all fields.
        from custTable
        where custTable.AccountNum == '4000';
}
```

If the preceding select statement does not find a record in cache, it will expand the field to contain all fields, not just the *creditRating* field. This ensures that the fetched record from the database contains values for all fields before it is inserted into the cache. Although performance when fetching all fields is inferior compared to performance when fetching a few fields, this is regarded as acceptable because the performance gain in subsequent use of the cache outweighs the performance loss from populating it.

> **Tip**   You can disregard the use of the cache by calling the *disableCache()* method on the record buffer with a Boolean *true* parameter. This forces the application runtime to look up the record in the database, and it also prevents the application runtime from expanding the field list.

The Dynamics AX application runtime creates and uses caches on both the client tier and the server tier. The client-side cache is local to the rich client, and the server-side cache is shared among all connections to the server, including connections coming from rich clients, Web clients, the Business Connector, or any another connection.

 The cache used depends on which tier the lookup is made from. If the lookup is made on the server tier, the server-side cache is used. If the lookup is executed from the client tier, the client first looks in the client-side cache; if nothing is found, a lookup is made in the server-side cache. If there is still no record, a lookup is made in the database. When the database returns the record to the server and on to the client, the record is inserted into both the server-side cache and the client-side cache.

The caches are implemented using AVL trees (which are balanced binary trees), but the trees are not allowed to grow indefinitely. The client-side cache can contain a maximum of 100 records for a given table in a given company, and the shared server-side cache can contain a maximum of 2,000 records. When a new record is inserted into the cache and the maximum is reached, the application runtime removes approximately 5 to 7 percent of the oldest records by scanning the entire tree.

> **Note**   You cannot change the maximum number of records to be cached in metadata or from the X++ code.

The scenarios that repeat lookups on the same records and expect to find the records in cache may therefore suffer performance degradation if the cache is continuously full—not only because records will not be found in the cache because they were removed based on the aging scheme, forcing a lookup in the database, but also because of the constant scanning of the tree to remove the oldest records. The following X++ code shows an example in which all *SalesTable* records are looped twice, and each loop looks up the associated *CustTable* record. If this X++ code were executed on the server and the number of *CustTable* record lookups was more than 2,000, the oldest records would be removed from the cache, and the cache would not contain all *CustTable* records when the first loop ended. When the code loops through the *SalesTable* records again, the records might not be in the cache, and the selection of the *CustTable* record would continue to go to the database to look up the record. The scenario would therefore perform much better with fewer than 2,000 records in the database.

```
static void AgingScheme(Args _args)
{
    SalesTable salesTable;
    CustTable custTable;
    ;
    while select SalesTable order by custAccount
    {
        select custTable          // Fill up cache.
            where custTable.AccountNum == salesTable.CustAccount;
        // More code here
    }

    while select SalesTable order by custAccount
    {
        select custTable          // Record might not be in cache.
            where custTable.AccountNum == salesTable.CustAccount;
        // More code here
    }

}
```

> **Important**   If you test code on small databases, the preceding issue cannot be tracked
> by only tracing the number of statements parsed to the database. When you execute such
> code in a production environment, you can encounter severe performance issues because
> this scenario does not scale very well.

Before the Dynamics AX application runtime searches for, inserts, updates, or deletes records in the cache, it takes a mutually exclusive lock, which is not released until the operation is complete. This means that two processes running on the same server cannot perform these operations in the cache at the same time; only one process can hold the lock at any given time, and the remaining processes are blocked. Blocking occurs only when the application runtime accesses the server-side cache. So although the caching possibilities supported by the application runtime are useful features, they should not be abused. If you can reuse a record buffer that is already fetched, you should do so. The following X++ code shows the same record fetched twice: The second fetch uses the cache, even though the first fetched record buffer could have been used. When you execute the following X++ code on the server tier, the process might get blocked when the application runtime searches the cache.

```
static void ReuseRecordBuffer(Args _args)
{
    CustTable custTable;
    ;
    select custTable
        where custTable.AccountNum == '4000';

    // Some more code, which does not change the custTable record
```

```
    select custTable                              // The cache will be used, but
        where custTable.AccountNum == '4000';     // blocking might occur.
                                                  // Reuse the record buffer
                                                  // instead.
}
```

## The *EntireTable* Cache

In addition to the three caching methods described so far, a fourth caching option can be set on a table. This option is the *EntireTable*, which enables a set-based cache. The option causes the AOS to mirror the table in the database by selecting all records in the table and inserting them into a temporary table when any record from the table is selected for the first time. The first process to read from the table could therefore experience a longer response time because the application runtime reads all records from the database. Subsequent *select* queries then read from the entire-table cache instead of from the database.

A temporary table is usually local to the process that uses it, but the entire-table cache is shared among all processes that access the same AOS. Each company (as defined by the *DataAreaId* field) has an entire-table cache, so two processes requesting records from the same table from different companies use different caches, and both could experience a longer response time to instantiate the entire-table cache.

The entire-table cache is a server-side cache only. When requesting records from the client tier on a table that is entire-table cached, the table behaves as a *Found* cached table. If a request for a record is made on the client tier that qualifies for searching the record cache, the client first searches the local *Found* cache. If the record is not found, the client calls the AOS to search the entire-table cache. When the application runtime returns the record to the client tier, it inserts the record into the client-side *Found* cache.

The entire-table cache is not used when executing a *select* statement by which an entire-table-cached table is joined to a table that is not entire-table cached. In this situation, the entire *select* statement is parsed to the database. However, when *select* statements are made that access only the single entire-table cached table, or when joining other entire-table cached tables, the entire-table cache is used.

The Dynamics AX application runtime flushes the entire-table cache when records are inserted, updated, or deleted in the table. The next process, which selects records from the table, suffers a degradation in performance because it must re-read the entire table into cache. In addition to flushing its own cache, the AOS that executes the insert, update, or delete also informs other AOSs in the same installation that they must flush their caches on the same table. This prevents old and invalid data from being cached for too long in the entire Dynamics AX application environment. In addition to this flushing mechanism, the AOS flushes all the entire-table caches every 24 hours.

Because of the flushing that results when modifying records in a table that has been entire-table cached, you should avoid setting up entire-table caches on frequently updated tables. Rereading all records into the cache results in a performance loss, which could outweigh the performance gain achieved by caching records on the server tier and avoiding round trips to the database tier. The entire-table cache setting on a specific table can therefore be overwritten at run time when you configure the Dynamics AX application.

Even if the records in a table are fairly static, you might achieve better performance by not using the entire-table cache if the number of records in the table is large. Because the entire-table cache uses temporary tables, it changes from an in-memory structure to a file-based structure when the table uses more than 128 kilobytes (KB) of memory. This results in performance degradation during record searches. The database search engines have also evolved over time and are faster than the ones implemented in the Dynamics AX application runtime. It might be faster to let the database search for the records than to set up and use an entire-table cache, even though a database search involves round trips to the database tier.

## The *RecordViewCache* Class

The *RecordViewCache* class allows you to establish a set-based cache from the X++ code. The cache is initiated by writing the following X++ code.

```
select nofetch custTrans where custTrans.accountNum == '4000';
recordViewCache = new RecordViewCache(custTrans);
```

The records to cache are described in the *select* statement, which must include the *nofetch* keyword to prevent the actual selection of the records from the database. The records are selected when the *RecordViewCache* object is instantiated with the record buffer parsed as a parameter. Until the *RecordViewCache* object is destroyed, *select* statements will execute on the cache if they match the *where* clause defined when it was instantiated. The following X++ code shows how the cache is instantiated and used.

```
static void RecordViewCache(Args _args)
{
    CustTrans        custTrans;
    RecordViewCache recordViewCache;
    ;
    select nofetch custTrans                      // Define records to cache.
        where custTrans.AccountNum == '4000';

    recordViewCache = new RecordViewCache(custTrans); // Cache the records.

    select firstonly custTrans                    // Use cache.
        where custTrans.AccountNum == '4000' &&
            custTrans.CurrencyCode == 'USD';
}
```

The cache can be instantiated only on the server tier. The defined *select* may contain only equal-to (==) predicates in the *where* clause and is accessible only by the process instantiating the cache object. If the table buffer used for instantiating the cache object is a temporary table or it uses *EntireTable* caching, the *RecordViewCache* object is not instantiated.

The records are stored in the cache as a linked list of records. Searching therefore involves a sequential search of the cache for the records that match the search criteria. When defining *select* statements to use the cache, you can specify a sort order. This causes the Dynamics AX application runtime to create a temporary index on the cache, which contains the requested records sorted as specified in the *select* statement. The application runtime iterates the temporary index when it returns the individual rows. If no sorting is specified, the application runtime merely iterates the linked list.

If the table cached in the *RecordViewCache* is also record-cached, the application runtime can use both caches. If a *select* statement is executed on a *Found* cached table and the *select* statement qualifies for lookup in the *Found* cache, the application runtime performs a lookup in this cache first. If nothing is found and the *select* statement also qualifies for lookup in the *RecordViewCache*, the runtime uses the *RecordViewCache* and updates the *Found* cache after retrieving the record.

Inserts, updates, and deletes of records that meet the cache criteria are reflected in the cache at the same time that the Data Manipulation Language (DML) statements are sent to the database. Records in the cache are always inserted at the end of the linked list. A hazard associated with this behavior is that an infinite loop can occur when application logic is iterating the records in the cache and at the same time inserting new records that meet the cache criteria. An infinite loop is shown in the following X++ code example, in which a *RecordViewCache* object is created containing all *custTable* records associated with *CustGroup* '40'. The code iterates each record in the cache when executing the *select* statement, but because each cached record is duplicated and still inserted with *CustGroup* '40', the records are inserted at the end of the cache. Eventually, the loop fetches these newly inserted records as well.

```
static void InfiniteLoop(Args _args)
{
    CustTable         custTable;
    RecordViewCache   recordViewCache;
    custTable         custTableInsert;
    ;
    select nofetch custTable                   // Define records to cache.
        where custTable.CustGroup == '40';
    recordViewCache = new RecordViewCache(custTable); // Instantiate cache.

    ttsbegin;
    while select custTable                     // Loop over cache.
        where custTable.CustGroup == '40'
    {
        custTableInsert.data(custTable);
        custTableInsert.AccountNum = 'dup'+custTable.AccountNum;
```

```
        custTableInsert.insert();       // Will insert at end of cache.
                                        // Records will eventually be selected.
    }
    ttscommit;
}
```

To avoid the infinite loop, simply sort the records when selecting them from the cache; this creates a temporary index that contains only the records in the cache from when the records were first retrieved. Any inserted records are therefore not retrieved. This is shown in the following example, in which the *order by* operator is applied to the *select* statement.

```
static void FiniteLoop(Args _args)
{
    CustTable        custTable;
    RecordViewCache  recordViewCache;
    custTable        custTableInsert;
    ;
    select nofetch custTable                 // Define records to cache.
        where custTable.CustGroup == '40';
    recordViewCache = new RecordViewCache(custTable); // Instantiate cache.

    ttsbegin;
    while select custTable                   // Loop over a sorted cache.
        order by CustGroup                   // Create temporary index.
        where custTable.CustGroup == '40'
    {
        custTableInsert.data(custTable);
        custTableInsert.AccountNum = 'dup'+custTable.AccountNum;
        custTableInsert.insert();       // Will insert at end of cache.
                                        // Records are not inserted in index.
    }
    ttscommit;
}
```

Changes made to records in a *RecordViewCache* object cannot be rolled back. If one or more *RecordViewCache* objects exist, if the *ttsabort* operation executes, or if an error is thrown that results in a rollback of the database, the *RecordViewCache* objects still contain the same information. Any instantiated *RecordViewCache* object that is subject to modification by the application logic should therefore not have a lifetime longer than the transaction scope in which it is modified. The *RecordViewCache* object must therefore be declared in a method that is not executed until after the transaction has begun. In the event of a rollback, the object and the cache are both destroyed.

As described earlier, the *RecordViewCache* object is implemented as a linked list that allows only a sequential search for records. This involves a performance degradation in search when you use the cache to store a large number of records. The use of the cache should be weighed against the extra time spent fetching the records from the database where the database uses a more optimal search algorithm. This is especially true when you search only for a subset of the records; the application runtime must continuously match each record in the cache against the more granular *where* clause in the *select* statement because no indexing is available for the records in the cache.

However, for small sets of records, or for situations in which the same records are looped multiple times, *RecordViewCache* offers a substantial performance advantage compared to fetching the same records multiple times from the database.

## Limiting Field Lists

Most of the X++ *select* statements in Dynamics AX retrieve all fields on a record, although the values in only a few of the fields are actually used. The main reason for this coding style is that the Dynamics AX application runtime does not report compile-time or run-time errors if a field on a record buffer is accessed and it has not been retrieved from the database. The following X++ code, which selects only the *AccountNum* field from the *CustTable* table but evaluates the value of the *CreditRating* field and sets the *CreditMax* field, will not fail because the application runtime does not detect that the fields have not been selected.

```
static void UpdateCreditMax(Args _args)
{
    CustTable custTable;
    ;
    ttsbegin;
    while select forupdate accountNum from custTable
    {
        if (custTable.CreditRating == '')
        {
            custTable.CreditMax = custTable.CreditMax + 1000;
            custTable.update();
        }
    }
    ttscommit;
}
```

This code therefore updates all *CustTable* records to a *CreditMax* value of 1,000, regardless of the previous value in the database for the *CreditRating* and *CreditMax* fields. Adding the *CreditRating* and *CreditMax* fields to the field list of the *select* statement might not solve the problem because the application logic could still update other fields incorrectly. This is because the *update* method on the table could be evaluating and setting other fields on the same record.

**Important**    You could, of course, examine the *update* method for other fields accessed in the method and then select these fields as well, but new problems would surface soon. For example, if you customize the *update* method to include application logic that uses additional fields, you might not be aware that the X++ code in the preceding example also needs to be customized.

However, limiting the field list when selecting records does result in a performance gain because less data is retrieved from the database and sent to the AOS. The gain is even bigger if you can retrieve the fields by using the indexes without lookup of the values on the table. This performance gain can be experienced and the *select* statements written safely when you use the retrieved data within a controlled scope, such as a single method. The record buffer must be declared locally and not parsed to other methods as a parameter. Any developer customizing the X++ code can easily see that only a few fields are selected and act accordingly.

But to truly benefit from a limited field list, you must understand that the Dynamics AX application runtime sometimes automatically adds extra fields to the field list before parsing a statement to the database. One example was explained earlier, in the section titled "Caching." In this example, the application runtime expands the field list to include all fields if the *select* statement qualifies for storing the retrieved record in the cache. In another example that I explained in Chapter 12, the application runtime ensures that the fields contained in the unique index, used by the application runtime to update and delete the record, are always retrieved from the database.

To illustrate how the application runtime adds additional fields and how to optimize some *select* statements, the following X++ code is used as a basis. The code calculates the total balance for all customers in customer group '40' and converts it into the company's currency unit. The *amountCur2MST* method converts the value in the currency specified by the *currencyCode* field to the monetary unit of the company.

```
static void BalanceMST(Args _args)
{
    CustTable    custTable;
    CustTrans    custTrans;
    AmountMST    balanceAmountMST = 0;
    ;
    while select custTable
            where custTable.CustGroup == '40'
          join custTrans
            where custTrans.AccountNum == custTable.AccountNum
    {
        balanceAmountMST += Currency::amountCur2MST(custTrans.AmountCur,
                                                    custTrans.CurrencyCode);
    }
}
```

When the *select* statement is parsed to the database, it retrieves all *CustTable* record fields and all *CustTrans* record fields, even though only the *AmountCur* and *CurrencyCode* fields on the *CustTrans* table are used. The result is the retrieval of more than 100 fields from the database.

The field list can be optimized by simply selecting the *AmountCur* and *CurrencyCode* fields from *CustTrans* and, for example, only the *AccountNum* field from *CustTable*, as shown in the following code.

```
static void BalanceMST(Args _args)
{
    CustTable   custTable;
    CustTrans   custTrans;
    AmountMST   balanceAmountMST = 0;
    ;
    while select AccountNum from custTable
            where custTable.CustGroup == '40'
          join AmountCur, CurrencyCode from custTrans
            where custTrans.AccountNum == custTable.AccountNum
    {
        balanceAmountMST += Currency::amountCur2MST(custTrans.AmountCur,
                                                    custTrans.CurrencyCode);
    }
}
```

As explained earlier, the application runtime expands the field list from the three fields shown in the preceding X++ code example to five fields because it adds the fields used when updating the records. This happens even though neither the *forupdate* keyword nor any of the specific concurrency model keywords are applied to the statement. The statement parsed to the database therefore starts as shown in the following example, in which the RECID column is added for both tables.

```
SELECT A.ACCOUNTNUM,A.RECID,B.AMOUNTCUR,B.CURRENCYCODE,B.RECID
FROM CUSTTABLE A,CUSTTRANS B
```

To prevent retrieval of any *CustTable* fields, you can rewrite the *select* statement to use the *exists join operator*, as shown here.

```
static void BalanceMST(Args _args)
{
    CustTable   custTable;
    CustTrans   custTrans;
    AmountMST   balanceAmountMST = 0;
    ;
    while select AmountCur, CurrencyCode from custTrans
        exists join custTable
            where custTable.CustGroup  == '40' &&
                  custTable.AccountNum == custTrans.AccountNum
    {
        balanceAmountMST += Currency::amountCur2MST(custTrans.AmountCur,
                                                    custTrans.CurrencyCode);
    }
}
```

This code retrieves only three fields (*AmountCur*, *CurrencyCode*, and *RecId*) from the *CustTrans* table and none from the *CustTable* table.

In some situations, however, it might not be possible to rewrite the statement to use *exists join*. In such cases, including only *TableId* as a field in the field list will prevent the retrieval of any fields from the table. The original example is modified as follows to include the *TableId* field.

```
static void BalanceMST(Args _args)
{
    CustTable    custTable;
    CustTrans    custTrans;
    AmountMST    balanceAmountMST = 0;
    ;
    while select tableid from custTable
            where custTable.CustGroup == '40'
          join AmountCur, CurrencyCode from custTrans
            where custTrans.AccountNum == custTable.AccountNum
    {
        balanceAmountMST += Currency::amountCur2MST(custTrans.AmountCur,
                                                    custTrans.CurrencyCode);
    }
}
```

This code causes the application runtime to parse a *select* statement to the database with the following field list.

```
SELECT B.AMOUNTCUR,B.CURRENCYCODE,B.RECID
FROM CUSTTABLE A,CUSTTRANS B
```

If you rewrite the *select* statement to use *exists join* or only include *TableId* as a field, the *select* statement sent to the database retrieves just three fields, instead of more than 100. Therefore, you have much to gain in regard to performance by rewriting queries to retrieve only the necessary fields.

> **Best Practices**    A best practice warning is implemented in Dynamics AX 4.0 to analyze X++ code for the use of *select* statements and recommend whether to implement field lists based on the number of fields accessed in the method. The best practice check is made if (in the Best Practice Parameters dialog box) the AOS Performance Check under General Checks is enabled and the Warning Level is set to Errors And Warnings.

## Other Performance Considerations

You can further improve transactional performance by giving more thought to the design of the application logic. For example, ensuring that various tables and records are always modified in the same order will help prevent deadlocks and ensuing retries. Spending time preparing the transactions before starting a transaction scope to make it as brief as possible can reduce the locking scope and resulting blocking, and ultimately improve the concurrency of the transactions. Database design factors, such as index design and use, are also important. These topics are addressed in other books, however, so they are not discussed here.

# Dynamics AX Monitoring Tools

Without a way to monitor the execution of the implemented application logic, you would implement features almost blindly with regard to performance. Fortunately, the Dynamics AX development environment contains a set of easy-to-use tools to help you monitor client/ server calls, database activity, and application logic. These tools provide good feedback on the feature being monitored. The feedback is integrated directly with the development environment, making it possible for you to jump directly to the relevant X++ code.

## Monitoring Client/Server Calls

When you develop and test the Dynamics AX application, you can monitor the client and server calls by turning on the Client/Server Trace option, found on the Development tab in the Options dialog box, which can be accessed from the Tools menu. The Development tab shows the calls made that force the application runtime to parse from one tier to the other. Figure 17-1 shows an example of the client/server trace for one of the previous X++ examples.

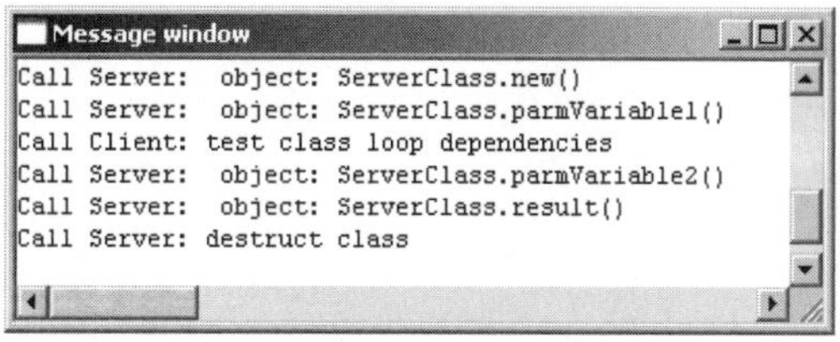

```
Message window                              _ □ ×
Call Server:   object: ServerClass.new()
Call Server:   object: ServerClass.parmVariable1()
Call Client: test class loop dependencies
Call Server:   object: ServerClass.parmVariable2()
Call Server:   object: ServerClass.result()
Call Server: destruct class
```

**Figure 17-1**   A client/server trace message window.

## Monitoring Database Activity

You can also trace the database activity when developing and testing the Dynamics AX application logic. Tracing can be enabled on the SQL tab in the Options dialog box. You can trace all SQL statements or just the long queries, warnings, and deadlocks. SQL statements can be traced to the Infolog, a message window, a database table, or a file. If statements are traced to the Infolog, you can use the context menu to open the statement in the SQL Trace dialog box, in which it is easier to view the entire statement, as well as the path to the method that executed the statement. The dialog box is shown in Figure 17-2.

You can open the Statement Execution Plan dialog box from the SQL Trace dialog box, as shown in Figure 17-3. This dialog box shows a simple view of the execution plan to help you understand how the statement will be executed by the underlying database.

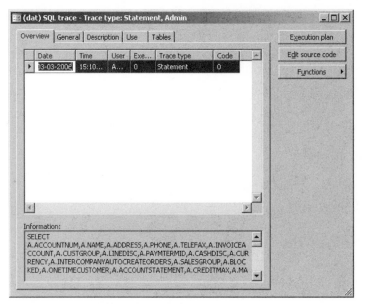

**Figure 17-2** The SQL Trace dialog box.

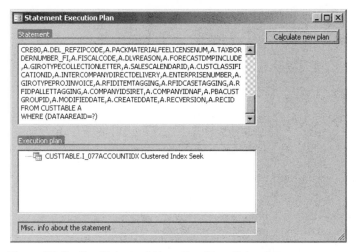

**Figure 17-3** The Statement Execution Plan dialog box.

**Important** To trace SQL statements, you must select the Allow Client Tracing On Application Object Server Instance option on the Tracing tab in the Server Configuration Utility.

From either of the two dialog boxes, you can copy the statement and, if you are using SQL Server 2000, paste it into SQL Server Query Analyzer to get a more detailed view of the execution plan. If the Dynamics AX application runtime uses placeholders to execute the statement, the placeholders are shown as question marks in the statement. These must be replaced by variables or constants before they can be executed in the SQL Server Query Analyzer. If the application runtime uses literals, the statement can be pasted directly into the SQL Server Query Analyzer and executed.

When you trace SQL statements in Dynamics AX, the application runtime displays only the DML statement. It does not display other commands sent to the database, such as transaction commits or isolation level changes. With SQL Server 2000, you can use the SQL Profiler to trace these statements using the event classes *RPC:Completed* and *SP:StmtCompleted* in the Stored Procedures collection, and the *SQL:BatchCompleted* event in the TSQL collection, as shown in Figure 17-4.

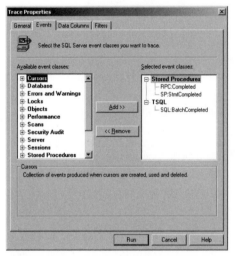

**Figure 17-4**   SQL Profiler trace events.

## The Code Profiler Tool

The previous version of Dynamics AX included a Code Profiler tool that could trace all method calls within a traced scenario and display the trace in a tree structure. You could traverse the tree to see the method calls made and their durations.

This tool is greatly enhanced in Dynamics AX 4.0. It calculates the profile much faster, and it includes a new view of the code profile, providing a better user experience. Figure 17-5 shows the new traverse view, in which each of the called methods in the profiled scenario appears in the top grid. The view also displays a duration count that shows the number of ticks that it took to execute the method and a method count that shows the number of times the methods have been called. The grid for parent calls and children calls shows the methods that called the specific method and the other methods calling the specific method, respectively.

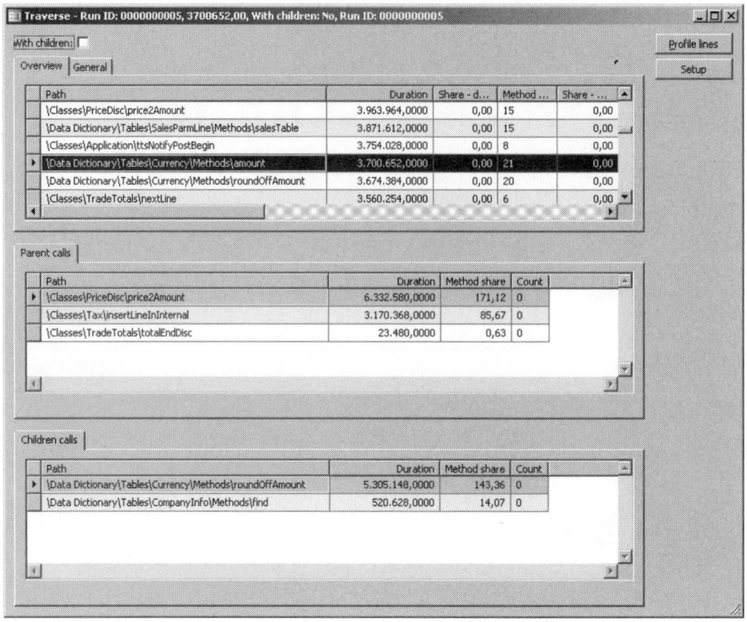

**Figure 17-5**    The Traverse view in the Code Profiler.

If you use the Code Profiler as a performance optimization tool, you can focus on the methods with the longest duration to optimize the internal structure of the method, or you can focus on the methods called the most and try to limit the number of calls to those methods. You can inspect the internal operation of the methods by clicking the Profile Lines button, which opens the view shown in Figure 17-6. This view shows the duration of every line in the method.

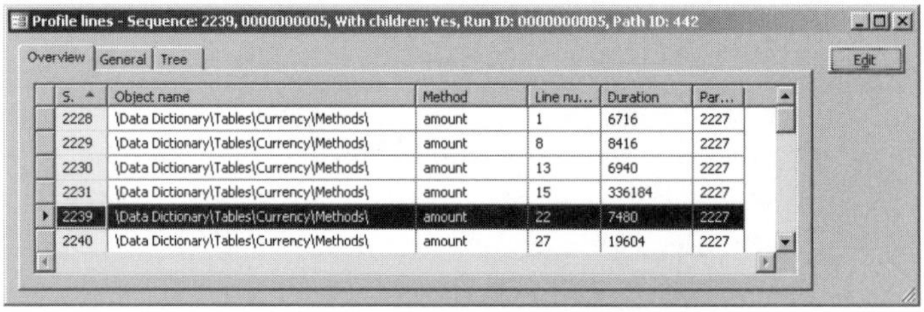

**Figure 17-6**    The Profile Lines view in the Code Profiler.

With these changes, the Code Profiler has become an important and powerful tool for finding issues such as problem areas in the X++ code, code that does not have to be executed in certain scenarios, and code that makes multiple calls to the same methods.

# Chapter Summary

Is poor performance an implementation issue with a feature, or is it a bug? It may depend on the user's expectations. You should therefore consider performance when implementing a feature, rather than trying to address performance issues with bug fixes. As described in this chapter, the Dynamics AX application development environment and runtime support a set of features that assist you with implementation of optimized application logic in a three-tier environment. This chapter also described a set of tools for monitoring the execution before releasing it to a production environment. However, it is not enough merely to know about the these tools—understanding the other software products that integrate with the Dynamics AX execution environment is equally important.

# Chapter 18
# Upgrade and Data Migration

The objectives of this chapter are to:

■ Describe an upgrade of Microsoft Dynamics AX 4.0 that includes modifications.

■ Explain how to apply a service pack or hotfix.

■ Discuss migration of data from a legacy system when implementing Dynamics AX.

## Introduction

This chapter provides an overview of how to upgrade from one version of Dynamics AX to a newer version in a live environment. This process includes upgrading of modifications to reflect the changes in the standard application and upgrading of the design and contents of the database to reflect schema changes.

An upgrade process can involve a change to a major version (this chapter describes an upgrade from version 3.0 to 4.0), or it can involve applying a service pack to the running version. The routine is basically the same in either case; however, the workload is much greater when changing major versions.

Single critical errors can be corrected by applying a hotfix. A hotfix is typically an export of a small number of application objects. A hotfix can also contain a new version of the executables.

Migration of data is the process of initializing a Dynamics AX environment with data from a legacy system. You perform this task when implementing Dynamics AX as a replacement for the previous enterprise resource planning (ERP) system.

# Upgrading from an Earlier Version

The upgrade process consists of six major steps:

1. Plan the upgrade.

2. Back up code and data.

3. Perform the code upgrade in a development environment.

4. Perform the data upgrade in a test environment.

5. Test the upgraded code and data.

6. Perform the production upgrade in the live environment.

> **Note**    The process of upgrading from version 3.0 to version 4.0 is thoroughly described in the Microsoft Dynamics AX 4.0 Implementation Guide supplied with the product. Refer to this document for all process-specific information.

## Upgrade Planning

Upgrade planning is often affected by decisions concerning the extensions or modifications made to the current version. When you have decided what must be upgraded, you will want to estimate the cost of upgrading the customer's application. The process of making the upgrade entails costs for resources used. It is critical to clear any potential costs with the customer before the work is started. If the costs outweigh the benefits of the upgrade, the customer might decide to postpone the upgrade.

An upgrade cost estimate requires a detailed analysis of the number and extent of modifications performed on the previous version of the standard application. A good starting point could be a list of the number of different types of application object in the current layer and the number of shadows, as illustrated in Figure 18-1. A shadow is an application object from the standard application that is modified. The modification is performed by making a copy of the object, which hides the original object. Any changes to the object in the lower layers will not be visible because it is shadowed by the modification.

Such a list can be generated by using the *UtilElements* table, which contains a record for each application object in each layer it represents. The preceding example contains quite a few objects in the current layer, but only a small fraction of these constitutes modifications to standard objects. Many of the shadows are object and instance methods, which are usually easy to upgrade. The main concern in the preceding example is the forms, which should be further analyzed to investigate the work involved for the upgrade.

The amount of time between when the production environment running the previous version is stopped and when the new upgraded production environment is started is critical for the customer because the ERP system will not be available during this time. The time spent depends on the amount of data, hardware, and infrastructure involved in the upgrade. The data upgrade performed in the test environment can be used as a guideline for the time that will be required, but only if the test is performed in an environment that is comparable to the production environment.

| Type | Counter | Shadows |
|---|---|---|
| Table | 21 | 8 |
| TableField | 69 | |
| TableFieldGroup | 32 | 8 |
| TableIndex | 14 | 1 |
| TableRelation | 2 | |
| TableInstanceMethod | 20 | 10 |
| TableStaticMethod | 7 | |
| TableMap | 2 | 2 |
| ExtendedType | 23 | |
| Enum | 6 | 3 |
| ConfigurationKey | 1 | |
| SecurityKey | 1 | |
| Macro | 2 | 1 |
| Class | 82 | 16 |
| ClassStaticMethod | 153 | 8 |
| ClassInstanceMethod | 1225 | 32 |
| Form | 32 | 17 |
| Report | 5 | 1 |
| Job | 12 | |
| Menu | 1 | |
| DisplayTool | 7 | |
| OutputTool | 4 | |
| ActionTool | 1 | |
| Grand Total | 1722 | 107 |

**Figure 18-1**   Modified application objects.

Figure 18-2 illustrates the steps in an upgrade across several environments.

The base for the upgrade is the live environment at the customer site. Because this environment runs live until the time of the production upgrade, you establish a copy of the 3.0 environment. You transfer code by copying the layer files. Use the 3.0 environment to prepare the modifications before the code upgrade. If, for example, you have modifications in the current application that prevent you from starting the new Dynamics AX 4.0 environment, you should work in the 3.0 environment to start the 4.0 environment with the layer files (with the extension .aod) from the current environment.

You establish the environment to be used for the code upgrade by installing Dynamics AX 4.0 and copying the modifications from the version 3.0 development environment. All .aod files from the production environment should be copied to the folder named Old in the version 4.0 environment. In the first step of the process, only the application files are transferred; processing of the data upgrade is postponed until the data upgrade step.

You test the data upgrade in a following step. The primary purpose of this environment is to verify the data upgrade scripts, including the extensions implemented during the code upgrade. A secondary objective is to get an estimate of the time needed to perform the live data upgrade.

Functional Test 4.0, as illustrated in Figure 18-2, is a copy of Data Upgrade Test 4.0. The test is often executed at the customer site. The purpose is to let end users verify that the functions used are still working correctly on their dedicated hardware setup.

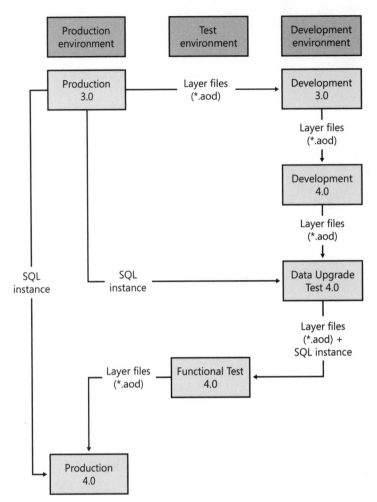

**Figure 18-2**   Steps in an upgrade.

Finally, you perform the live upgrade by copying the code from Functional Test 4.0 and the data from Production 3.0. You must get a new copy of the data because data will have changed since you started the upgrade.

## Backup of Code and Data

Performing an initial backup makes it possible to perform a rollback if something goes wrong. At a minimum, the backup should include the directory structure that holds the application; this includes all the layer files with the file extension .aod. A backup should also include a copy of the databases with the live data.

You should plan when you will perform backups during the upgrade process and what your backup process will include. Dynamics AX 4.0 provides a Version Control tool that helps you identify the versions of objects in the Application Object Tree (AOT).

# Code Upgrade in a Development Environment

This section describes the challenges that result from modifications to the standard application. This includes discussion of upgrading the code to comply with the changes in the standard application, as well as information about how to extend the data upgrade to include upgrade of the data in the tables and columns implemented by the modifications.

Making modifications to a Dynamics AX installation involves making copies of application objects from the lower layers. These copies form a shadow of the underlying application object. If the original object is modified in the new version, it will be hidden by the copy in the modified layer. A major task in the code upgrade process is to resolve such conflicts by merging the changes in the modification with the changes between the two versions. The .aod files hold the original and changed objects. For details, see the discussions about layers in the Microsoft Dynamics AX 4.0 Implementation Guide. Also study the contents of Appendix C, "Source Code Changes Required for Upgrade." The change of the *RecId* field from 32 bits to 64 bits requires some source code changes, and this appendix provides guidelines for that process.

The amount of work required to perform a code upgrade depends largely on the number of modifications. The first task in the process is to make sure not to spend time on upgrading unnecessary code. Some of the initial work should be performed in the original 3.0 development environment prior to establishing the 4.0 code upgrade environment.

If it is feasible, review the list of application objects in the current layer to identify unnecessary or obsolete modifications. Some of the modifications in the original version may be replaced by using new or changed functions in the standard application. You should consider keeping the tables and columns related to the original modification. The information that they stored can be used in the data upgrade to populate the tables and columns used by the standard application.

Placing modifications in multiple layers will complicate the upgrade. The code in each layer should be upgraded in its own environment. If you try to upgrade multiple layers in one environment, you cannot delete modifications in lower layers, which is sometimes appropriate in the code upgrade. As an alternative, you can consolidate all the layers into one, but doing so will create another challenge in regard to the IDs of the application objects because they are generated individually for each layer. One strategy is to consolidate the layers but keep the original IDs. This solves the problem, but it prevents use of the deleted layers for other purposes because some of the IDs related to this layer are already used. Another strategy is to change all IDs to comply with the consolidated layer. However, this introduces issues with the existing database, as will be explained shortly. Note that even if the primary purpose of the IDs is to support the synchronization, the IDs are also used as references in the data. If you choose to change the IDs, you should make an extension to the upgrade scripts to update the fields, which hold a reference to the changed ID.

You will experience a conflict if your modifications contain any application objects with names that are introduced by the new standard version. Duplicate database-related objects (such as tables, fields, or indexes) will cause a synchronization error. To resolve this, you must rename conflicting objects before you perform the upgrade.

If an object is not related to the database, a shadow is introduced in the new version that was not present in the previous version. The object must be included in the upgrade project because the shadow is presumably not correct because the original modification was not made by copying the object from the standard version. Conflicts of this type can be avoided by using a prefix while adding new application objects on the top level. Fields and other objects in added tables do not require this prefix because the conflict is resolved by prefixing the table. The same applies to methods on added classes.

In the code upgrade environment, the application files from the 3.0 environment are used when copying all the version 3.0 application files. The main task in the code upgrade environment is to resolve the conflicts collected in the upgrade project.

Sometimes an application object is inadvertently copied to the current layer. For example, if you browse a standard element in the AOT, the kernel assumes that you have modified the object, and it saves an identical copy in the current layer. If the object is modified in the new standard version, it will be shadowed by the copy in the current layer. If you specify that you want to delete obsolete objects while generating the upgrade project, shadows will be removed automatically and will not be included in the upgrade project.

There are four application object versions to consider when generating an upgrade project:

- **C4**  The object version on the current layer in version 4.0
- **L4**  The object version on the layer just below the current layer in version 4.0
- **C3**  The object version on the current layer in version 3.0
- **L3**  The object version on the layer just below the current layer in version 3.0

When an existing object was modified in the previous version, a copy was taken from the original layer (L3) and placed in your current layer (C3). In the upgrade process, the old layers are copied to the Old folder. The object in question in the new version (4.0) of the standard application is called L4, and the copy of the object that you modified is C4. Initially, C4 is equal to C3, but C4 should be modified (upgraded) to reflect the differences between L3 and L4.

Not all four versions of the application object need to be present. The flow chart in Figure 18-3 illustrates the criteria for inclusion in the upgrade.

The upgrade project includes all application objects that have been modified by you and that are changed between the two versions. This kind of conflict can be solved by using one of the following strategies:

- Re-implement the difference between L3 and C3 in L4.
- Implement the changes between L3 and L4 in C4.

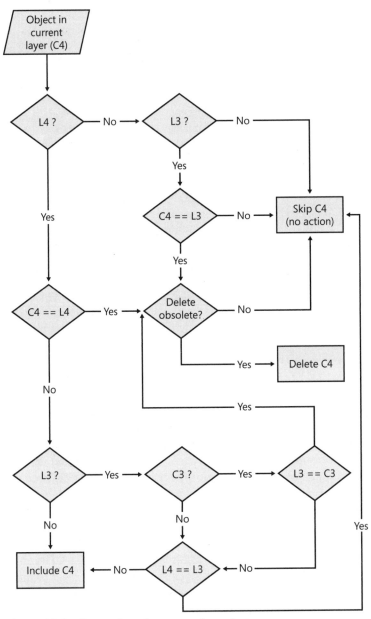

**Figure 18-3**   Generation of an upgrade project.

You can select a strategy individually for each application object. If you are in doubt, you should take the first approach because you are more familiar with the modifications performed in the previous version than you are with the changes in the lower layers.

You can compare L3 with L4 to analyze the changes in the standard application by using the Compare tool. The original modifications can be analyzed by comparing L3 with C3. C3 would initially be equal to C4 until C4 is modified during the code upgrade process.

Suppose that you discover that the only modification to a form is the addition of a new tab page with several new field groups and fields. The easiest way to re-implement this modification is to delete C4 and open a new window showing C3 by using the Add-ins menu. Then you can drag the tab page from C3 to L4 and save the result as a new version C4. You could also copy the source code in the Compare tool and paste it into the X++ editor.

Another interesting task is to find references to obsolete application objects in the modifications. You can find the references to the objects in the X++ code by using the compiler because the source code will still hold the name without the prefix. To find the references in the properties, you can use the Find tool. You can also use the Cross-Reference tool, but this requires you to make a global update including all the current modifications. You can activate the list of application objects from Tools\Development Tools\Cross Reference\ Names. Applying the filter DEL_* in the name column provides a list of all dropped objects. Unfortunately, all the fields in tables are cross-referenced to all dynamic query data sources on the same table. Consequently, you must ignore references to objects that originate from individual queries or queries embedded in a report.

When you modify the application, you change the X++ methods in some existing methods. Other methods are just referenced by a method call. Some of the methods referenced can have changed signatures (parameters). These are fairly easy to find because they will result in a compiler error during compilation of the method you modified. It is important to analyze changes in signatures and to comply with them.

The most difficult part of the code upgrade involves methods from the standard application that are referenced in the modified code whose contents, but not signatures, have changed. Such situations can result in errors when you test the upgraded code before applying it to the production environment. The important last step of a test upgrade should be a functional test that involves all the processes used by the customer. You might want to set up a test installation at the customer site and let regular users test their individual workflows.

## Data Upgrade in a Test Environment

The version upgrade typically includes some adjustments to the database. Some tables and columns become obsolete, and other tables and columns are added. The data contained in the obsolete tables and columns is often used to populate some of the newly added tables and columns. The data upgrade framework handles the upgrade of the data structure and data in the standard application, but you must handle any changes that affect the modified layers. This means that you must determine whether changes in the data structure will affect any modification in the application.

The data upgrade consists of two steps. One occurs before the new schema is applied, and the other occurs immediately after the schema changes are synchronized with the database. The pre-synchronization step prepares the existing data so that new unique indexes are not violated. When programming scripts are executed before synchronization, you cannot refer to new tables and fields, because they are not present in the database before the schema changes are applied.

The post-synchronization step populates the new tables and columns and updates the existing data where necessary. The tables and fields that are dropped are not deleted from the database when the schema changes are applied; they are merely renamed with the added prefix DEL_. This strategy allows for access to the data in the post-synchronization script. The tables and fields in question will be related to a configuration key, which can be disabled when the data upgrade is complete. When the key is disabled, the database is synchronized and the dropped tables and fields are deleted.

When Dynamics AX 4.0 is installed, the necessary scripts for upgrading the schema changes in the standard application are automatically installed as well. They will be executed when the upgrade checklist is executed.

**Tip**  For details on the upgrade checklist, see the Microsoft Dynamics AX 4.0 Implementation Guide.

Some of the modifications might also need data upgrade scripts. The following list describes situations that are solved by modifying and extending the upgrade scripts:

- The modifications in the previous version have introduced some data that is now present in the standard application. The column added in the previous version by the modifications should be used to populate the new column in the standard application. After the upgrade, both the standard application and the modifications with upgraded code should use the field in the standard application.

- The modifications in the previous version use standard application data that is no longer used by the standard application. If the data is still needed by the modifications, it should be transferred to a new table created during the code upgrade.

- The modifications in the previous version have added one or more entries to a base enumeration introduced by the standard application. The new version of the standard application has added one or more entries to the same base enumeration. If the numeric values of the entries conflict, an extension to the upgrade script should convert the values of the existing data to reflect the new values that result after adding the modified entries and merging the new version.

## Testing of Upgraded Code and Data

The purpose of the data upgrade test performed in a test environment is to:

- Ensure that all code upgrades are performed correctly.

- Ensure that no data upgrade errors will occur when performing the production data upgrade.

■  Measure the time used for performing the data upgrade, which is also the system down-time estimate you should use for the production data upgrade. Upgrades in the production environment typically have a narrow time window in which the task must be completed.

Some code and data upgrade problems can be identified and easily solved, but other problems cannot be identified automatically. Always perform a test of all your business-critical functions in Dynamics AX to ensure that they are working as expected after the upgrade. It is a good idea to involve your end users in this task, giving them an opportunity to become more familiar with the new version before it goes live. The process should be considered a learning experience, as well as a sign-off of the functionality.

## Production Upgrade in the Live Environment

The production upgrade process is similar to the data upgrade process performed in the test environment. But because the live data has been changed during the test, the process must be repeated from the beginning.

# Applying Service Packs and Hotfixes

This section explains how to apply service packs and hotfixes for Dynamics AX 4.0. The task is less complicated than upgrading to a major version because the number of changes is limited.

## Service Packs

Service packs are collections of bug fixes that are released at regular intervals. A Dynamics AX service pack typically includes a new kernel (executables) and one or more .aod files with the corrected application objects.

The advisability of applying a released service pack should depend on an evaluation of the benefits and costs of making the upgrade. You may skip one or more service packs and apply a later service pack, because the contents of the individual service packs are cumulative. For example, the contents of Service Pack 2 (SP2) include all corrections included with SP1. Also, an upgrade to the next version of Dynamics AX can normally be performed directly from any service pack.

Service packs are accompanied by detailed documentation to help you analyze the possible benefits of applying the service pack in the current installation. If only a few of the corrections are significant, you might consider extracting these application objects and importing them manually in the current layer. Remember to document this so that you can remove the objects from the current layer when you apply the next service pack. When you extract the application objects to an export file, you should remember to specify that you want to keep the original ID. This will allow you to apply a later service pack without having to change IDs.

The process of applying a service pack is much like upgrading to a new version. However, the number of changed application objects is smaller, and the changes to the database schema are minimal, so the number of upgrade scripts is also smaller. The tasks that you must perform when applying a service pack are the same as for a version upgrade, but each task typically takes less time.

## Hotfixes

A hotfix is a fix of a single severe error that must be corrected as soon as possible. Dynamics AX hotfixes are released on the Microsoft Dynamics PartnerSource portal. You should consider applying a hotfix only if the current installation is affected by the correction.

A hotfix can be an updated kernel (executable) or an export file that contains application objects. The export file is imported in the current layer of the installation. This means that the hotfix will be placed with the modifications. Before you apply a hotfix, you should determine whether the hotfix contains application objects that are already modified. You can use the Compare tool in the Import dialog box to examine the hotfix before the import executes. If it contains objects that are already modified, they should be merged with the changes performed in the hotfix.

Released hotfixes are typically added to the next service pack. If you have applied any hotfixes, you should remove them from the current layer when you apply the next service pack. If the change in the hotfix is identical to the change in the next service pack, you can delete the application object in the current layer when you generate the upgrade project.

## Migrating Data

Data migration is the process of transferring data from a legacy system to an initial implementation of Dynamics AX. Migration from a legacy system to Dynamics AX can include the steps illustrated in Figure 18-4.

The data migration process is composed of the following steps:

1. The requirements for the new Dynamics AX implementation arise from the customer and from the current legacy system.

2. The requirements are used as input for creating specifications of the necessary modifications to Dynamics AX.

3. The specifications are used as the guide for programming the necessary modifications, including implementation of scripts needed for data migration.

4. The data migration procedure is tested by transferring data from the live legacy system to a test environment.

5. A test environment is established at the customer site to test the functional modifications implemented and to verify that the data migration procedure is valid.

6.  Finally, a production environment in the new Dynamics AX installation is created. This includes the modifications previously tested. But the data could have changed in the legacy system during the process, so you must carry out a new live data migration while switching the production environment to Dynamics AX.

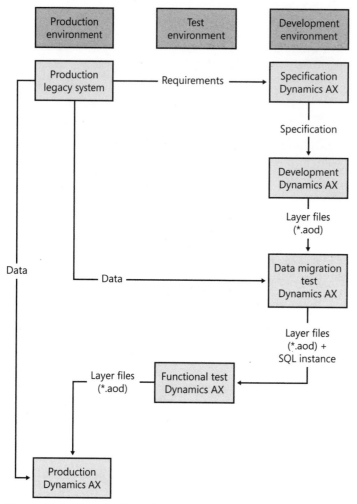

**Figure 18-4**   Steps in data migration.

# Data To Be Migrated

The data in a Dynamics AX database can be categorized as follows:

- Parameters and setup
- Main tables
- Worksheets

- Transactions
- Journals

## Parameters and Setup

The parameters and setup usually must be entered manually because they are specific to Dynamics AX. The legacy system will not contain corresponding data for all setup and parameters in Dynamics AX.

## Main Tables

The data in the legacy system that describes ledger accounts, customers, vendors, employees, and items is used to populate the corresponding tables in Dynamics AX.

## Worksheets

Worksheets that include ledger journals and inventory journals can be used to import opening figures regarding the ledger, customers, vendors, and inventory. Sales and purchase orders are also treated as worksheets in Dynamics AX because they specify future packing slips and invoices.

## Transactions

The transaction tables contain many relations between the individual records that cannot be reconstructed by importing data. The correct way to populate these tables is to import the transactions into a journal and post it.

## Journals

Journals include posted packing slips and invoices. If journals are posted in Dynamics AX, they will have references to the transactions in the ledger and inventory module. But if the data migration includes transfer of journals, they will not have these references, because the transactions can be populated with opening figures only. The transferred journals can still be used for inquiry and reporting without these relations to the transactions.

# Data Migration Techniques

Several data entry techniques can be used to migrate the data from a legacy system:

- Manual data entry
- Microsoft Office Excel export/import
- Data import
- Individually programmed import

The migration process typically includes a mix of all these techniques, as illustrated in Figure 18-5.

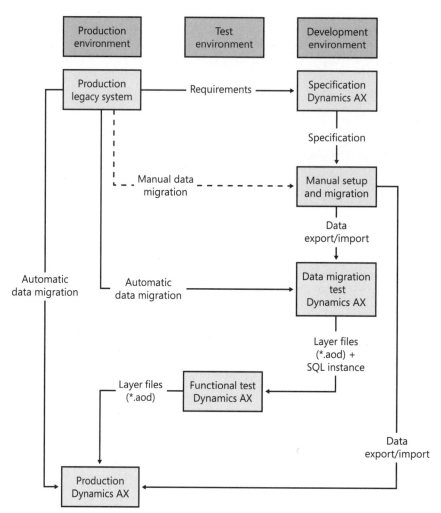

**Figure 18-5**   Data migration techniques and flow.

Some of the parameters and setup data will not exist in the legacy system. They must be specified and entered manually. As an alternative to manual entry, you can generate Office Excel templates from Dynamics AX, enter the legacy data in Excel, and import the Excel spreadsheets.

Part of the data in the legacy system will be of a static nature and will not change until the system is replaced by Dynamics AX. The import functionality can be used to import this data. However, the dynamic data can only be transferred to the final Dynamics AX version after the legacy system has been shut down. You must make a preliminary migration of this data to be able to test the implemented modifications and the routines for data migration. If it is possible to make an automated data migration of this data, you can avoid a great deal of manual work (which can be time-consuming and can introduce new errors) during the live migration.

Figure 18-5 illustrates how to avoid entering manual data directly into the environment, which is also the target of the automated migration. By making the manual data entry in a dedicated environment, you can repeat the process without repeating the manual entry. This also isolates the manual data to be transferred during the live migration, at which time it will be merged with the final version of the dynamic data from the legacy system.

## Manual Data Entry

Manual data entry is often used on smaller amounts of data. This data typically includes the setup of groups and other parameters that must be analyzed and designed while specifying the new implementation.

Many of the groups and parameters are used as mandatory foreign keys on accounts, customers, vendors, and items. You must define these keys before the main tables can be imported. Some of the parameters can be the same key for all records in a specific table; the value of the key are hard-coded in the import definition. Since the parameters are cached, you should be careful to reset the cache if the parameters are modified in a live environment.

If the reliability of the data in the legacy system is questionable, the manual transfer can be supplemented by a critical review of the data. This could include verification of the customer addresses, deletion of inactive accounts, and so on.

## Office Excel Export/Import

An alternative to manual entry of data into the Dynamics AX forms is the use of the Office Excel export/import function. This function generates Office Excel spreadsheets with templates and existing data from Dynamics AX. After modification, the spreadsheets can be imported back to Dynamics AX.

> **More Info**   For an in-depth description of the use of the Office Excel export/import function, refer to the online Help for Dynamics AX 4.0.

## Data Import

Another approach to data transfer is to generate comma-separated files from the legacy system and import these files by using the data import function in Dynamics AX. Use of the data import function is documented in the online Help for Dynamics AX 4.0.

## Individually Programmed Import

An alternative to using the parameter-controlled import mentioned in the preceding section is to create individual scripts to carry out the import. This requires some additional programming knowledge, but it can be a more flexible method because all functions and classes in the development environment will be available. This approach also allows for a more automated data migration that can be repeated without much manual work; this is beneficial if your migration is designed using multiple cycles of programming and testing of the data migration.

If you can access the data in the legacy system by using an ODBC connection, you might consider reading directly from the original data and inserting the data into the Dynamics AX database by using X++. This approach makes it possible to dynamically select data from different data sources in the legacy system.

When you program the import, you can choose to use the interface classes implemented in Dynamics AX as an alternative to inserting the physical records. The *AxBC* (business component) classes are especially useful when importing transactions into the worksheets. The following *AxBC* classes wrap the tables with the worksheet lines:

- *AxLedgerJournalTrans*
- *AxInventJournalTrans*
- *AxSalesTable* and *AxSalesLine*
- *AxPurchTable* and *AxPurchLine*

The *AxBC* classes have implemented *parm* methods for all the fields in the table and keeps track of which fields are assigned a value. When you save the record, the class tries to assign default values to the fields in which values were not assigned during the import. The classes will also assign the various number sequence IDs and line numbers. The following code example illustrates the use of *AxInventJournalTrans*.

```
InventJournalNameId     inventJournalNameId    = 'MOV';
InventJournalTable      inventJournalTable;
AxInventJournalTrans    axInventJournalTrans;
;

ttsbegin;

inventJournalTable.JournalNameId = inventJournalNameId;
inventJournalTable.insert();

axInventJournalTrans = new AxInventJournalTrans();

axInventJournalTrans.parmJournalId(inventJournalTable.JournalId);
axInventJournalTrans.parmTransDate(systemDateGet());
axInventJournalTrans.parmItemId('I1234');
axInventJournalTrans.axInventDim().parmInventLocationId('MAIN');
axInventJournalTrans.parmQty(100.00);
axInventJournalTrans.parmCostPrice(50.00);

axInventJournalTrans.save();

ttscommit;
```

When you import large amounts of data, pay attention to performance. As with upgrades from one version of Dynamics AX to another, the time between stopping the legacy system and starting the new system is critical for the customer. Using the interface classes to encapsulate data can increase the time needed for the import. To reduce the number of database calls, you can also use the *RcordInsertList* class to make  array inserts when you insert the physical records.

## Automated Data Migration

It is important that the part of the migration that must be executed after the legacy system is shut down and before the new system is running be automated as much as possible. One way to automate the process is to control the client by using XML files. When you activate ax32.exe, you can specify a startup command that will execute the commands in an XML file. Some of the possible commands are useful with respect to data migration. Here are a few examples of tasks that can be executed in this way:

- Make an import of application objects from a file.

- Activate data import with a specified file.

- Run a *main* method on a class.

## Data Model

Table 18-1 illustrates the destination of the data migration for the most common types of data.

**Table 18-1   Destination of Migrated Data**

| Information | Destination | Notes |
|---|---|---|
| Chart of accounts | *LedgerTable* *LedgerTableInterval* | The second table is used to specify setup of sum accounts. |
| Ledger transactions | *LedgerJournalTrans* | Migrate only opening amounts. The data in the journal are transferred to *LedgerTrans* when the journal is posted. Do not transfer amounts for customer, vendor, and inventory because they are generated when posting journals, as explained in this table. |
| Customers | *CustTable* | |
| Customer transactions | *LedgerJournalTrans* | Migrate only the opening amount or open transactions. |
| Vendors | *VendTable* | |
| Vendor transactions | *LedgerJournalTrans* | Migrate only the opening amount or open transactions. |
| Items | *InventTable* *InventTableModule* *InventItemLocation* | Each item should have three related records in *InventTableModule* and at least one record in *InventItemLocation* with the *InventDimId* specifying the blank inventory dimensions. |

Table 18-1 Destination of Migrated Data

| Information | Destination | Notes |
|---|---|---|
| Stock on hand | *InventJournalTrans* | The data in the journal are transferred to *InventTrans* when the journal is posted. |
| Bills of material | *BOMTable* *BOMVersion* *BOM* | The table BOMVersion relates the Bill of material to the items in *InventTable*. |
| Sales orders | *SalesTable* *SalesLine* | Migrate only open sales orders with no updated delivery or invoice. |
| Sales prices | *PriceDiscAdmTrans* | The data in the journal are transferred to *PriceDiscTable* by posting the journal. |
| Posted sales invoices | *CustInvoiceJour* *CustInvoiceTrans* | *InventTransId* should be blank for migrated invoices. |
| Purchase orders | *PurchTable* *PurchLine* | Migrate only open purchase orders with no updated delivery or invoice. |
| Purchase prices | *PriceDiscAdmTrans* | The data in the journal are transferred to *PriceDiscTable* by posting the journal. |
| Posted purchase invoices | *VendInvoiceJour* *VendInvoiceTrans* | *InventTransId* should be blank for migrated invoices. |
| Employees | *EmplTable* | |

# Chapter Summary

This chapter examined the process of upgrading from an existing installation to Dynamics AX 4.0, focusing on the issues introduced by the modifications to the standard application. An upgrade from one version to another is a major task; the installation of a service pack or a hotfix is less complicated, because the number of changes is limited. The initial implementation of Dynamics AX usually includes migration of data from a legacy system. This migration is typically performed by using a combination of tools and manually programmed scripts.

# Part IV
# Appendixes

# Appendix A
# Application Files

All application model elements are stored in application files in an application folder on a file system that is usually located on an Application Object Server (AOS). Deploying application extensions, customizations, and patches requires changes to the application files. Application files have the file extensions listed in the following table.

### Application File Extensions

| First letter | Second letter | Third letter |
|---|---|---|
| **A** (for "application") The file is an application file. | **O** (for "object") The file contains application model elements. | **D** (for "data") The file is a data file. The "data" designation is historical, not factual. The file can contain model elements, X++ source code, and corresponding byte code. |
| **K** (for "kernel") The file is a kernel (system) file and should not be modified. | **L** (for "label") The file contains label resources. | **I** (for "index") The file is an index file to a data file. If the index file is not found, the application server recreates it. |
| | **H** (for "help") The file contains online documentation. | **T** (for "temporary") The file contains data that will be written to a data file. |
| | **D** (for "developer help") The file contains online documentation for application developers. | **C** (for "cache") The file contains cached data. It can be deleted without compromising integrity—only performance is compromised. |
| | **T** (for "text") The file contains system text. This letter is used only in .ktd files. | |

In light of the preceding table, the following file extensions, which are drawn from the file types that typically make up a Microsoft Dynamics AX application, are readily comprehensible:

- The .aod files contain the application object data, or more precisely, the model element, X++ source code, and byte code data for a specific model element layer.

- The .aoi file contains the index to the .aod file.

- The .khd files contain kernel help data (system documentation in the Application Object Tree).

- The .ald files contain the application label data.

- The .alc files contain the application label cache.

**Note**  In Dynamics AX 4.0, the application object cache file is named .auc (application Unicode object cache). In earlier versions, it was named .aoc, which strictly followed the naming conventions outlined in the table. The new name reflects the fact that the objects are now stored in Unicode format.

The file name itself can also contain comprehensible information:

- All of the object, label, help, and developer help files contain model elements from specific model element layers. One file is created for each layer, and the layer name is part of the file name.

- All label, help, and developer help files are localizable. There is one file for each locale, and the locale is a part of the file name. Here are a few examples:

  - AxSys.aod

  - AxSysEn-us.ald

  - AxSysEn-us.ahd

**Note**  The Help system is different in Dynamics AX 4.0 than it was in earlier versions. The Help system used to be an integral part of the integrated development environment (IDE), using the internal editor to create Help topics. In Dynamics AX 4.0, Help is generated as stand-alone Help files (.chm files). Although the Help content must be customized and updated by using an external authoring tool, the IDE still contains elements of the application and system Help. For details about the documentation, refer to the Microsoft Dynamics AX SDK.

# Appendix B

# Microsoft SQL Server 2000, SQL Server 2005, and Oracle Database 10*g* Comparison

The following table shows the statements that are sent to the supported databases when database transactions are handled.

| Microsoft Dynamics AX 4.0 | SQL Server 2000 | SQL Server 2005 | Oracle Database 10*g* |
|---|---|---|---|
| First *ttsbegin* statement | SET TRANSACTION ISOLATION LEVEL READ COMMITTED | SET TRANSACTION ISOLATION LEVEL READ COMMITTED | No statement sent |
| First SQL DML statement inside a transaction scope | SET IMPLICIT_ TRANSACTIONS ON | SET IMPLICIT_ TRANSACTIONS ON | No statement sent |
| Final *ttscommit* statement | COMMIT TRANSACTION | COMMIT TRANSACTION | COMMIT |
| | SET TRANSACTION I SOLATION LEVEL READ UNCOMMITTED | SET TRANSACTION ISOLATION LEVEL READ COMMITTED | |
| *ttsabort* statement | ROLLBACK TRANSACTION | ROLLBACK TRANSACTION | ROLLBACK |
| | SET TRANSACTION ISOLATION LEVEL READ UNCOMMITTED | SET TRANSACTION ISOLATION LEVEL READ COMMITTED | |
| First SQL DML statement outside a transaction scope | SET IMPLICIT_ TRANSACTIONS OFF | SET IMPLICIT_ TRANSACTIONS OFF | No statement sent |
| *selectLocked(false)* | WITH (NOLOCK) hint added to SELECT statement | Not supported, so no hint added | Not supported, so no hint added |
| Select *optimisticlock concurrencyModel (ConcurrencyModel:: OptimisticLock)* | WITH (NOLOCK) hint added to SELECT statement | No hint | No hint |
| Select *pessimisticlock concurrencyModel (ConcurrencyModel:: PessimisticLock)* | WITH (UPDLOCK) hint added to SELECT statement | WITH (UPDLOCK) hint added to SELECT statement | FOR UPDATE OF clause added to SELECT statement |

| Microsoft Dynamics AX 4.0 | SQL Server 2000 | SQL Server 2005 | Oracle Database 10*g* |
|---|---|---|---|
| *readPast(true)* | WITH (READPAST) added to SELECT statement | WITH (READPAST) added to SELECT statement | Not supported, so no hint added |
| Select *repeatableread* *selectWithRepeatableRead* *(true)* | WITH (REPEATABLEREAD) added to SELECT statement | WITH (REPEATABLEREAD) added to SELECT statement | FOR UPDATE OF clause added to SELECT statement |

# Appendix C
# Source Code Changes Required for Upgrade

When you upgrade to Microsoft Dynamics AX 4.0 from an earlier version, you must make changes to the source code to ensure that the internal references comply with the new best practices. This includes code changes, metadata changes, and table modifications, as described in the following sections.

## Code Changes

For fields of the *int64* data type assigned to a 32-bit integer value, the assigned-to variable must be rewritten as a variable of the same type, or explicitly cast to an *int* value. For example,

```
int recId = table.recId;
```

must be rewritten like this:

```
RecId recId = table.recId;
```

When a variable that derives from *int64* is used as an index to an array, the code must be refactored to use a map. For example,

```
int array[,1];
array[table.recId] = 123;
```

must either be written as a map (in memory, used for few records), as shown here,

```
Map map = new Map(TypeId2Type(TypeId(recId)),Types::Integer);
map.insert(table.recId, 123);
```

or as a temporary table (on disk, used for many records), as shown here:

```
TmpTable tmp;
tmp.recIdRef = table.recId;
tmp.value    = 123;
tmp.insert();
```

For fields of the type *int64* that are placed into a collection class, as shown here,

```
Set set = new Set(Types::integer);
Set.insert(tableA.recId);
```

the code must be updated to use the appropriate data type, as shown here:

```
Set set = new Set (TypeId2Type(TypeId(recId)));
Set.insert(tableA.recId);
```

When a record ID is used inside a *pack* method, the code should be refactored to persist that record ID to a table field.

# Metadata Changes

You should notice that the extended data type *RefRecId* derives from the *RecID* system data type and will automatically be increased to 64 bits. The following are the extended data type requirements:

- Extended data types used by fields that contain *RecIDs* must derive from the *RecID* data type or one of its derived extended data types to automatically increase the extended data type to 64 bits.

- Extended data types used by fields that contain *RecIDs* must derive from the *RefRecID* extended data type or one of its derived types.

- Extended data types must define a relation to the *RecID* column of a table if:

  ❑ The extended data type has *RefRecId* as an ancestor type.

  ❑ The extended data type has a deterministic relationship to exactly one other table.

- Extended data types must not define a relation to the *RecID* column of a table if:

  ❑ It does not have *RefRecId* as an ancestor type.

  ❑ The extended data type, or one of its derived types, may be used to refer to *RecIDs* in more than one table.

- Extended data types used by fields that contain table IDs must derive from the *tableID* data type.

- Extended data types used by fields that contain table IDs should derive from the *RefTableId* extended data type.

# Table Modifications

The following are the required table modifications for upgrade:

- Table fields that contain a *RecID* (other than the system-defined *RecID* field itself) must be associated with an extended data type of *RefRecId* or one of its derived types.

> **Note**    The *RecID* extended data type should be used only by the system *RecID* fields.

- Table fields that contain a *RecID* (other than the system-defined *RecID* field) should be associated with an extended data type that is strictly derived from the *RefRecId* data type (not including the *RefRecId* data type itself).

- Existing table fields that have *RecID* or *RefRecId* as an ancestor and define their own deterministic single-field relation should have that relation removed.

- Relations must be defined for every table field associated with a *RecID*-derived extended data type (hereafter called *RecID-derived field*) that does not define its own single fixed-field relations. Fixed-field relations (defined with the Related Field Fixed option when adding a relation on an extended data type) are those in which the related table depends on the value of another field.

- If the table to which a *RecID*-derived field is related depends on the value of another field, and that other field contains an enumeration (or other value) to indicate the table to relate to for each row, one relation in the table must be defined for each value in the enumeration using a combination of a Related Field Fixed relation and a Normal relation.

- If the table to which a *RecID*-derived field is related depends on the value of another field, and that other field contains table IDs, one of the following approaches must be adopted:

  - ❑ A relation must be defined for each legal value of the field containing the table ID. (From inspecting the Application Object Tree, this is a very common approach.)

  - ❑ A single relation must be defined in the table to express that relationship in terms of the Common table.

- All fields that are used to refer to a table ID must be associated with the *RefTableId* extended data type or a derived type.

> **Note**    The *tableID* system type should be used only by the system-created *tableID* fields.

- All fields that are used to refer to a table ID should be associated with a type strictly derived from *RefTableId*.

# Glossary

The following list contains terms and abbreviations used throughout the book. For an in-depth terminology list, refer to the product documentation.

**ACID**  Abbreviation for Atomicity, Consistency, Isolation, Durability. *Atomicity:* Every operation in the transaction is either committed or rolled back. *Consistency:* When committed, the transaction should leave the database in a consistent state. *Isolation:* Any uncommitted changes are not visible to other transactions. *Durability:* After a transaction is committed, the changes are permanent, even in the event of system failure.

**.add**  The file extension for application developer documentation data. For details on application files, refer to Appendix A, "Application Files."

**.ald**  The file extension for application label data. For details on application files, refer to Appendix A, "Application Files."

**.ahd**  The file extension for application Help data. For details on application files, refer to Appendix A, "Application Files."

**AIF**  Abbreviation for Application Integration Framework.

**AOC**  Abbreviation for Application Object Cache.

**.aod**  The file extension for Application Object Data (AOD). Files with the extension .aod contain application objects—more precisely, the model element, X++ source code, and byte code data for a specific model element layer. An .aod file contains all the code for a layer and is used to distribute solutions.

**AOI**  Abbreviation for Application Object Index (index to the AOD).

**AOS**  Abbreviation for Application Object Server.

**AOT**  Abbreviation for Application Object Tree. The AOT is a development tool whose nodes are populated with the System Dictionary element metadata and X++ source code. Some elements in the tree are class and interface definitions that specify the structure and behavior of application logic and framework types. The top-level nodes in the AOT, such as Forms and Reports, are element categories that organize the elements of the dictionary.

**AUC**  Abbreviation for Application Unicode Object Cache.

**AutoDataGroup**  A control property that, if set to *Yes*, inherits the field group design dynamically from the specific table. This removes the option to further customize the group layout at the control level in the AOT, but you may do so from the code when the form is executed.

**AVL**  A data structure of self-balanced binary search trees. The term is named after its two inventors, G. M. Adelson-Velskii and E. M. Landis, who described it in their 1962 paper "An algorithm for the organization of information."

**_Axd_ classes**    Dynamics AX document classes.

**B2B**    Short for business-to-business.

**CLR**    Abbreviation for the Microsoft .NET Common Language Runtime.

**DataGroup**    A form and report control property that references a field group on a table.

**DDE**    Abbreviation for Dynamic Data Exchange.

**DML**    Abbreviation for Data Manipulation Language.

**EAI**    Abbreviation for enterprise application integration.

**element**    The unit in which metadata and source code are stored in the .aod file. The AOT contains many nodes, some of which are elements.

**element category**    A classification of elements. Category types include Forms, Reports, Classes, and Macros.

**enum**    Short for enumeration element.

**ERP**    Abbreviation for enterprise resource planning.

**field group**    A grouping of fields for a table with similar characteristics or purposes, used to optimize the design of forms and reports.

**GUID**    Abbreviation for globally unique identifier.

**IDE**    Abbreviation for integrated development environment.

**IIS**    Abbreviation for Microsoft Internet Information Services.

**information worker**    An individual who creates, uses, transforms, consumes, or manages information in the course of his or her work. Also referred to as IWorker or IW.

**IntelliMorph**    A control layout technology. The Dynamics AX runtime uses IntelliMorph to lay out controls on both rich client and Web client forms and reports.

**ISAM**    Abbreviation for indexed sequential access method. ISAM is a method for storing data for fast retrieval.

**.khd**    The file extension for kernel Help data. For details, refer to Appendix A, "Application Files."

**Liskov substitution principle**    A particular definition of subtype in object-oriented programming that was introduced by Barbara Liskov and Jeannette Wing in a 1993 paper titled "Family Values: A Behavioral Notion of Subtyping."

**LTRIM**    A SQL function that returns a character expression after removing leading blanks.

**MorphX**    The Microsoft Dynamics AX integrated development environment (IDE).

**MSMQ**    Abbreviation for Microsoft Message Queuing. MSMQ is a Microsoft technology that enables applications running at different times to communicate across heterogeneous networks and systems that may be temporarily offline.

**node**    The term used in the AOT for leaves and folders.

**object**   An instance of a type.

**OCC**   Abbreviation for optimistic concurrency control.

**OCI**   Abbreviation for Oracle Call Interface.

**ODBC**   Abbreviation for Open Database Connectivity.

**rich client**   The Dynamics AX client built using the Microsoft Windows Graphics Device Interface (GDI) API. The rich client is opened by executing Ax32.exe.

**RPC**   Abbreviation for remote procedure call.

**runtime**   The Dynamics AX runtime. The runtime comprises the virtual machine in which Dynamics AX objects and the Dynamics AX System API operate.

**System API**   The Dynamics AX System API. The System API is the system programming interface that X++ objects use to interact with Dynamics AX system objects.

**System Dictionary**   The host for all metadata and X++ source code that comprise a Dynamics AX application. The dictionary has a programmable Dynamics AX System API that can be used from X++ code. Elements of the dictionary are either composite, such as Form, Report, and Class, or primitive, such as method or class header. Elements are stored in Application Object Files and are loaded into the *UtilElement* table by the Dynamics AX runtime. Elements are copied between layers when there are modifications to lower-layered elements. Elements are also versioned with the version control system.

**table**   1. *Overloaded table semantics:* Table reference objects have overloaded semantics. For example, the `MyTable myTable;` variable can be interpreted both as a database record (`myTable.Field`) and as a cursor (`next myTable`). The base type for tables is *common*, and the methods for *common* are defined on the *XRecord* Dynamics AX system type. 2. *Temporary tables:* Temporary tables and database tables have different behaviors. Temporary tables are managed as ISAM database tables. Joining temporary tables and database tables requires that the temporary table be defined on the AOS, for example.

**type**   A type is a child of Kind. Types can be declared by name in X++. An element can be a type. For example, a table element or a class element may be a type, but not a form, macro, or method element.

**Web client**   The Dynamics AX client built on Web and Windows SharePoint Services technologies.

**X++**   The built-in Dynamics AX object-oriented programming language.

**XAL**   Abbreviation for Extended Application Language.

**.xpo**   The file extension for the export of Dynamics AX elements.

# Index

## Symbols

* (asterisk), 103
" (double quotation marks), referencing labels, 51
; (semicolon), 98
' (single quotation marks), referencing system text, 51

## A

absolute updates, 316
abstract method modifier, 117
access operators, 98
access permissions, 27
accessing data, 206–207
accessor methods, 166
ACID (atomicity, consistency, isolation, durability), 306
actions, 40
Active Directory directory service, 287
ActiveX controls, 365–367
add-ins, 40
addProp method, 251
Admin domain, 290
administration, record identifiers and, 324
AFC (Axapta Foundation Classes), 400
afterInit method, 366
aggregate functions, 105
AIF (Application Integration Framework), 8, 191, 213
    configuring endpoints, 230
    external applications, 18
AifConstraint objects, 232
AifEntityKey class, 230
AifServiceable interface, 215
alerts, 344–345
allocating record identifiers, 322
AllowAdd property, 280–281
AllowEdit property, 124
AllowNegative property, 123
AllowUserSetup property, 280–281
anytype type, 94, 97
.aoc files, 40
AOD (Application Object Directory), 194
.aod files, 88, 91
AOS (Application Object Server), 8
    integration technologies, 190
    transaction IDs, 308
AOS process pool, 308
AOSAuthorization property, 295
AOSValidateDelete method, 296

aosValidateDelete method, 348
AOSValidateInsert method, 296
aosValidateInsert method, 348, 441
AOSValidateRead method, 296
aosValidateRead method, 348
AOSValidateUpdate method, 296
aosValidateUpdate method, 348
AOT (Application Object Tree), 5, 23, 35, 36–41, 214
    adding controls to forms, 365
    AOT root node, 31
    Data Dictionary node, 28
    Global class, 400
    global session classes, 394
    job model elements, 92
    operational and programming elements, 26
    Web elements, 11
    Web node, 31
    Windows SharePoint Services integration, 265
AOT queries, 214–216
AOT root node, 31
APIs, protected, 196
appl object, 393–396
Application class, 344, 395
application developer tasks, 3
application elements, 5
application framework, 17–18
Application Hierarchy Tree, 78
Application Integration Framework. See AIF
        (Application Integration Framework)
application logic
    controlling, 428
    design considerations, 456
    monitoring database activity, 457
    transaction performance, 432–457
application model dictionary, 25
application model elements, 21, 25–34
application model layering, 13–17
    components, 13
    layer descriptions, 15
application modeling, 12
application modules, 26
application object cache, 40
Application Object Directory (AOD), 194
Application Object Layer, 41
Application Object Server (AOS), 8, 190
    MorphX debugger, 62
    transaction IDs, 308

# About the Authors

Hans Jørgen Skovgaard joined Microsoft in 2003 as product unit manager for the Microsoft Dynamics AX product line. As part of Microsoft's Navision acquisition process, Hans facilitated and managed the introduction of engineering excellence initiatives, aligned developer competence, created new teams, and organized training for new developers. Hans joined Microsoft with more than 20 years of professional software development and management experience. Prior to his engagement with Microsoft Dynamics AX, Hans was vice president of engineering at Mondosoft, a search engine company, for three years. Before that, he was vice president

of CRM development in the ERP company Baan for 10 years, during which time he architected a product configuration technology and associated tools. Hans has an MSc in AI (artificial intelligence) and an MBA from IMD, one of the world's leading business schools. Hans lives in Denmark with his wife, Nomi, and his three lovely daughters, Ristil, Simone, and Mikala. He holds a black belt in karate and is an avid mountain biker.

Arthur Greef is a software architect on the Microsoft Dynamics AX team at the Microsoft Development Center in Copenhagen, Denmark. Prior to working in this position in Denmark, he worked on the Microsoft Business Network product team that was part of bCentral in Redmond. Before he joined Microsoft in 1991, Arthur was chief architect at Edifecs, a small company that developed the XML business collaboration protocols for the RosettaNet Consortium, a standards organization for the information technology industry. He also held the position of chief architect for two years at the RosettaNet Consortium. During this time, he was on executive

loan from IBM, where he worked on e-commerce Web catalog and sales configuration products. Arthur has a BSc and an MSc in mechanical engineering from the University of Natal in South Africa, he has a PhD in industrial engineering from the University of Stellenbosh in South Africa, and he spent two years in an industrial engineering post-doctoral program at the University of North Carolina in the United States. Arthur has a passion for delivering innovative technology to mid-market manufacturing and distribution companies who need to manage their supply chains and who need to plan, schedule, and control their production and logistics activities.

Michael Fruergaard Pontoppidan joined Damgaard Data in 1996 as a software design engineer on the MorphX team, delivering the developer experience for the first release of Microsoft Dynamics AX after graduating from DTU (Technical University of Denmark). In 1999, he became the program manager and lead developer for the Application Integration and Deployment team that delivered on the Load 'n Go vision. For version 4.0, he worked as a software architect on version control, unit testing, and Microsoft's Trustworthy Computing initiative, while advocating code

quality improvements through Engineering Excellence, tools, processes, and training. He has been a highly rated and frequent speaker at technical briefings, conferences, and other road shows. Michael lives in Denmark with his wife, Katrine, and their daughter, Laura.

Lars Dragheim Olsen joined Damgaard Data in 1998 as a software design engineer for the Internet and Trade team. This was shortly after the first version of Microsoft Dynamics AX was released. While continuing his development work, he has since also held positions as program manager and project manager. His work has mainly focused on the Supply Chain Management modules within Dynamics AX and the integration of these modules with other modules, such as Financials and Project. During the development of version 4.0, he worked as a software architect, focused primarily on optimizing performance within the Supply Chain Management modules. Before working for Damgaard Data, Navision, and Microsoft, he worked for seven years as a system consultant on another ERP product. He lives in Denmark with his three children, Daniel, Christian, and Isabella, and his girlfriend, Camilla.

Palle Agermark joined Microsoft as an application developer in 2003 after spending more than 10 years in the ERP industry specializing in Concorde XAL and Microsoft Dynamics AX solutions. Palle works on the Control team and has primarily worked with the General Ledger, Accounts Receivable, and Accounts Payable feature areas. For Microsoft Dynamics AX 4.0, Palle worked as a developer in the following areas: unit testing, payment proposal, dimension hierarchy, the Financial Dimension Wizard, EU-115 Sales Tax Directive, and audit trail. Palle lives in Denmark with his wife, Rikke, and daughter, Andrea.

Per Baarsoe Jorgensen joined Damgaard Data in 1998 as a software design engineer for the Financials team, and he has delivered content for all releases of Microsoft Dynamics AX ever since. Over the years, he has held positions as team lead and lead developer for the Financials team. For version 4.0, he worked as lead developer on two teams that delivered the Alerts and Integration framework functionality. He has been a frequent speaker at Microsoft on Dynamics AX feature area implementations. He has more than 20 years of development experience; prior to his work with Dynamics AX, he was a development consultant for more than 10 years. Per lives in Denmark with his wife, Jeanette, and their two lovely daughters, Karoline and Natascha.

Thomas Due Kay is a program manager who joined Damgaard Data in 1997. In addition to program management, he has worked in various product areas such as product management, support engineering, and product quality management. For Microsoft Dynamics AX 4.0, he was involved in the development of version control integration, Microsoft Visio Unified Modeling Language add-on integration, user interface brush-up, re-branding, and many other technology-oriented features. He has also been deeply involved in Microsoft's Trustworthy Computing effort. He is a frequent speaker at customer and technical briefings, conferences, and other road shows. Thomas lives in Denmark with his wife, Theresa, and his two sons, Marcus and Lucas.

Karl Tolgu is a program manager for Microsoft Dynamics. He is responsible for the delivery of a variety of platform features in Microsoft Dynamics AX. Previously, Karl worked on project accounting modules in Microsoft Dynamics SL and Microsoft Dynamics GP. He has worked in the software industry in both the UK and the United States since graduating. He has held various software development management positions at Oracle Corporation and Niku Corporation. Karl resides in Seattle, Washington, with his wife, Karin, and three sons, Karl Christian, Sten Alexander, and Thomas Sebastian.

Mey Meenakshisundaram is a program manager on the Microsoft Dynamics product team who focuses on the Enterprise Portal. He has 14 years of experience in software engineering, consulting, and management, the last 5 of which were spent at Microsoft. Prior to his current role, he led the engineering team that developed and implemented the portal, content management, and sales operations systems for Microsoft Global Sales teams. He lives in Sammamish, Washington, with his wife, Amutha, and his children, Meena and Shammu. Mey regularly posts blog entries at *http://blogs.msdn.com/solutions*.

Bjørn Møller Pedersen works at thy:development, a Microsoft partner specialized in skills transfer related to development in Microsoft Dynamics AX. Bjørn joined Damgaard Data in 1990 as an application developer, so he has in-depth knowledge of the Dynamics AX application. He played an important part in the development of Concorde XAL from the first version and beyond, and he was later heavily involved in the transition from Concorde XAL to Dynamics AX. Since 1997, he has trained and coached Microsoft Dynamics partners in Dynamics AX. His focus is development, including quality assurance activities. Bjørn has an MSc degree in business administration, accountancy, and auditing.

# What do you think of this book? We want to hear from you!

Do you have a few minutes to participate in a brief online survey? Microsoft is interested in hearing your feedback about this publication so that we can continually improve our books and learning resources for you.

To participate in our survey, please visit:

## www.microsoft.com/learning/booksurvey

And enter this book's ISBN, 0-7356-2257-4. As a thank-you to survey participants in the United States and Canada, each month we'll randomly select five respondents to win one of five $100 gift certificates from a leading online merchant.* At the conclusion of the survey, you can enter the drawing by providing your e-mail address, which will be used for prize notification *only*.

Thanks in advance for your input. Your opinion counts!

Sincerely,

Microsoft Learning

**Microsoft** | Learning

*Learn More. Go Further.*